Essays on the Nature and State of Modern Economics

What do modern academic economists do? What currently is mainstream economics? What is neoclassical economics? And how about heterodox economics? How do the central concerns of modern economists, whatever their associations or allegiances, relate to those traditionally taken up in the discipline? And how did economics arrive at its current state? These and various cognate questions and concerns are systematically pursued in this new book by Tony Lawson. The result is a collection of previously published and new papers distinguished in providing the only comprehensive and coherent account of these issues currently available.

The financial crisis has not only revealed weaknesses of the capitalist economy but also highlighted just how limited and impoverished is modern academic economics. Despite the failings of the latter being more widely acknowledged now than ever, there is still an enormous amount of confusion about their source and true nature. In this collection, Tony Lawson also identifies the causes of the discipline's failings and outlines a transformative solution to its deficiencies.

Amongst other things, Lawson advocates for the adoption of a more historical and philosophical orientation to the study of economics, one that deemphasizes the current focus on mathematical modelling while maintaining a high level of analytical rigour. In so doing Lawson argues for a return to long term systematic and sustained projects, in the manner pursued by the likes of Marx, Veblen, Hayek, and Keynes, concerned first and foremost with advancing our understanding of social reality.

Overall, this forceful and persuasive collection represents a major intervention in the on-going debates about the nature, state, and future direction of economics.

Tony Lawson is Professorial Research Fellow of the Independent Social Research Foundation and Reader in Economics at Cambridge University, UK.

'This is a book of genuine originality, something that is rare in modern academia and all too often confused with mere novelty. Few thinkers can legitimately claim to have had a significant impact on their chosen field. Fewer still can claim to have substantively changed the terms of debate of that field. Tony Lawson is one of those few. These essays are for anyone with an interest in the future of the discipline.'

Jamie Morgan, *Reader in Economics, Leeds Beckett University; Co-editor,* Real-World Economics Review

'Tony Lawson has changed the conversation.'

Edward Fullbrook, *Executive Director of the World Economics Association*

'This book should be read by everyone concerned to remedy the deficiencies in economics exposed by the 2008 financial crisis. Through rigorous argument, Lawson shows that the answer is not more complex forms of mathematical modelling, but the adoption of ... methods that recognize the open-ended, relational, and processual character of economies.'

Diane Elson, *Professor of Sociology, University of Essex, UK*

'Economics is notorious for a slapdash approach to its own methodology, best epitomised by Friedman's infamous "assumptions don't matter" paper. Samuelson rightly satirised Friedman's position as "the F-twist", but despite this putdown, mainstream economists continue to use Friedman's obiter dictum as a way to escape having to consider the realism of their methods. Tony Lawson provides the "L-correction" to Friedman's "F-twist", by forcing economics to consider its ontology. If the L-correction works, the reformed discipline of Economics may differ from Lawson's expectations, but it can only be improved by having to confront its current unrealism.'

Steve Keen, *Professor and Head of Economics, History & Politics, Kingston University, London, UK*

'Tony Lawson is the enfant terrible of modern economic methodology. Whether you agree with him or not, he makes you think. This collection of (all but one) previously published papers is no exception. Highly recommended for all those with the slightest interest in the current state and nature of economic science.'

Dimitris Milonakis, *Professor of Political Economy and Dean of the Faculty of Social Sciences, University of Crete, Greece*

'There has been a growing sense of discontent with the economics discipline since the outbreak of the Global Financial Crisis. Tony Lawson argues that "the winter of our discontent" should be seen as much deeper than the current debate conveys—tracing much further back in time than

2008, and at more fundamental methodological and analytical levels. Lawson writes with clarity and with an intellectual passion. A must read for any student of economics and political economy.'

Peter Boettke, *Professor of Economics and Philosophy at George Mason University, USA*

'For many years now Tony Lawson, whose background includes mathematics and philosophy as well as economics, has been making a sustained critique of the methodology and approaches of modern economics. In this important book, which should be required reading for all serious economists, regardless of their approach, Lawson sets out starkly and systematically the substances of his criticisms. He outlines the way forward towards constructive approaches in teaching, research, and policy, allied with avenues for fruitful dialogue between the criticisers and the criticised alike.'

G.C. Harcourt, *Professorial Fellow, University of New South Wales, Australia*

Economics as Social Theory
Series edited by Tony Lawson
University of Cambridge

Social Theory is experiencing something of a revival within economics. Critical analyses of the particular nature of the subject matter of social studies and of the types of method, categories and modes of explanation that can legitimately be endorsed for the scientific study of social objects, are re-emerging. Economists are again addressing such issues as the relationship between agency and structure, between economy and the rest of society, and between the enquirer and the object of enquiry. There is a renewed interest in elaborating basic categories such as causation, competition, culture, discrimination, evolution, money, need, order, organization, power probability, process, rationality, technology, time, truth, uncertainty, value etc.

The objective for this series is to facilitate this revival further. In contemporary economics the label "theory" has been appropriated by a group that confines itself to largely asocial, ahistorical, mathematical "modelling". Economics as Social Theory thus reclaims the "Theory" label, offering a platform for alternative rigorous, but broader and more critical conceptions of theorizing.

Other titles in this series include:

1. **Economics and Language**
   Edited by Willie Henderson

2. **Rationality, Institutions and Economic Methodology**
   Edited by Uskali Mäki, Bo Gustafsson, and Christian Knudsen

3. **New Directions in Economic Methodology**
   Edited by Roger Backhouse

4. **Who Pays for the Kids?**
   Nancy Folbre

5. **Rules and Choice in Economics**
   Viktor Vanberg

6. **Beyond Rhetoric and Realism in Economics**
   Thomas A. Boylan and Paschal F. O'Gorman

7. **Feminism, Objectivity and Economics**
   Julie A. Nelson

8. **Economic Evolution**
   Jack J. Vromen

9. **Economics and Reality**
   Tony Lawson

10. **The Market**
    John O' Neill

11. **Economics and Utopia**
    Geoff Hodgson

12. **Critical Realism in Economics**
    Edited by Steve Fleetwood

13. **The New Economic Criticism**
    Edited by Martha Woodmansee and Mark Osteeen

14. **What do Economists Know?**
    Edited by Robert F. Garnett, Jr.

15. **Postmodernism, Economics and Knowledge**
    Edited by Stephen Cullenberg, Jack Amariglio and David F. Ruccio

16. **The Values of Economics**
    An Aristotelian perspective
    Irene van Staveren

17. **How Economics Forgot History**
    The problem of historical specificity in social science
    Geoffrey M. Hodgson

18. **Intersubjectivity in Economics**
    Agents and structures
    Edward Fullbrook

19. **The World of Consumption, 2nd Edition**
    The material and cultural revisited
    Ben Fine

20. **Reorienting Economics**
    Tony Lawson

21. **Toward a Feminist Philosophy of Economics**
    Edited by Drucilla K. Barker and Edith Kuiper

22. **The Crisis in Economics**
    Edited by Edward Fullbrook

23. **The Philosophy of Keynes' Economics**
    Probability, uncertainty and convention
    Edited by Jochen Runde and Sohei Mizuhara

24. **Postcolonialism Meets Economics**
    Edited by Eiman O. Zein-Elabdin and S. Charusheela

25. **The Evolution of Institutional Economics**
    Agency, structure and Darwinism in American institutionalism
    Geoffrey M. Hodgson

26. **Transforming Economics**
    Perspectives on the critical realist project
    Edited by Paul Lewis

27. **New Departures in Marxian Theory**
    Edited by Stephen A. Resnick and Richard D. Wolff

28. **Markets, Deliberation and Environmental Value**
    John O'Neill

29. **Speaking of Economics**
    How to get in the conversation
    Arjo Klamer

30. **From Political Economy to Economics**
    Method, the social and the historical in the evolution of economic theory
    Dimitris Milonakis and Ben Fine

31. **From Economics Imperialism to Freakonomics**
    The shifting boundaries between economics and other social sciences
    Dimitris Milonakis and Ben Fine

32. **Development and Globalization**
    A Marxian class analysis
    David Ruccio

33. **Introducing Money**
    Mark Peacock

34. **The Cambridge Revival of Political Economy**
    Nuno Ornelas Martins

35. **Understanding Development Economics**
    Its challenge to development studies
    Adam Fforde

36. **Economic Methodology**
    An historical introduction
    Harro Maas
    Translated by Liz Waters

37. **Social Ontology and Modern Economics**
    Stephen Pratten

38. **History of Financial Crises**
    Dreams and follies of expectations
    Cihan Bilginsoy

39. **Commerce and Community**
    Ecologies of social cooperation
    Robert F. Garnett, Jr., Paul Lewis and Lenore T. Ealy

40. **Essays on the Nature and State of Modern Economics**
    Tony Lawson

Essays on the Nature and State of Modern Economics

Tony Lawson

LONDON AND NEW YORK

First published 2015
by Routledge
2 Park Square, Milton Park, Abingdon, Oxon OX14 4RN

and by Routledge
711 Third Avenue, New York, NY 10017

Routledge is an imprint of the Taylor & Francis Group, an informa business

© 2015 Tony Lawson

The right of Tony Lawson to be identified as author of this work has been asserted in accordance with the Copyright, Designs and Patent Act 1988.

All rights reserved. No part of this book may be reprinted or reproduced or utilised in any form or by any electronic, mechanical, or other means, now known or hereafter invented, including photocopying and recording, or in any information storage or retrieval system, without permission in writing from the publishers.

Trademark notice: Product or corporate names may be trademarks or registered trademarks, and are used only for identification and explanation without intent to infringe.

British Library Cataloguing in Publication Data
A catalogue record for this book is available from the British Library

Library of Congress Cataloging in Publication Data
Lawson, Tony.
  The nature and state of modern economics / Tony Lawson.
  Includes bibliographical references and index.
  1. Economics—Study and teaching (Higher)   2. Economics.   I. Title.
  HB74.5.L39 2015
  330—dc23   2014036834

ISBN: 978-1-138-85101-6 (hbk)
ISBN: 978-1-138-85102-3 (pbk)
ISBN: 978-1-315-72441-6 (ebk)

Typeset in Palatino
by RefineCatch Limited, Bungay, Suffolk

Printed and bound in the United States of America by Publishers Graphics, LLC on sustainably sourced paper.

To Julien and Chloe

Contents

Preface		xii
Acknowledgements		xiii

1 Continuing myths and fallacies of modern economics — 1

2 Modern economics: the problem and a solution — 13

3 The nature of heterodox economics — 25

4 What is this 'school' called neoclassical economics? — 56

5 The current economic crisis: its nature and the course of academic economics — 105

6 Contemporary economics and the crisis — 130

7 Mathematical modelling and ideology in the economics academy: competing explanations of the failings of the modern discipline? — 142

8 Tensions in modern economics: the case of equilibrium analysis — 169

9 Soros' theory of reflexivity: a critical comment — 188

10 Ontology, modern economics, and pluralism — 204

11 The varying fortunes of the project of mathematising economics: an evolutionary explanation — 220

Index of names — 252
Index of subjects — 255

Preface

These essays are put together because, although there is some overlap across them, they do I think complement each other. Frequently, critics of one or other have castigated me for not mentioning or addressing matters that are in fact covered by other papers. So here a set of inter-relating papers are put together in a manner that hopefully comprises an integrated and reasonably coherent whole.

All chapters but the first are previously published. For permissions to republish the material included I am grateful to Anthem Press (chapter 2), the Cambridge Journal of Economics/Oxford University Press (chapters 3, 4 and 5), the World Economics Association (chapters 6 and 7), Routledge (chapters 8 and 10), Revue de Philosophie Économique/Vrin (chapter 9) and the European Journal of Economic and Social Systems/Lavoisier (chapter 11).

The papers have been written over a decade or more and so for intellectual input and support I am indebted to far more people than I can possibly remember. Individual chapters do though carry their own particular acknowledgements. However, in the endeavour of putting the chapters together (as well as that of writing the most recent contributions) I must thank the Independent Social Research Foundation for generous supportive funding.

Tony Lawson
Cambridge, August 2014

Acknowledgements

Sources of chapters:

1. *Continuing myths and fallacies of modern economics.* (2014). Previously unpublished.
2. 'Modern Economics: the Problem and a Solution', in Edward Fullbrook (ed.), *The Student's Guide to What's Wrong with Economics*, Anthem Press (an imprint of Wimbledon Publishing Company), (2004), pp. 21–32.
3. 'The Nature of Heterodox Economics', *Cambridge Journal of Economics*, (2006)(30): 2 (July), pp. 483–507.
4. 'What is this 'School' called Neoclassical Economics?'*Cambridge Journal of Economics*, (2013) 37(5), pp. 947–83.
5. 'The Current Economic Crisis: its Nature and the Course of Academic Economics', *Cambridge Journal of Economics*, (2009) 33(4), July, pp. 759–88.
6. 'Contemporary Economics and the Crisis', *Real-World Economics Review*, (2009) 50, pp. 122–31.
7. 'Mathematical Modelling and Ideology in the Economics Academy: competing explanations of the failings of the modern discipline?', *Economic Thought: History, Philosophy Methodology*, open access journal of the *World Economic Association*, (2012) 1(1), pp. 3–22.
8. 'Tensions in Modern Economics. The Case of Equilibrium Analysis', in Valeria Mosini (ed.), *Equilibrium in Economics: Scope and Limits*, (2007) London and New York: Routledge.
9. 'Soros's Theory of Reflexivity: A Critical Comment', *Revue de Philosophie Économique*, (2013) 14(1).
10. 'Ontology, Modern Economics and Pluralism' in Robert Garnett, Erik K. Olsen, Martha Starr (eds.), *Economic Pluralism*, (2010), pp. 99–113, London and New York: Routledge.
11. 'The Varying Fortunes of the Project of Mathematising Economics', *European Journal of Economic and Social Systems*, Volume 15, N°4 2001, pp. 241–68.

1 Continuing myths and fallacies of modern economics[1]

What is the nature of economic analysis as it is currently pursued in the academy and, intellectually speaking, in how healthy a state is the modern economics discipline? These, broadly, are the questions addressed in the papers collected below. Actually the state of health of the discipline, not least that of its hugely dominant mainstream project (and the latter project influences all else that goes on) is easily and quickly summarised. Intellectually, the discipline is in some disarray, short on explanatory successes, largely detached from its subject-matter, and seemingly without clear objectives or sense of direction. However, if the state of the discipline is easily in this way summarised, filling in the details, accounting for the repeated failures, and indicating how the discipline arrived at its current sorry situation, require a good deal of systematic analysis and elaboration.

The papers included below are concerned to address these and related issues. As such, they are generally explanatory in nature, albeit concerned to lay the foundations for transcending the discipline's continuing failings. They are also, though, somewhat critical in orientation. Although the object of this critical concern is most clearly seen to be the current hugely dominant mainstream project, the criticism levelled does extend significantly further. For this mainstream project is able to persist in its unhappy state and yet simultaneously remain hugely dominant and influential, in large part because of the workings of a set of persistent myths and fallacies many of which are accepted at least as much by heterodox critics of the mainstream as by the latter's own protagonists.

These myths and fallacies usually take the form of presuppositions that underpin more explicit beliefs and accepted practices, and as such they tend very often to go unnoticed, or, if noticed, they are rarely critically examined. It is because this is so that the objective of this current very short introductory chapter is given over to formulating some of these more fundamental preconceptions explicitly and in somewhat stark terms, placing them up front, and indicating in an equally stark manner why indeed they are erroneous.

There are likely various reasons that the errors of the sort that I have in mind do not receive greater critical examination. No doubt their perpetuation serves (whether wittingly or otherwise) certain vested interests at various levels. But an especially (and perhaps the most) significant factor is that modern economists, not least those who set themselves up as media commentators, policy advisors/analysts and the like, mostly (there are important exceptions) reveal themselves to be unwilling to do the philosophical legwork necessary to get to the nub of the issues involved.

Most of these individuals unhesitatingly presume that the recourse of criticising substantive claims (typically modelling assumptions) of others and thereafter substituting (equally questionable) alternatives of their own is always sufficient and proper procedure (the sort of error that I am here seeking to dispel). To the extent that a few of the individuals in question do reveal some awareness of somewhat philosophically oriented critiques, the resort typically is to avoid the effort of engaging by instead displaying overtly dismissive postures, suggesting for example that their formulators know no economics, have hidden agendas, cannot do the mathematics, are 'economic flat-earthers', merely hide behind terms ending in 'ism' and 'ology', and so forth. The inevitable consequence is that discussions of the state of the modern discipline remain largely superficial, criticism is mostly misdirected and overly tame, and supposed/proposed alternative approaches or projects (some of which receive significant financial backing) end up, in the main, being essentially more of the same.

It is thus with the aim of counterbalancing tendencies of the sort just noted that in this opening chapter I focus solely, and in an explicit and sustained fashion, on some of the various myths and fallacies that, in my assessment, individually or collectively, serve to obstruct serious attempts to transform modern academic economics into a more relevant, open-minded, serious and pluralistic discipline. I proceed, as I say, by way of formulating a number of them in simple and stark terms and placing them up front at the outset rather than (or before they appear) embedded in longer argumentative texts. In each case, after indicating briefly why I take the presupposition in question to be erroneous, I provide references to textual sources where the relevant argument is developed at length.

The myths and fallacies I have in mind run as follows:

Twenty common myths and/or fallacies of modern economics

Concerning the nature and problems of the discipline

1 *The widely observed crisis of the modern economics discipline turns on problems that originate at the level of economic theory and/or policy.*
   It does not. The basic problems mostly originate at the level of methodology, and in particular with the current emphasis on methods of mathematical modelling. The latter emphasis is an error given the lack of match of the methods in question to the conditions in which they are applied. So long as the critical focus remains only, or even mainly, at the level of substantive economic theory and/or policy matters, then no amount of alternative text books, popular monographs, introductory pocketbooks, journal or magazine articles, newspaper columns, blogs, new institutes or centres, alternative programmes or projects, conferences, workshops, plenary speeches, videos, comic strips or whatever, are going to get at the nub of the problems and so have the wherewithal to help make economics a sufficiently relevant discipline. It is the methods and the manner of their usage that are the basic problem. These methods more or less necessitate that the sorts of theories and policy formulations entertained are always (if implicitly) accounts of closed worlds inhabited only by isolated atoms (entities that always act with the same, separate and independent effect, whatever the context); social reality is easily shown to be quite different (see all the chapters below; also Lawson, 1997, 2003).

2 *The failings of modern economics emerged only with the recent economic crisis.*
   This is simply false. Economics has been in an intellectually sorry state for the last 50 years or so. The output of the discipline has long been explanatorily a failure, plagued with unrealistic assumptions, and produced by those with no real idea where the project is going. This has been the case indeed ever since the significant take up of methods of mathematical modelling in economics. Even certain prominent mainstream spokespeople, not least Nobel Memorial Prize Winners in Economics (for example Wassily Leontief, 1982; Milton Friedman 1999; or Ronald Coase, 1999), have, at least when adopting a reflective mode (in presidential speeches and such like), acknowledged this sorry situation over the years (see this volume, especially chapters 1, 5, 6, 7 and 11).

4 *Continuing myths and fallacies of modern economics*

3 *It is a failing of modern economics not to have predicted the timing of the recent crisis, (and given that so few did so, those who were successful should be lauded).*
Not really. Social reality including the future is open, so that successful event prediction is typically not much more creditable than winning a lottery. This is not to deny that we can understand many of the various tendencies in play at any time, not least those that are unsustainable. In the latter case we all know that something somewhere must 'give' in some way sooner or later. But when and how it all happens is usually highly contingent. Of course, as with all forms of betting, it is very often the case with economic forecasting that all possible outcomes are covered by the totality of forecasts made. Thus, at any given point in time there are usually some that can claim (with at least some subset of their projections) to have got it 'right' (in the sense that official figures or 'measurements' fall with the assumed-to-be-appropriate bounds of error attached to these forecasts) whatever the actual outcome (although these 'official figures' are frequently revised with time, albeit perhaps after reputations have been established). But as with most lucky gambles, those forecasts interpreted as successful are usually not followed by similar successes the next time around.

In any case, successful event prediction, if mostly infeasible in the social realm, is actually unnecessary (we can still successfully identify explanatory social causes), and also mostly unwanted (its impossibility being consistent with our ability to use explanatory insights to knowledgeably transform social reality to make the world a better place) (see this volume, chapters 6 and especially 7).

4 *The economics taught in modern universities is driven by right-wing or neo-liberal ideology.*
It is not. It is driven by a methodological ideology: that mathematical modelling is the only sound way to do economics. Throughout the modern academy the latter is widely accepted uncritically as 'common sense'. Most academic economists, in my experience, have little idea what neo-liberalism even means; nor do they care (see this volume, chapters 3 and especially 7)

5 *Dismissing the substantive theory and/or policy contributions of opponents with the label 'neoclassical' is helpful in pinpointing the problems of the discipline.*
It is not. Rarely is the term defined. And far from pinpointing or facilitating an understanding of any fundamental problem of the discipline it almost always detracts from doing so, through giving the impression that the problem is self-evidently essentially a matter of poorly, but freely constructed, theory or policy—that which is dismissed as neoclassical (see this volume, chapter 4). Not much better is the strategy of supposing that any approach labelled

heterodox or Post Keynesian or institutional or whatever, especially if it is a form of mathematical modelling, is necessarily any better *just because* it is so labelled. To transform the discipline in a constructive way it is necessary first to identify its problems; this is not achieved merely by signalling opposition or support for particular contributions through the use of unexplained labels (see this volume, chapter 4 [where it is argued that there actually is no neoclassical economic theory or policy]).

6 *Whatever may be the source of the discipline's problems we can always make progress by highlighting and chipping away at the lack of realisticness of prominent substantive assumptions (such as the familiar claims made about rationality, preferences, beliefs and states of the economy).*

I doubt it. To render mathematical modelling exercises tractable (to guarantee that embedded hypotheses are consistent with event correlations) economists must, as already noted, turn the 'agents' of their analyses into metaphorical atoms and situate them in isolated systems quite unlike those in which we actually live (see this volume, most chapters). This endeavour (given the actual nature of human beings and the social world) necessitates the making of assumptions that are inevitably mostly unrealistic. It is specifically absurd formulations of rationality and the like that serve the purpose of 'atomisation'.

Significantly however, although the cause of this lack of realisticness (i.e., the very use of inappropriate methods) goes unappreciated, *the fact of this lack of realisticness* of assumptions is usually acknowledge by everyone, including those who continually employ them, and frequently with regret; very often the assumptions made are interpreted as temporary devices that are expected to be improved upon in due course. Certainly, few if any modellers or mainstream 'theorists' have defended their rationality assumptions as realistic, and when pushed, do often substitute other (fixed) behavioural assumptions or formulations (e.g. alternative specifications of rationality; or those of limited rationality; or those even of irrationality [as for example proposed by neuro-economists and the like]) that serve similarly to 'atomise' the subjects of the analysis. In the same fashion, modern accounts of human beliefs (e.g. rational expectations) and economic states (e.g. equilibrium) work to facilitate model tractability or achieve various model consistency properties, and are rarely held by their formulators to be realistic (see all chapters, but especially chapters 4, 8 and 9).

In consequence, it is more or less futile for critics to think that inroads can be made by noting specific cases of assumptions that are unrealistic. Any lack of realisticness is rarely news; very often, as I say, it is regretted.

The insight that does seem like news, that does appear to go unrecognised by most, is that it is the emphasis on methods of

6 *Continuing myths and fallacies of modern economics*

mathematical modelling that is responsible for this persistent lack of realisticness, and that in an open complex social reality the production of unrealistic formulations is not a temporary contingent state but inevitable. Much better then to focus the critique on the modelling emphasis *per se* (see all chapters below, but especially 4, 8 and 9).

7 *The project of seeking to mathematise the economics discipline is a relatively modern one, and its dominance has been achieved through the project's significant explanatory successes.*

Not at all. It is a project that has been underway for over 200 years. And the current dominance of the mathematical modelling endeavour within the academic discipline owes nothing to explanatory successes (see this volume, especially chapters 1, 5, 6, 7 and 11), something to the manner in which mathematics was reinterpreted by mathematicians themselves in the early years of the last century (see Lawson 2003, chapter 10, or this volume, chapters 4, 7 and 11), and much to politics (see especially Lawson 2003, chapter 10 or this volume, chapter 7).

Concerning theoretical/philosophical issues

8 *Economics can and should avoid ontology.*

To the contrary, the recent neglect of ontology is a major reason the myths and fallacies of the sort here being criticised have prevailed. Ontology is the study of the nature of being. Like all forms of philosophy, ontology plays a ground clearing role for science. But this does not mean that scientists, whatever their domain of study, do not need to engage in it at significant moments in the advancing of causal, and indeed all other forms of, knowledge. Many physicists for example concern themselves with investigating the basic material of reality when they inquire into the *nature* of quantum fields, 'dark matter', particles and waves, mass, curved spacetime, quantum gravity, black holes, etc., all issues in ontology. Economics too has its more basic concerns. These include such matters as social relations, collective practices, social positions, community, capitalism, money, corporations, technology, gender, rights, obligations, human nature, care, trust, crises, economy, and so forth. Yet most economists, if inevitably occasionally referencing such categories, do rarely investigate their nature. However, it is impossible to provide much insight without at least some understanding of the nature of both social being in general and also the specific social phenomena being 'theorised'. These issues, all concerns of social ontological analysis, are easily shown to constitute part of the subject-matter of any would-be serious social science (see this volume chapter 5; also see Lawson, 2012a, 2012b, 2014a, 2014b, 2015a, 2015b).

9 *The division between modern mainstream economics and heterodox alternatives rests fundamentally on competing substantive and policy claims.*

It does not. It rests ultimately on very different ontological presuppositions (preconceptions, often implicit and unexamined, about the nature of social reality) combined with the fact that heterodox, but not mainstream, economists embrace pluralistic stances at the level of method (see this volume, especially chapter 3, but also chapters 4 and 9)

10 *To criticise/oppose the current mathematical modelling emphasis is to adopt an anti-mathematics stance.*

It is not. It is simply to point out that various tools (methods of mathematical modelling) are being used, and more or less exclusively so, in conditions (social reality) where these tools are generally inappropriate and more useful alternatives are available.

One of the many features that I find striking in the scene captured in Gustave Courbet's 1849 painting *The Stonebreakers* (depicted on the cover to this the book) is the seeming incongruity between the wielding of relatively light-weight handheld hammers and the task at hand—which is to break up rocks and stones in the process of creating a road through a hill or mountain. The use of mathematical modelling methods to address economic phenomena turns out to be at least as incongruous, and perhaps significantly more so. For when Courbet was painting, the hammers were conceivably used in the absence or unavailability of alternatives tools that were more appropriate to the allotted task; or at least this was likely the situation facing the older man and young boy depicted (individuals who in themselves seem equally ill-suited to the sorts of tasks undertaken). However, it is not clear that mathematical models, interpreted as tools for providing insight to social reality, have ever been found to be useful to this allotted task; and there have always been better more productive/fruitful alternatives readily available (as well as people skilled in their application).

The point is that if close study of the practices of the modern economics academy reveals a situation that is every bit as marked by monotony and (albeit in a different sense) impoverishment as Courbet's scene (and its portrayal is similarly irritating to the powers that be) the rendering of this situation in a realistic if somewhat stark manner is *not* to oppose (or be 'anti') the tasks or the tools. Rather it is to criticise the generalised matching of each to the other along with the societal causal conditions that underpin the continuing insistence/conviction that the identified tasks be addressed or tackled only in the depicted ways (see this volume, all chapters; and also Lawson, 2003, 2009a).

11 *To criticise/oppose the current mathematical modelling emphasis is to adopt an anti-science stance.*
   It is not. Mathematics is not essential (or inessential) to science; science involves using tools that are appropriate to the given task. A science of economics is perfectly feasible, and the current emphasis on mathematical modelling in economics serves, given the nature of social reality, mostly to prevent that potential from being realised (see this volume, chapters 1 and 9).

12 *To criticise/oppose the current mathematical modelling emphasis is to adopt an anti-pluralist stance.*
   It is not. Pluralism, I take it, is an orientation of support for variety at all levels, as well as of tolerance and respect for, and willingness to listen to, and to engage with, others. To criticise the current emphasis on mathematics is not to argue for keeping the approach of mathematical modelling out of the toolbox, or to refuse to engage its users. Rather it is to resist the dogma that *only* mathematical modelling methods should be, and be unquestioningly, utilised (and utilised however unrealistic the assumptions and explanatorily unsuccessful the whole endeavour; and despite the availability of more appropriate alternatives). It is, in other words, to resist one particular denial of pluralism, the version that currently dominates the discipline of economics (see this volume, chapters 6 and especially 10).

13 *The mathematical models of modern economics can be shown to generate insights about aspects of the real world, once or if these models are appropriately, albeit super-cautiously, interpreted.*
   This claim, where it is not totally banal, or a mere expression of hope and/or faith, is almost always based on a failure to recognise that, in most cases certainly, any insight attributed to the modelling endeavour was never actually a result of the latter, but rather achieved prior to model construction and incorporated into the modelling process (see especially Lawson, 2009a).

14 *Methods of mathematical modelling are, even if unnecessary, used in a neutral fashion, serving as just another language or heuristic device.*
   They are not used in a neutral fashion. They are tools. And like all tools they are appropriate for some tasks and conditions and not others. In certain contexts tools used inappropriately can be positively harmful. This has been (and is usually) the case with the application of mathematical methods in economics. It has forced the discipline into irrelevancy at best, whilst diverting resources away from potentially insightful alternative projects and applications. The claim that the mathematical methods adopted by economists are, or might conceivably be, employed as useful heuristic devices, serves, in the main, merely as an apology for this unhappy affair (see Lawson, 1997, 2003 and especially 2009a).

15 *Thought-to-be false assumptions and questionable modelling methods are justified and so useable if/where they generate agreeable conclusions, or anyway conclusions held to be true.*
This is incorrect, though seemingly widely believed even, or perhaps especially, amongst heterodox economists critical of the mainstream. That is, heterodox economists frequently suppose that although their modelling assumptions are (necessarily) false, their models are better (than those of their opponents) because the conclusions generated are held to be true. It may be true that 'all ravens are black'. But if this apparent truth is deductively generated from the assumptions that 'all ravens are vegetables' and 'all vegetables are black', we have added nothing to our understanding of ravens, vegetables or blackness; and nor have we provided explanatory support for the proposition that 'all ravens are black'. All deductive exercises that are so based on known absurd fictions, and this inevitably includes almost all mathematical modelling exercises in modern economics, are just as pointless. Certainly they add little to our understanding of social reality (see this volume, chapter 5 and 6).

Concerning proposals for constructively transforming the discipline

16 *The solution to making modern economics more relevant lies either in revising certain assumptions of mathematical models, or in a turn to more complex (in particular non-linear) forms of mathematical modelling, perhaps in the form of simulation analysis.*
It does not. This fallacy is based on a failure to see that the worldview presupposed by a reliance on these revised methods and forms is just as unrealistic (and indeed in essence is much the same) as that presupposed by more traditional ways of mathematical modelling. There is little reason to suppose that any of the novel modelling assumptions, modelling forms, model applications, or model estimation techniques currently on offer are of much use in the endeavour of rendering the discipline more relevant. The problem in all cases remains a mismatch of method and the conditions of application (see this volume all chapters). A continuing inability to recognise, or reluctance to accept, this fact of the situation explains the failure of the more recent 'alternative' projects interpreted as critical and 'new'. The *Institute for New Economic Thinking* (INET) sponsored by George Soros is a particular example. Although INET no doubt sponsors a few projects that do avoid the noted problems, in the main, and despite Soros' own best intentions (see this volume, chapter 9), the enterprise mostly fails to address the discipline's more fundamental problems, and indeed risks constituting an enormous waste of resources and opportunity (see chapters 5, 6 and 7).

17 *If conditions of experimental control do not hold in the social realm, then not only is science impossible, but all methods must be inadequate and not just mathematical modelling techniques. Thus in seeking to improve the discipline we might as well stick with the current emphasis on mathematical modelling.*

This is another view that is both pervasive and wrong. A social science can fruitfully concern it itself not only with much needed social ontological elaboration but also and especially with identifying unknown causes of significant phenomena, amongst other things (see Lawson, 2012a, 2012b). There are numerous ways of achieving such goals even in non-experimental contexts such as the social realm (see this volume chapter 2; see also Lawson, 2003, chapter 4; 2009b).

18 *Economics, including any transformed discipline, can and should avoid matters of ethics/morality.*

Both parts of this claim are false. Ethics and moral argument are unavoidable, so it is better and indeed vital to address moral and ethical concerns in an explicit, systematic and sustained fashion (see Lawson, 2013, 2014c). Even to contend otherwise is to engage in ethical/moral argumentation. Ethics, and specifically an ethics grounded in ontological analyses (of such matters as human nature, care, the nature of social organisation, and the possibilities for flourishing [of human and other living beings]), is essential for any suitably transformed more pluralistic, emancipated, economics (see especially Lawson, 2014c).

19 *Economics appropriately conceived is basically descriptive common sense, and this must be the basis of a transformed economics.*

This is not so. This mistaken view is unhelpfully widely promoted by various heterodox economists especially. Although mainstream and heterodox economists disagree on the value of descriptive common sense, the two are united in presuming that the latter is the only real alternative to methods of mathematical modelling (the latter being a methodological common sense to the mainstream—see this volume, chapter 6). This shared presumption is simply wrong. In fact, we all need seriously to raise our game and move way beyond common sense in all its forms; and in this both causal analysis and explicit, systematic and sustained projects in social ontology are likely essential (see this volume, most chapters; and also see chapters in Stephen Pratten 2014).

20 *The improving of economic teaching inevitably requires a good deal of prolonged, collective, formal discussion and debate over issues of substantive theory and policy*

This may be so, but I doubt it. Such an assessment seems to be underpinned by the idea that current academic economists, in constructing syllabuses, either conform to the uncaring atoms of their own theories or are ideologically biased at the level of theory and/or policy. I find neither to be typically the case. Rather, most modern economists are ideologically blinkered primarily by the idea that economics must be mathematical if it is to make a contribution. Even the lack of pluralism that so characterises the modern economics academy, stems mostly from a belief that to allow other methods into the toolbox will lead to a dumbing down of the discipline and a waste of resources.

Once the methodological error underpinning all this is revealed, or rather fully recognised, the potential is there in principle for the skills and energy of all the various participants in the economics academy to be harnessed to help fashion a more relevant discipline. Of course, new skills will likely need to be acquired by many. But we always must start from 'here'. In a process of successfully emancipating the discipline, the emphasis in the beginning will doubtless be as much upon supplementing, as upon replacing, existing courses, albeit likely involving the conversion of various currently compulsory courses into options (and also a change in styles of teaching [with the latter likely being rendered more interactive]). However, I do not anticipate that, with methodological blinkers removed, the task of providing relevant sets of courses in economics would be significantly more difficult (given time) than it is in any other open-minded, confident and successful discipline, where balancing acts regarding content taught are always to be performed—all disciplines must cope with issues of change in subject matter, competing interpretations and interests, and limited resources.

The pedagogical balancing act in an emancipated discipline of economics would presumably always be one of combining insights of the discipline regarded (albeit provisionally) as the more 'foundational' with any ongoing (possibly widely contested) advances regarded as contemporarily exciting and/or novel, taking into account local research and teaching expertise, skills and interests as well as the concerns of students; a transformed balancing act to that currently in play, but no less (or more) an inevitable balancing act.

The current problems, as I say, do not, in my assessment, derive in the main from an incapacity to care, or the sway of political ideology, or even an inability to find solutions. Rather, to repeat one last time, they stem from a pervasive and uncritical, indeed blinkered, belief in, and insistence upon, a simple and understandable, if ultimately mistaken, methodological dictum: that mathematical modelling is essential to any serious contribution to economics (see all the chapters that follow). It is in part with the intent of providing a focussed and sustained challenge to this dictum that the following papers or chapters are here collected together.

Note

1 I am grateful to the *Independent Social Research Foundation* for generous funding of the research upon which this chapter is based. For comments on an earlier draft I am also grateful to Phil Faulkner, Clive Lawson and Stephen Pratten.

References

Blaug, Mark (1997) 'Ugly Currents in Modern Economics', *Options Politiques*, September: 3–8.
Coase, Ronald (1999) 'Interview with Ronald Coase', *Newsletter of the International Society for New Institutional Economics*, Vol. 2, No. 1, Spring.
Friedman, Milton (1999) 'Conversation with Milton Friedman', in Snowdon B. and Vane H. (eds.). *Conversations with Leading Economists: Interpreting Modern Macroeconomics*, 124–44, Cheltenham: Edward Elgar.
Lawson, Tony (1997) *Economics and Reality*, London and New York: Routledge.
Lawson, Tony (2003) *Reorienting Economics*, London and New York: Routledge.
Lawson, Tony (2009a) 'On the Nature and Roles of Formalism in Economics', in Edward Fullbrook (ed.), *Ontology and Economics: Tony Lawson and His Critics*, London and New York: Routledge, chapter 12, pp. 189–231.
Lawson, Tony (2009b) 'Applied economics, contrast explanation and asymmetric information', *Cambridge Journal of Economics*, 33(3): 405–419.
Lawson, Tony (2012a) 'Ontology and the Study of Social Reality: Emergence, Organisation, Community, Power, Social Relations, Corporations, Artefacts and Money', *Cambridge Journal of Economics*, 36(2): 345–385.
Lawson, Tony (2012b) "Emergence and Social Causation" in John Greco and Ruth Groff (eds.), *Powers and Capacities in Philosophy*, London and New York: Routledge, pp. 285–307.
Lawson, Tony (2013) 'Ethical Naturalism and Forms of Relativism', *Society*, 50(6): 570–5.
Lawson, Tony (2014a) 'A Conception of Social Ontology', in Stephen Pratten (ed.), *Social Ontology and Modern Economics*, London and New York: Routledge.
Lawson, Tony (2014b) 'The Nature of Gender', in Stephen Pratten (ed.), *Social Ontology and Modern Economics*, London and New York: Routledge.
Lawson, Tony (2014c) 'Critical Ethical Naturalism: An Orientation to Ethics', in Stephen Pratten (ed.), *Social Ontology and Modern Economics*, London and New York: Routledge.
Lawson, Tony (2015a) "On the Nature of the Firm, including Peculiarities of the Corporation", *Cambridge Journal of Economics* (forthcoming).
Lawson, Tony (2015b) "The Modern Corporation: the Site of a Mechanism (of Global Social Change) that is Out-Of-Control?" Forthcoming in: Archer, Margaret (ed.), *Social Morphogenesis: Generative Mechanisms Transforming the Social Order*, New York: Springer.
Leontief, W. (1982) Letter in *Science* 217: 104–7.
Pratten Stephen (ed.) (2014) *Social Ontology and Modern Economics*, London and New York: Routledge.

2 Modern economics: the problem and a solution

Modern economics is not very successful as an explanatory endeavour. This much is accepted by most serious commentators, including many mainstream spokespeople (see e.g., Rubinstein, 1995, p. 12; Lipsey, 2001, p. 173; Friedman, 1999, p. 137; Coase, 1999, p. 2; Leontief, 1982, p. 104). In the words of Blaug: "Modern Economics is sick" (Blaug, 1997, p. 3). Certainly it seems desirable that we do better.

In order to determine whether we *can* do better, however, we need first to be clear *how* modern economics goes wrong and then to explain *why* it does. Once this is achieved, once we have identified the nature and cause(s) of the problem, we will be well placed to determine whether the failings of the discipline are in fact remedial. I briefly consider each of these three issues here.

The problem

So how does modern economics go wrong? It does so, I contend, simply through its practitioners seeking to utilise methods of analysis that are largely inappropriate for addressing material of the sort that lies within the social domain.

A fundamental insight here is that, for any method to be able to illuminate a domain of reality, the *nature* of the phenomena of that domain must be of a sort to render this feasible. There is a sense in which method must fit with the nature of its object. We can easily see, for example, that the nature of glass in the window is such as to allow a cotton cloth, but *not* a pneumatic drill, to serve as an appropriate tool for cleaning it. In similar fashion for a social research method to be relevant in a specific context the material to be studied must be of a sort as to make feasible the method's application.

The problem of modern economics, as I am interpreting it, then, stems from a neglect of this insight. Rather than starting with a question about an aspect of social reality and determining an appropriate method, modern economists usually start with a particular type of method and presume, mistakenly, that it must be appropriate to all social contexts.

The result is that, in their conceptions, modern economists end up distorting social phenomena just to render them open to treatment by their chosen approach.

What is the type of method that economists use that I am supposing is not entirely suitable, but which is effectively universally recommended even prior to determining the research question to be addressed?

If we open almost any modern economics textbook we quickly find references to procedures of formalistic economic modelling, central to which is the reliance upon functional relations. To the extent that economists concern themselves with phenomena such as consumption, production, investment or human well being, standard economic analyses involve the formulation of consumption, production, investment and utility *functions* respectively. It is this emphasis upon functional relations that I shall argue is inappropriate to the analysis of most social phenomena.

Now it does not take too much reflection to see that if an approach to economics that utilises mathematical functions is to be everywhere appropriate then social events must relate to each other in very specific (stable) ways.

Formally a function is defined as follows. If X is a set of numbers x and Y is a set of numbers y, and if rules are given by which, to each x in X, a corresponding y in Y is assigned, these rules determine a *function* defined for x in X.[1] Typically the value y that a function f takes for a particular x in X is written $f(x)$, so that $y = f(x)$.

The point, clearly, is that if a reliance on functions is to be an appropriate way to proceed in economics, event regularities or event correlations, i.e., regularities of the form 'whenever event x (or state of affairs) then event (or state of affairs) y', must be a commonplace in the social ream.

Functional relations and social phenomena

What are the reasons for supposing the emphasis on functional relations to be misplaced in economics?

One is simply empirical. Attempts so far to identify non-trivial, stable correlations between economic variables have mostly not succeeded. This is so despite the high-powered techniques of econometrics available to modern economists. Typically no sooner is an event regularity reported for the social realm than it is found to break down (see Lawson, 1997, chapter 7).

Actually, event regularities are even rather rare in the natural sciences too. To be precise most stable correlations that hold in the natural realm are restricted to situations of experimental control. For example, a table tennis ball will fall with a constant rate of acceleration when dropped in an experimentally produced vacuum, but rarely does so outside the experimental set up.

Why is this? It is simply because outside the experimental laboratory any object that is 'dropped' tends, in its movement, to be influenced by a range of causal factors. The wind, thermal forces, table tennis bats and much else may affect the movement of the ball. The point of an experimental set up is precisely to isolate a stable causal mechanism from the influence of countervailing mechanisms in order to identify better its properties. The event regularity produced correlates a triggering of a mechanism with its (isolated) effects. Of course if gravity were not a stable force an experimental event regularity would not occur anyway.

Such considerations suggest a second, more fundamental, reason for expecting the emphasis on functional relations in economics to be misplaced. For consideration of the experimentally produced event regularity leads us to recognise that at least three conditions must be satisfied if event regularities of the sort presupposed by the use of functional relations are to be guaranteed (as opposed to emerging fortuitously). And these seem unlikely to occur in the social realm, as we shall see.

What are the three conditions for an event regularity to be guaranteed? Simply put, the relevant domain of reality must consist of factors that are 1) intrinsically stable, 2) isolatable and 3) actually acting in a condition of isolation. Notice the last requirement is not superfluous to 2). We may be able experimentally to isolate gravitational forces, aerodynamic forces, thermal forces, and so on. However outside the laboratory all such forces and untold others simultaneously act on the autumn leaf making its actual path unpredictable. If an event regularity is to be achieved then isolation (and not just isolatability) at some level is required.

We might take note at this stage that, in the relevant philosophy-of-science literature, a situation in which many and changing causal mechanisms determine the course of events is referred to as open, whereas one in which a single mechanism is isolated, and an event regularity produced, is usually described as closed.

We are now in a position to see rather easily why economics, with its emphasis on functional relations, and so presumption of event regularities, does so poorly.

First of all, even if economic forces were intrinsically stable and isolatable there can be no presumption that they act in isolation. As I say, even in the natural realm, experimental intervention is required to achieve conditions of isolation. Thus in seeking to apply their modelling methods to all social situations economists are overlooking the special conditions required for such regularities even within natural science.

But the situation is more complex still. For rarely are social phenomena found to be either intrinsically stable in the way that some natural mechanisms seem to be, or isolatable.

Consider, first, the question of intrinsic stability. Now more or less by definition social phenomena depend on us for their existence. Without us there would still be natural forces like gravity, but no social phenomena like tables, chairs, cars, markets, universities, languages systems, and so forth. Let us consider the latter more closely. A language system is given to us at any moment and facilitates our speech acts. But, as I say, it also depends on us. And through individuals drawing on it when speaking, individuals, in total, come to reproduce the system in question and always, in part at least, transform it; whether intentionally or through error we continually change parts of it. The result is that the language system exists as a process of transformation or reproduction; this is its mode of being. It is intrinsically processual in nature. And a moment's reflection helps us realise that this is true too of the market, the school curriculum, ultimately the school itself, and everything else that is social. Although aspects of social life may be reproduced over sometimes significant regions of time and space, the sort of stability we attribute, say, to gravitational forces on the surface of the earth are unlikely to prevail.

The remaining requirement for the guarantee of an event regularity, namely that social causes be isolatable, appears to be at least as unlikely to be satisfied; the social realm seems intrinsically open and interconnected. Firms, money, markets, institutions, social relations, even individual identities, cannot be experimentally isolated from each other. Indeed most, if not all, social phenomena are actually *constituted* in their relations to something else. We cannot have employers without employees, teachers without students, parents without children, and so on; whenever any of us move into new positions, as students, employees, trade union members, etc., what we can and cannot do is determined by our relations to others.

In short, even opportunities for achieving event regularities within the confines of experimental analyses, conditions that are already rare in the natural sciences, seem unlikely in social research. Yet economists assume they occur anyway, and without any need for experimental intervention.

Economics as science

But is this analysis not rather debilitating for economics? Does it not undermine any hope that economics can be a science in the sense of natural science, or even a serious discipline at all? Actually this does not follow. Remember that even in natural scientific work the event regularities produced are mostly restricted to laboratory experiments. Yet this has not prevented the results of natural science, including experimental ones, being used successfully outside the experimental laboratory, in such activities as building bridges and sending rockets to the moon.

The reason this is possible is simply that even where experimental event regularities are produced these are not actually the real or primary objects of science. For the preceding discussion of experimental activity suggests that the primary objects of science are the underlying mechanisms that govern the directly perceivable events and states of affairs of the world. And unlike the (experimentally produced) event regularities the mechanisms responsible may operate inside and outside the experimental set-up alike. Thus the gravitational mechanism operates on autumn leaves (and table tennis balls) even as they fly over roofs and chimneys.

A working of a mechanism that so has its effects and makes its impact whatever the actual outcome (co-determined by countervailing factors) can be referred to as a *tendency*. It is clearly a knowledge of the gravitational mechanism or tendency, and not of events and their patterns *per se,* that helps us build bridges and send rockets to the moon.

So if the primary goal of science is not after all the sorts of event regularities produced in conditions of experimental control—but is the uncovering of causal mechanisms (like gravity) that govern the phenomena we can (or may be able to) experience directly (such as movements in table tennis balls and autumn leaves)—the failure to turn up many event regularities in the social realm clearly ought not to be viewed as an automatic bar to economics being a serious discipline or even scientific in the sense of natural science. This failure does, though, render the insistence of modern economic modellers on analysing the economy in terms functional relations somewhat questionable.

If event-regularities are mostly restricted to experimental situations we shall see below that non-experimental ways of identifying causal factors are perfectly feasible and common. Their uncovering is something that economists can succeed in as much as anyone else.

Explaining the problem

The question that arises at this stage is why we are in the situation in which we find ourselves. If the activity of economic modelling using functional relations, is so unsuccessful, and on reflection understandably so, why do economists persist in their modelling activities?

The answer is quite simple. Economists very much want to be viewed as scientific. But for reasons that I explore elsewhere (see Lawson, 2003, chapter 10) economists take the view that research can only qualify as scientific if it is formulated mathematically. And a deductive mathematics based on functional relations is the sort of mathematical system that economists have found easiest to handle.

Thus whilst other disciplines tend to be defined in terms of the nature of the materials or principles that are studied (for example chemistry is concerned with understanding the chemical aspect of the physical world including living organisms), economists mistakenly conceive of their discipline in terms of their chosen methodological approach.

Of course, we can now see that the belief that maths is essential to science is mistaken. As the discussion of experimental achievements above has demonstrated i) if there is any practice that is essential to science it is that of seeking to identify causes of phenomena of interest, whilst

ii) maths, certainly of the sort used by economists, is incidental to this endeavour, being mostly restricted to analysing cases of stable correlations. As we have also already seen such stable correlations are rare in the natural realm and even more so in the social.

It is likely that the fact that various phenomena regarded as economic are measurable encourages the misapprehension that mathematical discipline of relevance is possible. But beyond appreciating this fact of the situation, I suspect that most economists never for a moment question whether their preferred (mathematical) methods are appropriate to the material they address. They take it for granted that their methods and social reality 'fit' and that they themselves can be scientists in line with their own (mistaken) image of it, and thereafter they focus mostly on the potentialities of their chosen methods and such like. This indeed, is similar to an assessment made by Alfred Marshall rather a long time ago:

> [The mathematician's] concern is to show the potentialities of mathematical methods on the supposition that material appropriate to their use had been supplied by economic study. He takes no technical responsibility for the material, and is often unaware how inadequate the material is to bear the strains of his powerful machinery.
> (Marshall, 1920, p. 644)

Doing better

The final question to address is whether it is actually possible to do better. One conceivable justification for the insistence on mathematical modelling in economics that I want to dispose of quickly is that there just is no other way of proceeding.

Some commentators have reasoned that if each social phenomenon is really governed by many causal factors, where we cannot experimentally isolate the effects of any one of them, the only option available is to pretend that any social phenomenon of interest can be treated *as if* generated under conditions of the controlled experiment.

But there is a sense in which we often *can* isolate the effects of a single causal mechanism in such an *open* system. The controlled experiment is but a special case of a method I want to describe here, a method that, in its most abstract formulation, is appropriate to natural and social contexts alike. This is the method of *contrast explanation*. All we need for this method to work is a situation in which i) two outcomes are different ii) in conditions where it was expected that they would have been the same, resting on an assessment that they shared the same or a sufficiently similar causal history.

Alternatively put, in contrast explanation we seek *not* to explain some X, but to explain why some 'X rather than Y' occurred in a situation where Y was expected (given our understanding of the causal history of the relevant phenomenon). In such a situation we do not seek all the causes of X but the one that accounts for the departure from the Y that was anticipated.

Consider the onset of mad cows disease. In the late 1980s in the UK, a group of cows surprised everyone and confounded expectations in displaying unusual symptoms of an illness (such as wobbling their heads and falling over). Cows are complex animals, and many factors influence their behaviour. However, by comparing the conditions of the affected cows with others that revealed no symptoms, it was possible to standardise for the causes common to both groups, creating situation in which it was possible in effect to isolate and identify the cause of the difference, i.e., of the phenomenon of interest.

In the social realm specifically, surprises triggering explanatory endeavour often occur when we move to contexts (regions, countries, institutions, cultures) other than those with which we are very familiar. On doing so we may discover practices, ceremonies, meanings, and orientations, which are at variance with those with which we are acquainted. Of course, we usually also find very many commonalities too, presupposing similar causal conditions. By standardising for the latter when focusing on a specific contrastive experience, we can often figure out the causes (different rule systems, institutions, or social relations) for the unexpected outcomes.

Thus, if we travel, we may find that the inhabitants of some countries drive on a different side of the road to ourselves, treat as equal those who in our own locality are discriminated against (or vice versa), eat differently, etc., all of which allow us to infer something of the operative local rules and social relations.

Note too, that we can also seek to identify more than one of the various causes of any phenomenon. We can do this by comparing a given phenomenon with an array of different contrasts or 'foils', where feasible, considered one at a time. Elsewhere, for example, I have focussed on the immediate post Second World War productivity growth in the UK and contrasted this with different foils. When the foil utilised was the pre war productivity experience of the UK then the post war experience was found to be strikingly higher. This contrast can be explained by the post war specific expansion in world demand. When, however, the chosen foil was the rate of post war productivity growth in other comparable industrial countries, such as that of the old West Germany, the UK comparative experience was found to be strikingly poorer. The contrast now highlighted can be explained by the localised nature of collective bargaining in the UK compared to the centralised systems in West Germany and elsewhere (see Lawson, 1997, chapter 18 for detail).

We can now see that controlled experiments constitute a special case of contrast explanation. In outdoor research, such as in plant breeding experiments, a field may be divided into numerous plots with, say, some chemical compound applied to some plots only. If the average yield is higher in the plots where the compound is allocated we can conclude that it acts as a fertilizer, that it explains not the level of yield but the yield differential (our contrast).

In the outdoor experiment, the conditions in the field can vary throughout the growing season. The method works just because at any point in time the effects are the same throughout the field, except for the chemical compound whose properties are under investigation.

The indoor laboratory experiment is different only in that the background conditions are held constant throughout the period of the experiment, allowing a meaningful contrast between what happens prior to, and what occurs with, a mechanism being triggered.

But these experimental scenarios, though useful in science, are not necessary for success using the contrast explanatory approach. All we often need is an informed perspective giving us reason to expect two outcomes to be the same in a situation where the latter are found to be different. In that situation there is *prima facie* reason to suppose a single causal factor is responsible, and reason to expect that it can be identified (for a longer more detailed discussion, see Lawson, 2003, chapter 4).

The complexity of economic analysis

I have run through the method of contrast explanation first and foremost to indicate that causal analysis can proceed in the absence of closed systems. However, I should emphasise that explanatory analysis required to render any chosen contrast phenomenon of interest intelligible can take many forms. It may involve the identification of a hitherto non-existent local mechanism or set of conditions, or a reworking of previous understandings, including seeing connections or relations previously unnoticed, or even the elaboration of a highly abstract account of the workings of a system in its entirety. It all depends on context.

If, for example, the chosen contrast is highly context specific, say two local traders are selling the same product at different prices, the causal explanation is likely also to be a relatively localised factor. If instead, the contrast is of a sort that interested Marx, namely that after a point in history goods were mostly being produced for exchange in the marketplace (i.e., as commodities) rather than, as previously, for immediate use, the explanation (in Marx's case his theory of the emergence and nature of the capitalist mode of production) will be rather more extensive in its scope or reach of relevance.

Applied economics

Of course, economics is not restricted just to the identification of causal tendencies, whether these involve reference to simple mechanisms or economic totalities or systems. Economists may also be interested in specific outcomes.

Can we say much about concrete events? After a specific economic outcome has occurred it may be possible to work out how the different known mechanisms combined to produce it (much like a weather pattern can be explained after it has happened).

How about before the event? Can anything be said? The answer depends on context. If the situation is one in which two or three mechanisms or tendencies are thought to dominate a phenomenon of interest, perhaps a range of likely outcomes can be safely speculated.

More typically, though, it will be possible, in a given context, to do little more than identify the workings of a specific tendency of interest and speculate as to some of the likely countervailing tendencies. At the level of outcomes there is no option but to wait and see (notice that even this may be enough for policy purposes. Even if we do not know the workings of all mechanisms we may be able to identify those that work to produce greater unemployment, poverty, discrimination and other undesirable features, and so work on undermining their supporting conditions).

It is the deeper more abstract structures that, though never fixed, seem to be the more enduring. The price mechanism is more enduring than a set of prices; typically the university outlives any specific courses given. In serious economic research it is often the case that deeper structures will be taken as momentarily given and perhaps used to frame more detailed studies, although the insights of the latter will often facilitate a better or revised understanding of the former.

The broader analysis

What does all this entail for economists who wish to give a broader picture? It means they will need to move between different levels of abstraction, at some moments descending to speculations of concrete outcomes where it is believed the major forces of determination are fairly stable and mostly known; at other moments identifying the operation of significant tendencies in play and perhaps also noting offsetting counter-tendencies; and at further moments still retreating to yet higher levels of abstraction, specifically where the context makes so much difference both to precise outcomes and to the causal factors in play that little can be said short of empirically examining the details in context (and perhaps alerting the reader to this fact).

The above overview, though not comprehensive, indicates the sorts of analytical procedures that the best of economists have mostly tended to draw upon, most specifically those now associated with the modern heterodox traditions. Let me finish by giving some brief illustrations.

Precursors

When Thorstien Veblen, the figurehead of the (old) institutionalist school of economics (a heterodox tradition opposed to the modern mainstream), argued a century ago that social life was in large part a process, and specifically constituted by evolutionary processes of cumulative causation, he never tried to generalise the concrete details of social processes. Clearly to suggest that social life is largely processual is to generalise at a relatively high level of abstraction. However, Veblen was clear that if his general claim was correct, and that an evolutionary economics was inevitable, a turn to the latter actually meant abandoning the search for highly general self-contained systems of substantive economic theory (such as modern day economists mostly pursue with their reliance on functional relations). Indeed, Veblen concluded that an evolutionary economics would need to be highly empirical in nature, concerned with determining how actual social phenomena grow and change (he also erroneously thought that 'the body of economists' appreciated this and were already carrying through):

> Self-contained systems of economic theory, balanced and compendious, are no longer at the focal centre of attention; nor is there a felt need of such.... Meantime, detailed monographic and itemised inquiry, description, analysis, and appraisal of particular processes going forward in industry and business, are engaging the best attention of economists; instead of that meticulous reconstruction and canvassing of schematic theories that once was of great moment and that brought comfort and assurance to its adepts and their disciples. There is little prospect that the current generation of economists will work out a compendious system of economic theory at large.........
>
> ... The question now before the body of economists is not how things stabilise themselves in a 'static state,' but how they endlessly grow and change.
>
> (Veblen, 1925 [1954], p. 8)

When John Maynard Keynes, the figurehead of the post Keynesian school of economics (a further heterodox tradition opposed to the modern mainstream), argued that social life was characterised by uncertainty, and specifically that, as a result, investment decisions were especially sensitive to the current state of markets and investor confidence, he never tried to generalise these factors at the concrete level (to make the state of investor confidence the dependent variable in a functional relation or whatever). Rather, Keynes recommended an empirical assessment of markets and actual business psychology in any relevant context. In doing so, Keynes was aware that successful analysis necessarily moved between different levels of abstraction, according to the nature of the subject matter being considered:

> There is, however, not much that can be said about the state of confidence *a priori*. Our conclusions must mainly depend on actual observations of markets and business psychology. This is the reason why the ensuing digression is on a different level of abstraction from most of the book.
>
> (1973, p. 149)

And when Karl Marx theorised, and systematised as a 'general law', a mechanism working to cause profits to fall, he fully recognised that, if his theory was correct, this mechanism would typically be crossed if not annulled by countervailing forces. For this reason Marx described his law as expressing a tendency rather than an empirical actuality. Marx even stressed that in periods when profits actually fell there were likely countervailing forces preventing it falling faster. Indeed, he inquired into their nature:

> There must be some counteracting influences at work, which cross and annul the effect of the general law, and which give it merely the characteristic of a tendency, for which reason we have referred to the fall of the general rate of profit as a tendency to fall.
> The following are the most general counterbalancing forces: ...
>
> (Marx, *Capital*, volume III, chapter xiv)

Summary

The argument of this essay can be put simply. It is widely recognised that economics performs badly as an explanatory endeavour. The reason for this is that modern economists all too often seek to generalise in the wrong place, and specifically, given their desire to formulate functional relations, at the level of actual outcomes and their presumed correlations. The reason for this, in turn, is a widespread insistence on using the methods of mathematical-deductive modelling. And this latter phenomenon, in its turn, is motivated by a desire on the part of economists to be scientific coupled with the (erroneous) belief that mathematics is essential to all science. Once the latter belief is seen to be erroneous and the straightjacket of the insistence on mathematical-deductive modelling thrown off, methods can be taken up that seem capable of allowing economics to be both explanatorily successful and even scientific in the sense of natural science.

Note

1 Sometimes a function defined in X with values in Y is called a transformation or mapping of X into Y.

References

Blaug, Mark (1997) Ugly Currents in Modern Economics, *Options Politiques*, (Septembre): 3–8.

Coase, Ronald (1999) Interview with Ronald Coase, *Newsletter of the International Society for New Institutional Economics,* Vol 2, No. 1 (Spring).

Friedman, Milton (1999) Conversation with Milton Friedman in Snowdon B. and Vane H. (ed.), *Conversations with Leading Economists: interpreting modern macroeconomics,* 124–44, Cheltenham: Edward Elgar.

Kay, John (1995) Cracks in the Crystal Ball, *Financial Times,* September 29.

Keynes, John Maynard (1973) *The Collected Writings of John Maynard Keynes,* Vol. VII, *The General Theory of Employment Interest and Money,* Royal Economic Society.

Lawson, Tony (1997) *Economics and Reality,* London and New York: Routledge.

Lawson, Tony (2003) *Reorienting Economics,* London and New York: Routledge.

Leontief, Wassily (1982) Letter in *Science,* 217: 104–7.

Lipsey, Richard, G. (2001) Successes and failures in the transformation of economics *Journal of Economic Methodology,* Vol. 8, No. 2 (June): 169–202.

Marshall, A. (1920) *The Principles of Economics,* 8th Edition, London: Macmillan.

Marx, Karl (1974) *Capital: A Critique of Political Economy, Volume III: The Process of Capitalist Production as a Whole,* Edited by Engels F., London: Lawrence and Wishart.

Rubinstein, Ariel (1995) John Nash: the master of economic modelling, *Scandinavian Journal of Economics* 97(1): 9–13.

Veblen, Thorstein B. (1925 [1954]) 'Economic Theory in the Calculable Future', *American Economic Review,* Vol. XV, No. 1, Supplement, March. Reprinted in Ardzrooni, Leon (ed.) (1954) *Essays in our Changing Order,* New York: Viking Press (page references to the latter).

3 The nature of heterodox economics*

Introduction

Recent years have seen the emergence of numerous activities in economics identified first and foremost as heterodox. For example, 1999 witnessed the formation of the Association for Heterodox Economics (AHE), an organisation that now sponsors an annual conference, postgraduate training workshops and more.[1] In October 2002, The University of Missouri at Kansas City hosted a conference on 'The History of Heterodox Economics in the 20th Century'. December 2002 saw the inaugural conference of the Australian Society of Heterodox Economists (SHE) at the University of New South Wales. Six months later, in June 2003, back at the University of Missouri at Kansas City, ICAPE (the International Confederation of Associations for Pluralism in Economics) celebrated its ten-year birthday with its 'First World Conference on the Future of Heterodox Economics'. Soon after this, journals started devoting whole issues to the movement or its history. A *Heterodox Economics Newsletter* has since emerged.[2] At the time of writing, the University of Utah sports a Heterodox Economics Student Association (HESA) and, on the Internet, it is possible to find a large number of sites dedicated to promoting specifically 'heterodox economics' and providing significant relevant resources.[3]

So it seems that something called heterodox economics is alive and flourishing. My question here is what (sort of thing) is it? In asking this question, I do not wish to reify or fix the project. There is no reason at all to suppose that heterodox economics, any less than any other social phenomenon, is other than intrinsically dynamic and indeed ultimately transient. But I do take the view that things in process can still be known, if only as historical (and geographical and cultural) products. And I believe, and hope to show, that there can be gains to critical self-reflection upon the nature of that with which we are dealing or involved, at any point in time.

Among the very few who have questioned the nature of heterodox economics, it is recognised that heterodoxy serves, in the first instance, as an umbrella term to cover the coming together of, sometimes long-standing, *separate* heterodox projects or traditions. The latter include post-Keynesianism, (old) institutionalism, feminist, social, Marxian, Austrian and social economics, among others.

With this in mind, my initial question can be reformulated as an enquiry into whether there exists a (set of) trait(s) or causal condition(s), etc., that these traditions hold in common, over and above their all being projects in academic economics. For if there is a set of characteristics by virtue of which any tradition qualifies as heterodox (and determining whether this is so is my objective here), it is presumably included among the features, if any, that the often very differently oriented traditions share.

It is on this presumption that I shall proceed. The interpretation I defend is indeed one of unity within difference. It will be seen that to conceptualise and so identify heterodox economics is also to distinguish the mainstream against which it stands opposed. And thus to determine both is to distinguish economics from other disciplines, and so on. A process is thus set in train that stretches far beyond my original question. But I here explicitly step beyond a discussion of heterodox economics only to the extent that it is necessary to do so to get a reasonable initial assessment of its specific determinations.

1. The separate heterodox traditions

When we turn to the separate heterodox traditions, we find that the task of identifying the nature of any one of them is not straightforward. In fact, there is a good deal of debate within most, if not all, of the various traditions as to whether they constitute constructive programmes at all (see Peukert, 2001) or even coherent individual projects (see e.g., Hamouda and Harcourt, 1988). However, there do appear to be some prominent common features of all these separate traditions, even if some work is required in interpreting the implications. These prominent commonalities are, or include, the following:

1 a set of recurring fairly abstract tradition-specific themes and emphases;
2 a multiplicity of attempts within each tradition to theorise around its tradition-specific themes and to form policy stances, or else to determine tradition-specific main units of analysis or other methodological principles based on them. The results are often presented as the theory/policy stances, basic units of analysis, or methodological principles that constitute the relevant tradition's alternatives to those of the mainstream;
3 an *a posteriori* recognition that it is usually impossible to generate very large agreement within any given heterodox tradition on specific

'alternative' theories and policies or specific methodological stances, a recognition typically resulting in an (often begrudging) inference that, even within any one tradition, the only definite common ground in terms of achieved position, is an opposition to the mainstream or 'neoclassical' orthodoxy.

Consider, as an illustration, the case of post-Keynesianism. Few would doubt that various themes or emphases are prominent. I refer, for example, to the concern with fundamental uncertainty in the analysis of decision-making, the rejection of the idea that macro outcomes can be provided with micro-foundations, a significant emphasis on methodological analysis, a recognition of the importance of time, institutions and history, a frequent drawing on the writing of Keynes, and so forth (see, for example, Arestis, 1990; Davidson, 1980; Dow, 1992; Sawyer, 1988).

However, attempts to produce substantive theories, policies or methodological stances have usually led to such a degree of variation or competition that post-Keynesians, and their observers, have tended to conclude that indeed the only definite point of agreement among post-Keynesians is that they stand opposed to the mainstream or 'neoclassical' contributions. Consider the following assessments:

> Post-Keynesian economics can be seen as covering a considerable assortment of approaches. It has sometimes been said that the unifying feature of post-Keynesians is the dislike of neoclassical economics.
> (Sawyer, 1988, p. 1)

> [P]ost-Keynesian economics is often portrayed as being distinguished more by its dislike of neoclassical theory, than by any coherence or agreement on fundamentals by its contributors.
> (Hodgson, 1989, p. 96)

> It is less controversial to say what post-Keynesian theory is not than to say what it is. Post-Keynesian theory is not neoclassical theory.
> (Eichner, 1985, p. 51)

> [P]ost-Keynesians tend to define their program in a negative way as a reaction to neo-classical economics.
> (Arestis, 1990, p. 222)

> Some have argued that what unites post-Keynesians is a negative factor: the rejection of neoclassical economics.
> (Dow, 1992, p. 176)

What seems to be striking to outsiders of post-Keynesianism and neo-Ricardianism is that these two schools of thought and their major proponents only seem to have one cementing theme, their rejection of the dominant neoclassical paradigm.

(Lavoie, 1992, p. 45)

I think heterodox economists will recognise that the sorts of commonalities listed above, and illustrated for the case of post-Keynesianism, hold to a degree for all the heterodox traditions.[4] David Colander, Richard Holt and J. Barkley Rosser Jr appear to speak for many when they conclude that '[i]n economics, at least, beyond this rejection of the orthodoxy there is no single unifying element that we can discern that characterises heterodox economics' (Colander *et al.*, 2004, p. 492)

In short, we appear to reach an apparently widely shared assessment of heterodox economics only in terms of what it is not, or rather in terms of that to which it stands opposed; the one widely recognised and accepted feature of all the heterodox traditions is a rejection of the modern mainstream project.

Of course, such an oppositional stance should not altogether surprise us. For employment of the term heterodox entails precisely this. According to the *Shorter Oxford English Dictionary*, for example, the qualification heterodox just means '[n]ot in accordance with established doctrines or opinions, or those generally recognised as orthodox'.

However, this recognition need not imply that heterodoxy is purely reactive. Nor does it follow that there is little more to be said. Indeed, an explicit rejection of orthodoxy in any sphere is presumably undertaken for certain reasons. And a sustained opposition, such as we find in modern economics, leads us to expect that the reasons for resistance are deep ones. Further, in addition to explicitly formalised grounds for an opposition to any orthodoxy, there are often other less-than-clearly-unrecognised presuppositions. I think this is so with heterodox economics, as we shall see.

It is clear, though, that if we are to progress in our quest to understand the nature of heterodox economics, we need first to determine something of the nature of that to which the heterodox traditions stand opposed. Only with this achieved are we likely to be successful in identifying the basis of the heterodox opposition. That is, before we can elaborate the presuppositions of heterodox economics, we need some insight into the nature of the project to which heterodoxy stands so seemingly implacably opposed.

2. What is modern mainstream or orthodox economics?

Perhaps at this point the argument begins to get somewhat (more) contentious. For although most observers of modern economics do recognise that the discipline is dominated by a mainstream tradition, and is so to a degree that is rather striking, there is remarkably little sustained discussion or analysis of (as opposed to a few quick assertions about) the nature of that mainstream project (even though practising economists usually agree that they know it when they see it). Among the conceptions of the mainstream that are to be found the following two are perhaps the more prominent, though each, I believe, is ultimately unsustainable.

The first such conception of mainstream economics is as a project concerned primarily with defending the workings of the current economic system, a conception often systematised under the heading of 'mainstream economics as ideology'. A recent example is provided by Guerrien (2004). Although the term ideology is rarely defined, it carries the connotation of a theory adhered to irrespective of its method or level of justification (or lack of justification). It is maintained, rather, because of some purpose it serves. Guerrien (2004) writes in this context of a mainstream ungrounded insistence that '"market mechanisms" produce "efficient" results if you abstract from "frictions", "failures" etc.' (Guerrien, 2004, p. 15).

Kanth (1999) provides an insightful contribution that seems to interpret mainstream economics in a similar fashion. According to Kanth, mainstream economics (which he sometimes refers to as neoclassical economics) is deliberately 'rigged' so as to generate results that support the *status quo*:

> To state the moral: *the entire enterprise of neo-classical economics is rigged to show that laissez-faire produces optimal outcomes*, but for the disruptive operation of the odd externality (a belated correction) here and there.
> (Kanth, 1999, pp. 191–2, emphasis in the original)

How is this rigging said to be achieved? One component of the most common strategy is everywhere to stipulate that human beings are rational (meaning optimising) atomistic individuals. A second is the construction of theoretical set-ups or models specified to ensure that (typically unique) optimal outcomes are attainable.

This is not yet enough to 'show' that the overall economic system is itself optimal in any way. If the claim is that mainstream economists seek to defend the economic system *per se*, something more is required to guarantee this result. This, it is usually supposed, is achieved by the commonplace construction of an equilibrium framework, the latter being so specified that the actions of isolated optimising individuals somehow (tend to) work to bring an equilibrium position about. Thus Kanth, for example, refers to the 'economic science of capitalism' as 'simply *irrelevant* for being a fantasy world of an ideal rational, capitalism where all motions are mutually equilibriating, in a Newtonian co-ordination of the elements' (Kanth, 1999, p. 194).

There is little doubt that some mainstream economists approach their subject in the manner that Guerrien and others suggest. But most do not. And I do worry that portraying mainstream economics as driven by the goal of achieving results in these terms is overly conspiratorial. Nor is the presumption that mainstream results are consistent with an efficient or optimal social order even correct as a generalisation. Even those who have spent their careers studying models of equilibrium typically do not draw the sorts of inferences that can be used to justify the economic system.

Consider the conclusions of Frank Hahn, a major contributor to general equilibrium theory who has also been concerned to comment continually on the nature of the enterprise of equilibrium theorising. In both his Jevons memorial lecture entitled 'In Praise of Economic Theory' and the introduction to his collection of essays entitled *Macroeconomics and Equilibrium*, Hahn explicitly acknowledges that he everywhere adopts (1) an individualistic perspective, a requirement that explanations be couched solely in terms of individuals, and (2) some rationality axiom. But in referencing questions of economic order or equilibrium, Hahn further accepts *at most* (3) a commitment merely to the *study* of equilibrium states. Poignantly, Hahn believes equilibrium outcomes or states are rarely if ever manifest:

> [I]t cannot be denied that there is something scandalous in the spectacle of so many people refining the analyses of economic [equilibrium] states which they give no reason to suppose will ever, or have ever, come about. It probably is also dangerous. Equilibrium economics ... is easily convertible into an apologia for existing economic arrangements and it is frequently so converted.
>
> (1970, pp. 88–9)

Further, there are groups of economists, seemingly acceptable to the mainstream who, though adopting the individualist-rationalistic framework, seem determined from the outset to demonstrate the *weaknesses* of the current economic system. Those economists who are often described as 'rational-choice Marxists' seem to be so inclined.

Equally to the point if not more so, most economists who accept the individualist and rationalistic framework do not actually concern themselves with questions of equilibrium at all or, more generally, do not focus on the workings of the economic system as a whole. Most such economists, rather, concern themselves with highly specific or partial analyses of some restricted sectors or forms of behaviour. Moreover, to the extent that it is meaningful for the various results or theorems of these economists to be considered as a whole, or in total, the only clear conclusion to be drawn from them is that they are mostly wildly inconsistent with each other.

Notoriously, even econometricians using identical, or almost identical, datasets are found to produce quite contrasting conclusions. The systematic result here, as the respected econometrician Edward Leamer (1983) observes, is that 'hardly anyone takes anyone else's data analysis seriously' (p. 37).

If we turn away from econometrics to the mostly non-empirical 'economic theory' project, and look beyond its general equilibrium programme (which in any case has been in decline for some time now), there seems not even to be any agreement as to the project's purpose or direction. As one of its leading practitioners, Ariel Rubinstein, admits:

> The issue of interpreting economic theory is ... the most serious problem now facing economic theorists ... Economic theory lacks a consensus as to its purpose and interpretation. Again and again, we find ourselves asking the question 'where does it lead?'
> (Rubinstein, 1995, p. 12)

3. Mainstream economics as the study of optimising individual behaviour

So what are we to make of all this? How are we to understand the project of mainstream economics in a manner that can make sense of this more complex situation? An obvious alternative hypothesis to examine in the light of the discussion so far, perhaps, is that, if there is anything essential to the mainstream tradition of modern economics, it is merely a commitment to individualism, coupled with the axiom that individuals are everywhere rational (optimising) in their behaviour. Perhaps the mainstream is just so committed, but without any overall common purpose in terms of the sorts of substantive results that 'should' be generated?

This is the second reasonably widespread interpretation of the mainstream endeavour, and the chief alternative to the view that the mainstream project is one concerned to defend the workings of the economic system. It constitutes an assessment, in particular, that is probably the more dominant among modern historians of economic thought.

Perhaps this characterisation of the mainstream programme is closer to the mark. But in the end, it is not sustainable. There are numerous game theory contributions where rationality is no longer invoked, and seemingly not even meaningful. Mainstream economists are sometimes even prepared to assume that people everywhere follow fixed highly simple rules whatever the context (see references in Lawson, 1997, ch. 8). Moreover, some mainstream economists are prepared to abandon the individualist framework entirely if this will help make the 'economic theory' framework more productive in some way. As the 'economic theorist' Alan Kirman writes:

> The problem [of mainstream theorising to date] seems to be embodied in what is an essential feature of a centuries-long tradition in economics, that of treating individuals as acting independently of each other.
>
> (Kirman, 1989, p. 137)

Kirman adds 'If we are to progress further we may well be forced to theorise in terms of groups who have collectively coherent behaviour' (Kirman, 1989, p. 138).

So it is not obvious that even assumptions of individualism and rationality are ultimately essential to the mainstream position. Indeed, many (e.g., Davis, 2005) find with Colander *et al.* (2004) that '[mainstream] economics is moving away from strict adherence to the holy trinity—rationality, selfishness, and equilibrium—to a more eclectic position of purposeful behaviour, enlightened self-interest and sustainability' *(ibid.,* p. 485).

Do we, then, give up on our search for the essence of the current mainstream project? Some commentators believe so, with many concluding that the current mainstream is just too slippery a project to pin down. But I do not think that the latter is the case. Rather, I think that an essential distinguishing feature of the mainstream project of the last fifty years or more is identifiable and remaining in place even through the sort of (ongoing) changes recorded by Colander *et al.*, Davis and others, a matter to which I return below. What then do I take the mainstream to be?

4. The mathematising inclination

As I say, I believe there is a feature of modern mainstream economics that is essential to it. And it is an aspect so taken for granted that it goes largely unquestioned. This is just the formalistic-deductive framework that mainstream economists everywhere adopt, and indeed insist upon.

I am not suggesting that the mathematical framework goes unrecognised. This could hardly be the case. But the mathematical framework is usually only briefly noted at best; it is considered so essential that worries about its usefulness, or dispensability, if they are raised at all, tend to be summarily dismissed rather than seriously addressed. It is because mathematisation is understood as being so obviously desirable, indeed, that the project is rarely defined in such terms. Serious work, it seems to be supposed, could never be otherwise.

Consider just the (mainstream) economists already mentioned. Rubinstein notes in passing that (mainstream) economic theory 'utilises mathematical tools' without questioning the legitimacy of this. Kirman (1989), though acknowledging that 'the mathematical frameworks that we have used made the task of changing or at least modifying our paradigm hard, is undeniable', insists that 'it is difficult to believe that had a clear well-formulated new approach been suggested then we would not have adopted the appropriate mathematical tools' (Kirman, 1989, p. 137). Leamer, on noting a continuing 'wide gap between econometric theory and econometric practice', laments not being able to perceive 'developments on the horizon that will make any mathematical theory of inference fully applicable' (Leamer, 1978, p. vi; the idea that there may be relevant non-mathematical theories of inference is seemingly never contemplated). And Hahn probably most epitomises widespread sentiment when he declares of any suggestion that the typical emphasis on mathematics may be misplaced that it is 'a view surely not worth discussing' (Hahn, 1985, p. 18). In fact, Hahn later counsels that we 'avoid discussions of 'mathematics in economics' like the plague' (Hahn, 1992A; see also Hahn, 1992B).[5]

The truth is that modern mainstream economics is just the reliance on certain forms of mathematical (deductivist) method. This is an enduring feature of that project, and seemingly the only one; for the mainstream tradition it is its unquestioned, and seemingly unquestionable, essential core.

Consider some more observations. The worry of non-economist observers is often that descriptions or overviews by critics of modern mainstream economics are likely to be uncharitable caricatures. So I focus on more impressions of mainstream economists themselves. Richard Lipsey, an author of a best-selling mainstream economic texts book, acknowledges:

> to get an article published in most of today's top rank economic journals, you must provide a mathematical model, even if it adds nothing to your verbal analysis. I have been at seminars where the presenter was asked after a few minutes, 'Where is your model?'. When he answered 'I have not got one as I do not need one, or cannot yet develop one, to consider my problem' the response was to turn off and figuratively, if not literally, to walk out.
>
> (Lipsey, 2001, p. 184)

Just as tellingly, when William Thomson was recently invited by a leading mainstream journal to provide a piece entitled 'The young person's guide to writing economic theory', the taken-for-granted meaning of 'writing economic theory' is clear in the opening three sentences:

> Here are my recommendations for writing economic theory (and, to some extent, giving seminar presentations). My intended audience is young economists working on their dissertations or preparing first papers for submission to a professional journal. Although I discuss general issues of presentation, this essay is mainly concerned in its details with formal models.
>
> (Thomson, 1999, p. 157)

34 *The nature of heterodox economics*

Or consider assessments of some Nobel Memorial Prize winners in economics. Wassily Leontief observes critically how '[p]age after page of professional economic journals are filled with mathematical formulas ... Year after year economic theorists continue to produce scores of mathematical models and to explore in great detail their formal properties; and the econometricians fit algebraic functions of all possible shapes to essentially the same sets of data' (Leontief, 1982, p. 104). Friedman concludes that 'economics has become increasingly an arcane branch of mathematics rather than dealing with real economic problems' (Friedman, 1999, p. 137). And Coase finds that '[e]xisting economics is a theoretical [meaning mathematical] system which floats in the air and which bears little relation to what happens in the real world' (Coase, 1999, p. 2). And there are many other observers of this situation, too.[6]

5. The changing face of the mainstream

Perhaps it will be thought that changes in the mainstream project that are currently under way serve to undermine the assessment sustained above? Colander *et al.* (2004) (in their paper explicitly titled 'The changing face of mainstream economics') argue that the mainstream is currently being transformed quite significantly, and criticise heterodox economists for failing to notice such ongoing developments. Specifically, these authors criticise heterodox contributors for adopting an overly 'static view of the profession' (p. 486); for referring to the current mainstream as neoclassical; and for missing the 'diversity that exists within the profession, and the many new ideas that are being tried out' (p. 487). In contrast, Colander *et al.* insist that '[m]ainstream economics is a complex system of evolving ideas' (p. 489), and refer to the 'multiple dimensionalities that we see in the mainstream profession' (p. 489).

Now, as it happens, I mostly agree with each of these critical assessments. In my view, it has always been unhelpful to make reference to a 'neoclassical economics', a category rarely clearly defined, and always misleading. And diversity within the dominant tradition has never been absent. Further, as always in the past, changes in the dominant tradition (as elsewhere) are certainly currently under way. For example, I can acknowledge (with Colander *et al.*) that evolutionary game theory is redefining how (notions of) institutions are integrated into analysis; that ecological economics is redefining how rationality is treated; that econometric work dealing with the limitations of classical statistics is defining how economists think of empirical proof; that complexity theory is providing a new way to conceptualise equilibrium states; that computer simulations offer a new approach to analysis; that experimental economics is changing the way economists think about empirical work, and so on.

But it remains the case that these and all other widely sanctioned examples of ongoing change, diversity, novelty, complexity, evolution and multi-dimensionality, etc., are occurring within the framework of formalistic modelling. The insistence on mathematical–deductive modelling prevails in all cases; the essential feature of the recent and current mainstream remains intact.

In fact, Colander *et al.* have noticed this aspect of 'the changing face of mainstream economics' themselves. I am not sure they fully appreciate the significance of their observation (they give it little emphasis) but in any case they acknowledge that:

> modern mainstream economics is open to new approaches, as long as they are done with a careful understanding of the strengths of the recent orthodox approach and with a modelling methodology acceptable to the mainstream.
>
> (Colander *et al.*, 2004, p. 492)

Perceiving an 'elite' within the mainstream that determines which new ideas are acceptable, Colander *et al.* also write:

> [o]ur view is that the current elite are relatively open minded when it comes to new ideas, but quite closed minded when it comes to alternative methodologies. If it isn't modelled, it isn't economics, no matter how insightful.
>
> (Colander *et al.*, 2004, p. 492)

And they add, with reason: '[s]pecifically, it is because of their method, not their ideas, that most heterodox find themselves defined outside the field by the elite' (Colander *et al.*, 2004, p. 492).

In any case, an examination of ongoing developments soon enough reveals that they too ultimately provide support for my assessment that the mainstream project of modern economics must be characterised in terms neither of substantive results (such as demonstrating the desirability of the current economic order) nor of basic units of analysis (rationalistic or optimising individuals), but of its *orientation* to method. This is my first major contention: the mainstream project of modern economics just is an insistence, as a discipline-wide principle, that economic phenomena be investigated using only certain mathematical–deductive forms of reasoning. This is the mainstream conception of proper economics. It is the one feature or presupposition[7] that remains common to (if not always explicitly formulated in) all contributions regarded as mainstream, remaining in place throughout all the project's theoretical fads and fashions.

6. The nature of heterodox economics

What follows for our understanding of heterodox economics? If the latter is first and foremost a rejection of modern mainstream economics, and the latter consists in the insistence that forms of mathematical–deductive method should everywhere be utilised, then heterodox economics, in the first instance, is just a rejection of this emphasis.

Notice that this does not amount to a rejection of all mathematical–deductive modelling. But it is a rejection of the insistence that we all always and everywhere use it.

In other words, heterodox economics, in the first instance, is a rejection of a very specific form of methodological reductionism. It is a rejection of the view that formalistic methods are everywhere and always appropriate.

To say more about the nature of the heterodox traditions of modern economics, I think it is clear that we need to explain this opposition. And, as noted, we are concerned here with explaining an opposition that is sustained and enduring.

One conceivable explanation, I suppose, is that heterodox economists believe that methodological pluralism is desirable *per se* and no more needs to be said. But is that really all there is to it? After all, in some fields of physics, such as super string theory, mathematical methods seem actually to be universally applied, but without any sign of a heterodox opposition. In economics, by contrast, there clearly is a heterodox opposition to the mainstream. And the phenomenon to explain is not just that a heterodox opposition exists, but that it is, as noted, relatively widespread, firm, often highly vocal and enduring.

7. Accounting for the nature of the heterodox opposition

To make sense of the fact of a sustained and widespread opposition to the mainstream, I think we must acknowledge that it is at least in some part based on an assessment by heterodox economists and others that the mainstream approach is actually very rarely up to the task at hand. And, indeed, the mainstream project is perceived by many as being more or less systematically irrelevant (see especially Fullbrook, 2003, 2004; Howell, 2000).

Even mainstream contributors seem increasingly to be accepting the assessment that their project (albeit typically conceived just as economics) is not doing too well in a general sense, and may actually be not very appropriate in the way it is done. Once more considering only those mainstream spokespeople already noted, Rubinstein (1995, p. 12) notes the explanatory and predictive weaknesses of the mainstream project, while Leamer (1983, p. 37) draws attention to a disparity of mainstream theory and practice. Coase, as we have seen, concludes that '[e]xisting economics is a theoretical system which floats in the air and which bears little relation to what happens in the real world' while, according to Leontief, the mathematical formulae with which economists fill economic journals lead 'the reader from sets of more or less plausible but entirely arbitrary assumptions to precisely stated but irrelevant theoretical conclusions', while econometricians fail 'to advance, in any perceptible way, a systematic understanding of the structure and the operations of a real economic system' (Leontief, 1982, p. 104).

8. Ontology

Now how could a project in modern economics turn out to be as systematically deficient as these commentators and others appear to find it? I want to suggest that a compelling (and perhaps the only plausible) explanation of it is that the sorts of methods on which the mainstream put so much emphasis are just not appropriate for dealing with social material, given the latter's nature. This is my second central thesis.

Here we get to the topic of ontology. Ontology is the study of, or a theory about, the basic nature and structure of (a domain) of reality. We all adopt ontological stances, and the acceptance of any method of analysis carries with it certain ontological preconceptions. As Marx says somewhere, microscopes and chemical reagents are not appropriate to the analysis of economic forms. I suspect most of us would agree with this assessment. But the point is a general one. All methods of analysis are appropriate to some sorts of material but not others. This is as true of mathematical methods as others. My claim here is that the explanation of the poor showing of much of modern economics is that mathematical methods are being imposed in situations for which they are largely inappropriate.

In due course, I shall argue further that it is an appraisal that mathematical methods are mostly inappropriate to social analysis that ultimately underpins the heterodox opposition. In short, I am contending that *the essence of the heterodox opposition is ontological in nature*. This, indeed, will be my third central thesis.

Although I shall address this third contention below, let me immediately emphasise that, if it does indeed constitute a correct assessment, I do not claim that the ontological orientation of the heterodox opposition has always been, or is always, recognised. To the contrary, I believe that one reason that the heterodox traditions have been less effective than their case appears to warrant is precisely that the ontological nature of their opposition has rarely been made sufficiently clear. Let me elaborate these various contentions.

9. The preconceptions of modern mainstream economics

I start by examining the implicit ontological presupposition of the modern mainstream project, thereby indicating the worldview that I believe is, in effect, being opposed by heterodox contributors.

We can note, first, that the sorts of formalistic methods that economists wield mostly require, for their application, the existence (or positing) of closed systems, i.e., those in which (deterministic or stochastic) event regularities occur. Mainstream economics is thus a form of *deductivism*. By deductivism I mean any form of explanatory endeavour that relies upon (which seeks or posits) closed systems.

Actually, mainstream economics is slightly more specific than this: it is a version of deductivism that posits functional relations presupposing *closures of causal sequence*. The latter are closed systems in which the events correlated are such that one set (conceptualised as 'independent variables') are considered to stand in the causal history of the remaining events (the 'dependent variable'). Thus a standard formulation of, say, a 'consumption function', which typically involves the correlation of household expenditure with household disposable income, posits the latter as a factor standing in the causal history of the former.[8]

Of course, the fact that formalistic modelling methods require the identification or construction of event regularities of some sort is well recognised by mainstream economists. Allais (1992), taking the association of deductivist modelling and science for granted, expresses the conventional situation well:

> The essential condition of any science is the existence of regularities which can be analysed and forecast. This is the case in celestial mechanics. But it is also true of many economic phenomena. Indeed, their thorough analysis displays the existence of regularities which are just as striking as those found in the physical sciences. This is why economics is a science, and why this science rests on the same general principles and methods of physics.
>
> (Allais, 1992, p. 25)

But if Allais correctly points to the need for modern mainstream economists to identify or formulate social event regularities, his description of the situation of modern economics is actually quite wrong in two of its aspects. Econometricians repeatedly find that correlations of the sort formulated are no sooner reported than found to break down; social event regularities of the requisite kind are hard to come by (see Lawson, 1997, ch. 7). And, it is just not the case that 'striking' event regularities of the sort Allais appears to reference, and which modern mainstream economists pursue, are essential to science. Their prevalence is a precondition for the mathematical–deductivist methods that economists emphasise as having relevance, but the application of these methods cannot be equated to science (see Lawson, 2003, ch. 1). Here, though, I merely note that any presumption of the universal relevance of mathematical-modelling methods in economics ultimately presupposes the ubiquity of (strict) event regularities.

10. Atomism and isolationism

But this is not the end of the ontological preconditions of methods of mathematical–deductivist modelling as employed in modern economics. A further important feature, which is less often recognised (or at least rarely explicitly acknowledged), is that the dependency of mathematical–deductivist methods on closed systems in turn more or less necessitates, and certainly encourages, formulations couched in terms of (i) isolated (ii) atoms. The metaphorical reference to atoms here is not intended to convey anything about size. Rather the reference is to items which exercise their own separate, independent and invariable (and so predictable) effects (relative to, or as a function of, initial conditions).

Deductivist theorising of the sort pursued in modern economics ultimately has to be couched in terms of such 'atoms' just to ensure that under given conditions x the same (predictable or deducible) outcome y always follows. If any agent in the theory could do other than some given y in specific conditions x—either because the agent is intrinsically structured and can just act differently each time x occurs, or because the agent's action possibilities are affected by whatever else is going on—the desire to pursue deductive inference would be frustrated.

Notice that this assessment is not novel, at least with regard to econometrics. It is in effect that advanced by Keynes over 60 years ago, albeit using a slightly different terminology. Thus, in response to an invitation from the League of Nations to review Tinbergen's early work on business cycles, Keynes writes:

> There is first of all the central question of methodology,—the logic of applying the method of multiple correlation to unanalysed economic material, which we know to be non-homogeneous through time. If we are dealing with the action of numerically measurable, independent forces, adequately analysed so that we were dealing with independent atomic factors and between them completely comprehensive, acting with fluctuating relative strength on material constant and homogeneous through time, we might be able to use the method of multiple correlation with some confidence for disentangling the laws of their action . . .

In fact, we know that every one of these conditions is far from being satisfied by the economic material under investigation . . .

> To proceed to some more detailed comments. The coefficients arrived at are apparently assumed to be constant for 10 years or for a larger period. Yet, surely we know that they are not constant. There is no reason at all why they should not be different every year.
>
> (1973, pp. 285–6)

The point then, however unoriginal, is that the ontological presuppositions of the insistence on mathematical modelling include the restriction that the social domain is everywhere constituted by sets of isolated atoms.[9]

Now it is immediately clear, I think, that this latter restriction *need* not characterise the social realm. I want to suggest indeed that the noted conditions for closure (a world of isolated atoms) may actually be rather rare in the social realm. I draw this conclusion on the basis of an *(a posteriori* derived) theory of social ontology, a conception of the nature of the material of social reality defended elsewhere (especially in Lawson, 1997, 2003). I shall not provide a *defence* of this ontology here but merely give a brief overview of some the central components of it that are relevant to the purpose at hand.

11. A theory of social ontology

By *social reality* or the social realm, I mean that domain of all phenomena whose existence depends at least in part on us. Thus, it includes items such as social relations which depend on us entirely, but also others like technological objects, where I take technology to be (or anyway to be included within) that domain of phenomena with a material content but social form.

Now if social reality depends on transformative human agency, its state of being must be intrinsically dynamic or *processual*. Think of a language system. Its existence is a condition of our communicating via speech acts, etc. And, through the sum total of these speech acts, the language system is continuously being reproduced and, under some of its aspects at least, transformed. A language system, then, is intrinsically dynamic, its mode of being is a process of transformation. It exists in a continual process of becoming. But this is ultimately true of all aspects of social reality, including many aspects of ourselves, including our personal and social identities. The social world turns on human practice.

The social realm is also highly *interconnected and organic*. Fundamental here is the prevalence of *internal* social relations. Relations are said to be internal when the relata are what they are and/or can do what they do, just in virtue of the relation to each other in which they stand. Obvious examples are relations holding between employer and employee, teacher and student, landlord/lady and tenant or parent and offspring. In each case, you cannot have the one without the other; each is constituted through its relation to the other.

In fact, in the social realm it is found that it is social positions that are significantly internally related. It is the position I hold as a university lecturer that is internally related to the positions of students. Each year, different individuals slot into the positions of students and accept the obligations, privileges and tasks determined by the relation. Ultimately, we all slot into a very large number of different and changing positions, each making a difference to what we can do.

The social realm is also found to be *structured*. By this I mean that it does not consist just in one ontological level. In particular, it does not reduce to human practices and other actualities but includes underlying social structures and processes of the sort just noted and [their] powers and tendencies.

A further fundamental category of the ontological conception I am laying out is that of *emergence*. A stratum of reality can be said to be emergent, or as possessing emergent powers, if there is a sense in which it (1) has arisen out of a lower stratum, being formed by principles operative at the lower level, (2) remains dependent on the lower strata for its existence, but (3) contains causal powers of its own which are both irreducible to those operating at the lower level and (perhaps) capable of acting back on the lower level.

Thus, organic material emerged from inorganic material. And, according to the conception I am defending, the social realm is emergent from human (inter)action, though with properties irreducible to, yet capable of causally affecting, the latter.

Finally, the stuff of the social realm is found, in addition, to include *value* and *meaning* and to be *polyvalent* (for example, absences are real).

This broad perspective, as I say, is elaborated and defended elsewhere. But I doubt that, once reflected upon, the conception is especially contentious. Nor in its basic emphasis on dynamism and organicism or internal-relationality is it especially novel. However, it should be clear that, if the perspective defended is at all correct, it is *prima facie* quite conceivable that the atomistic and isolationist preconceptions of mainstream economics may not hold very often at all.

That said, I emphasise that the possibility of closures of the causal sequence kind, i.e., of the sort pursued by modern mainstream economists, cannot be ruled out a priori. Certainly, there is nothing in the ontological conception sketched above which rules out entirely the possibility of regularities of events standing in causal sequence in the social realm. But the conception sustained does render the practice of universalising a priori the sorts of mathematical–deductivist methods economists wield somewhat risky if not foolhardy, requiring or presupposing, as it does, that social event regularities of the relevant sort are ubiquitous.

Equally to the point, in discussing the nature of modern mainstream economics above, we saw in passing that it is not in an entirely healthy state; indeed, I think it is fair to say that, intellectually, it is in a state of disarray. In particular, it performs badly according to its own explanatory and predictive criteria, and is plagued by theory–practice inconsistencies. In the foregoing discussion we have an explanation. For if the conception of social ontology sketched above does not altogether rule out the possibility of social event regularities of the sort in question occurring here and there, it does provide a compelling explanation of the *a posteriori* rather generalised lack of (or at best limited) successes with mathematical–deductivist or closed-systems explanatory methods to date

I do not doubt that mathematical–deductive methods have many desirable features. But the ability of a set of methods to help us understand social reality matters too. The problem with the mainstream stance is that the ontological preconditions of its formalistic methods appear to be not only *not* ubiquitous in the social realm, but actually rather special occurrences. If we knew both that social life was everywhere atomistic, and also that for any type of outcome we could effectively isolate a fixed set of causes (treating all other causal processes as a kind of stable, non-intervening or homogeneous backdrop), we should have grounds for feeling confident in the emphasis that mainstream economists place on the sorts of deductivist methods they use. However, our best ontological analysis suggests that closures are a special case of social ontology, while our *a posteriori* experience is that this special case seems not to come about very often at all.

12. Implications for heterodox economics

So how does all this bear on the central topic of this essay? Specifically, how does this help us understand heterodox economics? My claim is that something like the alternative ontology described above (and defended elsewhere: see Lawson, 1997, 2003) systematises the implicit preconceptions of the various heterodox traditions, and ultimately explains their enduring opposition to the mainstream. This was my third basic thesis already noted.

I repeat that I do not claim that such an ontological orientation is always explicit in heterodox contributions.[10] Indeed, the term ontology itself is rarely mentioned. At least this has been so until recently.[11] I contend, though, that the sorts of emphases that are prominent clearly do presuppose something like the ontological position I have described above.

Thus, briefly, the post-Keynesian emphasis on fundamental uncertainty is easily explained if openness is a presupposition, just like the institutionalist emphasis on evolutionary method and on technology as a dynamic force (and on institutions as a relatively enduring feature of social life—see Lawson, 2003) are explained if it is presupposed that the social system is a process, and the feminist emphasis on caring and interdependence presupposes an ontology of internal relationality, among other things. The dominant emphases of the separate heterodox traditions, in other words, are just manifestations of categories of social reality that conflict with the assumption that social life is everywhere composed of isolated atoms; as I say, they are categories best explained by an implicit attachment to something like the social ontology outlined above.

As I have also already noted, the heterodox ontological presuppositions are rarely rendered explicit. Part of my contention here is that they should be. Mainstream economists have found it all too easy to find closed-system substitutes for heterodox claims or emphasises, once it is admitted that heterodox economists have made a point. Thus, uncertainty is mapped onto risk; evolutionary concepts are shorn of their Darwinianism and reinterpreted in terms of the requirements of non-linear or game theory modelling; care for others becomes a variable in a utility function; and so on.

The fact that heterodox economists resist the mainstream reformulation of their concepts of uncertainty, evolutionary developments, care, institutions and history, etc., reveals that heterodoxy is not so much committed to the latter categories *per se*, as that it insists on their possessing the ontological properties of openness, processuality and internal-relationality, etc. that I have elaborated above. Once the heterodox groups make their attachment to this ontology explicit, the mainstream's transformative manoeuvres are pre-empted. The heterodox challenge becomes at once more powerful and less easily bypassed or seemingly accommodated.

I return to these sorts of considerations in due course. But, for the time being, I want to re-emphasise the point that the feature that drives the heterodox opposition to an insistence on mathematical formalism is an implicit worldview at odds with that which the formalistic methods presuppose. Thus I am arguing that, collectively, heterodox economists are primarily motivated, in their opposition to the mainstream, by ontological (not epistemological) considerations. Specifically, I believe we can explain the heterodox resistance to the mainstream incorporation of their key categories (uncertainty, evolutionary change, caring relations, etc.) only by recognising that the latter are really defended as manifestations of, and that heterodox economists carry commitments to, an underlying ontology of openness, process and internal-relationality. The latter is an ontology which mainstream economists simply cannot accommodate as long as they insist on employing only mathematical–deductivist methods.

13. The nature of heterodoxy

I have suggested, then, that the various heterodox traditions can be identified as heterodox through a recognition of the fact that they advance claims or practices or orientations which are either concrete manifestations of, or presuppose for their legitimacy, a social ontology of the (seemingly coherent) sort set out above. *In short, the set of projects currently collected together and systematised as heterodox economics is, in the first instance, an orientation in ontology.*

Of course, the heterodox projects on which I am focussing present themselves as projects in economics; I suspect many contributors would resist the idea that their traditions are to be understood as first and foremost an acceptance of the orientation in ontology that, I am suggesting, distinguishes them as heterodox. Indeed, this latter orientation has rarely been explicitly acknowledged anyway, at least until recently, as I have pointed out.[12] However, once we start looking at the more substantive orientations of the heterodox groups, we are confronted with issues that begin to distinguish various heterodox contributions from each other.

At this point a new question of interest arises. If an implicit commitment to the ontological conception described above renders heterodoxy coherent as a collective project, is it the case that the included traditions can each claim individual and distinctive coherency, with the latter being achieved at a more substantive level than ontology?[13] It is this question that I now address.

14. Distinguishing the heterodox traditions

It will be remembered that I earlier noted of each separate heterodox project that except for its basic guiding emphasis there is much internal debate and disagreement over substantive theories and policy stances, as well as over appropriate basic units of analysis and other methodological principles. This situation, indeed, has led some to question whether projects like post-Keynesianism (e.g., Hamouda and Harcourt, 1988) or old institutionalism (see Rutherford, 2000) can be regarded as coherent. I now want to propose a conception or interpretation of these heterodox traditions that can make sense of, and indeed ground, the fact of competing conceptions or theories and methodological claims within any one separate heterodox tradition, while simultaneously rendering the separate heterodox traditions individually coherent.

I have so far argued that the coherence of each separate project *as a form of heterodoxy* is achieved just by recognising each project as being committed broadly to the sort of ontological conception discussed earlier. With regard to distinctions, I contend that the heterodox traditions *can* be coherently identified and distinguished from each other, but *not* according to any specific theories or policy proposals favoured and defended, nor in terms of any features of the economy held to constitute the most basic units of analysis, nor according to any other specific substantive or methodological claim.

Rather, I suggest that the most, and perhaps only, tenable basis for drawing distinctions between the various heterodox projects is *according to substantive questions raised or problems or aspects of the socio-economic world thought sufficiently important or interesting or of concern as to warrant sustained and systematic examination*. That is, I suggest that the separate projects be characterised according to the features of socio-economic life upon which they find reason continually to focus their study.

In other words, if ontology can account for the distinctions between the heterodox traditions and the modern mainstream, i.e., if *ontological commitments identify post-Keynesians, institutionalists, feminist economists and others as heterodox*, it is their particular *substantive orientations, concerns and emphases, not answers or principles*, that *distinguishes the heterodox traditions from each other.* The latter is my fourth and final basic thesis or contention.

Before I elaborate upon it, let me quickly set this contention in the context of the conception of economics I defend in *Reorienting Economics* (Lawson, 2003). For I believe there are parallels to be drawn. Mainstream economics, of course, has implicitly defined the discipline in terms of method. The obvious alternative approach is to identify the different sciences not according to methods they employ but according to the nature of the material(s) or principles with which they are concerned. Thus physicists study certain physical principles, biologists study life processes, and so on.

Now the social ontology described above provides a conception of properties of all social phenomena (of being open, structured, intrinsically dynamic in a manner dependent on social transformation, and highly internally related though social relations); there is no reason to suppose that there exists an economic sphere or any other sub-domain of the social realm with phenomena devoid of such properties. This recognition supports a contention I defend elsewhere (Lawson, 1997, 2003) that the materials and principles of social reality are the same across economics, sociology, politics, anthropology, human geography, and all other disciplines concerned with the study of social life. Hence I think we must accept that there is no legitimate basis for distinguishing a *separate* science of economics. Rather, economics is best viewed as at most a division of labour within a single social science.

What is that division of labour? I think that the answering of this question must start from a cognisance of the history of the discipline, though guided by ethical considerations such as inclusivity. In *Reorienting Economics* (Lawson, 2003), my strategy is to seek to synthesise the main accounts (of Mill, Marshall and Robbins) traditionally regarded as competing contenders. In doing so, the conclusion I reach is that economics is best characterised as the division of social theory or science primarily concerned with studying all social structures and processes bearing upon the material conditions of well-being.[14] This view is easy to sustain, but in its detail it does not concern the present discussion. For whether or not the specifics of the latter suggestion are accepted, the broader point of relevance here is that, if economics is to be distinguished as a strand of social research, it cannot be according to its own ontology, methodological principles or substantive claims, but in terms only of its particular focus of interest (I elaborate on all this in Lawson, 2003, ch. 6).

It is in a similar fashion that I am proposing that the various heterodox economic traditions might also be considered as divisions of labour, albeit as divisions now within economics. It is the mainstream project that has purported to provide general theories at a substantive level, as well as setting down supposedly universal methodological principles. Heterodox economics can, and I believe should, avoid adopting the mainstream criteria of success uncritically. My suggestion is that just as economics (like all other disciplines) is appropriately conceived as a programme of research, not a set of answers or principles, the same holds for the heterodox traditions within economics.

Specifically, I have at several points noted that each separate heterodox tradition has tended to emphasise various features of social reality regarded as fundamental or of significant interest (even if attempts to theorise around these features are highly variable and competitive). I now propose that each individual heterodox tradition be identified precisely with these sorts of general features and emphases, conceived of as constituting topics for research.[15]

Thus, post-Keynesians, given their previous emphases, might be distinguished according to their concern with the fact of fundamental uncertainty stemming from the openness of social reality. Such a focus could take in the implications of uncertainty or openness for the development of certain sorts of institutions, including money, for processes of decision-making, and so forth. At the level of policy, the concern may well include the analysis of contingencies that recognise the fact of pervasive uncertainty, given the openness of the social reality in the present and to the future, etc. For those influenced by Keynes, especially, a likely focus is how these matters give rise to collective or macro outcomes, and how the latter in turn impact back on individual acts and pressures for structural transformation, etc.

By similar reasoning, I believe that it is best to distinguish institutionalism, *not* according to claims along the lines that institutions or evolutionary processes constitute main units of analysis or some such but, given that project's traditional concern with evolutionary issues, in terms of its interest in *examining how* social items change and/or endure over time. From such a perspective, those aspects of social life that are most enduring, such as institutions and habits, are particularly significant. So too are the interactions of factors such as institutions and technology in the process of reproduction and change (see Lawson, 2005).

Austrians may perhaps be best identified according to their emphasis on studying the market process and entrepreneurship in particular, or perhaps in line with the attention given by this project to the role of intersubjective meaning in social life, and so on.

And feminist economics is best distinguished, I believe, in terms of analyses of issues such as care, etc. And indeed this ties in with how feminist analysis has tended to proceed. To focus on care, of course, is to be concerned with social relations. Very often feminist economists have identified their own project as one that first of all concerns itself with women as subjects (which may include, for example, giving attention to differences among women, as well as between genders) and takes a particular orientation or focus, namely on the position of women (and other marginalised groups) within society and the economy. But this focus, of course, is inherently relational. It includes an attention to the social causes at work in the oppression of, or in discrimination against, women (and others), the opportunities for progressive transformation or emancipation, questions of (relations of) power and strategy, and so forth. And this orientation has inevitably meant a significant attention, within feminist economics, to relational issues that historically have been gender related, such as looking after children, and indeed, the nature of family structures in specific locations.[16]

In any case, the foregoing is mainly suggestive. I should finally perhaps emphasise (though it is hopefully apparent throughout) that, although I am arguing that each heterodox tradition be distinguished according to a traditional set of concerns and emphases (rather than answers or methodological principles), I do not want to suggest that each somehow works with isolated components of society or economy. The object or subject matter of social theory/science, no less than economics, is an interrelated whole (in process). To focus competently on specific aspects requires an understanding of the totality (just as the investigation of any specific aspect of the human body presupposes some prior understanding of its functioning within the whole). There is no part of the social realm that does not have an economic aspect (although social reality does not reduce to its economic aspects). And, similarly, there is no part of social life that cannot be viewed under the aspect of its degree of openness, or its processuality/fixity, or the nature of its social-relationality, etc. In other words, on the conception laid out each of the various heterodox traditions is viewed as approaching the same totality but with a distinguishing set of concerns, emphases, motivating interests and (so) questions. And, ideally, each will be achieving results that warrant synthesising[17] with the findings of others (again see Lawson, 2003, especially Part III).

15. Conclusion

In questioning the nature of heterodox economics, I have advanced and defended four basic theses or contentions. These can be summarised as follows.

1   The nature of the enduring modern mainstream project which the heterodox traditions continue to oppose, and against which they must ultimately identify themselves as heterodox, is set not in terms of its substantive results or basic units of analysis, but according to its *orientation* to method. The mainstream project of modern economics just is an insistence, as a discipline-wide principle, that economic

phenomena be investigated using only (or almost only) certain mathematical–deductive forms of reasoning.
2 The often noted intellectual failings and limitations of this mainstream project arise just because its *emphasis* on mathematical–deductivist reasoning is inappropriate given the nature of social material. In other words, the ontological presuppositions of these methods do not everywhere match the nature of social reality.
3 The heterodox opposition is based on a (albeit often no more than implicit) grasping of the situation expressed in the just noted second contention. In other words, modern heterodoxy is, *qua* heterodoxy, first and foremost an orientation in ontology. It is to be distinguished from the mainstream by its willingness to approach theory and method in a manner informed by available insights into the nature of social reality.
4 The individual heterodox traditions are rendered distinct from each other by their particular substantive orientations, concerns and emphases, not by theoretical claims or results, empirical findings, methodological principles or policy stances.

The perspective sustained in this essay will surely be contested, not least by those economists who prefer to view themselves as heterodox but who believe that mathematical–deductivist reasoning is desirable in itself. But in the absence of any more coherent or empirically adequate thesis on the nature of modern heterodoxy, the broad thesis advanced here does have something to commend it. In particular, the set of contentions defended allows, without any obvious tension, a way of distinguishing the various heterodox traditions, collectively from the mainstream and individually from each other, in a manner that does not compromise their coherence as fruitful traditions in economics.

Notes

* This chapter previously published as Tony Lawson, The nature of heterodox economics, *Cambridge Journal of Economics* (July 2006) 30(4): 483–505 first published online December 9, 2005, doi:10.1093/cje/bei093 by permission of Oxford University Press/on behalf of The Cambridge Political Economy Society © Cambridge Political Economy Society.
1 For an account of how the Association for Heterodox Economics was formed, see Lee (2002).
2 Go to http://l.web.umkc.edu/leefs/htn.htm
3 See, for example, http://www.orgs.bucknell.edu/afee/hetecon.htm, which currently lists various heterodox economics associations, heterodox economics journals, heterodox publications (news, commentary and analysis), and heterodox discussion groups
4 Briefly consider, for example, the project of old institutionalism, or anyway the manner in which it is commonly perceived. To speed up matters, let me rely on the commentary of the institutionalist historian Malcolm Rutherford. In his

view, '[a]ll attempts to define American institutionalism, whether in terms of a set of key methodological or theoretical principles or in terms of the contributions of [major contributors] . . . have run into problems with apparent disparities within the movement' (Rutherford, 2000, p. 277). Rutherford notes the 'dramatic differences' in the methodological principles, theoretical positions and definitions of major contributors, and recognises the impression this has given: '[i]nstitutionalism easily appears as incoherent, as little more than a set of individual research programs with nothing in common other than a questioning of orthodox theory and method' (Rutherford, 2000, pp. 277–8). Thus Mark Blaug has stated that institutionalism 'was never more than a tenuous inclination to dissent from orthodox economics' (Blaug, 1978, p. 712), and George Stigler has claimed that institutionalism had 'no positive agenda of research', 'no set of problems or new methods', nothing, but 'a stance of hostility to the standard theoretical tradition'. This view still finds wide currency—for example Oliver Williamson has recently argued that [in the light of its failures elsewhere] 'the older institutional economics was given over to methodological objections of the orthodoxy' (Williamson, 1998, p. 24).

5   Even Kanth notes the emphasis on mathematics but without quite appreciating its essentiality: 'The apparent rigour of mathematics was recruited avidly by neoclassicism to justify and defend its truistic, axiomatic, and almost infantile, theorems that deeply investigated but the surface gloss of economic life. Indeed, for the longest time, Marxists (in the U.S.) had to live in the academic dog-house for not being familiar with matrix algebra, until keen (if not always scrupulous) Marxist minds, with academic tenures at stake, realised the enormous (and inexpensive) potential of this tool for restating Marxian ideas in formalised language and instantly acquiring the gloss of high science, the latter-day pundits of repute here being Roemer in the U.S. and Morishima in England, who were of course soon emulated by a host of lesser lights to whom this switch in language alone promised hours of (well funded) computerised fun and games.

   Of course, all the formalisms did not advance a critical understanding of the organon of Marxian system, and its many difficulties, one iota; but it did succeed in generating grudging respect for the Marxist by the even more facile and shallow savants of neo-classicism' (Kanth, 1999, p. 189).

6   William Baumol focuses on hurdles facing students in particular: '[t]hese days few specialised students are allowed to proceed without devoting a very considerable proportion of their time to the acquisition of mathematical tools, and they often come away feeling that any piece of writing they produce will automatically be rejected as unworthy if is not liberally sprinkled with an array of algebraic symbols' (Baumol, 1992, p. 2).

   Roger Guesnerie focuses on research: '[m]athematics now plays a controversial but decisive role in economic research. This is demonstrated, for example, by the recourse to formalisation in the discussion of economic theory, and increasingly, regardless of the field. Anyone with doubts has only to skim the latest issues of the journals that are considered, for better or worse, the most prestigious and are in any case the most influential in the academic world' (Guesnerie, 1997, p. 88).

   And Robert Solow admits that: 'Today if you ask a mainstream economist a question about almost any aspect of economic life, the response will be: suppose we model that situation and see what happens . . . modern mainstream economics consists of little else but examples of this process' (Solow, 1997, pp. 39–58). Of course, heterodox economists do often capture the situation best. Consider the very apt assessment of Diana Strassmann, the editor of *Feminist Economics*. Like other heterodox economists, Strassmann certainly does not reduce economics to mathematical formalism but notices that this is an essential feature of the mainstream:

> 'To a mainstream economist, theory means model, and model means ideas expressed in mathematical form. In learning how to "think like an economist," students learn certain critical concepts and models, ideas which typically are taught initially through simple mathematical analyses. These models, students learn, are theory. In more advanced courses, economic theories are presented in more mathematically elaborate models. Mainstream economists believe proper models—good models—take a recognizable form: presentation in equations, with mathematically expressed definitions, assumptions, and theoretical developments clearly laid out. Students also learn how economists argue. They learn that the legitimate way to argue is with models and econometrically constructed forms of evidence. While students are also presented with verbal and geometric masterpieces produced in bygone eras, they quickly learn that novices who want jobs should emulate their current teachers rather than deceased luminaries.
>
> Because all models are incomplete, students also learn that no model is perfect. Indeed, students learn that it is bad manners to engage in excessive questioning of simplifying assumptions. Claiming that a model is deficient is a minor feat—presumably anyone can do that. What is really valued is coming up with a better model, a better theory. And so, goes the accumulated wisdom of properly taught economists, those who criticize without coming up with better models are only pedestrian snipers. Major scientific triumphs call for a better theory with a better model in recognizable form. In this way economists learn their trade; it is how I learned mine.
>
> Therefore, imagine my reaction when I heard feminists from other disciplines apply the term theory to ideas presented in verbal form, ideas not containing even the remotest potential for mathematical expression. 'This is theory?' I asked. 'Where's the math?' (1994, p. 154).

7 Essentially, the principle in question is a concrete universal underpinning the plethora of individual and singular contributions that collectively make up the mainstream output.
8 For a sustained discussion of the different forms of closed systems, including closures of causal sequence, see Lawson (2003, esp. chs 1, 2 and 4).
9 Most typically, such deductivist modelling endeavour encourages a specific conception of atomistic human agents (social atomism) where these are the sole explanatory units of social analysis (methodological individualism).
10 Though there are exceptions, such as Paul Davidson's concern with (non) ergodic systems (see Davidson, 1991, 1994, 1996).
11 Of course, where critics of the mainstream see the latter as substantive ideology, the emphasis on ontology promoted here can be viewed as a distraction (see, for example, Guerrien, 2004).
12 I do not wish to imply that individuals working mostly within heterodox traditions in economics could not themselves make a contribution to philosophical ontology. On philosophical matters, the flow of insights can be both ways between projects in ontology and the heterodox traditions in economics. Indeed, currently, there is real blossoming of insightful output by heterodox economists and others critically interacting with and seeking to shape (at the least the application of) the sort of ontological perspective described above, a perspective often systematised as critical realism in economics. See, in particular, Arestis *et al.* (2003), Beaulier and Boettke (2004), Davis (2004), Dow (1999, 2003), Downward *et al.* (2003), Downward and Mearman (2003A, 2003B), Dunn (2004), Finch and McMaster (2003), Fine (2004), Graça Moura (2004), Hands (2004), Hargreaves Heap (2004),

Kuiper (2004), Lee (2003), Lewis (2004A, 2004B), McKenna and Zannoni (1999), Nell (2004), Olsen (2003), Pagano (2004), Pinkstone (2003), Rotheim (1999), Setterfield (2003) and Smithin (2004).

13 I might note at this stage that there is surprisingly little comparative work in the literature that focuses on connections and distinctions between the various heterodox traditions. Some recent exceptions do exist (e.g., Danby, 2004.) But there is a need for far more. Some insights can be gained though by considering those who have compared and likened one heterodox tradition (e.g., Beaulier and Boettke, 2004; Dunn, 2004; Kuiper, 2004;) or more (e.g., Austen and Jefferson, 2004) with the ontological conception described above.

14 More specifically, I suggest that economics is: 'the identification and study of the factors, and in particular social relations, governing those aspects of human action most closely connected to the production, distribution and use of the material conditions of well-being, along with the assessment of alternative really possible scenarios.'

15 Such suggestions seem broadly substantiated explicitly by certain recent reflections of some heterodox thinkers concerned with the nature of the particular project with which they are associated (see Lewis, 2004).

16 Of course, the question 'what is feminist theory?' is highly discussed among feminist writers and generates various often very different responses. For a critical survey of the question that reaches a not dissimilar assessment to the very general suggestion advanced here, see Beasley (1999).

17 I use the word loosely. If findings are inconsistent, forms of critical resolution are clearly required.

Bibliography

Allais, M. 1992. The economic science of today and global disequilibrium, in Baldassarri, M. *et al.* (eds), *Global Disequilibrium in the World Economy*, Basingstoke, Macmillan

Arestis, P. 1990. Post-Keynesianism: a new approach to economics, *Review of Social Economy*, vol. XLVIII, no. 3, 222–46

Arestis P., Brown, A. and Sawyer, M. 2003. Critical realism and the political economy of the euro, in Downward, P. (ed.), *Applied Economics and the Critical Realist Critique*, London and New York, Routledge

Austen, S. and Jefferson, T. 2004. 'Comparing Responses to Critical Realism', mimeo, Curtin Business School, Perth, Western Australia

Baumol, W. J. 1992. Towards a newer economics: the future lies ahead!, in Hey, J. D. (ed.) 1992, *The Future of Economics*, Oxford, Blackwell

Beasley, C. 1999. *What is Feminism?*, London, Sage

Beaulier, S. A. and Boettke, P. J. 2004. The really real in economics, in Lewis, P. (ed.), *Transforming Economics: Perspectives on the Critical Realist Project*, London and New York, Routledge

Blaug, M. 1978. *Economic Theory in Retrospect*, 3rd edn, Cambridge, Cambridge University Press

Coase, R. 1999. Interview with Ronald Coase, *Newsletter of the International Society for New Institutional Economics*, vol. 2, no. 1

Colander, D., Holt, R. P. and Rosser, J. B. Jr 2004. The changing face of mainstream economics, *Review of Political Economy*, vol. 16, no. 4, 485–500

Danby, C. 2004. Towards a gendered post Keynesianisam: subjectivity and time in a non-modernist framework, *Feminist Economics*, vol. 10, no. 3, 55–76

Davidson, P. 1980. Post Keynesian economics, *The Public Interest, Special Edition*, 151–73, reprinted in Bell, D. and Kristol, I. (eds), *The Crisis in Economic Theory*, New York, Basic Books, 1981

Davidson, P. 1991. Is probability theory relevant for uncertainty?, *Journal of Economic Perspectives*, vol. 5, no. 1, 129–43

Davidson, P. 1994. *Post Keynesian Macroeconomic Theory*, Aldershot, UK, Edward Elgar

Davidson, P. 1996. Reality and economic theory, *Journal of Post Keynesian Economics*, vol. 18, no. 4, 479–508

Davis, J. B. 2004. The agency-structure model and the embedded individual in heterodox economics, in Lewis, P. (ed.), *Transforming Economics: Perspectives on the Critical Realist Project*, London and New York, Routledge

Davis, J. B. 2005. Heterodox economics, the fragmentation of the mainstream and embedded individual analysis, in Garnett, R. and Harvey, J. (eds), *The Future of Heterodox Economics*, Ann Arbor, MI, University of Michigan Press

Dow, S. C. 1992. Post Keynesian school, in Mair, D. and Miller, A. (eds), *Comparative Schools of Economic Thought*, Aldershot, Edward Elgar

Dow, S. C. 1999. Post Keynesianism and critical realism: what is the connection?, *Journal of Post Keynesian Economics*, vol. 22, no. 1, 15–33

Dow, S. C. 2003. Critical and economics, in Downward, P. (ed.), *Applied Economics and the Critical Realist Critique*, London and New York, Routledge

Downward, P. (ed.) 2003. *Applied Economics and the Critical Realist Critique*, London and New York, Routledge

Downward, P. and Mearman, A. 2003A. Critical realism and econometrics: interaction between philosophy and post Keynsian practice, in Downward, P. (ed.), *Applied Economics and the Critical Realist Critique*, London and New York, Routledge

Downward, P. and Mearman, A. 2003B. Presenting demi-regularities: the case of post Keynesian pricing, in Downward, P. (ed.), *Applied Economics and the Critical Realist Critique*, London and New York, Routledge

Dunn, S. P. 2004. Transforming post Keynesian economics: critical realism and the post Keynesian project, in Lewis, P. (ed.), *Transforming Economics: Perspectives on the Critical Realist Project*, London and New York, Routledge

Eichner, A. S. 1985. *Towards a New Economics: Essays in Post-Keynesian and Institutionalist Theory*, London, Macmillan

Finch J. H and McMaster, R. 2003. A pragmatic alliance between critical realism and simple non-parametric statistical techniques, in Downward, P. (ed.), *Applied Economics and the Critical Realist Critique*, London and New York, Routledge

Fine, B. 2004. Addressing the critical and the real in critical realism, in Lewis, P. (ed.), *Transforming Economics: Perspectives on the Critical Realist Project*, London and New York, Routledge

Friedman, M. 1999. Conversation with Milton Friedman, pp. 124–44 in Snowdon, B. and Vane, H. (eds), *Conversations with Leading Economists: Interpreting Modern Macroeconomics*, Cheltenham, Edward Elgar

Fullbrook, E. (ed.) 2003. *The Crisis in Economics: Teaching, Practice and Ethics*, London and New York, Routledge

Fullbrook, E. (ed.) 2004. *A Guide to What's Wrong with Economics*, London, Anthem Press

Graça Moura, M. da 2004. A note on critical realism, scientific exegesis and Schumpeter, in Lewis, P. (ed.), *Transforming Economics: Perspectives on the Critical Realist Project,* London and New York, Routledge

Guerrien, B. 2004. Irrelevance and ideology, *Post-autistic Economics Review,* no. 29, 6 December 2004, article 3, http://www.btinternet.com/~pae_news/review/issue29.htm

Guesnerie, R. 1997. Modelling and economic theory: evolution and problems, pp. 85–91 in D'Autume, A. and Cartelier, J. (eds), 1997, *Is Economics Becoming a Hard Science?* Cheltenham, Edward Elgar

Hahn, F. 1970. Some adjustment problems, *Econometrica,* vol. 38, January; reprinted as pp. 1–17 in *Equilibrium and Macroeconomics,* Oxford, Basil Blackwell

Hahn, F. 1984. *Equilibrium and Macroeconomics,* Oxford, Basil Blackwell

Hahn, F. 1985. 'In Praise of Economic Theory', 1984 Jevons Memorial Fund Lecture, London, University College

Hahn, F. H. 1992A. Reflections, *Royal Economics Society Newsletter,* vol. 77

Hahn, F. H. 1992B. Answer to Backhouse: Yes, *Royal Economic Society Newsletter,* vol. 78, no. 5

Hamouda, O. F. and Harcourt, G. C. 1988. Post-Keynesianism: from criticism to coherence? *Bulletin of Economic Research,* vol. 40, January, 1–34; reprinted in Pheby, J. (ed.) *New Directions in Post-Keynesian Economics,* Aldershot, Edward Elgar, 1989

Hands, D. W. 2004. Transforming methodology, critical realism and recent economic methodology, in Lewis, P. (ed.) 2004

Hargreaves Heap, S. 2004. Critical realism and the heterodox tradition in economics, in Lewis, P. (ed.), *Transforming Economics: Perspectives on the Critical Realist Project,* London and New York, Routledge

Hodgson, G. M. 1989. Post-Keynesianism and institutionalism: the missing link, pp. 94–123 in Pheby, J. (ed.), *New Directions in Post-Keynesian Economics,* Aldershot, Edward Elgar

Howell, D. 2000. *The Edge of Now: New Questions for Democracy and the Network Age,* London, Macmillan

Kanth, R. 1999. Against Eurocentred epistemologies: a critique of science, realism and economics, in Fleetwood, S. (ed.), *Critical Realism in Economics: Development and Debate,* London and New York, Routledge

Keynes, J. M. 1973. *The Collected Writings of John Maynard Keynes, Vol. XIV, The General Theory and After: Part II Defence and Development,* Royal Economic Society

Kirman, A. 1989. The intrinsic limits of modern economic theory: the emperor has no clothes, *Economic Journal,* vol. 99, no. 395, 126–39

Kuiper, E. 2004. Critical realism and feminist economics: how well do they get along?, in Lewis, P. (ed.), *Transforming Economics: Perspectives on the Critical Realist Project,* London and New York, Routledge

Lavoie, M. 1992. Towards a new research programme for post-Keynesianism and new-Ricardianism, *Review of Political Economy,* vol. 4, no. 1, 37, 78

Lawson, T. 1997. *Economics and Reality,* London and New York, Routledge

Lawson, T. 1999. Developments in economics as realist social theory, in Fleetwood, S. (ed.), *Critical Realism in Economics: Development and Debate,* London and New York, Routledge

Lawson, T. 2003. *Reorienting Economics,* London and New York, Routledge

Lawson, T. 2005. The nature of institutional economics, *The Evolutionary and Institutional Economic Review,* vol 2, no. 1, 7–20

Leamer, E. E. 1978. *Specification Searches: Ad Hoc Inferences with Non-experimental Data,* New York, John Wiley

Leamer, E. E. 1983. Let's take the con out of econometrics, *American Economic Review,* 34–43

Lee, F. S. 2002. The association for heterodox economics: past, present and future, *Journal of Australian Political Economy,* no. 50, 29–43

Lee, F. S. 2003. Theory foundation and methodological foundations of post Keynesian economics, in Downward, P. (ed.), *Applied Economics and the Critical Realist Critique,* London and New York, Routledge

Leontief, W. 1982. Letter, *Science,* vol. 217, 10–47

Lewis, P. (ed.) 2004. *Transforming Economics: Perspectives on the Critical Realist Project,* London and New York, Routledge

Lewis, P. 2004A. Transforming economics? On heterodox economics and the ontological turn in economic methodology, in Lewis, P. (ed.) 2004

Lewis, P. 2004B. Economics as social theory and the new economic sociology, in Lewis, P. (ed.), 2004

Lipsey, R. G. 2001. Successes and failures in the transformation of economics, *Journal of Economic Methodology,* vol. 8, no. 2, 169–202

McKenna, E. J. and Zannoni, D. 1999. Post Keynesian economics and critical realism: a reply to Parsons, *Journal Post Keynesian Economics,* vol. 22, no. 1, 57–71

Nell, E. J. 2004. Critical realism and transformational growth, in Lewis, P. (ed.), 2004

Olsen, W. 2003. Triangulation, time and the social objects of econometrics, in Downward, P. (ed.), *Applied Economics and the Critical Realist Critique,* London and New York, Routledge

Pagano, U. 2004. The economics of institutions and the institutions of economics, in Lewis, P. (ed.), 2004

Peukert, H. 2001. On the origins of modern evolutionary economics: the Veblen legend after 100 years, *Journal of Economic Issues,* vol. XXXV, no. 3, 543–56

Pinkstone, B. 2003. Critical realism and applied work in economic history: some methodological implications, in Downward, P. (ed.), *Applied Economics and the Critical Realist Critique,* London and New York, Routledge

Rotheim, R. 1999. Post Keynesian economics and realist philosophy, *Journal of Post Keynesian Economics,* vol. 22, no. 1, 71–104

Rubinstein, A. 1995. John Nash: the master of economic modelling, *Scandinavian Journal of Economics,* vol. 97, no. 1, 9–13

Rutherford, M. 2000. Understanding institutional economics: 1918–1929, *Journal of the History of Economic Thought,* vol. 22, no. 3, 277–308

Sawyer, M. 1988. *Post-Keynesian Economics,* Aldershot, Edward Elgar

Setterfield, M. 2003. Critical realism and formal modelling: incompatible bedfellows?, in Downward, P. (ed.), *Applied Economics and the Critical Realist Critique,* London and New York, Routledge

Smithin, J. 2004. Macroeconomic theory, critical realism and capitalism, in Lewis, P. (ed.), *Transforming Economics: Perspectives on the Critical Realist Project,* London and New York, Routledge

Solow, R. 1997. How did economics get that way and what way did it get? *Daedalus,* Winter, vol. 26, no. 1

Strassmann, D. 1994. Feminist thought and economics; or, what do the Visigoths know?, *American Economic Review, Papers and Proceedings,* 153–8

Thomson, W. L. 1999. The young person's guide to writing economic theory, *Journal of Economic Literature,* vol. XXXVII, 157–83

Williamson, O. E. 1998. Transaction cost economics: how it works: where it is headed, *De Economist,* vol. 146, April, 23–58

4 What is this 'school' called neoclassical economics?*†

1. Introductory observations

More than a century ago, Thorstein Veblen introduced the term 'neoclassical' into economics *prima facie* to characterise a particular 'school'. The latter quotation marks were provided by Veblen himself, suggesting that there may be a sense, however, in which the object of focus was not really a school of thought at all. Even so, Veblen certainly had in mind the nature of the output of a set of contributors, as we shall see.

Currently, the term 'neoclassical' pervades the discourse of academic economics, being employed to denote a range of substantive theories and policy stances. It does not take too much research or reflection, however, to realise that not only is the Veblenian heritage typically not acknowledged (and conceivably not always appreciated) but the term is invariably employed rather loosely and somewhat inconsistently across different contributors.

For many the act of describing an economic contribution as neoclassical is considered a form of criticism, though usually when the term is so used it is so without explanation or elaboration; it mostly signals dissent.[1] In similar fashion those who accept the term for their own output seem very often, and again mostly without definition or explanation, to suppose that any contribution they make is neoclassical in nature.

There are numerous more careful or systematic interpreters of the term, found typically (though not exclusively) amongst methodologists and/or historians of thought, who do seek to elaborate its meaning rather more cautiously. Here two strategies dominate.

First, there are those who suppose that intrinsic to the notion of neoclassical is a sense of both continuity and difference with something called classical economics. Certainly, if the category neoclassical economics is to be maintained it does seem *prima facie* reasonable to expect this to be the case. Yet those historians of thought and others who focus on this expectation[2] typically conclude that the criterion is not met and, most especially, that contributions classified as neoclassical fail to reveal meaningful *continuity* with any conception of classical economics.[3]

Second, there are those interpreters of the term who prioritise internal coherence (rather than continuity with some classical tradition) and instead seek to systematise any analytical features that are common to, or generative of, those contributions most widely accepted as somehow quintessentially neoclassical.

The conceptions developed by the latter set of interpreters do have significant features in common. Perhaps the most notable is the highly abstract nature of the characterisations advanced, very often taking the form of a set of 'axioms' or 'meta-axioms' or perhaps a 'meta-theory'. Additional commonalities are that the axioms identified tend to make reference to individuals as the units of analysis and indicate something of the states of knowledge and/or forms of typical behaviour of these individuals. In addition it is often the case that certain supposed (typically equilibrium) states of the economic system get a mention.

Thereafter, however, agreement is harder to find and significant variety creeps in. Sometimes individual knowledge is assumed to be in some sense 'perfect' or 'complete', sometimes systematically limited, and very often knowledge specifications do not figure explicitly at all. Behaviour is often treated as rational in some technical sense, though not always, and where it is, there is significant variety in the particular specifications. Further, there is wide disparity over whether equilibrium states are part of the essential framework of neoclassicism, and, where they are accepted as so, disagreement as to whether such states are held axiomatically always to prevail, or whether their possible existence is a matter of study, or something else; and so on. In short there is significant variety of interpretation of the term 'neoclassical economics' even across the more cautious interpreters.[4]

No less significant is the observation that the various substantive categories (rationality, equilibrium) which frequently occur across the conceptions of these more cautious interpreters seem to be in declining use in modern economics discourse, and despite the continuing prevalence of the category neoclassical economics. Others have noted the same developments. Thus David Colander *et al.* (2004), for example, insist that modern 'economics is moving away from strict adherence to the holy trinity—rationality, selfishness, and equilibrium—to a more eclectic position of purposeful behaviour, enlightened self-interest and sustainability' (Colander *et al.*, 2004, p. 485); an assessment shared by John Davis (2005), amongst others.

If current use of the term 'neoclassical' has lost touch with its original meaning, does not live up to its billing of signalling continuity with a classical school and is not consistently or usefully interpreted even by those who seek internal coherence, it seems to be additionally the case that there is no real need for such a term anyway, at least not for capturing major developments and/or approaches within the modern economics academy.

The reason for so concluding is that the major research groupings or divisions of study of modern economics are more than adequately characterised without employing the term. Certainly the contemporary discipline is dominated by a mainstream tradition. But whilst the concrete substantive content, focus and policy orientations of the latter are highly heterogeneous and continually changing,[5] the project itself is adequately characterised in terms of its enduring reliance, indeed unceasing insistence, upon methods of *mathematical modelling*. In effect it is a form of *mathematical deductivism* in the context of economics.[6] Deductivism is just the doctrine that all explanation be expressed in terms of 'laws' or 'uniformities' interpreted as (actual or 'hypothetical') correlations or event regularities (see later discussion and Lawson, 2003).

Moreover if the contemporary mainstream project is appropriately characterised as one of mathematical modelling in economics, a form of mathematical deductivism, each of the various academic heterodox traditions that stand opposed to this hugely dominant mainstream project has its own self-identifying label, including post-Keynesianism, feminist economics, (old) institutionalism, Marxian economics, Austrian economics, social economics and numerous others. It is thus *prima facie* unclear that the designation 'neoclassical economics' is anywhere required.

1.1 Why it matters

But so what? Does any of this matter? After all, it might be argued, in all spheres of human activity many categories are seemingly used rather loosely and without agreement, but appear to do little harm; this, it might thereby be supposed, is the case with the use of term 'neoclassical' in modern economics.

I suspect that in most contexts of human interaction more clarity is preferable to less. Of course, (lexical) ambiguity can sometimes be useful (for example, when an author does not want to reveal too much early on in a text) as can ambivalence (when a contributor is unable to weigh up the arguments and seeks to avoid making a commitment prematurely)[7]; I doubt that either are ever entirely avoidable whatever a contributor's intentions. In addition the meanings of many (if not most) categories do evolve to an extent over time, and in any case may, in part at least, be determined (and so revealed only) in use. Certainly there is no desire here to reify or underplay nuance or performativity and so forth. However in the current situation the manner in which, and wide disparity in the ways, the term 'neoclassical' is applied is not only productive of severe obfuscation, and seemingly increasingly so, it is also, or so I shall argue, positively debilitating of the discipline not least through hindering effective critique. Indeed, a major motivation of this article is precisely an assessment that the looseness with which this central term is interpreted (along with the toleration of this looseness) is a major factor inhibiting progress in economic understanding.

Not only is the economy in crisis but, as is now widely recognised, so is the discipline of economics itself. Yet the debate over the nature of the latter's problems, weaknesses and limitations has so far been mostly fairly superficial; indeed, it is apparent that within the academy there has been very little if any significant progress. A major reason for this, I will be arguing, is that loose and varying interpretations of 'neoclassical' theorising, especially when standing in as forms of criticism and dismissal, actually serve to distract sustained reflective attention from the real, or more systematic, causes of the discipline's failings.

If I am correct in my assessment here that the term is not only without obvious use but also debilitating (the latter, as I say, being a contention defended later), a seemingly reasonable reaction is to suggest jettisoning the category neoclassical economics altogether, as indeed has been the recourse of a few commentators (for varying reasons) previously.[8]

This in effect has tended to be my own previous orientation; I have rarely if ever employed the term in previous writings. But I have often been criticised for this, not least because a stance of non-recognition or non-engagement through avoidance is taken to be, if not itself confusing then insufficiently critical (Fine, 2004; Bernard Guerrien, 2004), or even accommodating, of results maintained under the neoclassical head. Perhaps, too, the non-appearance (rather than an explication) of the term 'neoclassical' in analyses seeking to identify and illuminate the causes of problems of the discipline has in itself encouraged some to treat the latter analyses less seriously. Although I shall argue that theorising and policy stances labelled neoclassical are not the primary causes of the discipline's problems, I accept (below) they may often be manifestations of it; so that determining the relation of at least the seemingly most coherent account of neoclassical to the real causes of the discipline's problems, will hopefully provide practical insight. Moreover I am aware that there is interest in, and I suspect there may be value to determining, how a conception of the contemporary mainstream economics as a form of mathematical deductivism, a conception I have long advanced, relates to at least the seemingly most sustainable conception of neoclassical economics. Furthermore, there is simply a repeatedly observed questioning of the nature of neoclassical thinking.

For various reasons, then, I take the opportunity here to elaborate that interpretation of the term that I believe to be the most sustainable. Let me stress at the outset that I do actually believe that a coherent construal is possible. I might also add that I am sympathetic to the idea that elaborating a coherent interpretation of such a pervasive term is an interesting intellectual project in itself. I also think it an intrinsically interesting exercise to systematically re-examine Veblen's purposes in formulating the term. But primarily, and more practically, the reason for seeking a coherent conception here is to facilitate clarity in the hope and expectation that, one way or another, this can contribute to advancing the discipline. If merely avoiding the use of the term is considered unhelpful and misleading for the reasons just given, then seeking as coherent an account as is feasible seems the obvious alternative recourse. Either way (if not through discarding the term altogether then through rendering it coherent), my aim is to help remove certain significant obstacles that obstruct the path of seriously addressing those factors that are the more fundamental causes of the modern discipline's increasingly widely recognised and indeed very widespread problems.

There is little point, of course, in my merely asserting a novel or alternative conception of neoclassical economics. Rather, any interpretation worth maintaining must fit at least the criteria implicit in criticising current uses above. The conception I advance does so. In particular I argue for an interpretation that is (developmentally[9]) consistent with the historical origins of the meaning of the term given it by Veblen; is both continuous with, as well as different from, a meaningful conception of classical economics; is not only consistent with but in a sense encompasses seemingly all the explicit modern interpretations, not least those put forward by the more careful/cautious contributors and indeed, makes sense of and explains the latter; renders equally intelligible the contradictions of the wider, looser literature; possesses a clear referent, one that is currently without a category name; and is useful in at least (through all the foregoing) bringing clarity to academic discussion.

Obviously, I cannot, any more than anyone else, stipulate that a specific interpretation of the term be accepted, but I can hope to persuade that a particular version is more adequate than others, at least in terms of its ability to satisfy all of the various criteria of coherence already elaborated. Indeed, in terms of satisfying the noted criteria I suspect that the conception defended here may be as good as it gets. Whether this is ultimately good enough for the purposes laid out, and indeed whether the fact of a coherent interpretation of the term renders it worth persevering with, are matters that I also examine in due course.

In presenting and defending the interpretation I have in mind, Veblen's initial conception is an obvious starting point. Unfortunately, Veblen's conception needs a fair bit of elaboration to convey its essential meaning. This in part, I suspect, explains why it seems rarely to be seriously discussed or even acknowledged. I believe, though, that there are significant rewards to treating Veblen's analysis on these matters explicitly and systematically, to recovering his basic message. This I attempt to accomplish eventually below (where I find that in the few cases Veblen is referenced on the matters before us, standard interpretations of his intentions are not quite right). Before I turn to such matters, however, I want first to expand a little on a central claim made in the introductory overview, concerning the real causes of the discipline's problems. The issues involved are likely not overly familiar to everyone; some of them require argumentation; many of them, as we eventually see, are highly relevant at some level for understanding Veblen's own conception of the neoclassical 'school'.

2. The real source of the discipline's problems

I have suggested that a widespread loose usage of the phrase 'neoclassical economics' or 'neoclassical theorising', especially in criticism, has tended to deflect from the real source of the discipline's problems, so I had better indicate here what the latter is and how the slack use of the category neoclassical economics hinders effective critique.

The source (as opposed to immediate manifestations) of the problems of the discipline of modern economics lies not at the level of substantive theorising at all but at the level of methodology and social ontology (the study, or a theory, of the nature of social reality). Modern economics, as has already been noted, is dominated by a mainstream tradition that insists on the repeated application of methods of mathematical modelling. The models actually employed, like all tools, are useful in some conditions and not in others. As it happens the sorts of conditions under which the modelling methods economists have employed would be useful are found to be rather uncommon, and indeed unlikely, occurrences in the social realm. Alternatively put, the ontological presuppositions of the heavy emphasis on mathematical modelling do not match the nature of the 'stuff' of the social realm. The heavy use of these tools in conditions for which they are found to be inappropriate both explains the repeated explanatory failings of the discipline as well as why formulations are of a nature that are typically recognised by almost everyone as rather unrealistic. That, in summary, is the real cause of the discipline's problems.[10]

Let me briefly elaborate some of the detail of the argument. It can be noted first that mathematical methods and techniques of the sort employed by economists (use of functions, calculus and so forth) presuppose regularities at the level of events. Whether the latter are *a priori* hypothesised or *a posteriori* 'detected', the successful application of economist's mathematical tools require event regularities or correlations. Systems in which such event regularities occur can be called *closed*. Deductivism, as already noted, is just the doctrine that all explanation be couched in terms of such (closed systems of) event regularities. Modern mainstream economics, if to repeat, is just a form of mathematical deductivism.

A social ontology or worldview that guarantees such event regularities is a world of isolated atoms. The term 'atom' here refers to anything that (if triggered) has the same independent effect whatever the context. Formulations couched in terms of atomistic factors allow the deduction and/or prediction of events. Or rather, they do so if nothing is allowed to interfere with the actions of the atoms. So to guarantee that at the theory level outcomes are truly predictable and/or deducible, the atoms must be assumed to act in isolation from any countervailing factors that could interfere with the outcomes.

This is the usual implicit ontology of mainstream mathematical modellers: a system of isolated atoms; indeed, a ubiquity of such systems. Very often specific substantive constructions employed take the form of conceptions of optimising (atomistic) individuals isolated in 'worlds' that each contains a unique set of optima, whereby the outcomes of agent interactions can be deduced. However, the latter type of set-up is not compulsory. Assumptions to the effect that individuals follow fixed rules are common, as are (or including) the algorithmic constructions of agent-based modelling and such like. But in almost all cases, the concrete theoretical specifications of economic mathematical modellers are implicitly in terms of—and so constrained to be formulations of—worlds of isolated atoms.

If there are exceptions to the latter sorts of formulations, these arise in the few exercises where the emphasis on mathematical modelling is retained but the modellers seek to avoid the usual unrealistic (atomistic and isolationist) conceptions by downgrading the role of theorising almost entirely. In such cases attempts are usually made to avoid theorising in terms of causal factors altogether as the emphasis is placed more on data information than theorising, as or where faith is placed, as with some modern approaches to econometrics, in more or less simply uncovering event regularities.[11]

Once, however, we change tack and give primary attention not to mathematical modelling but to studying more directly the actual nature of social reality, a quite different and clearly more explanatorily powerful or superior conception emerges. According to this alternative social ontology, causality always matters, and a more complex, processual account tends to dominate.

The conception of social ontology I have in mind is processual in that social reality, which itself is an emergent[12] phenomenon of human interaction, is recognised as being (not at all atomistic in the sense just noted but rather) highly transient, being reproduced and/or transformed through practice; social reality is in process, essentially a process of cumulative causation (see Lawson, 2012a). Furthermore, social reality is found to be composed of emergent phenomena that (far from being isolatable) are actually constituted in relation (that is, are internally related) to other things, and ultimately to everything else (for example, students and teachers, *qua* students and teachers, are constituted in relation to each other; so are employers and employees, landlords/ladies and tenants, creditors and debtors and so forth;[13] so, too, money, markets, firms and so forth are internally related under capitalism, and inherently transient). Constitutive social relations in short are a fundamental feature of social reality. So, social reality consists of emergent phenomena, constituting highly internally related causal processes.[14] For ease of exposition in what follows I often simply refer to this alternative worldview as a causal-processual or causal-historical ontology or some such.

Even this sketch, though unavoidably brief, is sufficient to indicate that from the perspective of the latter alternative ontology, the closed-system atomist and isolationist requirements of economic modelling are everywhere violated. In fact, the alternative ontology in question is more complex still, for the social world is additionally characterised by meaning, value and so on.

This latter conception, as I demonstrate elsewhere (see especially Lawson, 2003, chapter 2), is, if to repeat, significantly explanatorily superior as an account of the nature of social reality to the implicit worldview of systems of isolated atoms presupposed by the mainstream emphasis on certain techniques of mathematical modelling. It follows, accepting the alternative conception, that the failings of the discipline arise just because economists everywhere are seeking to provide analyses of a social system that is, amongst other things, open (in the sense of not consisting in event regularities), processual and highly internally related, in terms of formulations that require that the social realm be treated as if made of closed systems of isolated atoms. So, in summary, the real source of the discipline's problems is the very emphasis on mathematical modelling that defines the mainstream, an emphasis that usually results in formulations implicitly constrained to be consistent with a deficient social ontology.

2.1 The mainstream/heterodox contrast and the category neoclassical economics

I noted in the introductory overview that if the mainstream project is usefully characterised as a form of mathematical deductivism, the heterodox traditions are already self-identifying without employment of the term 'neoclassical'. Matters would be analytically neat if the mainstream/heterodox differentiation coincided with the contrasting ontological conceptions already sketched and that it was recognised as doing so. Unfortunately, at least in terms of recognition, matters are not quite so straightforward. Let me elaborate a little, for the issues involved, we eventually see, also bear significantly on Veblen's conception of neoclassical economics.

Although the heterodox traditions of modern economics do, on grounds of pluralism at least, oppose the noted mainstream insistence on methods of mathematical modelling, this opposition to the mathematical emphasis is not always viewed as a sufficient basis, or even sometimes as any basis, for identifying heterodoxy *qua* heterodoxy, just because the ontological implications of this mathematical emphasis are not always recognised.

64 The 'school' of neoclassical economics

Rather, on the surface at least, the heterodox antagonism to mainstream contributions is typically manifested not in terms of ontology at all but as a reaction to the project's substantive theoretical and policy claims. These of course are easily seen to be unrealistic and lacking explanatory power. But then so are the substantive theories accompanying more or less all mathematical modelling endeavours of modern economics. Although various commentators often suggest otherwise, the academic discipline of economics has been characterised by explanatory failure along with clearly unrealistic formulations for rather a long time now.[15] In this context the term 'neoclassical' plays a role, in distracting from the nature of the limitations of modelling *per se*. With more or less all theories attached to models being necessarily unrealistic in significant ways (due to the isolationist atomistic underpinnings), it is all too easy for any contributor to dismiss any particular set of results or claims that clashes with his or her own beliefs as neoclassical (or perhaps as insufficiently neoclassical) and quickly run up alternative (equally unrealistic) formulations that generate preferred conclusions.

Such activity serves to convince hardly anyone to change their minds on anything, of course. Yet it pervades the modern discipline. In this way much if not most academic economic debate remains extraordinarily superficial, certainly insufficiently radical, not least at the level of policy analysis. The practices of labelling varying sets of theories neoclassical helps sustain this superficiality precisely through encouraging the impression that the source of all problems lies at the level of substantive theories, with questionable claims and hypotheses reflecting no more than their formulator's erroneous beliefs about economic behaviour. In this way, any critical observer is encouraged in the view that there is no need to get beyond the level of substantive theorising and model building. In consequence, the more basic problems at the level of ontology remain insufficiently examined and indeed mostly neglected, so the emphasis on mathematical modelling remains largely unquestioned.[16]

Yet there is something of a paradox in all this. Although debates and critiques within modern economics do in this way tend to remain overly superficial, on closer examination it is also apparent that the more sustainable causal ontology of openness, process, significant internal relationality and so on is nevertheless regularly, if often only implicitly, recognised, most especially by heterodox practitioners (see Lawson, 2006a). Or at least this alternative social ontology is often acknowledged in some manner within heterodox pronouncements and more general forms of reasoning. Indeed, specific heterodox traditions have tended to emphasise, or focus centrally and repeatedly on, different aspects of it; or rather, they have systematically focussed on features that clearly presuppose it. Thus post-Keynesians effectively recognise the all prevailing openness (or the rarity of closed systems) in their significant and enduring concern with uncertainty; feminist economists highlight relationality especially, not least in their concern with theorising issues of care, discrimination and oppression; institutionalists continually interest themselves in systematically studying both change and stability in social life, not least through their emphasis on technology and institutions; Marxian economists concentrate especially on elaborating the nature of the specific emergent internally related totality in motion that is capitalism; and so on (on all this see Lawson, 2003, chapter 7; 2006a).

In fact, a good deal of sustained heterodox research is couched in conceptual frameworks consistent with the sort of causal-processual ontological conception just described. All too often, however, this goes hand in hand with a lack of realisation that methods of mathematical modelling require formulations that are in severe tension with this ontology. This lack of realisation both underpins a misapprehension of the source of the unrealistic nature of many competing claims, as well as the recourse of many heterodox economists to using mathematical modelling methods in seeking to advance insights obtained by other means (see Lawson, 2009a, 2009b).

Reinforcing the confusion of this whole situation are frequently repeated accompanying assertions to the effect that a reliance on mathematical methods is somehow analytically neutral, that mathematics is no more than a language, or mathematical models are heuristic devices or some such—none of which withstand critical scrutiny (see Lawson, 2009c).

Of course, because heterodox economists typically prioritise the search for relevance rather than mathematical prowess *per se,* a result is that those heterodox economists who engage in mathematical modelling are, unlike their mainstream counterparts, usually very willing to acknowledge as legitimate (i.e., do not reject as unscientific or not 'proper' economics) the various insightful analyses by others that are not mathematical in any way. The defining feature of the mainstream is the *insistence* on methods of mathematical modelling.

In large part, however, heterodox economists who resort to forms of mathematical modelling fail to appreciate the tension between the ontological presuppositions of this activity and the sort of worldview they otherwise tend to acknowledge. Or where within heterodoxy, a continuing faith in, and/or resources allocated to, exercises in mathematical modelling are not accounted for by an inattention to ontological preconceptions of methods, the explanation is seemingly that the individuals in question entertain hopes of identifying certain contexts in which local closures (facilitating the appropriate use of mathematical methods) do, temporarily, obtain. Either way, the more fundamental problems of the discipline are usually sidestepped with the result that the inappropriate emphasis on mathematical modelling methods remains largely unchallenged.

So, to take stock, both the fundamental failings and the main divisions of modern economics can at some level be expressed in terms of ontological orientations. Or at least this is the real basis for the heterodox opposition to mainstream contributions. However, the picture is muddied by the fact that seemingly not all heterodox economists appreciate that methods of mathematical modelling carry ontological presuppositions, let alone presuppositions (closed systems of isolated atoms) that are inconsistent with worldviews broadly professed. A result is that the picture, if reasonably coherent at the level of ontological distinctions and grounding, is far less so in terms of actual practice. Whether or not the latter identified tension is a weakness of the conception maintained, it represents a theme to which I return in due course and suggest a critical re-evaluation.

A factor that contributes to the preservation of this confused situation is a constant if uncritical repetition of the refrain, at least within heterodoxy, that neoclassical (substantive) theorising is the cause of the problems, even though there is the noted lack of clarity over the meaning of such a term. This activity serves to focus attention on conflicts at the level of substantive theorising and policy formulation, and thereby away from the deeper fundamental tensions at the level of ontology that inhibit systematic progress on all sides of modern debate.

It is thus against the backdrop of this situation that I seek to elaborate a coherent conception of the term 'neoclassical economics', indicating how it relates to the various strands of the discipline. This later task seems at least an appropriate and useful—and perhaps a necessary—undertaking if, as here, the goal is to help facilitate more effective critique within the current context, and thereby at least a possibility of progress in understanding.

I turn, then, to develop a conception of neoclassical economics that meets the criteria of coherence laid out in the introductory overview and can be viewed, in that sense at least, as more sustainable than the alternatives so far considered. To motivate the interpretation of neoclassical economics I have in mind, I focus specifically on the analysis originally provided by Veblen. I do so not merely to emphasise historical lineage but also because Veblen's analysis and concerns prove extremely useful to achieving an interpretation that retains current relevance as well as overall coherence, as we will see.

3. Veblen's project

Those individuals or groups who formulate novel categories do so, of course, for purposes of drawing out similarities and differences that they regard as significant within a body of phenomena they are concerned to examine. A first objective here is to identify Veblen's larger purpose in coining the term 'neoclassical', to uncover the sorts of concerns that interested him and relative to which he felt it advantageous to draw certain distinctions.

This is a topic rarely addressed at any length. Those who acknowledge Veblen as the originator of the term mostly report that he introduces it to distinguish Marshall's marginalism, or at least to distinguish a marginalist tradition for which Marshall is a central or typical proponent. For these observers, the emphasis tends to be on Marshall's intention of continuing a form of economics that Veblen labels classical, justifying the formulation neoclassical.[17] However, as already noted, these same observers mostly conclude that no significant commonality between the two projects actually exists.[18] Other contributors emphasise instead that the point of introducing the term 'neoclassical' is not merely to express commonality but also to differentiate, specifically to differentiate economists like Marshall from those whom Veblen labels Austrian.[19]

There is some insight to all of this. However, a close examination of the original text, I shall argue, reveals that Veblen holds neither that Marshall typifies the neoclassical contribution nor that Marshall and/or those grouped with him are the only continuers of the classical tradition in question, nor even that it is Marshall's marginalism *per se* that determines his neoclassical credentials. I also argue that Veblen does after all establish a coherent and sustainable account of continuity between the contributions of those he labels neoclassical and those he interprets as classical; and that in so doing, Veblen is indeed also very concerned to establish distinctions between projects, albeit not especially with drawing a distinction between the line of thinking designated neoclassical and Austrian contributions. In fact, to emphasise this latter distinction before others is to miss almost the entire point of Veblen's analysis.

Clearly I need to substantiate these introductory remarks as well as provide grounds for an alternative assessment. In seeking to do so I start by elaborating the nature of Veblen's broader project. That is, before turning to Veblen's actual introduction and use of the term 'neoclassical', I examine at some length the issues that motivate his analysis including the sorts of distinctions he seeks to draw.

3.1 Metaphysical preconceptions

In the 1900 paper in which the category neoclassical is first introduced, Veblen's ongoing relevant concerns are actually signalled by the paper's title: 'Preconceptions of Economic Science'. The sorts of preconceptions Veblen has in mind here are precisely those already discussed above, namely, the ontological presuppositions held by contributors to economic science. Veblen here (and in other papers written at the time, including his famous 'evolutionary essay' [1898] as well as two earlier papers also titled the 'Preconceptions of Economic Science' [1899a, 1899b]) uses the term 'metaphysics' rather than 'ontology', seeking to tease out the 'underlying metaphysics of scientific research and purpose' (1900, p. 241); but his meaning of metaphysics is the same as that of ontology as used here.

68 *The 'school' of neoclassical economics*

Throughout these papers Veblen's primary focus is not substantive theory but, as these titles suggest, the metaphysical preconceptions underpinning economic theorising.

Veblen's specific concern is to identify or distinguish competing 'grounds of finality' of economic contributions, meaning the conceptions of scientific formulations held as proper and providing the standard whereby analyses that conform might be regarded as potentially complete.

In the course of the three 'preconceptions' papers, Veblen at length traces out how 'changes which have supervened in the preconceptions of the earlier economists constitute a somewhat orderly succession' (Veblen, 1900, p. 240), the most interesting feature of which has been a gradual change over time in the received 'grounds of finality' presupposed in economics:

> The feature of chief interest in this development has been a gradual change in the received grounds of finality to which the successive generations of economists have brought their theoretical output, on which they have been content to rest their conclusions, and beyond which they have not been moved to push their analysis of events or their scrutiny of phenomena. There has been a fairly unbroken sequence of development in what may be called the canons of economic reality; or, to put it in other words, there has been a precession of the point of view from which facts have been handled and valued for the purpose of economic science.
> (Veblen, 1900, p. 240)

Motivating this analysis, however, is a concern to distinguish and contrast two specific and basic 'grounds of finality for science' especially. These relate to conceptions of science that Veblen usually terms 'taxonomic' and 'evolutionary' science, with the former taxonomic conception being 'the economics handed down by the great writers of a past generation' (Veblen, 1899a, p. 121) and the latter evolutionary conception described as 'modern'.

Put simply, for Veblen a taxonomic science is a science of normalities or of the normal case. It presupposes normality in or underpinning and grounding the course of events.[20] This contrasts with, and indeed can be said to be the antithesis[21] of, a historical or evolutionary or 'matter of fact' orientation to science that presupposes nothing more than cumulative causal sequence. In the latter case any outcome or event is always caused by something that went before it, but is not in conformity with some pre-ordained pattern or regularity, nor in a manner serving some normative or laudable purpose and so forth.

Veblen notes in this regard that the evolutionary scientist 'is unwilling to depart from the test of causal relation or quantitative sequence' (1898, p. 377), inquiring of everything only 'why?', and seeking an answer in terms of cause and effect. For the taxonomic economist, in contrast, 'this

The 'school' of neoclassical economics 69

ground of cause and effect is not definitive' (1898, p. 378). Rather, the ultimate term in the systematisation of knowledge is something like a 'natural law', or an association of phenomena, an empirical generalisation, or possibly a correlation regarded as 'natural' or 'normal' or a 'consistent propensity' with any exceptions regarded as mere disturbing factors.

Veblen interprets all lines of economics up until the time he is writing, including those systematised as classical, as being essentially taxonomic in this sense. He has two related concerns in producing the set of three papers titled the 'Preconceptions of Economic Science' as well as his 'evolutionary essay'. The first is to trace how preconceptions of normality and regularity have changed and been rationalised in different periods, culminating with the classical economists of recent standing. The second and more important purpose is to examine how conceptions of normality in economics have fared in the face of the influence of the wider modern evolutionary sciences. In regard to the latter objective his concern is with understanding whether the taxonomic emphasis will continue to shape the methods of economic science:

> The question of interest is how this preconception of normality has fared at the hands of modern science, and how it has come to be superseded in the intellectual primacy by the latter day preconception of a non-spiritual sequence. This question is of interest because its answer may throw light on the question as to what chance there is for the indefinite persistence of this archaic habit of thought in the methods of economic science.
> (Veblen, 1898, p. 379)

In the endeavour of tracing out earlier preconceptions of normality and regularity, Veblen first notes how the 'more archaic metaphysics of the science, [...] saw in the orderly correlation and sequence of events a constraining guidance of an extra-causal, teleological kind' (1900, p. 255). That is, the order that was experienced in social life was in effect interpreted as pre-ordained and external to the events unfolding. Starting from an analysis of this 'archaic metaphysics', Veblen at length traces out gradual changes in the underlying ontological preconceptions, running through those of the Physiocrats, Adam Smith, the utilitarian economists (especially Jeremy Bentham), and culminating in the more recent British contributors such as John Stuart Mill and especially John Elliott Cairnes.

A notable feature of the changing metaphysics throughout the period Veblen discusses is a continuous dissolution of 'animistic' preconceptions, a giving up of the idea that there is a spiritual force directing or guiding all developments including those classed as economics:

> The history of the science shows a long and devious course of disintegrating animism,—from the days of the scholastic writers, who

discussed usury from the point of view of its relation to the divine suzerainty, to the Physiocrats, who rested their case on an 'ordre naturel' and a 'loi naturelle' that decides what is substantially true and, in a general way, guides the course of events by the constraint of logical congruence. There has been something of a change from Adam Smith, whose recourse in perplexity was to the guidance of 'an unseen hand,' to Mill and Cairnes, who formulated the laws of 'natural' wages and 'normal' value.

(Veblen, 1898, p. 381)

As my intention here is to elaborate Veblen's notion of neoclassical economics and indicate its continuity with (as well as departure from) a classical economics, the segment of this history of metaphysics on which I mostly focus concerns precisely those developments in economics that Veblen systematises as classical.

It can be immediately noted that Veblen's use of this latter term is non-standard or anyway non-universal. As is well known, Karl Marx coined the term, or rather the category, 'classical political economy' in his *Contribution to the Critique of Political Economy* (Marx, 1977). Marx used it to denote that strand of economics, originating in France with Pierre le Pesant, sieur de Boisguilbert (1646–1714), running through William Petty (1772–1823) and reaching its high point with the contributions of Adam Smith and David Ricardo (1772–1823), where the focus is on the deeper structures of capitalism and in particular social relations, including relations of production. In coining the term, Marx sought to emphasise a contrast with the 'vulgar economy' that followed thereafter which puts aside any interest in real relations of production and focuses instead on superficial appearances.[22]

It is this latter set of contributions, Marx's vulgar economy, which Veblen essentially identifies as classical economics (as more or less did John Maynard Keynes and others later on). More specifically, for Veblen, the classical school consists in those British economists that came after, but were influenced by, Adam Smith and culminated with those contributors that were to precede Marshall, most notably Mill and Cairnes.

Given that I explore Veblen's thinking and quote various passages by him, I take it as given in the discussion of the next two sub-sections that the referent of the term 'classical' conforms to Veblen's usage, although in due course I briefly return to the issue of these differing conceptions of classical and any bearing the fact of the difference has on a viable interpretation of the category neoclassical economics.

3.2 Veblen's classical economics

Thus interpreted, classical economics, to now use Veblen's rather than Marx's characterisations of the different strands of thought, is differentiated from its forerunners at a substantive level in that its focus is primarily no longer on production but on the 'pecuniary side of life' constituting 'a theory of a process of valuation' (Veblen, 1898, p. 424).

However, it is the metaphysical preconceptions of contributors to classical economics that most characterises the latter for Veblen, and he primarily focusses on them. These do develop somewhat over time, starting with 'remnants of natural rights and of the order of nature' but becoming 'infused with that peculiarly mechanical natural theology that made its way into popular vogue on British ground during the eighteenth century and was reduced to a neutral tone by the British penchant for the common-place—stronger at this time than at any earlier period' (Veblen, 1899b, p. 424).

Thus Veblen is explicit in regarding the significant difference between the early classical economics in the form of the utilitarianism and the contributions of Adam Smith, its forerunner, to lie neither in any attachment to a utilitarian viewpoint *per se* nor in any substantive conclusions or policies but in metaphysical preconceptions (Veblen, 1899b, pp. 411–12). For Smith the ultimate ground of economic reality is the design of God; the economic order is divinely instituted, and human beings are suitably deferential. For contributors to classical economics, in contrast, the ultimate grounds are human nature and processes of valuation. For the utilitarian version of classical economics specifically, the ultimate ground lies in a simplistic hedonistic conception of the nature of human beings conceived essentially in terms of maximising pleasure and minimising pain:

> After Adam Smith's day, economics fell into profane hands [. . .] the next generation do not approach their subject from the point of view of a divinely instituted order; nor do they discuss human interests with that gently optimistic spirit of submission that belongs to the economist who goes to his work with the fear of God before his eyes [. . .].
>
> With Adam Smith the ultimate ground of economic reality is the design of God, the teleological order; and his utilitarian generalizations, as well as the hedonistic character of his economic man, are but methods of the working out of this natural order, not the substantial and self-legitimating ground. [. . .] Of the utilitarians proper the converse is true, [. . .]. The substantial economic ground is pleasure and pain: the teleological order (even the design of God, where that is admitted) is the method of its working out.
>
> (Veblen, 1899b, pp. 411–12)

In the course of the development of classical economics, as Veblen conceives it, the spiritual or 'animistic preconception was not lost, but it lost tone' and 'partly fell into abeyance'. It was mostly evident in 'the unavowed readiness of the classical writers to accept as imminent and definitive any possible outcome which the writer's habit or temperament inclined him to accept as right and good.' Veblen thus writes of 'the visible inclination of classical economists to a doctrine of the harmony of interests' and their readiness to 'state their generalizations in terms of what ought to happen' (1899b, pp. 424–25).

An operative term here is 'generalisations'. These are fundamental to the classical contributions as Veblen views them. However, uncovering these generalisations is not a straightforward matter. In discussing how they are derived, Veblen draws attention to a norm of procedure especially important to the later classical economics. Although the approach is heavily empirical, it involved not the direct observation of event regularities but their careful construction via interpreting the evidence at hand. Let me elaborate this assessment a bit.

In fact, Veblen is of the clear view that later 'avowedly classical economists', notably Cairnes and J S Mill, are essentially empiricists, who, in seeking their (empirical) correlations or laws, exclude all ideas of teleology or even causal continuity. Thus Veblen (1900, p. 251) writes of 'the abiding faith which these empiricists had in the sole efficacy of empirical generalization' in which all notions of organic connection or causal continuity are to be avoided. Rather, they construe 'causal sequence to mean a uniformity of co-existences and successions simply' (Veblen, 1900, p. 252).[23]

However, such empirical regularities, then as now, were nowhere in evidence. The novelty of the contributors of this period is to interpret regularities as the product of laborious interpretation:

> But, since a strict uniformity is nowhere to be observed at first hand in the phenomena with which the investigator is occupied, it has to be found by a laborious interpretation of the phenomena and a diligent abstraction and allowance for disturbing circumstances, whatever may be the meaning of a disturbing circumstance where causal continuity is denied.
>
> (Veblen, 1900, pp. 252–53)

The perspective or set of preconceptions that ground this interpretive activity is summed up by the idea that all things ultimately tend towards (even if they are temporarily disturbed from) ends or patterns that the common sense of any era holds to be valuable or worthy. This, says Veblen, is the 'standpoint of the classical economists in their higher or definitive syntheses and generalizations' (1898, p. 382). It is described as a standpoint of 'ceremonial adequacy', not least because the 'ultimate laws and principles which they formulated were laws of the normal or the natural, according to preconception regarding the ends to which, in the nature of things, all things tend'; the latter in turn being ends that 'the instructed common sense of the time accepts as the adequate or worthy end of human effort' (1898, p. 382).

Veblen's assessment of the later avowedly classical economists, then, is that their scientific preconceptions of normality took the form essentially of correlations or event regularities, albeit regularities about the normal or natural, understood as that which common sense determines as desirable. However, these had to be carefully read into actual economic outcomes. This is a method of analysis, peculiar to these classical economists, that, according to Veblen, renders them a 'deductive school', and their science taxonomic:

> What is peculiar to the classical economists in this respect is their particular norm of procedure in the work of interpretation. And, by virtue of having achieved a standpoint of absolute economic normality, they became a 'deductive' school, so called, in spite of the patent fact that they were pretty consistently employed with an inquiry into the causal sequence of economic phenomena. The generalization of observed facts becomes a normalization of them, a statement of the phenomena in terms of their coincidence with, or divergence from, that normal tendency that makes for the actualization of the absolute economic reality. This absolute or definitive ground of economic legitimacy lies beyond the causal sequence in which the observed phenomena are conceived to be interlinked. It is related to the concrete facts neither as cause nor as effect in any such way that the causal relation may be traced in a concrete instance. It has little causally to do either with the 'mental' or with the 'physical' data with which the classical economist is avowedly employed. Its relation to the process under discussion is that of an extraneous—that is to say, a ceremonial—legitimation. The body of knowledge gained by its help and under its guidance is, therefore, a taxonomic science.
> (Veblen, 1899b, p. 425)

The preconceptions of normality that underpin the analysis, to repeat, are that economic developments conform to correlations, albeit correlations that express features that common sense determines as desirable and can be apprehended only though significantly reinterpreting the evidence. As Veblen had earlier observed in his 'evolutionary essay':

> The ways and means and the mechanical structure of industry are formulated in a conventionalised nomenclature, and the observed motions of this mechanical apparatus are then reduced to a normalised scheme of relations. [. . .] With this normalised scheme as a guide, the permutations of a given segment of the apparatus are worked out according to the values assigned the several items and features comprised in the calculation; and a ceremonially consistent formula is constructed to cover that much of the industrial field. This is the deductive method. The formula is then tested by comparison with observed permutations, by the polariscopic use of the 'normal case';

and the results arrived at are thus authenticated by induction. Features of the process that do not lend themselves to interpretation in the terms of the formula are abnormal cases and are due to disturbing causes. In all this the agencies or forces causally at work in the economic life process are neatly avoided. The outcome of the method, at its best, is a body of logically consistent propositions concerning the normal relations of things—a system of economic taxonomy.

(Veblen, 1898, pp. 383–84)

Laws, then, are but laws of the normal case, sometimes interpreted as hypothetical or abstract, and this science, to repeat, is taxonomic.

> The laws of the science, that which makes up the economist's theoretical knowledge, are laws of the normal case. The normal case does not occur in concrete fact. These laws are, therefore, in Cairnes's terminology, 'hypothetical' truths; and the science is a 'hypothetical' science. They apply to concrete facts only as the facts are interpreted and abstracted from, in the light of the underlying postulates. The science is, therefore, a theory of the normal case, a discussion of the concrete facts of life in respect of their degree of approximation to the normal case. That is to say, it is a taxonomic science.
>
> (Veblen, 1900, pp. 254–55)

Given this concern with the non-empirical normal or natural, it is unsurprising that a central category for describing economic states should be that of equilibrium. Thus Veblen in total traces the interpretations of normality from extra-causal teleological guidance of the ancients to the modern-day search for correlations and suchlike, as well as theories concerning conditions of economic equilibrium:

> The earlier, more archaic metaphysics of the science, which saw in the orderly correlation and sequence of events a constraining guidance of an extra-causal, teleological kind, in this way becomes a metaphysics of normality which asserts no extra-causal constraint over events, but contents itself with establishing correlations, equivalencies, homologies, and theories concerning the conditions of an economic equilibrium.
>
> (Veblen, 1900, p. 255)

Importantly for the issues before us, Veblen assesses that at the time he is writing, economics is experiencing change and moving in the direction of an evolutionary science. However, the degree of change achieved is regarded by Veblen as not yet sufficient for economic science to qualify as evolutionary, with hallmarks of taxonomic thinking remaining dominant:

The process of change in the point of view, or in the terms of definitive formulation of knowledge, is a gradual one; and all the sciences have shared, though in an unequal degree, in the change that is going forward. Economics is not an exception to the rule, but it still shows too many reminiscences of the 'natural' and the 'normal,' of 'verities' and 'tendencies,' of 'controlling principles' and 'disturbing causes' to be classed as an evolutionary science.

(Veblen, 1898, p. 381)

3.3 Veblen's conception of neoclassical economics

All that has been said on Veblen's concerns to this point, of course, has been motivated by a need to set the scene for a discussion of what Veblen might mean by the category 'neoclassical'. As we shall see, Veblen also refers to the same project intermittently as modernised or even quasi-classical economics.

Fundamental to Veblen's use of the term 'neoclassical' are precisely the metaphysical or ontological grounds of finality of science that form the focus of the three 'preconceptions' papers, and in particular the contrasting preconceptions associated with taxonomic science on the one hand and with causal-historical or evolutionary science on the other. It is important to recall that Veblen believed himself to be writing at a time of transition in relation to the matters that concerned him (see Lawson, 2003, chapter 8). Although, as we have seen, Veblen motivates his preconceptions papers by enquiring into the possible persistence of the taxonomic approach, and certainly concludes that an adequate basis in evolutionary thinking has yet to be achieved, he elsewhere basically expresses the view that an evolutionary orientation to economics, and indeed to all social and political science, is ultimately unavoidable; specifically, 'The social and political sciences must follow the drift [towards becoming evolutionary sciences], for they are already caught in it.'[24]

In this assessment, Veblen has so far been proven to be quite wrong. When introducing the term 'neoclassical economics', Veblen is uncertain as to which of various projects that coexisted at that time will most endure, or, as he puts it, survive the processes of 'natural selection'. Nor is he clear as to which of the various contending contributors will be most involved in 'continuing the main current of economic speculation and inquiry'. Nor even is he intending to give any relative evaluation of the specific claims of the two or three main 'schools' of theory; or at least, he intends not to do so beyond noting one obvious comparative 'finding'. However, it is in the context of noting this obvious finding that the term 'neoclassical' first appears. The relevant passage runs as follows:

> With respect to writers of the present or the more recent past the work of natural selection, as between variants of scientific aim and animus

and between more or less divergent points of view, has not yet taken effect; and it would be over-hazardous to attempt an anticipation of the results of the selection that lies in great part yet in the future. As regards the directions of theoretical work suggested by the names of Professor Marshall, Mr. Cannan, Professor Clark, Mr. Pierson, Austrian Professor Loria, Professor Schmoller, the group,—no off-hand decision is admissible as between these candidates for the honor, or, better, for the work, of continuing the main current of economic speculation and inquiry. No attempt will here be made even to pass a verdict on the relative claims of the recognised two or three main 'schools' of theory, beyond the somewhat obvious finding that, for the purpose in hand, the so-called Austrian school is scarcely distinguishable from the neo-classical, unless it be in the different distribution of emphasis.

(Veblen, 1900, pp. 260–61)

So Veblen does indeed introduce the term 'neoclassical' in a passage that indicates a 'school' that it is not the same as the Austrian. He does so, however, only to point out that for 'the purpose in hand' the neoclassical and Austrian school are actually 'scarcely distinguishable'.

What is this 'purpose in hand'? It is, as it has been throughout the three preconception essays, to determine the accepted 'grounds of finality' or the ontological preconceptions of science, of groups of economists. In particular, Veblen is concerned to examine if and how the taxonomic orientation is giving way to evolutionary thinking or science. In the passage that immediately continues that just noted, he substitutes 'modernised' for 'neo' in qualifying classical, indicating that he regards the terms as equivalent, and makes it very clear that with regard to this 'purpose in hand' the interesting and significant contrast (to neoclassical economics) is provided *not* by the Austrians but by the 'historical and Marxist schools':

The divergence between the modernised classical views, on the one hand, and the historical and Marxist schools, on the other hand, is wider,—so much so, indeed, as to bar out a consideration of the postulates of the latter under the same head of inquiry with the former. The inquiry, therefore, confines itself to the one line standing most obviously in unbroken continuity with that body of classical economics whose life history has been traced in outline above. And, even for this phase of modernised classical economics, it seems necessary to limit discussion, for the present, to a single strain, selected as standing peculiarly close to the classical source, at the same time that it shows unmistakable adaptation to the later habits of thought and methods of knowledge.

(Veblen, 1900, p. 261)

Whatever else neoclassical economics is, then, it is clearly not on par with the historical or Marxist schools. But if neoclassical economics and the 'modernised classical school' are the same project, it is equally apparent (from the final sentence of the last noted passage) that Veblen is intending to limit discussion not to neoclassical thinking as a whole but to a single 'strain' of it. It is in consideration of this single strain or subset of neoclassical thinking, we will see, that Marshall enters the picture.

What is the nature of this 'strain'? According to Veblen, although the producers of neo- or modernised classical economics stand 'peculiarly close to the classical source' they are differentiated from their classical predecessors in being aware of and positively oriented to evolutionary thinking. The strain or subgroup on which Veblen focuses includes those who best exemplify this positive orientation. This is his meaning in observing of this 'strain' that 'it shows unmistakable adaptation to the later habits of thought and methods of knowledge'.

3.4 Marshall and Keynes

In identifying this specific strain (which shows unmistakable adaptation to the historical or evolutionary approach) Veblen proceeds merely by illustrating it with reference to two of its developers. One is the philosopher of science John Neville Keynes (the father of John Maynard Keynes), the other is the economist (and Keynes family friend) Alfred Marshall:

> For this later development in the classical line of political economy, Mr. Keynes's book may fairly be taken as the maturest exposition of the aims and ideals of the science; while Professor Marshall excellently exemplifies the best work that is being done under the guidance of the classical antecedents.
>
> (Veblen, 1900, pp. 261–62)

So Marshall's contributions do not so much *typify* neoclassical economics as represent a specific strand of it that represents the best work done within that line of thinking, in effect moving it further away from its taxonomic classical heritage. The contributions of both Keynes and Marshall are presumably singled out because, under the principle of charity, if a line of thinking is to be criticised for its fundamental nature, and this indeed is Veblen's intention, it is always better to illustrate with the best of work in that line.

Veblen certainly discusses these noted contributors at some length. But his main point throughout is that no matter how ready they are to acknowledge causal processes, and in particular causal histories of structures like institutions in line with causal-processual ontology underpinning historical and evolutionary science, even Keynes and Marshall are unable in practice to break with the taxonomic ideal of science, particularly at the level of

78 The 'school' of neoclassical economics

method, and this prevents the achievement of a meaningful account of the genesis and developmental continuity of such phenomena.

Veblen is clearly positively disposed towards aspects of the stances adopted by both Keynes and Marshall. He acknowledges of Keynes, for example, that not only does he interpret the aims of modern economic science as having 'less of the 'hypothetical' character assigned it by Cairnes (that is, as dealing less closely with the ascertainment of the normal case), he also takes 'fuller account of the genesis and developmental continuity of all features of modern economic life' giving 'more and closer attention to institutions and their history'.

Nevertheless a break with taxonomy is not achieved in practice. Rather,

> There is a curious reminiscence of the perfect taxonomic day in Mr. Keynes's characterisation of political economy as a "positive science," the sole province of which is to establish economic uniformities.
>
> (Veblen, 1900, p. 264)

Moreover, observes Veblen,

> in this resort to the associationist expedient of defining a natural law as a "uniformity," Mr. Keynes is also borne out by Professor Marshall.
>
> (Veblen, 1900, p. 265)

So the taxonomic approach that typifies the classical school survives even in the writings of Keynes and Marshall, albeit the case that notions of normality no longer express economic developments considered desirable but rather those situations, now considered to exist at the level of the actual course of events, that conform to empirical regularities or economic uniformities. This, of course, is all quite inconsistent with Veblen's conception of evolutionary thinking.

Indeed, although (or perhaps because) Marshall is apparently more adapted to modern science than most economists, he is interpreted by Veblen as being especially inconsistent on these matters. For, despite observing that Marshall occupies himself with investigating the nature of institutions and is positively disposed to incorporating insights of evolutionary thinking, Veblen also observes that throughout this work the 'taxonomic bearing is, after all, the dominant feature' (Veblen, 1900, p. 263).

This is not to say that Marshall is not considered to make a substantial contribution. Indeed, Veblen even suggests that despite 'survivals of the taxonomic terminology, or even of the taxonomic canons of procedure' the latter 'do not hinder the economists of the modern school from doing effective work of a character that must be rated as genetic rather than taxonomic' (Veblen, 1900, p. 265).[25] The problem, though, according to Veblen, is that the evolutionary thinking is in the end rather superficial; in particular there is little attempt to fashion relevant methods of analysis. The special 'strain' of neoclassical thinking represented by Keynes and Marshall is singled out precisely to illustrate that even this most adapted and aware strain (which 'exemplifies the best work that is being done under the guidance of the classical antecedents') fails to get beyond taxonomic science at the level of method.

In short, a feature of contributions of both Keynes and Marshall that is significant with regard to the sorts of issues that interest Veblen is a tension bordering upon inconsistency. It is a tension between method and ontology/metaphysics (or more accurately between the ontological presuppositions of taxonomic method and a causal-processual social ontology).

Certainly Veblen finds in these contributors a greater awareness (than is revealed by the earlier classical economists) of issues that are central to the historical evolutionary approach of the sort he favoured, but taxonomy in terms of method remains dominant.

It is precisely this tension, which is first illustrated using the contributions of Keynes and Marshall that I take to be the essence of neoclassical economics, according to Veblen. In other words, the defining feature of all neoclassical economics is basically an inconsistent blend of the old and the new; it is in effect an awareness of the newer metaphysics of processual cumulative or unfolding causation, combined with a failure to break away from methods of the older taxonomic view of science that are in tension with this modern ontology.

Neoclassical economists are classical in their acceptance of a taxonomic orientation to science that does not rely on the design of God, albeit a taxonomic stance now primarily revealed at the level of method. But at that level of explicit ontological or metaphysical preconception, neo-classical economists reveal unmistakable adaptation to the viewpoints of the evolutionary sciences, warranting the qualifier 'neo'.

3.5 Neoclassical economics more generally

Within neoclassicism, it is the strain or subset of neoclassical thinking represented by Marshall and Keynes that in Veblen's assessment is the more adapted to evolutionary thinking. As such Marshall and Keynes are viewed as the more scientifically advanced contributors to, rather than as typifying, neoclassical economics, though even these do not escape the classical taxonomic heritage. Equally, however, Veblen is clear that an air of evolutionism does characterise all neoclassical output, allowing it in fact to be associated at least superficially with work of the early generation of Darwinians. Hence the tension or inconsistency revealed to be present in Keynes and Marshall does characterise all of neoclassical argumentation. Specifically neoclassical economists have done little to develop or to apply methods of analysis that are appropriate to evolutionary preconceptions:

80 *The 'school' of neoclassical economics*

> All this gives an air of evolutionism to the work. Indeed, the work of the neo-classical economics might be compared, probably without offending any of its adepts, with that of the early generation of Darwinians, though such a comparison might somewhat shrewdly have to avoid any but superficial features. Economists of the present day are commonly evolutionists, in a general way. They commonly accept, as other men do, the general results of the evolutionary speculation in those directions in which the evolutionary method has made its way. But the habit of handling by evolutionist methods the facts with which their own science *is* concerned has made its way among the economists to but a very uncertain degree.
>
> The prime postulate of evolutionary science, the preconception constantly underlying the inquiry, is the notion of a cumulative causal sequence; and writers on economics are in the habit of recognising that the phenomena with which they are occupied are subject to such a law of development. Expressions of assent to this proposition abound. But the economists have not worked out or hit upon a method by which the inquiry in economics may consistently be conducted under the guidance of this postulate.
>
> (Veblen, 1900, pp. 265–66)

At best neoclassical economists have limited their analyses to aspects of the social world that appear least unpromising for handing with taxonomic methods. This, on occasion at least, is how Veblen describes Marshall specifically, that is, as merely limiting the scope of economics to the few situations where the conditions of such a taxonomic approach may conceivably prevail. In particular, where some innovation has occurred the taxonomic approach of this sort, with its 'statements of uniformities', may be able to say something of the conditions of survival of the innovation, though even here Veblen remains sceptical:

> Taking Professor Marshall as exponent, it appears that, while the formulations of economic theory are not conceived to be arrived at by way of an inquiry into the developmental variation of economic institutions and the like, the theorems arrived at are held, and no doubt legitimately, to apply to the past, and with due reserve also to the future, phases of the development. But these theorems apply to the various phases of the development not as accounting for the developmental sequence, but as limiting the range of variation. They say little, if anything, as to the order of succession, as to the derivation and the outcome of any given phase, or as to the causal relation of one phase of any given economic convention or scheme of relations to any other. They indicate the conditions of survival to which any innovation is subject, supposing the innovation to have taken place, not the conditions of variational growth. The economic laws, the 'statements

of uniformity,' are therefore, when construed in an evolutionary bearing, theorems concerning the superior or the inferior limit of persistent innovations, as the case may be. It is only in this negative, selective bearing that the current economic laws are held to be laws of developmental continuity; and it should be added that they have hitherto found but relatively scant application at the hands of the economists, even for this purpose.

(Veblen, 1898, p. 266)[26]

Finally, it is not merely Keynes and Marshall who abandon the idea that correlations carry some kind of normative appeal; it is a feature of neoclassical economics more generally. Economics remains taxonomic for neoclassical economists essentially because of the presumed form of its results, as presupposed by its methods of correlation analysis. Only now the correlations or uniformities that are produced or sought-after are interpreted (if ultimately somewhat mysteriously) as laws of everyday conduct:

> In consonance with this quasi-evolutionary tone of the neo-classical political economy, or as an expression of it, comes the further clarified sense that nowadays attaches to the terms 'normal' and economic 'laws.' The laws have gained in colorlessness, until it can no longer be said that the concept of normality implies approval of the phenomena to which it is applied. They are in an increasing degree laws of conduct, though they still continue to formulate conduct in hedonistic terms; that is to say, conduct is construed in terms of its sensuous effect, not in terms of its teleological content. The light of the science is a drier light than it was, but it continues to be shed upon the accessories of human action rather than upon the process itself. The categories employed for the purpose of knowing this economic conduct with which the scientists occupy themselves are not the categories under which the men at whose hands the action takes place themselves apprehend their own action at the instant of acting. Therefore, economic conduct still continues to be somewhat mysterious to the economists; and they are forced to content themselves with adumbrations whenever the discussion touches this central, substantial fact.

(Veblen, 1900, pp. 267–68)

In summary, I am suggesting that Veblen introduces the term 'neoclassical' to distinguish a line of thinking that is ultimately characterised by possessing a degree of ontological awareness whilst persevering with a methodology inconsistent with this awareness; it is a line of thinking identified precisely by this ontological/methodological tension or inconsistency. Its practitioners recognise that social reality is a historical process of cumulative causation, but nevertheless continue to rely upon methods that require of reality that it conforms to given correlations, that render the science as still taxonomic.

As I noted earlier, deductivism is the term used to designate any explanatory reliance on methods that presuppose event correlations. Veblen's neoclassical economists, then, can be characterised as acknowledging the social world everywhere as historical, as processual, but nevertheless simultaneously treating it using taxonomic and specifically deductivist methods that presuppose that social reality is anything but.

It warrants emphasis that, so interpreted, Veblen's neoclassical economics is neither identical to nor subsumes marginalist economics under its head. Of course all versions of marginalist economics are taxonomic. But not all contributors to marginal economics, at least 100 years ago, adopt or reveal adherence to the sort of causal-processual ontology that Veblen attributes to the neoclassicals. Veblen's main focus in discussing theorising under the marginalist head is John Bates Clark. But Clark's position is interpreted as basically classical, or at least a near derivative that is *not* distinguished by some revealed support for a causal-processual metaphysics.[27]

In short, neoclassical economists approach the analysis of social reality armed with inappropriate tools, with the result that they fail to illuminate, or at best they limit the scope of economics to those few cases, if any, where localised stabilities or uniformities may occur. Whatever else it may be, neoclassical economics, according to Veblen, is a line of thinking that falls short of determining methods that are appropriate to addressing the causal-processual nature of social reality that its practitioners nevertheless, at some level, widely recognise.

Although recognition of a causal-processual ontology is regarded by Veblen as an advance of neoclassical over classical thinking, the persistence with taxonomy (in the form of deductivism) is the dominating feature that determines the form of the research findings. That is why it makes sense for Veblen to have characterised the project or strand of thinking in question not, say, as post- or counter-classical, but as modernized or neoclassical, signalling that it constitutes a continuation of the same basic taxonomic project, at least at the level of method, even if its 'adepts' at some level hold to a worldview ultimately inconsistent with such a taxonomic orientation.

Parenthetically, the interpretation of the term 'neoclassical' that I am advancing here may remain coherent even if or where, instead of Veblen's interpretation of classical economics, Marx's alternative and original interpretation of classical is preferred.[28] For on both interpretations, the term 'neoclassical' expresses a tension between method and ontology, and in both cases neoclassical is seen to be both a continuation of, as well as a departure from, classical thinking. The difference is that on Veblen's interpretation it is the adherence to taxonomic method that expresses the continuity of the later neoclassical economists with classical thinking, whereas on Marx's interpretation it is the recognition of a causal-processual ontology that plays this role. Alternatively put, for Veblen the causal-processual ontological commitments account for the prefix 'neo-' in neoclassical, whilst from the point of view of Marx's interpretation the overly taxonomic (deductivist) orientation to method might be said to legitimise its use. Either way, as I say, the label 'neoclassical economics' seems not entirely inappropriate.[29]

4. The rise of mathematical modelling in economics

In viewing neoclassical economics as founded on inconsistency, Veblen expected it ultimately to prove unsustainable. Indeed, as already noted, he thought that the social and political sciences were already caught up in processes leading to the inexorable rise of evolutionary science, or anyway of science grounded in an ontology of causal processes (Veblen, 1898, pp. 396–97; Lawson, 2003, chapter 8), a development that would have entailed the relative demise of all overly taxonomic (including deductivist) approaches. What Veblen could not foresee is that taxonomy in the form of deductivism specifically was later to acquire a new lease of life by way of unprecedented developments in the field of mathematics.

Ever since the Enlightenment various economists had been seeking to mathematise the study of the economy. In this, at least prior to the early years of the twentieth century, economists keen to mathematise their discipline felt constrained in numerous ways, and not least by pressures by (non-social) natural scientists and influential peers to conform to the 'standards' and procedures of (non-social) natural science, and thereby abandon any idea of constructing an autonomous tradition of mathematical economics. Especially influential, in due course, was the classical reductionist programme, the idea that all mathematical disciplines should be reduced to or based on the model of physics, in particular on the strictly deterministic approach of mechanics, with its emphasis on methods of infinitesimal calculus. Moreover, the intellectual context throughout was one in which, amongst these scientists and mathematicians in particular, there was an enduring belief that mathematical methods were unlikely to be of relevance to the analysis of society (on all this, see Lawson, 2003, chapter 10).

However, in the early part of the twentieth century changes occurred in the interpretation of the very nature of mathematics, changes that caused the classical reductionist programme itself to fall into disarray. With the development of relativity theory and especially quantum theory, the image of nature as continuous came to be re-examined in particular, and the role of infinitesimal calculus, which had previously been regarded as having almost ubiquitous relevance within physics, came to be re-examined even within that domain.

The outcome, in effect, was a switch away from the long-standing emphasis on mathematics as an attempt to apply the physics model, and specifically the mechanics metaphor, to an emphasis on mathematics for its own sake.

Mathematics, especially through the work of David Hilbert, became increasingly viewed as a discipline properly concerned with providing a pool of frameworks for *possible realities*. No longer was mathematics seen as the language of (non-social) nature, abstracted from the study of the latter. Rather, it was conceived as a practice concerned with formulating systems comprising sets of axioms and their deductive consequences, with these systems in effect taking on a life of their own. The task of finding applications was henceforth regarded as being of secondary importance at best, and not of immediate concern.

This emergence of the axiomatic method removed at a stroke various hitherto insurmountable constraints facing those who would mathematise the discipline of economics. Researchers involved with mathematical projects in economics could, for the time being at least, postpone the day of interpreting their preferred axioms and assumptions. There was no longer any need to seek the blessing of mathematicians and physicists or of other economists who might insist that the relevance of metaphors and analogies be established at the outset. In particular it was no longer regarded as necessary, or even relevant, to economic model construction to consider the nature of social reality, at least for the time being. Nor, it seemed, was it possible for anyone to insist with any legitimacy that the formulations of economists conform to any specific model already found to be successful elsewhere (such as the mechanics model in physics). Indeed, the very idea of fixed metaphors or even interpretations, came to be rejected by some economic 'modellers' (albeit never in any really plausible manner).[30]

The result was that in due course deductivism in economics, through morphing into mathematical deductivism on the back of developments within the discipline of mathematics, came to acquire a new lease of life, with practitioners (once more) potentially oblivious to any inconsistency between the ontological presuppositions of adopting a mathematical modelling emphasis and the nature of social reality. The consequent rise of mathematical deductivism has culminated in the situation we find today.

5. Implications for the contemporary situation

It will no doubt be apparent by now where I am headed with all this. I am suggesting that central to Veblen's characterisation of neoclassical economics is a particular tension or inconsistency—specifically, a tension of ontological perspective and method (or the latter's ontological presuppositions) that, as I noted at the outset, is a prevalent feature of much economics produced today. Certainly the interpretation of the term in this manner is useful in that it picks out the practices of a prominent group of modern economics. Moreover, it picks out a group and a set of practices that are so far unidentified by any label and yet arguably warrant being so identified to draw attention to the inconsistencies of the positions taken.

Somewhat ironically, then, albeit particularly advantageously, if the suggested interpretation of the term 'neoclassical' is accepted, usage of the category would serve to draw attention to precisely that inconsistency (of preconceptions of certain modelling practices with otherwise revealed ontological commitments) which the manner of its current usage helps obfuscate. The effect, in short, would be to reverse the term's current role in the discipline; its usage would contribute to identifying, revealing and/or signalling the tension in question, rather than, as at present, serving to mask or otherwise divert attention from it.

I do not suggest that the content of the taxonomic endeavour of Veblen's time matches the content of modern taxonomic endeavour or even that the latter is at all uniform or consistent. Nor do I pretend that Veblen possessed anything like the developed account of the causal-processual social ontology outlined earlier and defended elsewhere. He only rarely mentions social relations for example; nor does he advance a systematic theory of an emergent social reality. He does, though, recognise that social reality is not well characterised by conceptions of normality at the level of or underpinning actual events and indeed observes that actual social events advance typically in causal sequence only. Nor, as already noted, do I suggest that Veblen anticipated that taxonomic science would persist in economics in the form of mathematical deductivism. But the tension he identifies remains evident and still warrants attention. As such, it is not unreasonable to hold that there is usefulness, in addition to any historical legitimacy, to employing the term 'neoclassical economics' to express this particular tension.

There are clearly many currently who both adhere to taxonomic and specifically deductivist methods and yet at some level also acknowledge the open causal-processual nature of social reality. The central difference between the current situation and that which Veblen addresses is that deductivism today, the production of formulations couched in terms of event-level uniformities, is, to repeat once more, more pervasively bound up with the drive to mathematise the discipline; it takes the form of methods of mathematical modelling.

5.1 The coherence of the conception of neoclassical

So is it really the case that I am suggesting that all mathematical modellers in modern economics who at some level appear to subscribe to the causal-processual worldview, including those who self-identify as heterodox, are appropriately characterised as (modern-day) neoclassical economists? I re-emphasise that the group under focus here is not the set of mathematical deductivist modellers *per se*, but that subset of the latter who at some level simultaneously accept a historical or causal-processual ontology.

I certainly think this is the most coherent rendering of the category of neoclassical economics in that it constitutes a strategy, and seemingly the only one, that allows the term to be interpreted in a manner that meets all the criteria earlier set out. Let me briefly elaborate how it does so.

The interpretation provided is clearly developmentally consistent with historical lineage, as we have seen; indeed, I suggest that it is effectively Veblen's conception. Moreover it expresses a strand of thinking that is both continuous with and a departure from a position that has been prominently characterised as classical. It also possesses a meaningful referent or object of analysis, namely, that group of economists who at some level accept the causal-processual ontology yet for some reason feel unable, unwilling or unmoved to abandon deductivism. It is *prima facie* useful just in that it picks out and identifies a group of economists that are prominent and significant in their impact on the contemporary discipline and economy but currently have no alternative identifying label. Finally the interpretation I am proposing not only generalises all the loose attributions of neoclassical, as well the alternative contending systematic conceptions, revealing them to be in effect special cases of deductivism, of the taxonomic approach to economics, but can make sense of the form of the latter more cautious systematisations as well. Let me now elaborate the latter claim a little.

From the perspective of the conception set out, the explanation of the nature and variety, as well as the limitations, of the accounts of the term advanced by the more cautious/careful interpreters is that the latter have resulted from attempts to uncover the most general, core or generative features of contributions widely regarded as neoclassical whilst their formulators were mistakenly working under the apprehension that these features must be stated in substantive economic terms.

I suggest that the core feature of neoclassical economics is adherence not to any particular substantive features but to deductivism itself in a situation where the general open-processual nature of social reality is widely recognised at some level. Certainly Veblen's central focus and concern is with *pre*conceptions (of economics) rather than conceptions (of economics). Thus from the perspective of this understanding the presumption that the core features must lie at the level of substantive-economic specification, even if it takes a highly abstract form, is, as I say, mistaken. The result is that these more cautious interpreters of neoclassical economics have come as close to the interpretation I propose as seems feasible whilst sticking to the self-imposed constraint of interpreting neoclassical economics only in substantive economic terms.

I re-emphasise that deductivism entails reliance on correlations. The desire to theorise in a manner that produces results taking the form of correlations or event regularities in turn encourages the treatment of economics in terms of systems of isolated atoms. At the same time, the traditional view of the object of economics is in terms of consumption (demand) and production (supply). Thus I am suggesting that the varying conceptions of neoclassical economics outlined earlier (in Section 1) are explained as attempts to steer as close as possible to the above features, namely, correlations involving closed systems of isolated atoms, whilst maintaining a concern with consumption and production, that is, whilst acting under the erroneous constraint of characterising neoclassical economics in terms of substantive economic categories.

The point here of course is that although the deductivist orientation encourages substantive formulations that are implicitly in terms of isolated atoms, there is no unique way of generating them. This explains the sorts of conceptions held, and/or conclusions reached, both by those who have sought to establish commonalities between Veblen's classical and neoclassical economics and by those who have sought to draw out general or generative features of prominent (if often recent) accounts widely regarded as neoclassical.

Thus, turning first to those in the former group, we can see that they have failed to find continuity in Veblen's conceptions of classical and neoclassical just because continuity has been sought at the level of the 'substantive content' (Aspromourgos, 1986, p. 269) of theories (whether in economics or psychology) or of 'economic ideas' (Fayazmanesh, 1998, p. 90), but not at the level of accepted preconceptions of science. In this Veblen's focus on the continuing taxonomic emphasis with its implicit ontological presuppositions is overlooked. Yet it is precisely an adherence to the latter by Marshall and others that constitutes the features that render the latter contributors continuous with the classical tradition.

If we turn to the second group, namely, those that have sought to categorise neoclassical economics through seeking generalities across prominent contributions, we can just as equally make sense of, and indeed explain, the sorts of results produced here. Commonalities arise because these interpreters, in seeking generality across numerous contributions, have formulated their conceptions in highly abstract terms, whereby, given the ontological constraints of the reliance on methods of mathematical modelling on the contributors on which they focus, these abstract accounts have tended to take the form of varying versions of isolated human individuals–as–atoms, with specifications concerning knowledge and behaviour serving precisely to constrain conceptions of human beings so as to render them atomistic. Yet significant variation is nevertheless equally found across the versions of neoclassical economics so determined just because there is no unique way to generate substantive formulations consistent with the taxonomic and specifically deductivist orientation, that is, of producing substantive claims that presuppose closed systems of isolated atoms.

The atomistic condition for a closure requires only that the (atomistic) factors in question have the same separate and independent effect whatever the context. Rendering formulations of human individuals so that they are atomistic in this sense is the purpose of and mostly achieved via the rationality assumption/axiom, of course. But there are various versions even of the latter. In some cases the specification of this (rationality) constraint is absurdly unrealistic (as when individuals are assumed to be continuous calculative optimisers); in other cases it is overly simplistic (as when individuals are assumed to be merely fixed-rule followers). The feature in all this that warrants emphasis (and tends to be overlooked) is that the primary purpose of any rationality axiom is just to fix individual behaviour in some way to render it atomistic and so tractable. The precise (set of) assumption(s) whereby this is done is secondary to this requirement.

This is why some of the more careful interpreters of neoclassical economics have recognized that all that is needed in this regard is 'an acceptance of some rationality axiom' (see, for examples, Hahn, 1984, 1985). Alternative interpretations of neoclassical economics that have individuals continually following maximising behaviour in the name of rationality no doubt capture a good deal of the actual literature, but stipulations do not need to be this specific. We can now also see why others have been (even) more cautiously abstract, for only fixity of response to stimuli is actually required in the process of satisfying conditions of closure (i.e., in which event regularities can be derived). Of course there are numerous different specifications that will achieve this.

We can further explain the widely varying assessments of and uncertainty concerning the need to include some notion of equilibrium theorising in the characterisation of neoclassical economics. For although theorising in terms of this category is usually of a sort that can be regarded as taxonomic in Veblen's sense, and is a practice pursued by Marshall and since figured widely in the economics literature, a concern with equilibrium theorising is not in and of itself an integral part of any modern mathematical deductivist framework. Rather, in the context of modern economics especially, equilibrium is basically a solution concept, given a system of equations. Where such a system is generated under deductivist thinking, a question that can in some contexts be meaningfully addressed is whether the resulting set of equations are mutually consistent. Is there a vector of values consistent with them all? The solution concept, especially where prices are involved, is often called an equilibrium state; when economists enquire whether an equilibrium state exists, they are merely inquiring as to whether a set of equations has a solution (see Lawson, 2005, 2006b). In this manner we can understand why, at least from a mathematical point of view, such a concern may be of interest, and thereby we can explain the (former) high frequency of appearance of the category equilibrium in the economics literature. However the set of steps involved in examining whether there exists a solution to a set of equations is not *per se* a requirement of adhering to deductivism and is notably absent from many contributions widely perceived as neoclassical. So we can easily understand why some of the more cautious interpreters never mention equilibrium in their definition of neoclassical economics (for example, Weintraub, 2002), whilst others accept no more than a qualified 'commitment to study equilibrium states' (for example, Hahn, 1984, 1985).

From the perspective set out, all other looser interpretations of neoclassical economics can equally be rendered intelligible, including those that seek to tie the category to laissez-faire ideology, or to competing claims about the functioning of markets, or use it to promote notions of efficiency and so on. In contemporary economics, all designations are applied to substantive claims and policy proposals formulated in accordance with the constraints of taxonomic, essentially mathematical modelling exercises, so that where commitment to a social system as being causal processual in nature are is at some level implied, all are appropriately characterised as neoclassical according to the conception I am advancing.

Perhaps the interpreter of neoclassical economics that comes closest to the conception defended here is Fine (2006). Consistent with deductivism being the problem, Fine does not interpret neoclassical in terms of the particular specifications of human beings or states of the economy or whatever that have been adopted to guarantee that event regularities can be derived; rather, he interprets neoclassical economics in terms of the regularities themselves, or at least in terms of functions expressing them. Thus for Fine the defining feature is the 'technical apparatus or architecture' the 'most fundamental' of which is 'the use of utility and production functions'. From this perspective, Fine is able to recognise that additional common objects of focus like equilibrium states are encouraged but not necessary:

> Enduring commitment to this technical apparatus explains the persistence but not the necessity of equilibrium, efficiency, laissez-faire ideology, the optimising individual and so on. To a large extent, even those approaches on the edge within the mainstream take this technical apparatus at least as point of departure, adding other forms of behaviour or modifying technical assumptions or, because institutions, history, path dependence, aggregation now matter, glorifying previous inconveniences as the way forward to add wrinkle or complexity.
>
> (Fine, 2006, p. 3)

Where Fine's analysis proves deficient is that his emphasis on utility and production functions forces him to interpret other manifestations of deductivism as merely 'wrinkles or complexity'. In truth modern mathematical economists have gone way beyond resting their attention on demand and supply conditions in the economy as a whole. Yet still the deductivism remains, generating, as always, unrealistic formulations. These are readily dismissed by heterodox critics, very often as being neoclassical. Now, at least where recognition of causal-processual ontology is at some level revealed, this designation can be rendered coherent.

6. Taking stock and reassessment

In short, I am suggesting that there are three basic divisions of modern economics that can be discerned in the actual practices of modern economists. These are:

1. those who both (i) adopt an overly taxonomic approach to science, a group dominated in modern times by those that accept mathematical deductivism as an orientation to science for us all, and (ii) effectively regard any stance that questions this approach, whatever the basis, as inevitably misguided;
2. those who are aware that social reality is of a causal-processual nature as elaborated above, who prioritise the goal of being realistic, and who fashion methods in the light of this ontological understanding and thereby recognise the limited scope for any taxonomic science, not least any that relies on methods of mathematical deductive modelling; and
3. those who are aware (at some level) that social reality is of a causal-processual nature as elaborated above, who prioritise the goal of being realistic, and yet who fail themselves fully to recognise or to accept the limited scope for any overly-taxonomic approach including, in particular, one that makes significant use of methods of mathematical deductive modelling.[31]

If members of group 1 not only include but (with the pervasive modern dogmatic insistence on methods of mathematical modelling) more or less reduce to the contemporary mainstream; and those in group 2 constitute the coherent core of modern heterodoxy; it is members of group 3, again mostly made up by those that utilise mathematical methods, that most qualify as modern neoclassical economists. Groups 1 and 3 are both overly taxonomic in Veblen's sense whilst only members of group 2 are coherently engaged in Veblen's idea of historical or often broadly evolutionary or modern science.

6.1 What to do with the category of neoclassical economics?

To return to a question already posed but not really answered, am I seriously suggesting that we employ the term 'neoclassical' to refer to the third of the identified groups of economists, which will clearly include many who self-identify as heterodox? I repeat that I am certainly suggesting that to use the term 'neoclassical' in this fashion is the most appropriate, and a coherent, use of the category for the reasons already given; although a better categorisation might be non-dogmatic taxonomists or non-dogmatic deductivists, in contrast with the dogmatic (mathematical) taxonomists/deductivists that are the mainstream.

If used in this way, then as noted, the term would serve no longer to mask but to bring repeatedly to the fore a basic tension that lies at the core of the discipline's problems. It is a tension that a consideration of Veblen's analysis reveals has long been in play. Using the term in this manner may encourage thereby a somewhat more critical orientation or greater reflexivity on the part of those unreasonably enamoured of any overly taxonomic emphasis at the substantive level, including especially any form deductivism. So there are certainly grounds for doing so.

All things considered, however, in the end I do not really think it reasonable to distinguish or identify any group on the grounds of a shared fundamental inconsistency. My aim here, in reporting my findings, is, in the end partly rhetorical, namely, to point out that if coherence in use is required, then according to the seemingly most sustainable conception, many of those who use the term 'neoclassical' as an ill-defined term of abuse can be viewed ultimately as engaged in unwitting self-critique. But I am hoping, more fundamentally, that it is enough in this manner to communicate (in a yet further way) that in modern economics there prevails largely unrecognised a basic tension between ontology and method, one that hinders serious attempts to overcoming the real problems of the discipline.

My suggestion, then, is that rather than distinguish/identify a group on the grounds of a fundamental inconsistency in (ontological) theory and (methodological) practice, the term 'neoclassical economics' should be dropped from the literature, as a few others have already suggested. In other words, I return to my previously held position, albeit now re-evaluated in the light of possessing a seemingly (and perhaps the only) coherent notion of the category of neoclassical economics. All the various questions or lines of reasoning that served to motivate the quest for a coherent interpretation are effectively answered or otherwise already addressed. But once addressed there seems to me to be emergent further grounds, now, to abandon the term. Given that the term as interpreted here signals intrinsic inconsistency, or at best severe tension, it is more reasonable, and significantly less uncharitable, to focus on displaying the latter as a seemingly genuine if long-lasting error than to apply a label with negative connotations to those who implicitly make it, as if implying that they consciously choose to be permanently in error. I doubt that many knowingly wish to build a school on the foundation of an inconsistency.

In this I also suspect that I am continuing in the spirit of Veblen. When Veblen uses the term, as we have seen, it was not intended to denote a school of thought at all; he merely wished to focus, in one specific paper,

92 The 'school' of neoclassical economics

on one line of thinking (which he expected to be highly transient) that had come out of classical reasoning (as he interpreted it), was open to ongoing (broadly evolutionary) scientific developments of his day but had not yet adjusted scientific method accordingly. The prefix 'neo-' is employed by Veblen just as a serviceable adjective for this discussion and was interchanged with qualifiers like 'modernised', 'quasi' and perhaps others.

Certainly I am not aware that Veblen uses the term 'neoclassical' outside the preconceptions paper in which it is introduced, and I suspect that he would be astounded at the widespread use of the term throughout the discipline today. Veblen's point when coining the term was simply to bring to prominence the limitations for economics of persevering with the taxonomic ideal in science and in particular with adopting a taxonomic science in the form of seeking uniformities at the level of events. That there are problems with adopting any overly taxonomic approach was a central message found in various of his numerous methodological essays, not least in the preconceptions paper in which the term 'neoclassical' is coined; whatever the fate of the category neoclassical, it is a message that is certainly no less relevant today.

7. Conclusion

Throughout his methodological writings, Veblen is acutely aware that all scientific undertakings carry within them metaphysical preconceptions regarding the 'grounds of finality' to which results must conform to be regarded as potentially satisfactory. Two basic approaches are distinguished: the (overly) taxonomic and the (broadly) evolutionary. The difference between them is 'a difference of spiritual attitude or point of view'; 'it is a difference in the basis of valuation of the facts for the scientific purpose, or in the interest from which the facts are appreciated' (Veblen, 1898, p. 377). The only preconception of the modern, broadly evolutionary historical scientist is that events unfold in causal sequence. Thus the 'modern scientist is unwilling to depart from the test of causal relation or quantitative sequence', and in responses to all questions of economics the modern scientist 'insists on an answer in terms of cause and effect'. In contrast the taxonomic scientist insists on (or holds preconceptions of science requiring) something more, whether that something extra takes the form of outcomes regarded as natural or normal or laudable, tendencies to these outcomes, ameliorative trends, or simply correlations at the level of events. Mathematical deductivism is just the very dominant contemporary form.

I have suggested, drawing on Veblen, that the most coherent interpretation of neoclassical economics is of an inconsistent stance of 1) recognising the historical processual ontology of unfolding causal sequence at the level of events, whilst simultaneously 2) seeking to combine this recognition with a taxonomic orientation in the form of deductivism at the level of method that is inappropriate to it. That is, I suggest that interpreted most coherently, the category designates a deep tension, the very one that the current loose usage of the term serves to mask.

Even if the foregoing does identify a coherent interpretation of neoclassical economics, I suggest further that it is likely better, on balance, to abandon the category. Though others have reached a similar conclusion, they are often quick to stress that in dropping the term they do not wish to imply criticism of any content the term may be used to express.[32] In contrast, I suggest that the reason to discard the term (or otherwise to employ a coherent interpretation) is precisely to facilitate more appropriate and telling criticism, than hitherto in evidence, of the content of modern economics including any expressed though the term itself. This indeed is the point of this exercise of attempted clarification.

The contemporary discipline of economics, most now agree, has lost its way. It is easy enough to demonstrate that this is due largely to the widespread contemporary persistence with methods of mathematical modelling (whether through mainstream insistence or through heterodox confusion/optimism) in conditions where this persistence is unwarranted. The ultimate solution, and, as Veblen clearly saw, basis for any relevant economics, lies first in uncovering the nature of social reality, and second, and certainly no less important, in taking seriously any ontological or metaphysical insights so uncovered in fashioning the methods of economic science. It is to understand the nature of society and then to ensure that research methods are appropriate to that nature. It is to render actual a situation that Veblen long ago thought inevitable. More concretely, it is to replace the current, yet long outlived fixation on seeking or constructing accounts of event correlations with a serious concern to develop an ontologically grounded causal-explanatory social science.

Notes

[*] This chapter previously published as Tony Lawson, What is this 'school' called neoclassical economics? *Cambridge Journal of Economics* (2013) 37(5): 947–983 first published online June 20, 2013, doi:10.1093/cje/bet027 by permission of Oxford University Press/on behalf of The Cambridge Political Economy Society © Cambridge Political Economy Society.

[†] For helpful comments on an earlier draft of this article, I am grateful to Lynne Chester, Nuno Martins, Dimitris Milinakis, Jamie Morgan, Roy Rotheim and four referees of the *Cambridge Journal of Economics*. I am also indebted to the Independent Social Research Foundation for generous financial support.

1 Not infrequently those who use the label to designate others are in turn often so labelled themselves by their opponents. Thus Paul Krugman (2009) refers to 'monetarist' and 'freshwater economist' opponents as neoclassical, whilst he in turn is criticised by Steve Keen (2012) as being neoclassical; and so on.

2 Almost universally amongst those who seek to uncover a significant element of continuity between neoclassical and classical economics, neoclassical economics is interpreted as a set of 'marginalist' theories and classical economics is used to designate whatever came before it. Unfortunately, however, the term

'marginalism' is itself variably interpreted. Some commentators use the category for Alfred Marshall's contributions; others for the contributions of William Stanley Jevons, Carl Menger and Léon Walras; and still other others for marginalism in general, including the writings of John Hicks and Paul Samuelson, and especially the latter's (Hicks-inspired) supposed 'grand neoclassical synthesis'. For a brief but systematic coverage of the various interpretations of marginalist economics, see especially Antonietta Campus (1987). For a discussion of marginalism in relation to interpretations of neoclassical specifically, see Tony Aspromourgos (1986).

3 Certainly this is the view of most scrutinisers of claims to continuity. Thus Maurice Dobb (1973, p. 248), for example, examines Joan Robinson's description of marginalist theories of distribution as neoclassical and finds it so unlike (his conception of) classical economics that he suggests that *counter-classical* would be a better designation. In similar fashion Joseph Schumpeter (1954) examines the 'habit, which has developed especially in the United States, of describing the "marginalist" theories as neo-classic', but concludes (focussing on the 'pure-theory' aspect in particular) that 'there is no more sense in calling the Jevons-Menger-Walras theory neoclassic than there would be calling the Einstein theory neo-Newtonian' (1954, p. 919). Milan Zafirovski defends at length the thesis 'that this neoclassical nomenclature for marginalism was problematic to the extent that marginalism, especially its early version in Walras, Menger, and especially Jevons, was a non- and even counter- or "anti-classical" rather than "newly" classical, as the term neoclassical would suggest' (Zafirovski, 1999, p. 46). And Aspromourgos (1986) finds that it was 'only with Hicks and Stigler, in the 1930s and 1940s, that the term was extended to embrace marginalism in general' finding however that 'Neither of them offered any substantial notion of continuity between classics and marginalists' (p. 266). This literature is usefully summarised by Aspromourgos (1986), who himself does notably turn to Veblen to locate the origin of the term 'neoclassical', suggesting that for Veblen, the 'central figure in this neoclassical school is Marshall' (1986, p. 266). Searching for continuity of neoclassical with the classical school at the level of substantive content, however, Aspromourgos concludes that Veblen fails to provide it in the essay in which the term 'neoclassical' is coined; instead 'Only in a later essay does Veblen suggest some substantive content for the continuity he perceived' (Aspromourgos, 1986, p. 266); even this Aspromougos seems to find unsatisfactory (see especially Aspromourgos, 1986, p. 269). Finally, I note too that Sasan Fayamanesh (1998) focuses almost exclusively on Veblen and examines three possible interpretations of what continuity may have meant for him, but concludes that 'none [. . .] presents a clear and viable argument in support of the continuity of economic ideas' (Fayamanesh, 1998, p. 90).

4 Consider first the view of Frank Hahn, someone who identifies with the label 'neoclassical'. Although not always consistent (compare Hahn, 1982, p. 354, with specifications found in Hahn, 1984, 1985), Hahn (1984, 1985) identifies the following restricted set of features of the 'neoclassical' economic theory project as essential: (1) an individualistic perspective, a requirement that explanations be couched solely in terms of individuals; (2) an acceptance of some rationality axiom; and (3) a commitment to the study of equilibrium states. Here the category equilibrium is explicitly referenced, though noticeably there is no presumption that an equilibrium state 'holds' or 'exists' in any sense. Rather, for Hahn, the task of determining whether an equilibrium state exists in some model is precisely the sort of activity intended by a commitment to the study of such states. Turning to a view from the history of economic thought, Roy Weintraub (2002) rather suggestively concludes that 'we are all neoclassical

now'. The reason for this assessment, it seems, is that supposedly all academic economists teach neoclassical economics to students; for this is the substantive content of modern economic textbooks that all economic teachers use. This content, we are informed, is, or conforms to, a meta-theory, meaning 'a set of implicit rules or understandings for constructing satisfactory economic theories', and any substantive theory consistent with this meta-theory qualifies as neoclassical. The particular set of understandings or 'fundamental assumptions' that render a theory neoclassical are: '1. People have rational preferences among outcomes. 2. Individuals maximize utility and firms maximize profits. 3. People act independently on the basis of full and relevant information. Theories based on, or guided by, these assumptions are neoclassical theories' (Weintraub, 2002). Notably, and in contrast to Hahn, Weintraub nowhere in his definition makes reference to the study of equilibrium states. A second difference is the insistence by Weintraub that individuals possess 'full and relevant information'. Turning next to a view from economic methodology, Christian Arnsperger and Yanis Varoufakis (2006) take the view that the essence of neoclassical economics reduces to three meta-axioms: 'It is hard to imagine how any standardly trained economist could deny that her theoretical practices digress from the three methodological moves mentioned above: *Methodological individualism, methodological instrumentalism and methodological equilibration.* For simplicity we shall henceforth refer to them as *the neoclassical meta-axioms.*' Notice that the third metaaxiom is simply 'the axiomatic imposition of equilibrium'. In their analyses, Arnsperger and Varoufakis, in agreement with those already noted, conclude that any axioms about individual behaviour are unable to guarantee equilibrium states, but, believing such states to be essential to neoclassical theorising, make the fact of equilibrium states an axiomatic assumption. No claim about individuals possessing full information is seemingly included. Turning finally to some views from the heterodox traditions, Geoffrey Hodgson, who has contributed much to institutionalist economics, offers the following interpretation drawing on the observations of Gary Becker: 'Let us attempt to identify the key characteristics of neoclassical economics; the type of economics that has dominated the twentieth century. One of its exponents, Gary Becker (1976, p. 5) identified its essence when he described "the combined assumptions of maximizing behavior, market equilibrium, and stable preferences, used relentlessly and unflinchingly." Accordingly, neoclassical economics may be conveniently defined as an approach which: (1) assumes rational, maximizing behaviour by agents with given and stable preference functions, (2) focuses on attained, or movements towards, equilibrium states, and (3) is marked by an absence of chronic information problems' (Hodgson, 1999, p. 29). In contrast, the Marxian economist Ben Fine insists that neoclassical economics is not couched in terms of rationality or equilibrium specifications or indeed any specifications regarding features of 'agents' or states of the economy. Rather it is essentially: 'the technical apparatus or architecture established by the mainstream from the marginalist revolution onwards. Most fundamental is the use of utility and production functions, with accompanying assumptions to allow the theory to proceed regardless of any other considerations—methodology, realism, other theory, empirical evidence *and* mathematics—to the contrary' (Fine, 2006, p. 2). Clearly, each of these conceptions, though sharing some features with a selection of others, is unique in various ways. There is no consensus on interpretation, nor *prima facie* is there any obvious basis for choosing between them; in particular there is not an interpretation provided that seems to generalise or generate the others. Of course all I offer here is an indicative selection of assessments for purpose of illustration.

5 On all this see especially Lawson (2012b). Others have emphasised the same features. For example, Colander et al. (2004) emphasise the 'changing face of mainstream economics' and criticise heterodox economists for failing to notice such ongoing developments. Specifically, these authors criticise heterodox contributors for adopting an overly 'static view of the profession' (p. 486); for simplistically referring to the current mainstream as neoclassical; and for missing the 'diversity that exists within the profession, and the many new ideas that are being tried out' (p. 487). In fact, Colander et al. insist that 'Mainstream economics is a complex system of evolving ideas' (2004, p. 489), and refer to the 'multiple dimensionalities that we see in the mainstream profession' (p. 489). They acknowledge though that the mainstream is tied to its mathematical modelling methodology.
6 Interestingly, none of those who seek seriously and systematically to characterise neoclassical economics appear to do so according to the use of mathematical modelling *per se* (see note 5, for example); of course it was long after Veblen was writing that such modelling practices became dominant in economics.
7 Or a contributor may have something to hide.
8 See, for example, Hicks (1983, pp. xiii–xiv), Aspromourgos (1986, p. 296), Colander (2000, p. 127), or Fayazmanesh (1998, p. 75).
9 As already noted, few categories remain entirely fixed in their meaning over time. However there is a sense in which those that prove helpful evolve systematically in the light of new understandings, changing conditions and evolving related needs. This is a case of (the broader notion of) developmental consistency (see Lawson, 1997, 2003 for a discussion of this notion).
10 On all this, see especially Lawson (1997, 2003, 2012b).
11 For a good discussion of this sort of (de-privileging of theory) approach to econometrics, see Katerina Juselius (2010).
12 'Emergence' is a term that expresses the appearance of novelty or something previously absent or unprecedented. Emergent causal properties are often the primary focus of the philosophy-leaning literature that employs the category, though where they exist they must be the properties of something, an emergent entity or some such. An emergent entity, where addressed, is usually found, or anyway held, to be composed out of elements deemed to be situated at a different (lower) level of reality to itself, but which have (perhaps through being modified) become organised as components of the emergent (higher level) entity or causal totality. 'Emergence', then, as widely interpreted is ultimately a compositional term and involves components being organised rather than aggregated. Elsewhere I argue that social phenomena, though emergent from and always dependent on non-social natural phenomena are causally and ontologically irreducible to the latter (see especially Lawson, 2013b, but also 1997, 2012a, 2013a).
13 All such constitutive relations are relations of power couched in terms of differing rights and obligations (see Lawson, 2012a, 2013a).
14 For a comprehensive account, again see for example Lawson (2003, chapter 2; 2012a, 2013a). For discussions of the causal and ontological irreducibility of emergent social processes see especially Lawson (2012a, 2013a, 2013b).
15 The discipline has been in such a state for more than half a century indeed (see, e.g., Lawson, 2003, chapter 1).
16 Thus we find the same old mistakes being repeated even in projects like the setting up of the Institute for New Economic Thinking (INET), an organisation whose stated intention is precisely to transform the discipline of economics in the light of its failings to provide much understanding of the ongoing crisis. Although George Soros, the founder of the institute, does reveal an awareness

that the reliance on mathematics may at least be something to question (see, e.g., Soros, 2009; Lawson, 2010), for most of his close associates the idea that there might be something problematic about the emphasis on forms of mathematical technique does not appear even to cross their minds. This is easily seen, for example, from a quick scan of the numerous presentations made at the inaugural (2010) conference, held at Kings College Cambridge (all the numerous contributions are posted on the INET website or can be found on YouTube. See, for example, http://ineteconomics.org/initiatives/conferences/kings-college or http://www.youtube.com/watch?v=SdZgD1DCNq4). Almost all presentations focus on modelling methods and details. The one issue that is rarely even hinted at is that we might also question the very emphasis on mathematical modelling itself; the discussion throughout is only and continually about how economists should go about finding 'better' mathematical models (for a discussion of the 2010 INET presentations, see Lawson, 2012b).

17 For example, Aspromourgos takes the view that 'The term was coined by Veblen in 1900, and subsequently employed by others, in order to characterise the Marshallian version of marginalism. This is a "satisfying" result, to the extent that Marshall, more than any of the other marginalist founders, sought to present his theory as having a substantial continuity with classical economics' (1986, p. 266). After a few paragraphs Aspormourgos adds, 'After Veblen, a number of other early instances of the term [neoclassical] amount to a broad acceptance of Veblen's view and therefore need not detain us in detail. They all place Marshall at the centre of a neoclassical economics and there is ample evidence that they derived from Veblen' (1986, pp. 266–67). Aspromourgos mentions in particular that on this matter 'Hamilton (1923), Homan (1928, pp. 262, 387, 401) and Mitchell (1967, vol. ii, pp. 208, 215, 217–218, 220) evidently followed Veblen's lead' (1986, p. 267). Fayazmanesh (1998) avaces a different interpretation to that of Aspromourgos but is still of the view that 'The term "neoclassical" was coined by Veblen apparently based on the assumption that the marginal school is a continuation of the 'classical school' (p. 92).

18 One of the more positive assessors is Aspromourgos, who allows a part of what he takes to be Veblen's basis of commonality to be correct 'to an extent': 'Veblen conceived Marshallian economics to be "neoclassical" because it had in common with the classics a utilitarian approach and employed a hedonistic psychology. To an extent this argument was correct, at least with regard to the utilitarianism'.

19 Although frequently heard, I am not sure this is a view often sustained by serious historians of thought. Nevertheless it is regularly found in 'popular' or easy access sources. For example, at the time of writing an initial draft of this article (July 2012) the Wikipedia entry on 'Neoclassical Economics' informs us that 'The term was originally introduced by Thorstein Veblen in 1900, in his article "Preconceptions of Economic Science", to distinguish marginalists in the tradition of Alfred Marshall from those in the Austrian School'. See http://en.wikipedia.org/wiki/Neoclassical_economics. Moreover, if this sentence found in Wikipedia is in turn entered in quotation marks into Google, we find it repeated identically in several thousand additional sources.

20 Of course, Veblen is quite aware that all sciences deal to some degree in taxonomy meaning classification, his own contributions included. He is critical, though, of taxonomy for the sake of taxonomy: 'There is no intention here to decry taxonomy, of course. Definition and classification are as much needed in economics as they are in those other sciences which have already left the exclusively taxonomic standpoint behind. The point of criticism, on this head,

is that this class of economic theory differs from the modern sciences in being substantially nothing but definition and classification. Taxonomy for taxonomy's sake, definition and classification for the sake of definition and classification, meets no need of modern science. Work of this class has no value and no claims to consideration except so far as it is of use to the science in its endeavor to know and explain the processes of life' (Veblen, 1908a, pp. 112–13). In a later passage where he discusses hedonistic science, it is clear that by a 'system of taxonomic science' specifically, he means: 'a science of normalities. Its office is the definition and classification of "normal" phenomena, or, perhaps better, phenomena as they occur in the normal case. And in this normal case, when and so far as the laws of nature work out their ends unvitated, nature does all things well. This is also according to the ancient and authentic canons of taxonomic science' (Veblen, 1908a, p. 122).

21 Veblen notes of himself that 'In speaking of this matter-of-fact character of the modern sciences it has been broadly characterized as "evolutionary"; and the evolutionary method and the evolutionary ideals have been placed in antithesis to the taxonomic methods and ideals of pre-evolutionary days' (Veblen, 1899a, p. 123).

22 Or as Marx (1974) writes: 'Once for all I may here state, that by Classical Political Economy, I understand that economy which, since the time of W. Petty, has investigated the real relations of production in bourgeois society in contradistinction to vulgar economy, which deals with appearances only, ruminates without ceasing on the materials long since provided by scientific economy, and there seeks plausible explanations of the most obtrusive phenomena, for bourgeois daily use, but for the rest, confines itself to systematizing in a pedantic way, and proclaiming for everlasting truths, the trite ideas held by the self-complacent bourgeoisie with regard to their own world, to them the best of all possible worlds' (1974, chapter 1, note 33).

23 According to Veblen: 'Nothing of the nature of a personal element was to be admitted into these fundamental empirical generalizations; and nothing, therefore, of the nature of a discretionary or teleological movement was to be comprised in the generalizations to be accepted as "natural laws." Natural laws must in no degree be imbued with personality, must say nothing of an ulterior end; but for all that they remained "laws" of the sequences subsumed under them. So far is the reduction to colorless terms carried by Mill, for instance, that he formulates the natural laws as empirically ascertained sequences simply, even excluding or avoiding all imputation of causal continuity, as that term is commonly under-stood by the unsophisticated. In Mill's ideal no more of organic connection or continuity between the members of a sequence is implied in subsuming them under a law of causal relationship than is given by the ampersand. He is busied with dynamic sequences, but he persistently confines himself to static terms. Under the guidance of the associational psychology, therefore, the extreme of discontinuity in the deliverances of inductive research is aimed at by those economists—Mill and Cairnes being taken as typical—whose names have been associated with deductive methods in modern science. With a fine sense of truth they saw that the notion of causal continuity, as a premise of scientific generalization, is an essentially metaphysical postulate; and they avoided its treacherous ground by denying it, and construing causal sequence to mean a uniformity of co-existences and successions simply' (Veblen, 1900, p. 252).

24 In fact Veblen concludes his evolutionary essay as follows: 'The later method of apprehending and assimilating facts and handling them for the purposes of knowledge may be better or worse, more or less worthy or adequate, than the earlier; it may be of greater or less ceremonial or aesthetic effect; we may be

moved to regret the incursion of underbred habits of thought into the scholar's domain. But all that is beside the present point. Under the stress of modern technological exigencies, men's every-day habits of thought are falling into the lines that in the sciences constitute the evolutionary method; and knowledge which proceeds on a higher, more archaic plane is becoming alien and meaningless to them. The social and political sciences must follow the drift, for they are already caught in it' (1898, pp. 396–97).

25 More expansively, Veblen writes: 'But this and other survivals of the taxonomic terminology, or even of the taxonomic canons of procedure, do not hinder the economists of the modern school from doing effective work of a character that must be rated as genetic rather than taxonomic. [. . .] Professor Marshall shows an aspiration to treat economic life as a development; and, at least superficially, much of his work bears the appearance of being a discussion of this kind. In this endeavor his work is typical of what is aimed at by many of the later economists. The aim shows itself with a persistent recurrence in his Principles. His chosen maxim is, "Natura non facit saltum," [nature takes no leaps]—a maxim that might well serve to designate the prevailing attitude of modern economists towards questions of economic development as well as towards questions of classification or of economic policy. His insistence on the continuity of development and of the economic structure of communities is a characteristic of the best work along the later line of classical political economy' (Veblen, 1900, p. 265).

26 Without mentioning, and perhaps unaware of, Veblen's earlier critique, Stephen Pratten (1998) provides a thesis on Marshall that is highly consistent with Veblen's assessment. Veblen, as noted, takes the view that by adhering to taxonomic methods Marshall is forced to concentrate at best on areas or topics, if any, where taxonomic analysis seems less unreasonable. Pratten argues this same thesis at length and in detail. Most fundamentally, Pratten notes that on publishing his *Principles* in 1890, Marshall anticipates that a second volume will follow, an anticipation still in place a decade later when Marshall is explicitly conceiving of this project as involving a 'biological perspective' (in place of the mechanical stance of the earlier analysis). The second volume never appeared, of course, and the reasons for this have been much debated in the history of economic thought. Pratten's contribution is to explain this puzzle in terms of the inconsistency between Marshall's ontology and method. Specifically, noting how Marshall's project of achieving a 'biological perspective' entailed taking seriously the sort of causal-processual ontology discussed here, Pratten demonstrates that the feature that was 'preventing Marshall from realizing his planned program of research lay in his conception of the nature of science—a conception that was simply inadequate to his chosen project' (Pratten, 1998, p. 122). Thus Pratten traces how Marshall's commitment to a taxonomic (constant conjunction or correlation seeking) conception of science 'feeds into characteristic trajectories in certain parts of his substantive analyses' (where the method seems least unpromising) but 'systematically diverts [Marshall] from more fruitful paths'. The result is that those 'aspects of Marshall's work that are not propelled by this standard perspective are not systematically developed' (Pratten, 1998, p. 123). Pratten concludes: 'Marshall's continuing commitment to the standard constant conjunction view [of the form of scientific results] represents one obvious constraint blocking his analysis of economic change, organic development, and so forth. More specifically, I have argued that Marshall's project of promoting, within a proposed second volume of the *Principles*, an economics more sensitive to the nature of its subject matter is frustrated by his inability to shrug off this inherited conception of science' (1998, pp. 158–59).

27 Thus, in a paper titled 'The Limitations of Marginal Utility', notably published nine years after the final preconceptions paper, Veblen notes of this version of marginalism in particular:

'The limitations of the marginal-utility economics are sharp and characteristic. It is from first to last a doctrine of value, and in point of form and method it is a theory of valuation. The whole system, therefore, lies within the theoretical field of distribution [. . .].

Within this limited range marginal utility theory is of a wholly statical character. It offers no theory of a movement of any kind, being occupied with the adjustment of values to a given situation. Of this, again, no more convincing illustration need be had than is afforded by the work of Mr. Clark, which is not excelled in point of earnestness, perseverance, or insight. For all their use of the term "dynamic", neither Mr. Clark nor any of his associates in this line of research have yet contributed anything at all appreciable to a theory of genesis, growth, sequence, change, process, or the like, in economic life [. . .]. They have had something to say as to the bearing which given economic changes, accepted as premises, may have on economic valuation, and so on distribution; but as to the causes of change or the unfolding sequence of the phenomena of economic life they have had nothing to say hitherto; nor can they, since their theory is not drawn in causal terms but in terms of teleology.

In all this the marginal utility school is substantially at one with the classical economics of the nineteenth century, the difference between the two being that the former is confined within narrower limits and sticks more consistently to its teleological premises. Both are teleological, and neither can consistently admit arguments from cause to effect in the formulation of their main articles of theory [. . .].

The infirmity of this theoretical scheme lies in its postulates which confine the inquiry to generalisations of the teleological or "deductive" order. These postulates, together with the point of view and logical method that follow from them, the marginal utility school shares with other economists of the classical line—for this school is but a branch or derivative of the English classical economists of the nineteenth century. The substantial difference between this school and the generality of classical economists lies mainly in the fact that in the marginal utility economics the common postulates are more consistently adhered to at the same time that they are more neatly defined and their limitations are more adequately realized' (Veblen, 1909, pp. 620–22).

In the final paragraph, Veblen clearly does allow of the marginal utility school that it may be derivative (rather than a branch) of the English classical economists of the nineteenth century. But as I say, if there is a difference it is not that marginalists are thought to reveal acceptance of a causal processual ontology. Rather it reflects the marginalists' greater consistency in treatment of common postulates.

28 I am grateful to Nuno Martins for drawing this to my attention.

29 Of course the pattern being drawn may seem overly forced if, say, we acknowledge certain taxonomic elements in Smith and take him to be typical of 'classical political economy', as Marx interprets the latter. However, emphasis matters. Indeed Marx's point in comparing his classical political economy with 'vulgar economy' (essentially Veblen's classical economists) is primarily to stress the former's dominant concern with underlying causal structures and especially social relations *in opposition to* vulgar economy's preoccupation with the superficiality of mere appearances and correlations and the like. Moreover, if we follow numerous observers and interpret Marx as not merely critically transforming but also developing, and so in effect working *within*, the classical political economy tradition (see, for example, Kurz, 2010; Martins, 2012), then any overly taxonomic elements in earlier contributors such as Adam Smith

might in consequence (arguably) be interpreted as contingent, non-necessary features of that classical political economy *tradition* anyway. Certainly, Marx for his part repeatedly rejects attempts (that he too found in Smith) to naturalise the political economy of capitalism or to represent generalities of capitalism by appeal to universalities of natural law. Marx's own understanding of capitalism, as I interpret him, is in the main an inherently historical system-in-process, that is anarchic, crisis prone, and subject to a non-predetermined trajectory of development; and so is essentially non- (certainly non-overly) taxonomic or teleological. (However Veblen, it must be noted, mostly seems to interpret Marx differently on these issues, or anyway as non- or insufficiently Darwinian; see especially Veblen, 1906.)

30 It is worth noting that Veblen was never oblivious to how a desire on the part of some to employ mathematical methods tended to preserve the taxonomic (specifically deductivist) emphasis. Indeed (writing eight years after the preconceptions papers but prior to the developments within the field of mathematics), Veblen observes that the main argument against the causalist ontology of evolutionary thinking (and so its implications for method) is that causal forces cannot be directly observed (they are merely 'metaphysical' postulates) and so should be discounted. He is aware that such a stance is apparent even amongst some 'modern scientists'. But Veblen observes that it is especially evident amongst those disposed to employing mathematical functions. Thus although he regards as established the characterisation of reality as a process of consecutive causal change, he acknowledges that it 'is by no means unusual for modern scientists to deny the truth of this characterization, so far as regards this alleged recourse to the concept of causation' (1908b, p. 33) and 'even deny the substantial continuity of the sequence of changes that excite their scientific attention'. Notably:

'This attitude seems particularly to commend itself to those who by preference attend to the mathematical formulations of theory and who are chiefly occupied with proving up and working out details of the system of theory which have previously been left unsettled or uncovered. The concept of causation is recognized to be a metaphysical postulate, a matter of imputation, not of observation; whereas it is claimed that scientific inquiry neither does nor can legitimately, nor, indeed, currently, make use of a postulate more metaphysical than the concept of an idle concomitance of variation, such as is adequately expressed in terms of mathematical function' (Veblen, 1908b, p. 33).

Veblen actually sets about demonstrating that such arguments are untenable, that we all implicitly or explicitly must invoke notions of causal powers and continuity (again, see Lawson, 2003, chapter 8).

31 Edward Fullbrook (2009, pp. 6–7) lists some possible strategies for those who recognise the relevance of the ontology in question but are resistant to adapting methods appropriately.

32 Colander (2000), for example, takes steps to 'declare the term neoclassical economics dead', but immediately adds: 'Let me be clear about what I am sentencing to death—it is not the content of neoclassical economics' (p. 1469).

Bibliography

Arnsperger, C. and Varoufakis, Y. 2006. What is neoclassical economics?, *Post-Autistic Economics Review,* no. 38, article 1

Aspromourgos, T. 1986. On the origins of the term 'neoclassical', *Cambridge Journal of Economics,* vol. 10, 265–70

Becker, G. S. 1976. *The Economic Approach to Human Behavior,* Chicago, University of Chicago Press

Campus, A. 1987. Marginalist economics, in Eatwell, J., Milgate, M. and Newman, P. (eds.), *The New Palgrave: A Dictionary of Economics,* London, Macmillan

Colander, D. 2000. The death of neoclassical economics, *Journal of the History of Economic Thought,* vol. 22, no. 2, 129–43

Colander, D., Holt, R. P. and Rosser, J. B. 2004. The changing face of mainstream economics, *Review of Political Economy,* vol. 16, no. 4, 485–500

Davis, J. B. 2005. Heterodox economics, the fragmentation of the mainstream and embedded individual analysis, pp. 53–72 in Garnett, R. and Harvey, J. (eds.), *The Future of Heterodox Economics, Essays in Honour of Paul Dale Bush,* Ann Arbor, University of Michigan Press

Dobb, M. 1973. *Theories of Value and Distribution since Adam Smith,* Cambridge, Cambridge University Press

Fayazmanesh, S. 1998. On Veblen's coining of the term 'Neoclassical', in Fayazmanesh, S. and Tool, M. R. (eds.), *Institutionalist Method and Value,* vol. 1, London, Edward Elgar

Fine, B. 2004. Addressing the critical and the real in critical realism, pp. 202–26 in Lewis, P. (ed.), *Transforming Economics: Perspectives on the Critical Realist Project,* London, Routledge

Fine, B. 2006. 'Critical realism and heterodoxy,' mimeo, SOAS, available at http://eprints.soas.ac.uk/7024/

Fullbrook, E. 2009. Introduction to ontology and economics: Tony Lawson and his critics,' pp. 1–12 in E. Fullbrook (ed.), *Ontology and Economics: Tony Lawson and His Critics,* London, Routledge

Guerrien, B. 2004. Irrelevance and ideology, *Post-autistic Economics Review,* no. 29, article 3

Hahn, F. H. 1982. The neo-Ricardians, *Cambridge Journal of Economics,* vol. 6, 353–74

Hahn, F. H. 1984. *Equilibrium and Macroeconomics,* Oxford, Basil Blackwell

Hahn, F. H. 1985. *In Praise of Economic Theory,* Jevons Memorial Fund Lecture, delivered at University College, London

Hamilton, W. H. 1923. Vestigial economics, *New Republic,* 4 April

Hicks, J. R. 1983. *Classics and Moderns* (Collected Essays on Economic Theory, vol. 3), Oxford, Basil Blackwell

Hodgson, G. M. 1999. False antagonisms and doomed reconciliations, in *Evolution and Institutions: On Evolutionary Economics and the Evolution of Economics,* Cheltenham, Edward Elgar, 23–45

Homan, P. T. 1928. *Contemporary Economic Thought,* New York, Harper and Brothers

Juselius, K. 2010. Time to reject the privileging of economic theory over empirical evidence? A reply to Lawson, *Cambridge Journal of Economics,* vol. 35, 423–36

Keen, S. 2012. Instability in financial markets: sources and remedies, paper presented at Berlin meetings of the Institute for New Economic Thinking (INET), available at http://ineteconomics.org /sites/inet.civicactions.net/files/keen-steve-berlin-paper.pdf [date last accessed 1 July 2012]

Krugman, P. 2009. How did economists get it so wrong?, *New York Times Magazine,* 2 September, available at http://www.nytimes.com/2009/09/06/magazine/06Economic-t.html?pagewanted=all [date last accessed 1 July 2012]

Kurz, H. D. 2010. Technical progress, capital accumulation and income distribution in classical economics: Adam Smith, David Ricardo and Karl Marx, *European Journal of the History of Economic Thought*, vol. 17, no. 5, 183–222

Lawson, T. 1997. *Economics and Reality*, London, Routledge

Lawson, T. 2003. *Reorienting Economics*, London, Routledge

Lawson, T. 2005. The (confused) state of equilibrium analysis in modern economics: an (ontological) explanation, *Journal for Post Keynesian Economics*, vol. 27, no. 3, 423–44

Lawson, T. 2006a. The nature of heterodox economics, *Cambridge Journal of Economics*, vol. 30, no. 2, 483–507

Lawson, T. 2006b. Tensions in modern economics. The case of equilibrium analysis, pp. 133–49 in Mosini, V. (ed.), *Equilibrium in Economics: Scope and Limits*, London, Routledge

Lawson, T. 2009a. The current economic crisis: its nature and the course of academic economics, *Cambridge Journal of Economics*, vol. 33, no. 4, 759–88

Lawson, T. 2009b. Contemporary economics and the crisis, *Real-World Economics Review*, vol. 50, 122–31

Lawson, T. 2009c. On the nature and roles of formalism in economics: reply to Hodgson, pp. 189–231 in Fullbrook, E. (ed.), *Ontology and Economics: Tony Lawson and His Critics*, London, Routledge

Lawson, T. 2010. '*Soros's theory of reflexivity: a critical comment*', mimeo, Cambridge, forthcoming in Revue de Philosophie Economique

Lawson, T. 2012a. Ontology and the study of social reality: emergence, organisation, community, power, social relations, corporations, artefacts and money, *Cambridge Journal of Economics*, vol. 36, no. 2, 345–85

Lawson, T. 2012b. Mathematical modelling and ideology in the economics academy: competing explanations of the failings of the modern discipline?, *Economic Thought: History, Philosophy and Methodology*, vol. 1, no 1

Lawson, T. 2013a. Emergence and social causation, pp. 285–307 in Greco, J. and Groff, R. (eds.), *Powers and Capacities in Philosophy*, London, Routledge

Lawson, T. 2013b. Emergence, morphogenesis, causal reduction and downward causation, pp. 61–84 in Archer, M. (ed.), *Social Morphogenesis*, New York, Springer

Martins, N. 2012. Sen, Sraffa and the revival of classical political economy, *Journal of Economic Methodology*, vol. 19, no. 2, 143–57

Martins, N. Forthcoming. Classical surplus theory and heterodox economics, *American Journal of Economics and Sociology*, vol. 73, no. 1

Marx, K. 1974. *Capital: A Critical Analysis of Capitalist Production*, vol. 1, Engels, F. (ed.), London, Lawrence and Wishart

Marx, K. 1977. *A Contribution to the Critique of Political Economy*, Moscow, Progress Publishers.

Mitchell, W. C. 1967. *Types and Economic Theory*, 2 vols., Dorfman, J. (ed.), New York, Kelley

Pratten, S. 1998. Marshall on tendencies, equilibrium, and the statical method, *History of Political Economy*, vol. 30, no. 1, 122–63

Schumpeter, J. A. 1954. *History of Economic Analysis*, Schumpeter, E. B. (ed.), London, George Allen and Unwin

Soros, G. 2009. *The Crash of 2009 and What it Means: The New Paradigm for Financial Markets*, New York, Public Affairs

Veblen, T. 1898. Why is economics not an evolutionary science?, *Quarterly Journal of Economics,* vol. 12, no. 4, 373–97

Veblen, T. 1899a. The preconceptions of economic science I, *Quarterly Journal of Economics,* vol. 13, no. 2, 121–50

Veblen, T. 1899b. The preconceptions of economic science II, *Quarterly Journal of Economics,* vol. 13, no. 4, 396–426

Veblen, T. 1900. The preconceptions of economic science III, *Quarterly Journal of Economics,* vol. 14, no. 2, 240–69

Veblen, T. 1906. The Socialist Economics of Karl Marx and His Followers, *Quarterly Journal of Economics,* vol. 20, no. 4, 575–95

Veblen, T. 1908a. Fisher's capital and income, *Political Science Quarterly,* vol. 23

Veblen, T. 1908b. The evolution of the scientific point of view, *University of California Chronicle,* vol. 10, no. 4; reprinted in Veblen, T. 1990. *The Place of Science in Modern Civilisation,* New Brunswick, NJ, Transaction Publishers (page references to the latter)

Veblen, T. 1909. The limitations of marginal utility, *Journal of Political Economy,* vol. 17, no. 9, 620–36

Weintraub, E. R. 2002. Neoclassical economics, in *Concise Encyclopaedia of Economics,* Library of Economics and Liberty, Liberty Fund

Zafirovski, M. 1999. How 'neo-classical' is neoclassical economics? With special reference to value theory, *History of Economics Review,* winter, 1–15

5 The current economic crisis: its nature and the course of academic economics*†

1. Introduction

As the current economic crisis continues and seemingly deepens it is not unusual to find groups of academic economists being attributed a share of the blame. A significant amount of this emanates from other academic economists. Those whose proposals have been largely ignored by policy makers in recent times are now finding that their voices are being heard, at least in the popular media. And they are not refusing the opportunity to say 'I told you so', suggesting that if only those in power had listened to us or me, rather than to them or s/he, things would not have gone so wrong.

Mostly this criticism focuses on the substantive economic theories and policies that previously have been in favour. Seemingly little attention is given to the modes of analysis that have been utilised in support of these positions. Yet method matters. And in my assessment the sorts of methods that prevail in modern economics, whilst fundamental to understanding how recently prominent theories have been sustained, do not carry the warrant that their widespread usage seems to presuppose. In consequence, I am especially concerned that the critics avoid now filling academic journals with contributions that make the same more fundamental, essentially methodological, mistakes as their economic opponents, albeit in slightly different guise.

For many years now, economic policy analysis emanating from the academy has been framed mostly in terms of properties of mathematical deductivist models. This modelling activity has not provided too much insight (see Lawson, 1997, ch. 19; 2003A, ch. 1). The anticipated response against which I want to caution is the substitution of yet more formalistic models, albeit models reflecting alternative economic hypotheses, in place of those that have hitherto been dominant. For the more fundamental problem of recent years, I shall argue, is not so much the use of specific inappropriate models, but the emphasis on mathematical deductivist modelling *per se*. Such models can provide limited insight at best into the workings of the economy (or any other part of social reality). Indeed, I will suggest that the formalistic modelling endeavour mostly gets in the way of understanding.

Clearly an opening up of the economics academy to methods other than those of mathematical deductivist modelling, though an appropriate response if I am correct, will not, in and of itself, lead us out of the crisis. But in that almost all academic resources in economics have, in recent years, been devoted to this mathematical activity, the resources that would thereby be rendered available to relevant academic enquiry, a situation not occurring for very many decades, must be a stimulus to any solution.

I do go further and indicate an alternative non-formalistic framework that I believe can serve the purpose of analysing the current situation. I also identify various fundamental mechanisms and developments that have contributed significantly to the crisis. But this section is primarily illustrative. A comprehensive analysis would require a different paper.

2. Background

Before indicating why the emphasis on mathematical modelling in modern economics is problematic, let me first observe that in economic journals the formalistic modelling activities seem currently to be continuing unabated. If my methodological concerns outlined below are valid, and if the crisis provides an opportunity for change, the most prominent academic economic journals are seemingly not yet responding. However, academic articles tend to have a significant publication lag, and so it may be too early to say; to this point, in fact, analyses of the crisis appear to be mostly restricted to the popular media.[1] However there are academic economic papers in circulation on the internet that are seemingly intended for journal publication. Here, too, the modelling emphasis appears to be maintained. One paper though, and a seemingly influential one, does at least address the issue of economic modelling explicitly. And I think it may be useful to motivate my discussion by first very briefly focusing on this contribution, if only to indicate that my concerns cannot yet be put aside as no longer relevant.

The paper in question is by David Colander, Hans Föllmer, Armin Hass, Michael Goldberg, Katerina Juselius, Alan Kirman, Thomus Lux and Brigitte Sloth (2008), and is aptly titled 'The Financial Crisis and the Systemic Failure of Academic Economics'. This paper, by a set of established, mainstream leaning, and clearly concerned, economists, seems by all accounts to have been especially widely circulated, and, as I say, is proving influential.[2] As such it may well be highly indicative of current thinking and evaluation.

As might be expected, the paper in question carries significant insight. Colander *et al.* inform us that they 'trace the deeper roots' of the crisis to economists' 'insistence on constructing models that, by design, disregard the key elements driving outcomes in real-world markets' (p. 1). In their view 'the current academic agenda has largely crowded out research on the inherent causes of financial crises' (p. 2). And their central emphasis is that '[m]ost models, by design, offer no immediate handle on how to think about or deal with this recurring phenomenon', namely crises (p. 2).

Getting down to details, these influential critics focus in part on the use of mathematical models by investors.[3] Mainly, though, Colander *et al.* focus on the formalistic modelling activities within the academy. Turning to specific claims built into modern economic models these authors single out the 'the twin assumptions of "rational expectations" and a representative agent' as particularly unrealistic. The assumption of rational expectations imparts a form of consistency between (i) the modeller's conception of a section of reality, and (ii) the conception of reality held by agents whose expectations form part of the content of that model. It assures that, within any such model, expectations cannot be systematically wrong. The assumption of a representative agent allows that theorising need only be in terms of a single average or representative individual.

In challenging these assumptions Colander *et al.* call for more realistic specifications, based, as they present it, on empirical insight. They summarise reporting that 'it seems to us that much of contemporary empirical work in macroeconomics and finance is driven by the pre-analytic belief in the validity of a certain model'.

Having identified some obvious problems with currently dominant economic practice, how do these authors suggest that matters be improved? Early on in the paper these authors make critical reference to their own conception of 'standard models'. And they make it very clear that the only acceptable way of proceeding is developing new formalistic models in their place, ones that are appropriate for our current exceptional times:

> The implicit view behind standard models is that markets and economies are inherently stable and that they only temporarily get off track. The majority of economists thus failed to warn policy makers about the threatening system crisis and ignored the work of those who did. Ironically, as the crisis has unfolded, economists have had no choice but to abandon their standard models and to produce hand-waving common-sense remedies. Common-sense advice, although useful, is a poor substitute for an underlying model that can provide much-needed guidance for developing policy and regulation. It is not enough to put the existing model to one side, observing that one needs, 'exceptional measures for exceptional times'. What we need are models capable of envisaging such 'exceptional times'.
>
> (Colander *et al.*, 2008, p. 2)

In the course of their argument, these authors go on to suggest a possible need for 'a different type of mathematics than that which is generally used now by many prominent economic models' (p. 3); and for giving back 'an independent role to expectations in economic models' (p. 9). In their view '[o]nce one acknowledges the importance of empirically based behavioral micro foundations and the heterogeneity of actors, a rich spectrum of new models becomes available [. . .] [allowing] one to study out-of-equilibrium dynamics and adaptive adjustments. Such dynamics could reveal the possibility of multiplicity and evolution of equilibria' (p. 9). They also conjecture, that '[i]f one accepts that the dispersed economic activity of many economic agents could be described by statistical laws, one might even take stock of methods from statistical physics to model dynamic economic systems' (p. 10). In terms of method, they 'recommend a more data-driven methodology' in which '[c]ointegrated VAR models could provide an avenue towards identification of robust structures within a set of data' (p. 11), adding that

> A chain of specification tests and estimated statistical models for simultaneous systems would provide a benchmark for the subsequent development of tests of models based on economic behavior: significant and robust relations within a simultaneous system would provide empirical regularities that one would attempt to explain, while the quality of fit of the statistical benchmark would offer a confidence band for more ambitious models.
> (Colander *et al.*, 2008, p. 11)

In short, these authors do not question the contemporary significant attention to formalistic modelling *per se*, but rather recommend the development of additional alternative mathematical models and techniques of mathematical deductivist modelling.

3. What is wrong with economists' modelling?

So it seems that any concerns I may have about the emphasis on formalistic modelling, assuming they are valid, ought not yet be put aside as redundant. However, are these concerns valid? Are they justified intellectually? What is wrong with the sort of response advocated explicitly by Colander *et al.*—and, of course, implicitly by many others as a presupposition of their practices?[4] Why do I suppose that mathematical deductivist modelling of the sort pursued by economists is a problem in itself?

The basic answer, elaborated at length elsewhere in philosophical terms (see e.g. Fullbrook, 2009; Lawson, 1997, 2003A), can actually be put very simply. But before giving the answer, let me anticipate and try and pre-empt a possible misunderstanding. The fundamental problem of modern economics, as I see it, is the mainstream *insistence* that mathematical modelling is the only useful, and the proper, way to do economics. It is this *insistence* on mathematical deductivist modelling that I am primarily seeking to criticise here. Although, for reasons I give below, I expect the enterprise to generate insight only rarely at best, I do not want to be equally dogmatic and assert that such modelling could never provide insight, or suggest that no one should ever experiment (see my various commentaries on this in Fullbrook, 2009, especially Lawson, 2009B).

My starting point, though, is that formalistic modelling has been mostly unsuccessful at providing insight (see Lawson, 2003A, ch. 1). The paper by Colander *et al.* discussed above points to the explanatory failures of the modelling project in times of crises, as well as to certain unhelpful unrealistic assumptions. The truth, though, is that the project of providing mathematical models of economic phenomena has proven to be explanatorily inadequate throughout its history, it is not something that has emerged with the crisis. Similarly, claims widely recognised as unrealistic are a feature of seemingly all mathematical deductivist endeavour in modern economics (again see Lawson, 2003A, ch. 1).

Why should this be? And specifically, why do I suppose that the emphasis on formalistic modelling is the problem? My answer, simply put, can be expressed in the following three propositions:

(i) The sorts of mathematical deductivist methods that economists use are, like all research methods, types of tools.
(ii) All tools are appropriate to dealing with but a limited set of tasks, involving a limited set of phenomena, in a limited set of contexts, and not others.
(iii) The nature and conditions of social reality are such that the forms of mathematical deductivist reasoning favoured by modern economists are almost entirely inadequate as tools of insightful social analysis.

I doubt that many would suggest that we seek to use pencils to cut hedges, telephones to dig gardens, forks to fly us to other countries. Yet pencils, telephones and forks can be very useful to us in certain contexts, with respect to very specific tasks and phenomena. Marx long ago observed that 'in the analysis of economic forms neither microscopes nor chemical reagents are of assistance' (1974, p. 90). There is reason to believe that mathematical deductive methods are equally of little assistance in the analysis of most social phenomena.

Why so? First note that the sorts of mathematical deductive methods that economists use presuppose event regularities or correlations. They require that events or states of affairs are connected as empirical regularities. More specifically, they require regularities that connect events standing in causal sequence, in order to deduce that this event happened because of, or followed from, that event (for example the increase/decrease in consumption or investment or earnings came about because of the increase/decrease in income or interest rates or productivity).

Second, it follows that economists in their theorising must produce conceptions that are consistent with such event regularity presuppositions. They require theories that guarantee that for any given conditioning event (or set of outcomes) X,[5] some predictable event Y inevitably follows (or at least does so on average, with something like a small distribution of outcomes around the mean).

Third, in practice economists meet this need by constructing theories couched in terms of isolated atoms. By atoms I do not mean something small, but something constructed as if it has the same independent invariable effect whatever the context. The assumption that such atoms are isolated, means that, if triggered, their effects are unimpeded by other factors, and so are deducible, or predictable, and so mathematically tractable. It is like assuming economic agents are like wind-up toy dolls that, once wound up and placed on a reasonably smooth surface such as a table, predictably walk forward, if nothing intervenes in their path. In modern economics, the wind-up doll is typically (though not necessarily) the supposedly optimising (perhaps representative) agent in the context of a closed scenario with a unique optimum.[6]

Parenthetically, we can note that this sort of practice is illuminated by considering the experimental practices within the natural sciences. In the experimental laboratory, scientists do often succeed in isolating stable causal mechanisms, allowing the latter to be triggered and their unimpeded effects examined. The assumed-to-be isolated and atomistic entities of modern economics are treated as if analogous to the experimentally isolated, intrinsically constant mechanisms that are the focus of the (experimental) natural sciences.

4. Critique

The essence of my criticism of the modelling emphasis is simply that the twin presuppositions of economic modellers that (i) empirical regularities of the sort required are ubiquitous, and (ii) social reality is constituted by sets of isolated atoms, are simply erroneous.

The repeated predictive failure of econometric forecasting models over the last 50 years is itself sufficient to cast significant doubt on the validity of the first presupposition. It is the empirical record that reveals that event regularities of the required sort are a relatively rare occurrence.

But actually, we can see that even in the natural sciences (where predictive testing is thought to be more successful), event regularities are not just sometimes observed in, but mostly *restricted* to, well-controlled experimental situations. This is precisely because conditions of experimental *intervention* tend to be required for intrinsically stable mechanisms to be isolated from countervailing factors. In the experimental laboratory it is indeed sometimes the case that event regularities are laboriously *produced*, correlating precisely the triggering of isolated intrinsically constant mechanisms and their unimpeded effects. But even in the controlled experiments of the natural sciences, attempts to bring about or reproduce such outcomes are also very often unsuccessful. Economists are thus seen to be rather heroic in assuming that scenarios that are laboured for in natural scientific experimentation, often involving great difficulty and subtlety, occur quite spontaneously everywhere in the social realm.

If event regularities hardly occur in the social realm, it does not take too much reflection to see that the second presupposition is also invalid, that the constituents of social reality can rarely be aptly portrayed as systems of isolated atoms.

If the ongoing crisis has served to emphasise one feature of the world economy it is surely that its numerous aspects or components are anything but isolated from each other. Developments in specific parts of the system have been found to immediately impact on developments in other parts, developments in one region to impact on those in others, and ultimately today's developments are closely related to what went before and will make a significant difference to the possibilities open to the future.

We cannot experimentally (or otherwise) isolate markets from monetary systems from firms and other processes of production, from state institutions including legislative and other regulatory processes, etc. Each is constitutively dependent on the others. And each human being is no less isolated. We are all of us inescapably socially situated and formed. We grow up to find ourselves gendered this way or that, of this nationality or that, and we become occupied as teachers or students, or as taxi-drivers or cleaners, as landlords/ladies or tenants, as employers or employees, etc. Each such position or status carries with it a set of community specific rights and obligations that bind us to, and indeed constitute us in relation to, others (teachers *qua* teachers only exist in relation to students, and vice versa, and similarly constitutive relations hold between employers and employees, landlords/ladies and tenants, etc.).

At the base of it all are accepted ways of doing things (some of which we call rules). We (as a community, either collectively or through representatives) accept in the sense of observe/act upon (whether or not we positively support or endorse) the creation of positions or statuses, that get allocated to certain individuals, and which are associated with positional powers or rights (allowed practices) and obligations (required practices). The network of accepted social positions and associated rights and obligations coordinates social life.

If social reality is composed of phenomena that are anything but isolated, so too everything is far from constant, or atomistic, but rather is in transformation. Think of language. The English language is a (typically unacknowledged) condition of the practices of all those currently speaking and/or writing English, and its reproduction and transformation is an (typically unintended) outcome of the same practices. This is how language exists: in process. That is its mode of being. It becomes and begoes through time, a complex structure continually being reproduced and transformed though practice. But what is true of language is true of everything else that is social (that is, everything whose existence depends on us): seminars, universities, personal identities, cities, financial systems, climatic systems and, ultimately, capitalism itself.

Social reality, then, is a relational totality in motion. It is also has depth or structure; the social relations, rules, positions, power structures and so forth discussed above, are typically immeasurable, out of phase with the practices they condition (for example motorway driving and speed limits) and at best known, but not seen, to exist. And, of course, social reality involves meaning, and values and much else.

Social reality, in other words, is of a nature that is significantly at variance with the closed systems of isolated atoms that would guarantee the conditions of mathematical deductivist modelling. That is why modern economics has continually failed on its own terms. It is also why, as a step on the road to this failure, economics is *inescapably* profuse with assumptions accepted by everyone as widely unrealistic, including, but certainly not reducing to, those highlighted by Colander *et al.*

So the more pressing and pervasive problem of modern economics, I suggest, is not a case of *this* particular set of mathematical deductivist models requiring substitution by *that* set. It is the emphasis on mathematical modelling *per se*.

5. What of models that get the 'right results' or 'address interesting questions'?

I should acknowledge that it is not only mainstream practitioners that will likely be resistant to (or uncomfortable with) my conclusions here. Heterodox economists *qua* heterodox economists, of course, differentiate themselves from the mainstream in *not* insisting that mathematical methods be everywhere employed (Lawson, 2003A, part III, 2006); pluralism in method is a chacteristic feature of this heterodoxy (Lawson, 2009A). And much heterodox output is indeed non-formalistic. Nevertheless the ontological grounding of the rejection of mainstream (modelling) contributions is rarely explicit and not always fully recognised. In consequence, at least amongst some individuals within the modern heterodoxy, it is not always appreciated that the acknowledged widespread implausibility and failing of modern economics is not just a contingent feature of a dominant set of models but an almost inevitable consequence of the practice of mathematical deductivist modelling *per se*. In heterodox circles I frequently encounter remarks like: these particular models seem OK because they get the right conclusions, or they address interesting questions, or it is always necessary in social science to make thought-to-be false assumptions so mathematical modelling (although not a method to be insisted upon) is not worse than any other form of analysis, and so forth.

I am suggesting that all such 'justifications' are basically untenable, and I worry that their uncritical acceptance within parts of heterodoxy may in itself be a contributory factor to the current unhappy situation. With this in mind I think it cannot be emphasised too strongly that the practice of allowing assumptions known or believed to be false, whilst unnecessary (see Lawson, 2003A, ch. 4), allows more or less any conclusion to be deduced, without adding to the latter's groundedness. In such a context, any evaluation that the question addressed is (or is not) an interesting one is simply irrelevant. Let me briefly elaborate.

Put starkly, if a desired and/or believed yet contested conclusion is derived by way of one or more claims that are believed to be false of our world, and of any really possible counterfactual world, but assumed in order to achieve model tractability, the only insight gained is into the properties of the model so constructed. Is there really much point to such an exercise? Certainly the analysis in itself provides no grounding or support for the preferred conclusion (however valid the conclusion may actually be). I suspect a supporter of a conclusion so reached would be dismissive if a second researcher used alternative but also accepted-as-false assumptions simply to undermine the preferred conclusion But models that allow the deduction of a preferred and/or believed conclusion by way of claims accepted as wildly unrealistic are *per se* no more tenable or insightful.

Obvious though the above observations may seem, it is nevertheless by way of inserting known to be unrealistic assumptions that preferred positions are often 'supported'. Consider the conclusion 'capital markets result in the correct determination/pricing of risk and return'. This viewpoint is especially pertinent here just because the liberalisation or deregulation of financial markets that I come on to discuss below are supported in classical finance theory by precisely this claim that capital markets are 'efficient' in the sense of pricing correctly, where the models used to generate the conclusion are acknowledged to be false. It is clearly this reliance on formal modelling, necessitating unrealistic assumptions, that allows certain dominant viewpoints to be sustained. For example, we find William Sharpe, a Nobel Memorial Prize Winner in economics, writing in his famous article on capital asset pricing that the inputs required to generate the conclusion are:

> highly restrictive and undoubtedly unrealistic assumptions. However, since the proper test of a theory is not the realism of its assumptions, but the acceptability of its implications, and since these assumptions imply equilibrium conditions which form a major part of classical

financial doctrine, it is far from clear that the formulation should be rejected[. . .].

(Sharpe, 1964, p. 434)

I hope it is clear that any claimed support for conclusions preferred in heterodox circles, for example that 'Keynesian demand management policy results in non-inflationary economic growth' would be equally vacuous. Certainly, it is quite inconsistent to accept a model on the basis of its results and yet to decry opponents' models derived on a similar basis. In all cases, to accept a believed-to-be-false model just because doing so enables a sought-after result to be generated is little more than self-serving opportunism. Mostly this manoeuvre only misleads those overly impressed with the use of formalism.

Of course, the previous few paragraphs present matters in a rather stark manner and, it may seem, in an overly cynical fashion too, just because it is implied that in all such exercises any resulting 'conclusion' is chosen first and underpin the sorts of assumptions made (i.e., those that allow the desired conclusion to follow). The problem remains, though, that even where any conclusion is not determined *a priori*, but results *a posteriori* from a rather complexly presented analysis, so long as that analysis includes assumptions that are known to be false of this, and any really possible, world the analysis itself gives no added credibility to any conclusion drawn. Yet if the social world is an open, structured, totality in motion, then any insistence upon the practice of mathematical deductivist modelling, with its implicit presupposition of a closed world (or systems) of isolated atoms, means that, most of the time at least, unrealistic claims of the sort in question are unavoidable.

In short, once the constraint of seeking to be realistic is given up, and the prioritisation of formalistic modelling usually necessitates this, there are a multitude of ways of being unrealistic. A mathematical modelling (or any other) exercise, which unavoidably generates accounts of factors acknowledged as (wildly) unrealistic, provides no grounding thereby for the conclusions reached, whatever our independent evaluation of the latter. In consequence, to the extent that we are interested in the way the real world is and works, none of us should be any more interested in a believed-to-be unrealistic mathematical deductivist model that supports a preferred (e.g. believed to be true) conclusion, than one that seems to negate it.

6. The way forward

So what is to be done? Implications clearly follow for reorienting (the practices of) the economics academy. A pertinent question here is whether the conception of the nature of social reality sketched above not only underpins a critique of the mainstream emphasis on formalistic modelling, but also points a way to understanding the nature of the financial crisis. A major contribution in this regard, I think, is an appropriate framework of analysis. Let me explore this contention a little.

I have suggested that social reality is an open, structured, totality in motion. It is a dynamic totality in which we all occupy positions that bind us to others through a network of rights and obligations.

This totality includes the financial system and anything we might want to call the economy. Within the network of accepted social positions and associated rights and obligations that coordinate social life, has arisen over time a measuring and accounting system bound up with something called money. The system that has evolved allows a subset of obligations and rights to emerge and proliferate taking the form of credit and debit. Alternatively put, amongst the numerous social positions in which individuals (including legal individuals called companies) find themselves, and which bind them to others and the rest of society, are very often those of debtor and creditor, and numerous individuals are often positioned as both.

A debtor owes a debt to a creditor and thereby is usually under an obligation to the latter in the sense of being duty bound at some stage to provide the latter with something of value. As such, markers of this debt (forms of 'money' or whatever) become valuable in themselves, and many types can be traded or exchanged, thus effecting a transference of specific rights to credit.

Such a system is stable and indeed functional only if the debtors are, and are considered to be, reliable, both in the sense of being committed to, and capable of, fulfilling the obligations involved. The system is thus based on trust and confidence on the part of creditors, and on promises, good intentions (or trustworthiness) and material credibility on the part of debtors.

Expectations and placements of trust, though, are easily disappointed. There is nothing in this system that prevents the level of borrowing, the expansion of credit/debt, from getting way beyond levels at which debtors can meet their obligations. Both debtors and creditors can be over-optimistic about investment possibilities that exist. Or the situation can easily change so that earlier seemingly profitable opportunities and decisions are rendered otherwise. In numerous ways there can be an expansion of credit/debt way beyond levels that the system is found *a posteriori* to be able to sustain. This is the scenario of the last 25 years or so, a period that has witnessed a massive expansion in credit/debt. When, in such a scenario, trust and confidence break down, we can have the sort of crisis such as we have recently witnessed.

Of course, the details of the recent period are complex, and a full understanding requires, amongst other things, a detailed analysis of the numerous structural transformations in the financial sector during this period, as well as an exploration of the nature of mechanisms whereby an expansion of credit/debt has occurred; but this brief sketch does, I believe, indicate the relevance of the framework.

7. Contributory factors

Although it is not strictly necessary, let me, for illustrative purposes, give a very brief sketch of certain mechanisms, consistent with this framework, that likely have contributed to the current crisis.[7]

Situations where borrowing and investing are fuelled by expectations of rising prices, only to be met by (a set of events causing) a reversal of expectations and indeed price movements, a period in which off loading of financial assets (often very quickly) occurs, resulting in a movement typically interpreted as a 'crash', are referred to as economic or financial or asset-price bubbles.

In recent times, it is conceivable, and seemingly likely, that such bubbles in part at least have been intentionally brought about. Large and powerful North Atlantic, and in particular Wall Street, investment banks have repeatedly bought and sold financial and real assets to create and exploit price shifts. The stimulation of asset-price bubbles is a form of this 'speculative arbitrage'.[8] Wall Street investment banks have been able to enter and influence specific markets, especially those emergent market economies of Eastern Europe with small bond or stock markets, first making large speculative profits, and then bursting the bubbles by withdrawing. With the later dot.com bubble these same banks found that they could equally gain financially from bubble bursting in home territory. The latest crisis must be seen, I think, as but the most recent bursting of a bubble, although this time with the banks themselves having been caught up in the fall out.

The bubble that has resulted in the 2007 credit crunch is significant not only for its size, but also for its nature. In previous over-lending induced crises both the source and scale of the problems have been easy to identify, allowing remedial steps of sorts to be taken. But at the heart of the 2007 debt bubble were the trading of *over-the-counter derivatives*, especially those taking the form of *collateralised debt obligations,* and these have served to confuse as to the true nature of the underlying situation

Derivatives are financial contracts or instruments that, as their name suggests, derive their value from that of something else. It is not necessary to own that 'something else'. So trading in derivatives is a form of pure gambling. Indeed, a bet placed on a horse in a race, where the horse is not owned, is essentially a form of derivative.

The *over-the-counter* nature of the derivatives means that trading is directly between two parties, with no exchange trading allowing the determination of 'market' prices. The over-the-counter derivative market is the largest market for derivatives, and, with most of the traders made up of banks, hedge funds and such like, the market is largely unregulated with respect to disclosure of information between the parties.

Collateralised debt obligations are a structured form of asset-backed security. They are asset backed in the sense that their worth and payments derive from a portfolio of fixed income underlying assets. They are structured in the sense of being divided into prioritised tranches with each tranche being assigned a different degree of riskiness. Those tranches that are considered the safest, designated 'senior tranches', receive the lowest rate of return; those that are the riskiest, designated 'junior tranches', generate the highest premium payments.

As I say collateralised debt obligations seem to have been at the centre of the recent crisis. And the process by which they were assessed for their 'riskiness' is a significant factor in understanding how.

It is important to recognise that the tranches were prioritised not in accordance with the values of the securitised assets underpinning (all) the various tranches, but according to how the different tranches were to absorb any losses emanating from the underlying portfolio. Specifically, where only some underlying assets defaulted the losses were in the first instance born by the most junior tranches. The senior tranches only absorbed losses after the junior claims had been exhausted. As the number of defaults increased, increasingly more senior tranches suffered too.

In short, the junior tranches generated higher premium payments, but the downside was that if defaults relating to the underlying assets occurred, the holders suffered losses *before* the holders of the senior tranches were similarly affected. Alternatively, the holders of the senior tranches, the supposedly least risky ones, received a lower risk payment, but would be the last to have their payments lost through non-performance of the underlying assets.

How was the riskiness of the tranches determined? This was undertaken by rating agencies, the main three being Moody's, Standard and Poor's and Fitch. Traditionally these agencies had focused their rating activities mostly on single-name corporate finance. However, with the rise of structured securities markets their activities expanded to include the evaluation of these assets. Somehow, these agencies expected to make meaningful independent evaluations of the creditworthiness of various entities, and rank them according to the rating scales AAA, AA, A, BBB, BB and so forth.

Very often these larger rating agencies offered 'credit rating advisory services' that essentially advised an issuer on how to structure its securities so as to achieve a given credit rating for a certain debt tranche. In consequence, it seems not unlikely that if the agency's advice was followed, the latter agency consequently felt obligated to provide the issuer with precisely that given rating.

Not surprisingly the banks choose very often to structure in such a manner as to achieve tranches with AAA ratings. In fact, in the last ten years the repackaging of assets has resulted in huge quantities of AAA-rated securities. Indeed, at one point roughly 60% of structured products were triple-A rated according to Fitch Ratings (2007) compared with less than 1% of corporate bond issues. And one result of all this was the generation of a perception (as it turned out, an illusion) that structured securities were comparable in terms of safety or riskiness with single-name corporate finance.

Notice, once more, that a triple-A rating of a tranche did not mean that it was necessarily backed by prime loans or assets. Indeed, it was quite possible for the opposite to be the case. It meant only that if the underlying assets stopped performing, the holders of the lowest rated tranches would lose out first, whilst holders of an AAA-rated tranche would continue to receive income the longest. If all the underlying assets failed at the same time, due, say, to a significant economic downturn, then clearly all tranches would become worthless simultaneously.

Of course, the analysis of the nature of social reality discussed at length above reveals that all risk assessment that purports to attach numerical probabilities or other measures or grades to assets is questionable. It is not just in the academy that such activities are pursued where conditions are *prima facie* inappropriate. Nevertheless the rating agencies purported to possess the relevant expertise to assign meaningful credit ratings and indeed profited from seeming to do so.

Furthermore, many potential investors were convinced by their results. Certainly a significant expansion in the issuance of structured securities was stimulated by a seeming ability on the part of investment banks to repackage otherwise risky collateral in this way to create supposedly 'safe' assets. Many of the tranches were viewed by investors as almost free of risk, and, as noted, effectively certified as being such by rating agencies.

Clearly, this process of pooling and repackaging of cash-flow-producing financial assets into structured securities, with the intention of their then being sold on to investors, was highly lucrative to many parties involved while the situation lasted; numerous agencies had incentives to facilitate a large flow of loans through the system, whatever their worth. High fee payments (which could not be recovered if things later went wrong) were received by mortgage brokers for providing the initial loans, by investment bankers who repackaged them as securities, by banks and other specialist groups who serviced them, by rating agencies who gave them high ratings, and then by insurance companies who guaranteed the holder of such securities against credit default.

But an additional advantage to the banks of all this lay in the the regulatory arbitrage that the collateralised debt obligations provided. Banks were able to expand leverage [the relationship of their assets (the amount lent out) to their equity or capital] in ways that were previously impossible. This expansion of leverage was a significant factor in allowing the investment banks and others to achieve greater pricing power in their trading activities, underpinning their bubble-inducing activities.[9] This is a complicated story that I can only briefly touch upon here.

Banks, of course, are, for various reasons, required to hold a minimum ratio of 'capital' to total assets, as a buffer against losses. Under the Basel accord,[10] banks are expected to maintain a minimum 8% buffer against a supposedly risk-adjusted measure of their assets (i.e. of their loans to others). Mostly, and particularly in the USA, this minimum ratio is interpreted as a target of 10%.

Clearly, any holding of capital is costly to the banks in the sense that it cannot be lent out at an interest. Yet over the recent past the creation of asset-backed securities of the form discussed above allowed the banks to increase their leverage substantially. It is important to see how this was achieved.

First, the very practice of securitisation made it possible for banks to avoid holding capital through their effectively becoming underwriters that, although making loans, could sell on these same loans to others. In this way assets became removed from the bank's balance sheet, so that formally there was no need for a percentage of their value to be held as a capital reserve (it is because of securitisation that there are significantly fewer deposits in the modern financial system than there are loans).

It is significant for what ensued, however, to note that the banks nevertheless held onto many of the asset-backed securities.

In part this was achieved through many banks creating off-balance sheet 'special purpose vehicles' or 'conduits', including structured investment vehicles. In this process the banks still brought risk back onto themselves, even if not shown on the balance sheet, by ways that are rather complicated and need not be entered into here (see, for example, Gowan, 2009).

Other banks, although also making loans and moving them off balance sheet by way of, securitisation, chose not to create special purpose vehicles but instead to reinvest in triple-A rated tranches of those same or similar products. For the AAA ratings of these securities meant a substantially lower capital requirement (as well as a premium on an apparently riskless security). The Basel accord in fact required of commercial banks that, for AAA-rated securities, the amount of capital held in reserve need only be half of that required for ordinary commercial or mortgage loans.

In addition, in 2004, Hank Paulson persuaded the Securities and Exchange Commission to pass measures relaxing the restrictions on leverage for large investment banks. Thereafter, these firms were allowed to decide their own leverage supposedly on the basis of their risk models (Gowan, 2009, p. 15). This facilitated an even larger leverage than for commercial banks.

8. The crisis

An outcome of all this was that collateralised debt obligations and other derivatives were distributed widely between the dominant institutions in the financial system, in particular the investment banks, as well as to their associated bodies including structured investment vehicles.

As it happens collateralised debt obligations were frequently made up of bundles of hundreds of loans of varied quality. They were perceived as relatively safe because, as noted, the rating agencies gave them a high rating. But in truth, the products so bundled came from hundreds of thousands of unidentifiable sources, and their credit worthiness and cash flow possibilities could not be determined. Being more or less completely opaque to those who bought them, and seemingly often intentionally so,[11] they were, at best, highly risky and in fact extremely precarious.

The situation was not one that could be permanently sustained. And in late 2007 the whole financial network came under strain, as various events, perhaps most notably a suspension of redemptions by BNP Paribas,[12] caused the viability of numerous financial instruments to be questioned. Soon the financial system as a whole was in some turmoil. Ratings of numerous financial assets were revised downwards; even many supposedly low risk super-senior debt tranches of the collateralised debt obligations came to be attributed junk status.

Once the money market and pension funds saw that some of the collateralised debt obligation arrangements were untenable, and then came to realise that there was no way of determining how much of the rest of the stockpile of collateralised debt obligations were more or less worthless, they off-loaded them quickly. The withdrawal of these funds from Wall Street investment banks and associated entities made it impossible for the banks to sustain the collateralised debt obligation 'market', thus contributing to the crash.

When the Wall Street banks tried to off-load their collateralised debt obligations, they found there were no takers for them. So the large banks too became victims of the crisis.

Of course, in theory the banks should not have been holding these assets. *Prima facie* the purpose of securitisation was to spread risk by distributing it away from the investment banks and across a large number of other investors. But the banks, as noted, kept the risky assets themselves. They used securitisation instead to circumvent the requirements on holding capital reserves, and thereby to expand their leverage in order to influence market pricing (whilst individual bankers, being remunerated through cash bonuses for short term gains rather than on the basis of long term profitability, had every incentive to enter into the risks involved).

The practices of credit rating agencies, too, have been a significant contributory factor to the whole situation. Had these agencies not been so willing to give ratings to illiquid, non-transparent, structured financial products such as collateralised debt obligations, and in particular had they not given such clearly unjustifiably high ones (for example had securities initially received the sorts of ratings they now carry), many pension and mutual funds would have been constrained by their own rules from buying them in the first place. These illiquid products are not easily traded on exchanges because there is no meaningful way to evaluate them. Thus, demand for them could not have developed in the way it did, had the rating agencies not provided the backing for them. Yet, as we have seen, the agencies were induced to give AAA ratings to a huge percent of tranches of collateralised debt obligations. And, to repeat, financial analysts, regulators and investors acted as if these ratings were as solid as the AAA ratings given to the safest corporate and government bonds. This allowed the financial boom in mortgage based securities to take place.

9. Background

All this is only a part of the story at best. And it begs many questions. How, for example, were the large investment banks able to generate the conditions described in the first place? An account of this would no doubt focus on the financial developments often systematised as economic or financial globalisation. These developments, notably the fiat dollar system, the ending of capital controls, and the free entry and exit of the major banks or operators in other financial systems, have undermined the capacity of most states to underwrite and control their own financial systems.

The volatility in foreign exchange markets following the breakdown of Bretton Woods, along with financial liberalisation, especially the abandonment of credit controls and the opening up of national financial systems to US operators, afforded an opportunity for a large and profitable expansion of Wall Street trading. It was these developments that, from the mid 1980s, allowed investment banks (traditionally companies that merely assisted other companies in raising financial capital in the capital markets, through such means as the issuance of stocks and bonds) increasingly to switch from trading securities on behalf of clients, to proprietary trading, that is, to actively trading various financial instruments with their own money as opposed to their customers' money, so as to make a profit in this manner for themselves.[13]

Through a series of 'financial innovations', some of which I have touched upon (involving the creation of new products and processes, institutional restructuring and oversight structures), Wall Street investment banks were able largely to escape regulatory constraints and expand their activities and profits significantly. They even constructed a shadow banking system in London alongside the regulated sector, and eventually pushed aside the local agencies and came to dominate the square mile.

I will not go on. Hopefully the brief sketch is enough to convince that the conception of the nature of social reality outlined above is likely relevant to understanding the story. To repeat the cautionary remark noted earlier, the details of the recent period are complex, and a full understanding requires, amongst other things a detailed analysis of structural transformations of the financial sector, along with the various mechanisms whereby the credit/debt was created; however, a focus on these sorts of issues does seem essential to the story.

10. Implications

The latter being so, and given the basic nature of the structures and mechanisms involved, it is clear that the recent crisis situation (like almost any social situation) is something that needs to be understood rather than modelled.

Pace Colander *et al.* (2008), it seems overly heroic to suppose that in order to capture the sorts of developments that occurred, all that is required of modern academic economics is a different type of mathematics, or internal 'theoretical' adjustments like the treating of a model's still isolated atoms as heterogeneous or as forming independent expectations; or focusing on the possibility of multiplicity and evolution of equilibria; or hoping that cointegrated vector autoregression (VAR) models will uncover robust structures within a set of data, and so forth.

At all points in, and stages of development of, the financial system, we are faced not with a ubiquity of regular behavioural patterns underpinned by isolated systems of human atoms, but with the perpetual emergence of novelty, not least at the level of relational structures,[14] underpinning transformed mechanisms and practices. This sort of continual emergence within a relationally structured, interconnected, totality in motion, is seemingly the essence of any financial system within capitalism.

Accepting the sort of framework I have begun to sketch above, it is apparent that the legitimate and feasible goal of economic analysis is not to attempt to mathematically model and perhaps thereby predict crises and such like, but to understand the ever emerging relational structures and mechanisms that render them more or less feasible or likely. Amongst other things, this requires an account of the background conditions against which ongoing developments are taking place. In the current context, this includes understanding how the credit expansion triggered by liberalised financial markets set the conditions for the current situation, and the assortment of developments and mechanisms by which it has come about.

Given this sketch briefly set out, it seems likely that any response to the crisis by those in positions of power will include seeking ways to (i) recreate trust and confidence on the part of creditors and (ii) transform modes of regulation to better control excesses on the part of creditors. Whatever measures will be imposed, greater 'transparency' of financial practices will no doubt be sought. More fundamental questions too may be raised. Should the credit institutions of capitalism facilitate social and economic development or be mainly concerned, as at present, with advancing funds to those concerned merely with making more money? Should nation states seek to regain more control over the banking system, not least as a seemingly more reliable means of supporting the financial system as a whole, and is the latter any longer even feasible in western industrial economies?

As it happens, the sorts of implications and concerns rendered likely given the above basic analysis do seem to be on the minds of many of those in positions of governmental or policy responsibility. But gaining clarity is not helped by debates over whether one form of largely irrelevant mathematical modelling endeavour better expresses the measurable aspects of human economic activity than another form of the same endeavour.

Although my purpose has not been to pinpoint the issue here, it seems likely that a reliance on formalistic modelling is as misleading in the finance industry, not least in the practices of the rating agencies, as it is in the academy. However, a systematic exploration of this issue must await another occasion.

Focusing for now on the economics academy specifically, it remains the case that the latter is dominated by a mainstream project that rarely allows courses to be taught that are not mathematical modelling oriented, even to undergraduates; and performance everywhere is measured only in terms of formalistic modelling output. The latter is regarded as fundamental for research recognition, academic appointments, promotions and everything else. The appropriate response here is clear and does not need spelling out. Suffice it to say that an intellectual opening up of the economics academy would be revolutionary indeed, allowing at least the possibility of genuine debate on all issues and the promise of progress and a freeing up of resources for relevant research that have long been allocated for practices that have little if any grounding or rationale or obvious practical benefit.[15]

11. Final comments: a return to Keynesianism in the academy?

As I write there is, in the economics academy and elsewhere, a renewal of interest in the writings of Keynes. Economic historians and post-Keynesians are indicating and lamenting the decline of Keynesian teaching in universities over the last 30 years or so; policy-oriented economists are seeking to revert to policies described as Keynesian. The *Economist* magazine even recently hosted an online debate on the topic 'We are all Keynesians now'.[16]

My concern is that in all of this the central problem may still be being overlooked. Given these developments, it is perhaps of interest to note that Keynes himself held similar worries to those expressed above concerning the relevance of formalism to the analysis of social phenomena. I have noted that in order to guarantee successes with methods of mathematical deductivist modelling, certain conditions are required that seem rarely to come about. This was also Keynes' view. An assessment that such conditions are unlikely to emerge in the relevant contexts, underpins his critique of aspects of G. E. Moore's ethics (see Lawson, 1993), his analysis of the relevance of probability judgements in his *A Treatise on Probability* (see Lawson, 2003B) and his critique of econometrics (Lawson, 2003A, 2003B). The latter was formulated even after the publication of his *A General Theory*, the book that so many cite as the inspiration for their 'Keynesian' modelling activities.

Given ongoing developments, this seems an opportune moment to recall Keynes' evaluation of the relevance of econometric techniques in particular, resting, as these techniques mostly do, on the method of multiple correlation. The context in which Keynes makes his evaluation is in response to an invitation from the League of Nations in the 1930s to review Tinbergen's early econometric work on business cycles. Here Keynes writes:

> There is first of all the central question of methodology—the logic of applying the method of multiple correlation to unanalysed economic material, which we know to be non-homogeneous through time. If we are dealing with the action of numerically measurable, independent forces, adequately analyzed so that we were dealing with independent atomic factors and between them completely comprehensive, acting with fluctuating relative strength on material constant and homogeneous through time, we might be able to use the method of multiple correlation with some confidence for disentangling the laws of their action. . . .
>
> In fact we know that every one of these conditions is far from being satisfied by the economic material under investigation. . . .
>
> To proceed to some more detailed comments. The coefficients arrived at are apparently assumed to be constant for 10 years or for a larger period. Yet, surely we know that they are not constant. There is no reason at all why they should not be different every year.
>
> (Keynes, 1973, pp. 285–6)

In my own analysis above I have identified, as the relevant conditions for correlation analysis to be guaranteed success, a world of isolated atoms. Perhaps viewing the assumption of isolation as obviously irrelevant, Keynes instead points to the need for a 'comprehensive' list of the required 'atomic factors'. But the underlying assessment is essentially the same (if a subset of all the potentially influential factors cannot be isolated from the others [the objective of a well-controlled experiment] then all the potentially influential factors must be included in any analysis). The point is that in examining the relevance of the method in question Keynes is concerned that it be appropriate to the material being studied, and he concludes that this is typically unlikely.

The hope has to be, then, that if the current crisis results in a shift in the economics academy in the direction of thinking associated with Keynes, it will mostly be a shift not to a form of mathematical modelling identified as Keynesian, but to a form of analysis that takes its leave from Keynes' critique of such modelling, certainly from a critique of any *insistence* that modelling of a mathematical deductivist type is the only way to proceed.

Notes

* This chapter previously published as Tony Lawson, The current economic crisis: its nature and the course of academic economics, *Cambridge Journal of Economics* (2009) 33(4): 759–777, doi:10.1093/cje/bep035 by permission of Oxford University Press/on behalf of The Cambridge Political Economy Society © Cambridge Political Economy Society.
† For helpful comments on an earlier draft of this paper I am grateful to Vinca Bigo, Stephen Pratten and to four anonymous referees of the *Cambridge Journal of Economics*.
1 In consequence, the debate noted at the outset has not itself involved forms of formalistic modelling. Economists (academic or otherwise) have always been prepared to avoid the formalism when invited to comment in the popular press. Very often, though, those academic economists so invited have risen to prominence, and qualify for such invitations, just because of their contributions to mathematical deductivist modelling. And typically they revert to their formalistic practices when returning their more 'serious' academic journal contributions.
2 Although to my knowledge not yet published, the paper has circulated widely and proven very influential in heterodox circles especially, being announced by its authors as the 'outcome of a week of intense discussions'. In fact at the time of writing there are internet sites devoted to its discussion (see http://economistsview.typepad.com/economistsview/2009/02/the-financial-crisis-and-the-systemic-failure-of-academic-economics.html), whilst its 'access statistics' on other sites are significant (see http:// econpapers.repec.org/paper/kudkuiedp/0903.htm)
3 They suggest that the use of formalistic models to quantify and hedge risk has encouraged commercial banks, investment banks and hedge funds to use more leverage (i.e., borrowing money to supplement existing funds for investment in such a way that the potential positive or negative outcome is magnified and/or enhanced) 'as if the very use of the mathematical methods diminished the underlying risk'. Quite reasonably, seemingly echoing recent formulations of Vinca Bigo (2008), these authors warn of the danger of what they call 'control illusion', suggesting that dominant emphasis on apparent 'mathematical rigor and numerical precision of risk management and asset pricing tools' results in a 'tendency to conceal the weaknesses of models and assumptions to those who have not developed them and do not know the potential weakness of the assumptions' (p. 6).
4 This is true of some heterodox economists too. See, for example, the blurb for the clearly formalistic book by Carl Chiarella *et al.* (2009) (see http://www.

routledgeeconomics.com/books/Financial-Markets-and-the-Macroeconomy-isbn9780415771009). Even Steve Keen's otherwise excellent recent analysis of the failure of modern economics to address the relevant issues seems to end up supporting a (different) sort of formalistic modelling: 'Fortunately, behavioural economics provides the beginnings of an alternative vision as to how individuals operate in a market environment, while multi-agent modelling and network theory give us foundations for understanding group dynamics in a complex society. They explicitly emphasise what neoclassical economics has evaded: that aggregation of heterogeneous individuals results in emergent properties of the group which cannot be reduced to the behaviour of any "representative individual" amongst them. These approaches should replace neoclassical microeconomics completely. The changes to economic theory beyond the micro level involve a complete recanting of the neoclassical vision. The vital first step here is to abandon the obsession with equilibrium. The fallacy that dynamic processes must be modelled as if the system is in continuous equilibrium through time is probably the most important reason for the intellectual failure of neoclassical economics. Mathematics, sciences and engineering long ago developed tools to model out of equilibrium processes, and this dynamic approach to thinking about the economy should become second nature to economists' (Keen, 2009, p. 5). At the same time, of course, there are heterodox contributions that avoid the formalistic emphasis. On the current crisis, see, e.g., Victoria Chick (2008), Sheila Dow (2008), and other contributors to the 2008, volume 27 edition of *Contributions to Political Economy*.

5 X can of course represent a vector of events $x_1...x_n$.
6 It may be thought (indeed a referee of an earlier version of this paper suggested) that general equilibrium theorising avoided the condition of isolation that I am identifying. But not really (see Lawson, 2005, 2007). The equilibrium framework typically comprises a number of equations. The theory underpinning each equation presupposes a closed world/system of isolated atoms. Equilibrium is typically a consistency criterion across (or a solution to) the set of equations. Moreover the question posed in such analyses is whether such a consistency property or 'equilibrium' or 'solution' exists as a mathematical feature of the equation system; there is typically nothing in the analysis to suggest that this is an outcome brought about by these individual atoms in the context of a world expressed (per impossible) by the set of equations.
7 In doing so I am well aware that if I do not give any illustrations of the sort of mechanisms to which I refer, I am open to the (all too familiar) charge of being overly abstract and thereby somehow necessarily cut off from the real world. Equally though, if I do attempt an illustration, no matter how partial, I run the risk of encouraging the idea that that the analysis rests on the content of this illustration, so that any subsequent critique of the latter is interpreted as a critique of the overall perspective. Both lines of reasoning are fallacious of course (see the discussion in Fullbrook, 2009, especially pp. 76–7). But given that the economic crisis may be most readers' dominant concern, let me throw caution to the wind and suggest a part of the substantive story of the crisis, hoping that the argument so far elaborated will not be thought to depend on the detail of what follows. For more detail, broadly consistent with the sketch provided here, see, e.g., Jamie Morgan (2009), which is especially comprehensive, or Peter Gowan (2009).
8 On this see also Nasser Saber (1999).
9 In addition bankers, being paid on short-term cash bonuses rather than long-term profitability, had little incentive to make allowances for a future possible scenario in which investors no longer wanted to hold onto the asset-backed securities.

10 A set of agreements set by the Basel Committee on Bank Supervision (so called because this Committee maintains its secretariat at the Bank of International Settlements in Basel, Switzerland and normally meets there) providing recommendations on banking regulations in regards to capital risk, market risk and operational risk. The purpose of the accords is to ensure that financial institutions have enough capital on account to meet obligations and absorb unexpected losses.

11 According to Satyajit Das (2006) 'in the [over the counter] market, dealers [ensure] that the clients do not know the true price of what is traded. The lack of transparency lies at the heart of derivative profitability. You deny the client access to up-to-date prices, use complicated structures that are hard for them to price, and sometimes just rely on their self-delusion' (p. 126). The same point is argued at length by Frank Partnoy (2003).

12 On August 9, 2007, the French BNP Paribas found it could not evaluate the market-to-market values of their securitised investments backed by subprime mortgages in three of their funds. In consequence subscription and redemptions were suspended. A press release by BNP Paribas included the following statement: 'The complete evaporation of liquidity in certain market segments of the US securitisation market has made it impossible to value certain assets fairly regardless of their quality or credit rating. The situation is such that it is no longer possible to value fairly the underlying US ABS assets in the three [...] funds. We are therefore unable to calculate a reliable net asset value ("NAV") for the funds. In order to protect the interests and ensure the equal treatment of our investors, during these exceptional times, BNP Paribas Investment Partners has decided to temporarily suspend the calculation of the net asset value as well as subscriptions/ redemptions, in strict compliance with regulations, for the following funds:

- Parvest Dynamic ABS effective 7 August 2007, 3 pm (Luxembourg time);
- BNP Paribas ABS Euribor and BNP Paribas ABS Eonia effective 7 August 2007, 1 pm (Paris time)'. See http://www.info-financiere.fr/upload/ FCCNS005647_20071016.pdf. In fact BNP's decision followed a similar one a week earlier by German fund manager Union Investment, which suspended redemptions in one of its funds that had exposure to the US subprime market through ABS investments. Union Investment argued that it did not want to be forced to sell assets in a market that would command steep discounts. Within days of BNP Paribas's decision several other European firms followed suit and froze funds.

13 The evolution of proprietary trading by investment banks eventually reached a point whereby the latter employed multiple desks of traders (often considered internal hedge funds within the investment bank, performing in isolation away from client-flow traders) devoted solely to this activity.

14 Indeed, in concentrating on mechanisms central to the crisis above I have perhaps underplayed the relationality of the picture. In the financial system, as elsewhere, everything is tied into everything else. Consider a situation wherein a pension fund P_1 wishes to invest billions of pounds sterling, say, in company C, but is constrained by its rules from doing so because the company only has a rating of BB. However, it can invest in this company if at the same time it takes out insurance (a credit default swap) with an AAA-rated insurance company X against company C defaulting. For, if C does then default, X will, in theory, pay up, and X is considered reliable because it is triple-A rated. Now not only may X not actually have the capital to pay up if company C defaults, but even it if does, very many pension companies, $P_1, P_2 \ldots P_N$, may have simultaneously insured with X to cover themselves if company C defaults. This

set-up is a nice little earner for X as long as C flourishes, but underpinning the situation may well be a debt obligation that X could not meet, should company C default. Even more striking, in order to insure against C with X, it is not necessary to have a stake in C. A hedge fund, H say, may just decide that company C seems likely to fail, and take out an insurance (credit default swap) to cover this happening. That is, H may essentially bet against company C's survival (just as X is essentially betting on the contrary). If C defaults there can clearly be a cascade effect. Even if X can afford to pay out to all companies that have taken out an insurance against this, its resulting loss of funds may cause the rating firms to downgrade it, causing pension funds to pull out and so forth. It will be clear that such a system is extremely highly interdependent, an unstable network in which a significant development in any one part will quickly reverberate throughout.

15 Of course, there are numerous further questions of relevance that cannot be addressed or even touched upon here, not least the question of how the economics academy arrived where it is, and how the situation is sustained. I have pursued these questions elsewhere (see especially Lawson, 2003A, ch. 10). For now it is enough for my purposes to emphasise the nature of the problem, and to caution against repeating the same essentially methodological errors.

16 See http://www.economist.com/debate/overview/140

Bibliography

Bigo, V. 2008. Explaining modern economics (as a microcosm of society), *Cambridge Journal of Economics,* vol. 32, no. 4, 527–54

Chiarella, C., Flaschel, P., Franke, R. and Semmler, W. 2009. *Financial Markets and the Macroeconomy: A Keynesian Perspective,* London, Routledge

Chick, V. 2008. Could the crisis at Northern Rock have been predicted? An evolutionary approach, *Contributions to Political Economy,* vol. 27, 115–24

Colander, D., Föllmer, H., Hass, A., Goldberg, M., Juselius, K., Kirman, A., Lux, T. and Sloth, B. 2008. 'The Financial Crisis and the Systemic Failure of Academic Economics', mimeo, available at http://www.debtdeflation.com/blogs/wp-content/uploads/papers/Dahlem_Report_EconCrisis021809.pdf [date last accessed 1 June 2009]

Das, S. 2006. *Traders, Guns and Money: Knowns and Unknowns in the Dazzling World of Derivatives,* Harlow, Prentice Hall

Dow, S. 2008. Mainstream methodology, financial markets and global political economy, *Contributions to Political Economy,* vol. 27, 13–30

Fitch Ratings. 2007. 'Inside the Ratings: What Credit Ratings Mean', August, available at http:// www.bankwatchratings.com/descargas/ratings.pdf [date last accessed 1 June 2009]

Fullbrook, E. 2009. *Ontology and Economics: Tony Lawson and his Critics,* London and New York, Routledge

Gowan, P. 2009. Editorial. Crisis in the heartland: consequences of the new Wall Street system, *New Left Review,* January/February, 5–29

Keen, S. 2009. Mad, bad and dangerous to know, *Real-world Economics Review,* no. 49, 12 March, 2–7, available at http://www.paecon.net/PAEReview/issue49/Keen49.pdf [date last accessed 1 June 2009]

Keynes, J. M. 1973. *The Collected Writings of John Maynard Keynes,* Vol. XIV, The General Theory and After: Part II Defence and Development, St Andrews, Royal Economic Society

Lawson, T. 1993. Keynes and Conventions, *Review of Social Economy,* vol. LI, Summer, 174–201

Lawson, T. 1997. *Economics and Reality,* London and New York, Routledge

Lawson, T. 2003A. *Reorienting Economics,* London and New York, Routledge

Lawson, T. 2003B. Keynes's realist orientation, in Runde, J. and Mizuhara, S. (eds), *Perspectives on the Philosophical Underpinnings of Keynes's Economics: Probability, Uncertainty and Convention,* London and New York, Routledge

Lawson, T. 2005. The (confused) state of equilibrium analysis in modern economics: an (ontological) explanation, *Journal for Post Keynesian Economics,* vol. 27, no. 3, Spring, 423–44

Lawson, T. 2006. The nature of heterodox economics, *Cambridge Journal of Economics,* vol. 30, no. 2, 483–507

Lawson, T. 2007. Tensions in modern economics. The case of equilibrium analysis, in Mosini, V. (ed.), *Equilibrium in Economics: Scope and Limits,* London and New York, Routledge

Lawson, T. 2009A. Heterodox economics and pluralism, pp. 93–129 in Fullbrook, E. (ed.), *Ontology and Economics: Tony Lawson and his Critics,* London and New York, Routledge

Lawson, T. 2009B. On the nature and roles of formalism in economics, pp. 189–231 in Fullbrook, E. (ed.), *Ontology and Economics: Tony Lawson and his Critics,* London and New York, Routledge

Marx, K. 1974. *Capital: Volume 1, Frederick Engels,* London, Lawrence and Wishart

Morgan, J. 2009. *Private Equity Finance: Rise and Repercussions,* Basingstoke, Palgrave Macmillan

Partnoy, F. 2003. *Infectious Greed,* New York, Times Books

Saber, N. 1999. *Speculative Capital: The Invisible Hand of Global Finance,* London, Pearson Education

Sharpe, W. 1964. Capital asset prices: a theory of market equilibrium under conditions of risk, *The Journal of Finance,* vol. XIX, no. 3, 425–42

6 Contemporary economics and the crisis

The fundamental failing of modern economics, or at least of its dominant mainstream project, is not that it was unable successfully to predict the recent crisis but that it is ill-equipped to illuminate much that happens in the economy at any time.

The latter is an assessment that I have advanced and defended on numerous occasions (e.g., Lawson, 1997, 2003). Contemporary mainstream economics relies almost exclusively on certain methods of mathematical deductivist modelling; indeed it insists that formalistic modelling is the proper way to do economics. My contention, defended elsewhere at length, is simply that these methods are in fact largely irrelevant to addressing social reality, and it is the insistence that such methods be everywhere utilised that accounts for the continuing sorry intellectual state of much of the modern discipline.

Recently, I advanced a framework of analysis that, I suggested, is generally relevant for social analysis, including understanding the nature of the recent 'crisis' (Lawson, 2009a). In the course of developing the arguments of the paper containing that framework, I took the opportunity to critically reference a contribution by David Colander, Hans Föllmer, Armin Hass, Michael Goldberg, Katerina Juselius, Alan Kirman, Thomus Lux, and Brigitte Sloth (2008). I did so because the latter paper appeared to me to send the signal that the crisis teaches us that we need to develop different versions of the mathematical models than those hitherto used to guide policy. Although the Colander et al (2008) paper, as might be expected from such a collection of authors, is insightful, the noted response, I believe, is not the best one. Because the paper seemed to have been influential, not least in heterodox circles, I used it as a kind of foil to set out my alternative account. I was, and remain, particularly concerned that the very recent apparent rise in popularity of seemingly radical substantive theories, most especially those that are counted as Keynesian, should not be used merely to develop alternative mathematical models to those previously dominant.

If my arguments about the limitations of formalism are correct, it follows that the situation of modern economics represents a very significant misallocation of resources – almost all are given over to the mathematical modelling project. Yet the seriousness of this unhappy state of affairs seems still to go largely unappreciated. So when the editor of this journal, Edward Fullbrook, invited me to produce a short paper that covered some of the same ground as in Lawson (2009a), I was happy enough to comply. However the invite was rather unusual in its details. It proposed a debate of sorts between myself and Colander et al covering those particular aspects on which we appear to disagree. Further, this debate was to take the form not of a direct engagement but of each set of contributors marshalling or summarising arguments of our earlier papers to address the statement below formulated by Fullbrook himself. This then explains the orientation of what follows. The statement in question runs as follows.

> *It is agreed that the current economic crisis has shown that the standard models of academic economics are seriously wanting. Should the main emphasis of reform be on developing new formal models or to an opening up of economics to methods other than traditional modelling?*

I start by considering the evaluation of the current situation contained in the first sentence of Fullbrook's formulation.

> It is agreed that the current economic crisis has shown that the standard models of academic economics are seriously wanting.

I assume that Edward Fullbrook uses the category of 'standard models' here just because, and in the same way that, it figures in the contribution of Colander et al (2008). These latter authors introduce the notion when writing: "The implicit view behind standard models is that markets and economies are inherently stable and they only temporarily get off track" (p. 2). In consequence, these authors argue, the standard models are incapable of successfully addressing the crisis.

Now whether or not certain specific models warrant being distinguished as 'standard' on the basis of their economic content, a feature of the situation of academic economics that is undeniable is that for a long time now the category 'modelling' has become synonymous with mathematical deductivist reasoning. The latter association, if questionable methodologically, is indeed a modern 'standard'. Thus any set of 'standard models' that Colander et al (2008) may identify according to the substantive content will be examples of mathematical deductive formulations.

My contention, explained and defended below, is that the fundamental problem of modern economics lies in its emphasis on formalistic modelling per se. So from this perspective, Fullbrook's evaluation above, or the assessment of Colander et al upon which Fullbrook seems to be drawing,

132 Contemporary economics and the crisis

is somewhat misleading, and in fact encourages an overly narrow focus and response.

I do not dispute the evaluation that the specific models that Colander et al (2008) designate standard 'are seriously wanting'; this is hardly contentious. The point, rather, is that just about all economic outcomes bearing on these (and any other sets of mathematical deductivist) models have indicated this for years, the economic crisis no more than anything else. And the reason (I will argue) is precisely the inappropriateness of the mathematical form of modelling per se as a general method of social analysis.

From this perspective, my concern is that by putting the emphasis on specific so-called standard (mathematical) models, the response (to the failure to illuminate the crisis) that is encouraged is that it is sufficient to put resources into developing alternative (less 'standard') mathematical-deductivist models (with the hope of accommodating [and perhaps even predicting] crises specifically).

Of course, the noted likely response of developing alternative formalistic models is only encouraged rather than necessitated by Fullbrook's and Colander et al's formulations. As the second part of Fullbrook's statement explicitly recognises, in practice the option of developing alternative approaches that do not take the form of mathematical modelling is not precluded. But with the culture and reward structure of modern economics so oriented to mathematical modelling, the formulation easily promotes precisely the noted reaction.

This indeed is the message imparted by the paper by Colander et al (2008). As I am supposed to be debating with these authors let me elaborate this assessment a little. There is a tendency in modern economic methodology (that I regard as unfortunate) which is to seek wherever possible to please all sides (or anyway to avoid upsetting any side) to any debate. The outcome, typically, is that either nothing or everything is supported, so that methodological advance is rarely made. I am not sure if being part of this tendency is the intention of Colander et al. Certainly, I note that they avoid stating explicitly or directly that any new approach is best formulated in terms of models interpreted as forms of mathematical deductivist reasoning. And although they certainly display support for modelling activities, I suppose that if pressed (especially if addressing a heterodox audience) they might suggest that they do not equate modelling to mathematical reasoning. But whatever the intention of Colander et al, or the interpretation they may prefer to put on their piece, I believe the signal they actually send, given the prevailing context, is support for yet more mathematical modelling. Let me indicate some of the reasons why I say this.

First, and most noticeably, having focussed on the failings of 'standard models', models that are inherently formalistic (the two assumptions Colander et al criticise specifically, namely rational expectations and the representative agents, are formulated precisely to render mathematical models tractable), Colander et al never raise the possibility that formalism in the academy (as opposed to the finance industry) may itself be the problem. For anyone at all aware of modern methodological discussion, this omission in itself is rather striking, and certainly telling.

Second, Colander et al adopt a prominent mainstream strategy and indeed mainstream language in ridiculing, rather than seriously engaging, alternative practices or 'remedies' to those employing 'standard' or other forms of models. As is well known, mathematical modellers tend to dismiss any contribution that is not formulated mathematically in derisory terms, such as 'hand waving'. This is the precisely the recourse of Colander et al:

> Ironically, as the crisis has unfolded, economists have had no choice but to abandon their standard models and to produce hand-waving common-sense remedies. Common-sense advice, although useful, is a poor substitute for an underlying model that can provide much-needed guidance for developing policy and regulation.
>
> (p. 2)

The authors may or may not want to commit themselves on the meaning of the category 'model', but, as I say, expressing support for undefined 'underlying models' that are contrasted to hand waving in the context of modern academic economic discussion certainly encourages the reading that yet more mathematical deductivist reasoning is being advocated.

Third, the various specific constructive suggestions advanced are mostly (and most easily) interpretable as suggestions for revised formalistic models or formalistic modelling strategies and techniques. Thus, Colander et al suggest a possible need for "a different type of mathematics than that which is generally used now by many prominent economic models"(p. 3); that "considerable progress has been made by moving to more refined models with e.g., 'fat tailed' Levy processes as their driving factors" (p. 6); they argue for models that allow "one to study out-of-equilibrium dynamics and adaptive adjustments" adding that "Such dynamics could reveal the possibility of multiplicity and evolution of equilibria" (p. 9). They also conjecture, that "If one accepts that the dispersed economic activity of many economic agents could be described by statistical laws, one might even take stock of methods from statistical physics to model dynamic economic systems" (p. 10). In terms of method, they "recommend a more data-driven methodology" in which "data-analytical tools and specification tests" are employed, adding that "clustering techniques such as projection pursuit [. . .]might provide alternatives for the identification of key relationships and the reduction of complexity on the way from empirical measurement to theoretical models" (p. 11); furthermore, "Cointegrated VAR models could provide an avenue towards identification of robust structures within a set of data" (p. 11), adding that:

> A chain of specification tests and estimated statistical models for simultaneous systems would provide a benchmark for the subsequent development of tests of models based on economic behavior: significant and robust relations within a simultaneous system would provide empirical regularities that one would attempt to explain, while the quality of fit of the statistical benchmark would offer a confidence band for more ambitious models.
>
> (p. 11)

And so on. I will not go on, not just because we may not have a dispute here (Colander et al may or may not resist my interpretation of them as ultimately contributing to sustaining the formalistic emphasis), but more significantly because, as I say, the primary concern of my earlier paper was not the contribution of Colander et al anyway, but the possible responses of heterodox economists.

However, whether or not their support for yet more formalism is a signal that Colander et al intended to send, I do regard it as a significant weakness of their paper that it fails to criticise explicitly the modern emphasis on formalism, or even to acknowledge the possibility that formalism per se may be the source of the failings of the modern discipline.

But to return to the main theme here, my worry was, and remains, that, as the crisis seems to allow a more significant voice than hitherto to heterodox lines of thinking, advocates of the latter may succumb to the temptation to focus on producing merely a revised set of mathematical deductivist models. Thus, for example, I worry that post Keynesians say may respond to the challenges before us by mostly advocating a different, supposedly Keynesian, form of mathematical-deductivist modelling.

Heterodoxy and mathematical modelling

The sense in which various traditions like post Keynesians are heterodox is precisely that they reject the mainstream or orthodox doctrine that methods of mathematical modelling should be used more or less always, and by all of us, whatever the context (I have defended this conception of heterodoxy at length elsewhere – for example Lawson, 2006). And heterodox economists have repeatedly rejected the particular models produced by the mainstream because they are recognised as being unrealistic in some significant way.

However, it is clear from a perusal of the range of heterodox writing and thinking that not all heterodox economists accept that the central problems of modern economics stem from the activity of mathematically modelling social phenomena per se. Nor is there uniformity within heterodoxy over the nature of the problem of unrealisticness in mainstream modelling.

Some heterodox economists seem to focus on the unrealisticness of mainstream conclusions; others on the wildly unrealistic nature of mainstream assumptions. Some economists in the former group seem to suppose that the realisticness or otherwise of assumptions is not really an issue; that even if a model is based on accepted-as-unrealistic assumptions, so long as it produces acceptable (for example, supposedly Keynesian) conclusions, then the whole analysis is satisfactory, and provides additional support for the preferred (because already accepted as true) conclusions. Economists in the second group seem to suppose that it is possible to construct mathematical deductive economic models that are capable of being explanatorily successful once, and whenever, the economic theorising is transformed in a manner that is more acceptable to the thinking of members of heterodox traditions.

The position adopted by the former group is, in truth, little more than crass opportunism. For if the constraint of employing only claims regarded as realistic is lifted, and I will argue that pursuance of the project of constructing mathematical-deductivist models of social phenomena more or less necessitates this, then for any preferred conclusion X, it is always a trivial matter to find a set of assumptions that facilitate a model consistent with X. I dealt with this issue in the earlier paper Lawson (1997a) and will not take space doing so again here. But it should be enough to point out that, so long as assumptions accepted-as-unrealistic are tolerated, it is not only trivially easy to choose assumptions that facilitate the construction of a model that is consistent with some preferred or desired or believed conclusion X, it is equally trivially easy to produce assumptions that facilitate the construction of a model consistent with the conclusion 'not X'. If a supporter of X thinks the procedure is somehow valid or useful in the first case, he or she must accept this is so in the second case too. Of course, the move is illegitimate in both cases. If we want to generate support for X it is necessary to do so on the basis of theorising and explanatory work that is not (regarded by everyone as) unrealistic.

So I turn, here, to consider the second possible response that concerns me, namely the allocating of available resources to yet more mathematical modelling activity, albeit of a sort that seeks to employ a different form (or set of theories) of economics. I do not suggest that such a response could never be the correct one (I return to this below). Certainly I do not suggest that post Keynesians or whoever should never try and develop insightful models (again I return to this below). But there are reasons to suspect that this response is unlikely very often to prove especially successful or useful. Let me briefly indicate what they are.

The problem with mathematical-deductive modelling of social phenomena

My basic contention here is that with a bit of reflection both on the nature of social reality, and also on the sorts of conditions that must hold for the mathematical methods in question to have utility, we can not only better understand and explain the failings of the latter methods in the hands of modern mainstream economists, but also recognise that such methods are unlikely very often to provide insight no matter what substantive economic theories are used in their construction.

Simply put the sorts of mathematical deductivist methods in question are restricted in their applicability to closed systems, meaning those in which event regularities or correlations occur, whereas not only have such closures been found rarely to occur in the social realm, but also we have good reason to suppose they will remain uncommon.

In fact, closures are relatively uncommon even in the natural sciences. As it happens, outside astronomy, most of the event regularities known to natural science occur in conditions of controlled laboratory experimentation – or experimental closures. They arise when an experimenter succeeds in isolating/insulating an intrinsically stable mechanism from the effects of countervailing factors. Under such conditions a regularity can be produced correlating the triggering of the mechanism with its unimpeded effects.

Two conditions for guaranteeing a closure are apparent in this experimental case. The first is that we are dealing with a mechanism that is intrinsically constant. The second is that a situation can be engineered ensuring that this mechanism, if triggered, acts in relative isolation. We can refer to these as conditions as respectively the intrinsic and extrinsic closure conditions.

Although, other, perhaps very different, sets of sufficiency conditions are possible in principle, it is difficult to imagine what they might be in practice; and more to the point it is these two conditions – the intrinsic and extrinsic closure conditions – that mainstream economists mostly, if implicitly, seek to satisfy in their theorising around their economic models.

Of course whereas experimental natural scientists work laboriously to achieve the isolation of a relevant mechanism, economic modellers heroically assume that such isolations of intrinsically constant causal factors occur quite spontaneously in the social realm, and indeed are even ubiquitous.

However, it is easy enough to see that the phenomena of social reality by and large are such that the two conditions identified are unlikely very often to be satisfied.

Consider the extrinsic condition first. Instead of existing in isolation almost all social phenomena are in fact constituted in relation to each other. It is easy enough in modern capitalism to see the internal relationality of markets and money and firms and governments and households, etc; all depend on and presuppose each other. It would be futile and meaningless to seek to isolate any one from the influence of the others. But human individuals as social beings are likewise formed in relation to others. All slot into positions, where all positions are constituted in relation to other positions. Thus employer and employee presuppose each other, as do teacher and student, landlord/lady and tenant, parent and child, gendered man and woman, and so on. We all slot into, and are moulded through the occupancy of, a multitude of such positions, deriving real interests from them, and drawing upon whatever powers or rights and obligations are associated with those positions. So social reality is an interdependent, network, it is an internally related totality, not a set of phenomena each existing in relative isolation.

Nor does the hope of satisfying the intrinsic condition for a closure seem any more promising. For everything social (that set of phenomena whose existence depends on us) is constantly being transformed. Think of a language such as English. At any point in time it exists as a (largely unacknowledged) resource to be drawn upon in our speech acts and so forth. But through the sum total of all people simultaneously drawing on it, the language is (largely unintentionally) reproduced and in part transformed. It thus exists as a process, as something that is constantly being reproduced and transformed through practice. This is its mode of being; it is intrinsically dynamic and subject to transformation. But a moment's reflection reveals that all social phenomena share this mode of being: universities, towns, pollution, society at large, each and every organisation, our positions and their associated powers, our embodied personalities and everything else. So a satisfaction of the intrinsic condition for a closure again is something not to be taken for granted.

Of course social reality is more complex still. It contains meaning and value and so forth. But enough has been said to account for the general empirical failings of modern mainstream economics with its emphasis on mathematical modelling (as well as its employment of bizarre assumptions such as rational expectations, representative agents, two commodity worlds and all the rest that are maintained). This general failure is a result of the constant endeavour to present the phenomena of social reality that are really open, relational and processual as if instead they are closed, intrinsically constant and effectively isolated or insulated from each other.

So what is the response? This brings me to the second part of Fullbrook's formulation, to his question following the initial evaluation. It reads:

> Should the main emphasis of reform be on developing new formal models or to an opening up of economics to methods other than traditional modelling?

Irrespective of the arguments set out above, and no matter how successful or unsuccessful the project of mathematical deductivist modelling, the case can be made for 'an opening up of economics to methods other than traditional modelling'. The current dogmatic constraint on how we all can proceed is undesirable whatever the state of the discipline were found to be in terms of explanatory successes. If mathematical-deductivist methods were found to be useful at providing insight I suspect most of us would choose to use them. But it is vital to a healthy, intellectual, progressive enterprise that the ability so to choose does actually exist.

However, not only is such choice mostly absent, but so are the successes at providing insight. And I have suggested an explanation as to why. In the light of analysis set out, I not only support 'an opening up of economics to methods other than traditional modelling' but I believe too that this should be the 'main emphasis of reform'. Indeed, my central purpose here is precisely to caution against the usual response to failure which is to insist that the main emphasis of reform be on developing new formal models.

As it happens I am pessimistic that the sorts of mathematical-deductive methods that economists employ will ever provide much insight, for the reasons given above. However, let me emphasise that I do not thereby suggest that the development of new formal models and so forth be in any sense or form precluded. I support any situation where each individual is able to follow his or her own convictions in choosing which research path to follow. I am certainly not wishing to suggest that we replace one form of dogmatism by another. Although I am convinced by the analysis above, it could yet be found to quite wrong. And even if it is correct, the intrinsic and extrinsic conditions, as I have acknowledged, are only sufficient conditions for a closed system supporting an event regularity to emerge. A failure to satisfy them does not rule out the possibility of an emergent closure.

Indeed, an event regularity could even arise by accident. Though seemingly unlikely, it is impossible to rule out a priori a situation in which numerous complex, different and changing, observable and unobservable, transient and less transient, causal factors combine in such a way that, over a period of time and/or space, an event regularity is observed.

This seemingly unlikely outcome, in effect, is what macro economists hope for when they seek correlations in highly aggregated time series or cross-section data, where the different data points are produced in often quite different conditions and contexts. In such cases, the exercise (often systematised through theorising a representative agent) is based on little more than a heroic expression of faith, or maybe hope. Ultimately, just about all applied modelling endeavour utilises data that are aggregated to some extent and drawn from very different contexts, being produced by often very different causal mechanisms. Thus the recourse to little more than unreasoned faith and optimism is a pervasive characteristic of the modern discipline quite generally. Even so, my point here is that economists proceeding in this fashion may yet strike it lucky. This cannot be ruled out in theory. So let the (mathematical) modellers keep trying.

But in the case of certain alternative approaches to such formalism, there is, in addition to faith and hope, both reason to expect explanatory successes especially where methods are tailored to conditions actually found to characterise the social realm, as well as evidence that such methods have already been fruitful (see Lawson, 2009b). So there is reason for the alternative approaches to be given some serious attention.

Institutional considerations

So far I have concentrated mostly on what might be termed the intellectual failing of modern economics, namely the misconception that utilising methods of mathematical modelling are a grounded, the best, and/or the only proper way of proceeding. But there is an additional, institutional, problem that explains why the failings of mathematical modelling have not led to a flourishing of alternative approaches, despite the demonstrated explanatory fruitfulness of some of the latter. This is simply that those with power allow almost no leeway for the undertaking of alternative approaches to formalistic modelling, despite the repeated failings of the latter, and indeed the demonstrated successes of alternatives (see e.g., Lawson, 2009b or various contributions to Fullbrook, 2009). Those with power act as very restrictive gate keepers.

This is a very significant obstacle to intellectual advance. As already noted I do believe that individuals should have the real choice to proceed as they see best fit. And I have no desire to see experimentation with formalism formally excluded. But I also suspect that if the noted dogmatism were overcome, if this gate keeping were to end, the emphasis on formalism would likely change very quickly without any 'legislation'. It seems to me anyway that many economists use mathematical deductivist methods just because this is what is required of them, not because of any deep belief in their relevance or utility. As is widely recognised, it is mostly only modellers that get appointments in university economic faculties; it is mostly only such modellers that get promoted; it is mostly only modellers that get research grants from certain sources; it is mostly only PhDs and post doctorate research taking the form of mathematical deductive modelling that get funded; it is mostly only this sort of research that can get published in core journals, etc. (This is presumably the reason too that many methodologists mostly hold back from criticising the mathematical emphasis.) Take away the insistence that only mathematical deductive modelling be supported and rewarded in the economics academy and I strongly suspect the composition of academic identities and practices will change very quickly, even if most of the current individual practitioners stay in place.

Of course, all of us should strive to maintain standards and seek to justify what we do. But this is precisely what the mainstream project currently fails to do. Mainstream modellers almost never justify the mathematical orientation of their endeavour, no matter what the extent of the failures of the latter. Nor is the modelling emphasis even questioned. When the results achieved are not successful, the response is almost always either to find a different set of questions to tackle, or to develop a different set of models, or modelling techniques, and so forth.

I might add that if some individual sincerely believes that there is good reason why experimenting with formalistic models is best not only for her or him, but for all of us too, that we all ought to be doing only mathematics, I am in favour of their receiving a platform; I support their being heard and accommodated generally. They may even be right, though I currently strongly doubt it for the reasons set out. The problem is not the arguing for a methodological position but the current refusal of the mainstream modellers to engage in methodological debate (whilst simultaneously withholding opportunities and resources from those with different methodological convictions).

Of course, the noted intellectual failing and the institutional problem of modern economics are connected. The latter no doubt is a response to the former (as well as a cause of its continuance). If modern mainstream economics were widely successful in providing insight then I suspect its proponents would be more susceptible to interaction, debate, openness and tolerance of others. But at this point in time institutional power is about all the mainstream practitioners have in their favour. So it is perhaps not unintelligible, if a little disappointing, that they should choose to wield it in such a defensive manner.

I might finally stress that in arguing for a more intellectual forum in the economics academy, in suggesting that we replace methodological dogmatism with a more modest pluralistic orientation, I am proselytising not against rigour, but against the narrow supposition that it only takes one form. The position I defend does not even constitute an argument against the study of social phenomena being scientific in the sense of natural science. To the contrary, it grounds an argument that such study can be so scientific in the relevant sense, once alternative practices are facilitated; although that is another story (see e.g. Lawson, 1997, 2003).

Conclusion

The project of mathematical modelling in modern economics has a long history of failure. This is now widely acknowledged, even amongst mainstream economists (see Lawson, 2003, chapter 1). Less widely emphasised is a repeated pattern of response to this failure. It runs in two parts, involving first an evaluation, and then an inference. The evaluation is that 'this specific set of mathematical models has performed badly because of that specific set of problems'. The standard inference is that the 'solution comes with finding an alternative set of mathematical models that overcome that specific set of problems'. The proposals of Colander et al for dealing with the phenomenon of the recent crisis are easily interpreted as merely the latest version of this 'solution'.

The concern I have with the evaluations and responses in question is that they detract from deeper ongoing problems. The first of these is that the sorts of practices of mathematical modelling that economists adopt seem continually to have failed to provide insight, and there are reasons to expect that things will not get better; that the methods themselves are inappropriate to social analysis. The second problem is that the economics academy is dominated by a mainstream group that posses, and utilises, a power to ensure that almost no approach except mathematical modelling is encouraged, published in core journals or otherwise rewarded.

My guess is that if an intellectual opening up of the academy can be achieved, an improvement in the relevance and utility of economics will quickly emerge as a matter of course. My concern is that so long as every failure is put down to limitations of a specific set of (formalistic) models, the explanatory weaknesses of the formalistic modelling process per se will continue to go relatively unchallenged, thus postponing yet further the day when the economics academy is transformed into the sort of open, honest and tolerant environment that seems essential for a generally successful economics to emerge.

References

Colander, David, Hans Föllmer, Armin Hass, Michael Goldberg, Katerina Juselius, Alan Kirman, Thomus Lux, and Brigitte Sloth (2008), "The Financial Crisis and the Systemic Failure of Academic Economics", unpublished mimeo, available at: http://www.debtdeflation.com/blogs/wp-content/uploads/papers/Dahlem_Report_EconCrisis021809.pdf

Fullbrook, Edward (editor) (2009) *Ontology and Economics: Tony Lawson and his Critics,* London and New York: Routledge.

Lawson, Tony (1997) *Economics and Reality,* London and New York: Routledge.

Lawson, Tony (2003) *Reorienting Economics,* London and New York: Routledge.

Lawson, Tony (2006) 'The nature of heterodox economics', *Cambridge Journal of Economics,* 30(2): 483–507.

Lawson, Tony (2009a) 'The current economic crisis: its nature and the course of academic economics', *Cambridge Journal of Economics,* 33(4): 759–77.

Lawson, Tony (2009b) 'Applied economics, contrast explanation and asymmetric information', *Cambridge Journal of Economics,* 33(3): 405–19.

7 Mathematical modelling and ideology in the economics academy: competing explanations of the failings of the modern discipline?

Introduction

One positive consequence of the ongoing economic crisis is that the intellectual malaise of the modern academic discipline of economics is becoming ever more widely recognised. Economics is a discipline that is marked by significant explanatory failure stemming from wildly unrealistic formulations, and has been for many years now (see Lawson, 2003, chapter 1).

The reference to specifically academic economics here is not incidental; I want to stress that throughout the discussion my concern is not economics in all its forms or manifestations but economics as it is pursued within the modern academy, which after all is the site from which most strands of the subject emanate.

Elsewhere I have put forward an explanation of the noted academic malaise that draws significantly on ontological theorising, i.e., on theorising the *nature* of (social) reality. Because my focus here is with examining the power of, and support for, an alternative explanation I do not want to rehearse my own position at length. But in brief, the explanation I elsewhere maintain is that the fundamental problem of modern economics is that methods are repeatedly applied in conditions for which they are not appropriate (see Lawson, 1997; 2003). Specifically, modern academic economics is dominated by a mainstream tradition whose defining characteristic is an *insistence* that certain methods of mathematical modelling be more or less always employed in the analysis of economic phenomena, and are so in conditions for which they are not suitable.

Fundamental to my argument is an assessment that the application of mathematics involves more than merely the introduction of a formal language. Of relevance here is recognition that mathematical methods and techniques are essentially tools. And as with any other tools (pencils, hammers, drills, scissors), so the sorts of mathematical methods which economists wield (functional relations, forms of calculus, etc.) are useful under some sets of conditions and not others.

The specific conditions required for the sorts of mathematical methods that economists continually wield to be generally applicable, I have shown, are a ubiquity of (deterministic or stochastic) closed systems. A closed system is simply one in which an event regularity occurs. Notice that these closures are as much presupposed or required by the 'newer' approaches to mathematical economics, those often referred to as non-linear modelling, complexity modelling, agent-based modelling, model simulations, and so on (including those developed under the head of behavioural or neuroeconomics), as they are by the more traditional forms of micro, macro and econometric modelling.

The most obvious scenario in which a prevalence of such closures would be expected is a world 1) populated by sets of atomistic individuals or entities (an atom here being an entity that exercises its own separate, independent, and invariable effect, whatever the context); where 2) the atoms of interest exist in relative isolation (so allowing the effects of the atoms of interest to be deducible/predictable by barring the effects of potentially interfering factors). Not surprisingly the latter two (ontological) presuppositions are easily shown to be implicit in almost all contemporary economic modelling contributions (see Lawson, 2003, chapter 1).

However, explicit, systemic and sustained (ontological) analysis of the nature of social reality reveals the social domain *not* to be everywhere composed of closed systems of sets of isolated atoms. Rather social reality is found to be an open, structured realm of emergent phenomena that, amongst other things, are processual (being constantly reproduced and transformed through the human practices on which they depend), highly internally related (meaning constituted through [and not merely linked by] their relations with each other – e.g., employer/employee or teacher/student relations), value-laden and meaningful, amongst much else (see Lawson, 2003 chapter 2).

Clearly if social phenomena are highly internally related they do *not* each exist in isolation. And if they are processual in nature, being continually transformed through practice, they are *not* atomistic. So the emphasis on the sorts of mathematical modelling methods that economists employ necessarily entails the construction of economic narratives – including the sorts of axioms and assumptions made and hypotheses entertained – that, at best, are always but highly distorted accounts of the complex phenomena of the real open social system (for lengthy elaborations of all this see e.g., Lawson, 1997; 2003; Edward Fullbrook, 2009). It is thus not at all surprising that mainstream contributions are found continually to be so unrealistic and explanatorily limited.

Employing the term *deductivism* to denote the thesis that closed systems are essential to social scientific explanation (whether the event regularities, correlations, uniformities, laws, etc., are either *a priori* constructions or *a posteriori* observations), I conclude that *the fundamental source of the*

144 *Mathematical modelling and ideology*

discipline's numerous, widespread and long lived problems and failings is precisely the emphasis placed upon forms of mathematical deductivist reasoning[1].

So much for my own assessment. Many heterodox economists clearly demur, and most of these seemingly hold to the view that a superior explanation of the state of modern economics is provided by focusing on the prevalence of a form of political-economic ideology. The real source of all the failings of the mainstream academic project, according to advocates of this view, is that ideology about how the economic system works gets in the way of explanatorily successful or realistic analysis.

Ideology is a term I have rarely employed, as various heterodox critics have pointed out[2]. Here I address the claim that ideology provides a better, or even an alternative, explanation of the modern academic economics' malaise to the one I have advanced and have briefly sketched above. In so doing I take the opportunity to explore the role of ideology in the practices and output of the modern economics academy more generally.

Ideology

The term *ideology* was seemingly coined by Count Destutt de Tracy in the late 18th century to define a "science of ideas". Few interpret the category in this way today, however. Almost universally, the current understanding is that the term ideology refers *not* to the study, but rather to the content, of certain sets of ideas, along with their consequences.

Thereafter, however, interpretations diverge, with very many alternatives to be found in the contemporary literature[3]. Even so, with a little systematising I think most interpretations can be seen either to presuppose, or to reduce to special cases of, two broad systemic conceptions. These are:

1. $Ideology_1$: a relatively unchallenged set of (possibly distorted or misleading) background ideas that every society or community possesses which forms the basis of, or significantly informs, general opinion or 'common sense', a basis that remains somewhat invisible to most of its members, appearing as 'neutral', resting on preconceptions that are largely unexamined. A consequence is that viewpoints significantly out of line with these background beliefs are intuitively seen as radical, nonsensical or extreme no matter what may be the actual content of their vision.
2. $Ideology_2$: a set of ideas designed, or anyway intentionally employed, in order to justify, preserve or reinforce some existing state of affairs, where this state of affairs is preferred, perhaps because it facilitates or legitimates various advantages for some dominant or privileged group, and where these ideas mostly work in the manner described by way of intentionally masking or misrepresenting the nature of reality.

Whether or not these two conceptions are sufficiently comprehensive with regard to the literature on ideology in general, as far I can discern they do cover the interpretations found in the economics literature (and are clearly apparent in the contributions of those who emphasise my apparent neglect of the role of ideology in modern economics). They also cover the viewpoints of many who never mention the term ideology. I should note, though, that those who adopt such a position, including those who explicitly emphasise ideology, frequently refer to (what I am calling) modern mainstream economics as neoclassical. The latter is again a term I rarely use, though I take it for the purposes of the current paper that both expressions are intended to refer to the same project, even if there is disagreement as to its nature.

The ideology theorists

According to those in effect employing the first conception of ideology, economic theory is found wanting just because, or where, its proponents act upon, but fail seriously to reflect upon, or to challenge, or to treat as other than a given, a set of background intuitions/ideas of *efficiently functioning markets* or some such. It is the latter intuitions/ideas that constitute the content of the ideology in question. Mainstream theories, it is held, are grounded in such intuitions; and it is just because they are inadequate to real world processes but so unquestioningly and almost unthinkingly maintained, that economics goes so wrong.

According to those instead employing the second interpretation, mainstream economists are viewed as the agents (rather than subjects) of ideology, advancing it with the purpose of sustaining the underlying economic system – so that the proposed *explanation* of the form of the mainstream lack of explanatory insight and so forth is just this desire to perpetuate the economic *status quo* using theories that are knowingly inappropriate to it.

These two contentions, though connected, are clearly not identical. In the first case, mainstream economists are viewed as the hapless dupes of the prevailing ideology. In the second case, these same economists knowingly and indeed conspiratorially provide, maintain and promote the ideology. Let me briefly give examples of each interpretation.

Ideology$_1$

A version of the former mainstream-as-manifestation-of-background-ideology interpretation is advanced for example by Bernard Guerrien (2004). Criticising my own contributions in particular, Guerrien writes:

> I am only going to consider Lawson's main criticism of neoclassical economics: its "lack of *realism*". I think that it is not the appropriate

objection: *all* theories lack realism, as they take into consideration only some aspects of reality. Everyone agrees on this, even neoclassical economists. The real problem with neoclassical theory is not its "lack of *realism*" but the "ideology" (a word Lawson never uses) that it smuggles in and carries with it

Having suggested that the real problem is not a lack of realism or (a better term) realisticness, Guerrien proceeds by agreeing that a lack of realisticness nevertheless *is* a problem, albeit, he supposes, mostly one that lies in the mainstream formulation of structure rather than its accounts of human agency. Guerrien understandably finds the formulations that abound to be somewhat absurd; in fact he goes as far as to talk of 'irrelevant' and 'stupid' models. His main concern, though, is not with the lack of realisticness *per se* but with the extreme nature of it; with why anyone – and specifically intelligent academics – would choose to reproduce and study constructions that can only be regarded as 'stupid':

> The question is [. . .]: how such intelligent people can propose – and endlessly study – such *stupid* models?

Guerrien answers his own question as follows:

> "I only see one reason for that: *ideology* (intuitive beliefs which render them blind)"

This is Guerrien's only elaboration of his understanding of the term. But it does suggest that Guerrien means something like a certain set of beliefs held by the community that are so intuitive in their appeal that their holders do rarely reflect upon them and are mostly blinded to the possibility that the beliefs in question might be wrong or even open to valid criticism[4].

What is this set of intuitive beliefs that Guerrien has in mind? Following his brief outline of what he means by ideology Guerrien writes:

> Here, the belief alluded to is that "market mechanisms" [. . .] produce "efficient" results – if you abstract from "frictions", "failures", etc. (ignoring these "imperfections" being, for neoclassical theorists, the principal reason of "lack of realism"). As there is a strong link between competitive equilibrium (that is, with auctioneer, etc.) and efficient states – link given by the two Welfare Theorems – then competitive equilibrium *must be* identified with "perfect market" (as both are supposed to be efficient). In some books (especially those on growth, in the "macro" mood – as those of Romer and Barro and Sala-I-Martin), perfect competition and an "omniscient" "representative agent" (or planner) choice are presented as giving the same results. How can a normal person make any sense of this?

Mathematical modelling and ideology 147

And Guerrien's answer to the question posed in the last sentence, in effect, is that we make sense of this by seeing mainstream economists as essentially cultural or economic dupes, unable to rise sufficiently above or beyond the prevailing ideology of their times.

Ideology$_2$

A rather more conspiratorial view of mainstream theory, as itself a form of ideology, is perhaps more common. The self-consciously heterodox *Real World Economics Review* (formerly the *Post-Autistics Review*) and its associated *Real World Economics Review* Blog are replete with contributions where the term ideology is used in this way. An illustrative example is provided by Peter Söderbaum (2009), who describes ideology explicitly as theory serving as a 'means' to achieve a political end:

> 'Ideology' stands for a 'means-ends philosophy' and is not limited to more or less established political ideologies like socialism, social democracy, social liberalism or neo-liberalism. In this sense, neoclassical economics clearly qualifies as an ideology and as such is more specific and precise than the political ideologies mentioned.
>
> Neoclassical economics tells us about the relevant actors in the economy (consumers, firms and government); about how to understand markets (supply and demand of commodities and of factors of production); about decision-making (optimization) and efficiency (usually a monetary concept or at best cost-efficiency). This way of understanding economics is clearly not neutral but specific in ideological terms.
>
> (p. 9)

Elsewhere a colourful statement of the more conspiratorial interpretation of economics as ideology is provided by Rajani Kanth (1999). Kanth, indeed, is quite explicit in the view that (mainstream) "economics is the ruling ideology of the capitalist system" (p. 191). Writing of (mainstream or 'neoclassical') economics as "this crown jewel of capitalist ideology" (p. 191); of "the inherent charlatanism of economic ideology" (p. 189), and so forth, Kanth elaborates as follows:

> To state the moral: *the entire enterprise of neo-classical economics is rigged to show that laissez-faire produces optimal outcomes*, but for the disruptive operation of the odd externality (a belated correction) here and there.
> (Kanth, 1999, pp. 191–2, emphasis in the original)

How is this rigging achieved? One component of the strategy is everywhere to stipulate that human beings are rational (meaning optimising) atomistic individuals. A second is the construction of theoretical set-ups or models specified to ensure that (typically unique) optimal outcomes are attainable.

There are indeed very many economists who do adopt the individualist framework and assumption that individual behaviour is optimal (in the sense of always deriving from optimising decisions in conditions where optimal outcomes are to be had). Perhaps most do. But this is not yet enough to show that the overall economic system is itself optimal in any way. If the claim is that mainstream economists seek to defend the economic system *per se*, something more is required to guarantee the result that the system is in a sense 'optimal'. This, it is supposed, is achieved by the commonplace construction of an equilibrium framework; the latter being so specified that the actions of isolated optimising individuals somehow (tend to) work to bring an equilibrium position about. Thus Kanth, for example, refers to the "economic science of capitalism" as

> simply *irrelevant* for being a fantasy world of an ideal rational, capitalism where all motions are mutually equilibriating, in a Newtonian co-ordination of the elements.
>
> (Kanth, 1999, p. 194)

In sum, two competing interpretations of the nature of ideology and how it connects to the mainstream tradition of modern economics can be found. The first supposes that mainstream economics is the more or less unrecognised product of ideology, the second sees mainstream economics as itself the ideology perhaps intentionally promoting deception.

If the two interpretations are radically different in their orientation, they do have something significant in common. They both characterise the mainstream project as primarily concerned with producing theories that express capitalism as an efficiently functioning, or otherwise desirable or optimal, system. Thus, according to both sets of accounts the lack of realisticness and so forth of mainstream economics arises just through that project's portrayal of the economy as an efficiently functioning or otherwise desirable system, a portrayal that is regarded by heterodox critics as being inconsistent with the way the social world really is.

In this manner the two groups ultimately provide somewhat similar explanations of the enduring failings of the modern mainstream, even if their accounts of the intentions of economists and manner in which ideology impacts are quite different.

An assessment of the political-economic ideology explanations

My own view is that neither of these explanations of the state of modern economics is sustainable. Remember the phenomenon before us is the generalised explanatory failure and lack of realisticness of formulations across the totality of the mainstream (macro, micro and econometric) output over a large number of years (again see e.g. Lawson, 2003, chapter 1).

It is one thing to suggest that mainstream economists mostly suppose that capitalism, as a market centred system, is somehow natural or normal or the best that can be achieved; but it is quite another thing to suppose that much of the output of these economists is even mainly concerned with such issues of political economy. It is a further step still to suppose that mainstream economists in their modelling endeavours everywhere either take it as a matter of unquestioning belief, or are motivated to demonstrate, that the social world in which we live is not merely defensible, but characterised by equilibrium or efficient markets or perfect competition, and so forth. In truth, the social system that is capitalism is, *qua* social system, barely ever even considered.

Moreover in those cases where economists do focus on questions of market or competitive equilibrium etc., the formulators of the models in question are often careful to stress that their theorising has little connection with the real world anyway and should not be used to draw conclusions about the latter, whether in terms of efficiency or for policy or whatever. Thus, Frank Hahn, a major contributor in this field, writes:

> it cannot be denied that there is something scandalous in the spectacle of so many people refining the analyses of economic [equilibrium] states which they give no reason to suppose will ever, or have ever, come about. It probably is also dangerous. Equilibrium economics [...] is easily convertible into an apologia for existing economic arrangements and it is frequently so converted.
>
> (1970, pp. 88–9)

Elsewhere, Hahn reveals in rather dramatic fashion what he feels should happen if people contemplate using such models for policy:

> When policy conclusions are drawn from such models, it is time to reach for one's gun.
>
> (Hahn, 1982, p. 29)

In truth in those cases where mainstream assumptions and categories are couched in terms of economic systems as a whole they are mainly designed to achieve consistency at the level of modelling rather than coherence with the world in which we live.

This concern for a notion of consistency in modelling practice is true for example of the recently fashionable rational expectations hypothesis, originally formulated by John Muth (1961), and widely employed by those that do focus on system level outcomes. The hypothesis proposes that predictions attributed to agents (being theorised about) are treated as being essentially the same as (consistent with) those generated by the economic model within which the same agents are theorised[5]. As such the proposal is clearly no more than a technique for (consistency in) modelling, albeit a bizarre one. Significantly any assertion that the expectations held (and so model in which they are imposed) are essentially correct, is a step that is *additional* to assuming rational expectations.

It is a form of modelling consistency (albeit a different one) that underpins the notion of equilibrium itself. In modern mainstream economics the category equilibrium has nothing to do with the features of the real economy (say with the balance of supply and demand – see e.g., Lawson, 2005; 2006). Economic models often comprise not single, but sets of, equations, each of which is notoriously found to have little relation to what happens in the real world. One question that nevertheless keeps economists occupied with such unrealistic models is whether the equations formulated are mutually consistent in the sense that there 'exists' a vector of values of some variable, say one labelled 'prices', that is consistent with *each and all* the equations. Such a model 'solution' is precisely the meaning of *equilibrium* in this context. As such the notion is not at all a claim about the world but merely a (possible) property that a set of equations may or may not be found to possess. The mainstream economist Huw Dixon gets it right when he summarises matters as follows: "At its most general, we can say that 'equilibrium' is a method of solving economic models. At a superficial level, an equilibrium is simply a solution to a set of equations" (Dixon, 1990, p. 356). In short, when mainstream economists question whether an equilibrium 'exists' they merely enquire as to whether a set of equations has a solution.

More to the point, however, the substantive content of mainstream theorising is far wider and more dynamic than a fixed focus on market mechanisms or on conceptions of competitive equilibrium and claims that the market mechanisms lead to efficiency, and such like.

In fact, most mainstream economists, as I say, have never concerned themselves much with the workings of the economic system as a whole (whether via an equilibrium framework or otherwise). The dominant concern, rather, has been, and remains, with highly specific or partial analyses of some highly restricted sectors or forms of behaviour. Very often the focus is on 'micro' decision making or 'behaviour'. Even (or perhaps especially) here though the contributions have more or less always been unrealistic and have rarely if ever generated (as opposed to imported) insight.

To the extent that it has ever been meaningful for the various disparate results or theorems of these economists to be considered as a whole, the clearest conclusion that can be drawn is that they are mostly wildly inconsistent with each other. So long as the assumptions are tractable mainstream theorists are free to posit anything they want no matter how unrealistic. Competing hypotheses abound, even by the same contributors in different contributions.

If we focus on empirical contributions, specifically, it is clear that there are few attempts to repeat the results of others, progress the results of others, or even acknowledge the results of others. Even econometricians using identical, or almost identical, data sets are regularly found to produce quite contrasting conclusions, usually with little attempt at explanation. The systematic result here, as the econometrician Edward Leamer (1983) observes, is that: "hardly anyone takes anyone else's data analysis seriously" (p. 37).

Furthermore, far from being a conspiracy or a uniformly misled project, mainstream economics lacks agreement even as to the project's purpose or direction. As one of its leading practitioners Ariel Rubinstein acknowledged more than a decade ago:

> The issue of interpreting economic theory is [...] the most serious problem now facing economic theorists. The feeling among many of us can be summarized as follows. Economic theory should deal with the real world. It is not a branch of abstract mathematics even though it utilises mathematical tools. Since it is about the real world, people expect the theory to prove useful in achieving practical goals. But economic theory has not delivered the goods. Predictions from economic theory are not nearly as accurate as those by the natural sciences, and the link between economic theory and practical problems [...] is tenuous at best. Economic theory lacks a consensus as to its purpose and interpretation. Again and again, we find ourselves asking the question 'where does it lead?'
>
> (Rubinstein, 1995, p. 12)

In short, the modern mainstream is not a project whose emphases and explanatory failures are mainly direct manifestations either of intentions to maintain attachment to the existing economic system, or of a blindness to its real nature. At the level of substantive theory, there is far more heterogeneity within mainstream theorising than Guerrien, Kanth and others allow, with relatively little attention focussed on the economic system as a whole, let alone given over to the theorising of its optimality. Indeed at the level of substantive theory the project is marked by overall incoherence and lack of cohesion amongst its various strands, and with significant uncertainty even as to what is worth pursuing.

In fact some recent close critical observers of the economic content of mainstream theories not only do not characterise the mainstream as ideological at the substantive level, but actually portray the mainstream project at this level as pluralist (see for example David Colander *et al.*, 2004 or John Davis, 2005). In truth I think this a polite way of saying that the projects flits from fad to fashion in the hope of achieving explanatory successes somewhere. But that aside, at least these authors recognise the obvious heterogeneity and change that characterises the project[6].

The one (and as far as I can see only) feature that has persistently and comprehensively marked all mainstream contributions, and continues to dominate, is the insistence that methods of mathematical modelling always be employed. And, significantly, *this emphasis is by itself sufficient to explain the mainstream deficiencies at all levels including that of economic content.* Specifically, and unlike explanations that seek to make ideology at the level of economic content the central factor, explanations in terms of the misplaced emphasis on mathematical modelling can account for mainstream inadequacies whether couched in terms of explanatory failure, unrealistic formulations, or the project's lack of direction; whether the economic focus is the system as a whole or very partial 'micro' situations; whether the modellers are or are not supporters of the *status quo*; whether or not data are employed; whatever the substance of the latest fad and fashion to preoccupy, and so on. In consequence, I see little reason in all of this to reject yet the assessment that the misplaced emphasis on mathematical deductivist reasoning provides the better explanation of the rather unhappy state of modern economics.

An alternative conception of ideology in the economics academy

I have considered the two conceptions of ideology that are most often associated with modern academic economists and I have argued that, in the political-economy garb in which these ideologies are usually presented by opponents of the mainstream, they do not serve easily to account for the explanatory failings of the discipline.

However in so concluding I must stress that it by no means follows that I suppose either that ideology is entirely absent from the modern economics academy, and specifically mainstream economics, or that questions of ideology have no bearing on the latter project's lack of explanatory power. Indeed I am of the definite view that ideology is rife and with significant consequences for mainstream explanatory performance. There are various issues to consider though.

First and foremost, I want briefly to indicate an alternative ideology, a version of ideology$_1$ (a set of background views manifest unquestioningly as if normal or neutral) that I believe does pervade the economics academy, one that is extremely widespread and indeed plays a significant contributory role in the failings of the discipline. But this is a set of beliefs that bears *not* directly upon the nature of the underlying economic system at all. Rather it *is precisely the doctrine that all serious economics must take the form of mathematical modelling.*

This ideology, as I am suggesting it to be, usually involves a presumption of an event-regularity-seeking (and so prediction-oriented) conception of science along with the complementary belief that mathematics is closely aligned with, and indeed essential to, such a science.

I must stress that the contention I am advancing here is not an arbitrary add-on adopted just because the focus of discussion is ideology. If I am right that the problems of modern economics stem first and foremost from the misplaced attachment to mathematical reasoning despite the record of failure so far, there must be a reason for this emphasis. That reason, I want to suggest, is, in large part at least, the unquestioning, uncritical, taken on trust as normal, blinkered orientation to employing mathematical techniques characteristic of most of those who pursue it. It is blindness to, or an unreasoned dismissive resistance to any suggestion of, any alternative to the idea that wielding mathematical techniques is both essential to science and compulsory if economics is to make a proper contribution. Such a stance amounts precisely to a system of beliefs that is itself a form of ideology (ideology$_1$).

Let me emphasise that I am quite aware that there are forms of mathematical systems, methods and techniques beyond those currently and/or traditionally prosecuted by economists. Deductivist forms, presupposing closures of the sort defined above, just happen to be those that economists (so far) find easiest to wield or otherwise most convenient. I do not argue that all forms of mathematical method (including those yet to be invented) must necessarily be inappropriate to social analysis – though I strongly doubt that any will ever prove of general use for addressing/illuminating the sort of capitalist social system in which we currently live. But this is not the issue. My point, rather, is that far from even contemplating, let alone exploring, alternative non-mathematical approaches – where various available alternatives are easily shown to be relevant to, and fruitful for, illuminating the real social system (for illustrations see for example Lawson, 2009a; 2003, chapter 4; 1997, chapter 18) – modern mainstream economists continually seek out mathematical techniques of some kind. It is, to repeat, this unwillingness or apparent inability seriously to contemplate the idea that a serious, fruitful and explanatorily successful (science) of economics might be developed that does not rely upon the application of mathematical methods and techniques of some form that indicates the dominant form of the actually prevalent ideology.

Ideology in action

It can be easily seen that the unquestioned emphasis on mathematical modelling is indeed a form of ideological blindness if a brief examination is made of cases where, for whatever reason, mainstream economists, whether in the form of a few critical contributors, or as a collective body, have come to critically address the explanatory failings of their project. For it is evident that the one feature that is almost never addressed in such endeavour is precisely the emphasis on the employment of mathematical techniques. Even in the very few cases that mainstream contributors recognise or acknowledge that criticisms of the mathematical-modelling emphasis have been made from outside their project, the latter criticisms tend to be summarily dismissed either without serious consideration, or at most with some vague referencing of alternative more appropriate mathematical techniques yet to be developed.

Let me first briefly consider examples of the latter, cases where the issue of the mathematical emphasis itself is at least broached in published mainstream commentaries. Amongst the very few examples I can find are by the 'theorists' Alan Kirman and Frank Hahn, surely amongst the most open-minded and reflective of mainstream economists. However, even in such cases any notion that the mathematical emphasis might be the problem is quickly dismissed rather than seriously entertained.

Kirman, for example, in critically examining the nature and poor performance of mainstream theorising focuses on the individualist emphasis of the enterprise. But in suggesting alternative ways for the mainstream to proceed it is clear that he regards methods of mathematical modelling *per se* as effectively indispensable. Thus, he writes:

> The argument that the root of the problem [...] [is] that we are confined by a mathematical strait jacket which allows us no escape, does not seem very persuasive. That the mathematical frameworks that we have used made the task of changing or at least modifying our paradigm hard, is undeniable but it is difficult to believe that had a clear well-formulated new approach been suggested then we would not have adopted the appropriate mathematical tools.
> (Kirman, 1989, p. 137)

I noted above that Frank Hahn does not hesitate to acknowledge that equilibrium theory tells us little about economic reality; and he is especially ill-disposed towards those that would seek to use mainstream models to draw policy conclusions or as a guide to practical action. But the idea that mathematics might be dispensable to economic thinking, or anyway overly emphasised, or commanding too high a proportion of the resources available for economic research, is not afforded serious reflection. To the contrary, he dismisses any suggestion that the modern emphasis on mathematical modelling may be misplaced as "a view surely not worth discussing" (Hahn, 1985, p. 18). And in a major speech to the Royal Economic Society he even counsels that we "avoid discussions of 'mathematics in economics' like the plague" (Hahn, 1992a; see also Hahn, 1992b).

If mainstream economists tend to be blind to, or to ignore, or at best to dismiss, external critiques of the mathematical emphasis how do they react in situations where they at least acknowledge explanatory failure? The ongoing economic crisis provides perhaps a unique insight to this.

Recently, possibly the largest numbers of mainstream self-critics ever have been driven to reassess their own practices as a result the ongoing economic crisis and widespread suspicion of, and concern for, if not outright condemnation of, academic economic output. Notably even amongst mainstream economists there have been increased calls for change and numerous claims advanced that changes have indeed been, or are being, made. The situation thus affords an unusual opportunity to assess which parts of academic economic practice are most readily regarded as open to transformation and which treated, consciously or subconsciously, as beyond, or anyway not in need of, critique.

A useful concentration or grouping of this unusually large set of mainstream critical reflections on the nature of modern academic economics is provided by the various contributions to the inaugural (2010) conference (held in Kings College Cambridge) of the *Institute for New Economic Thinking* (INET), the latter being an organisation set up precisely to transform economics in the light of the failings of the economics discipline to provide much understanding of the crisis.

Very many economists attended the conference, all apparently concerned critically to reconsider the nature of academic economics. It is in such a forum if anywhere that we might hope to find mainstream economists challenging all but the most obviously acceptable aspects of their theories, approaches and activities.

Although George Soros, who sponsors the Institute, shows some awareness that the reliance upon mathematics may at least be something to question (see e.g. Soros, 2009; Lawson, 2010), for most of his close associates the idea that there might be something problematic about the emphasis on forms of mathematical technique does not appear even to cross their minds (all the numerous contributions are posted on the INET website or can be found on Youtube[7]).

Consider for example the presentation by Joseph Stiglitz (2010[8]), a central contributor in the Institute. Stiglitz quickly focuses on the failure of most models to predict the crisis, he emphasises the need for predictive accuracy, and then he proposes a strategy of experimenting with different model assumptions, most of which are accepted as unrealistic, in order to come up with a best model in terms of forecast accuracy. Or rather Stiglitz makes reference to a "standard model" and declares that the critical question for "research strategy" is to decide which of the model's "many unrealistic assumptions" we "want to drop". Indeed, emphasising the need for pluralism Stiglitz suggests that we "investigate a number of different models where different assumptions are dropped". Stiglitz stresses that, in his view, dynamic models and stochastic models and general equilibrium models remain important for economics, even if it is necessary to revise some of their specifications. His overall preference is seemingly for analytic models or more complex stochastic models that can at least in principle accommodate human interactions (though other preferences for model specifications are listed).

Of relevance here is that, in all this, Stiglitz is seemingly open to entertaining an array of different modelling assumptions (albeit mostly unrealistic ones[9]), and so is also open to a degree about policy stances, etc., that might be adopted. The one issue that is not even hinted at, however, is that we might also question the very emphasis on mathematical modelling itself. Indeed the discussion throughout his presentation is only and continually about how economists should go about finding 'better' mathematical models. And this uncritical stance typifies the presentations made throughout the conference, as recorded on INET's website.[10]

Of course, mainstream economists like Stiglitz rarely, and perhaps have little opportunity to, explore in a sustained, serious or systematic way the issues of philosophy/methodology on which they sometimes pronounce. But the same reaction to the crisis is found even by methodologists of the mainstream that might be expected to look deeper and further. Thus in an influential paper entitled "The Financial Crisis and the Systemic Failure of Academic Economics", David Colander, Hans Föllmer, Armin Hass, Michael Goldberg, Katerina Juselius, Alan Kirman, Thomus Lux, and Brigitte Sloth (2008), provide an assessment that again questions anything and everything except the emphasis on formalistic mathematical modelling (see Lawson 2009b; 2009c).

Heterodoxy and mathematical modelling

In fact so apparently compelling is the belief system in question (that mathematical modelling is the proper way to do economics) that many heterodox economists too seemingly fall under its sway. Although heterodox modellers do not follow the mainstream in dogmatically insisting that we all everywhere adopt a mathematical orientation, it remains the case that many heterodox economists fail to recognise that the conceptions they find to be inadequate in mainstream theory owe something to the mainstream modelling emphasis; and these heterodox economists continue excessively (and often exclusively) to explore alternative mathematical models and forms of mathematical reasoning in the face of explanatory failures and unrealistic formulations.

The heterodox *Real-World Economics Review* has even seen fit to create a *Revere Award for Economics* given in large part for success in predicting the Global Financial Collapse, a move that may well further encourage the uncritical reliance on formalistic models and the predictive criterion of success[11]. And whilst the same journal and its associated blog do carry articles and comments that critically focus on the use of mathematics in economics, the dominant emphasis seems to be the exploration of novel, or currently non-standard, forms of mathematical technique[12].

Of course, I do not wish to (and indeed do not – see e.g. Fullbrook, 2009, especially chapter 12) discourage all experimentation with mathematical models and methods in all contexts, and certainly cannot insist that the use of methods of mathematical-modelling must always be devoid of insight, even if the arguments I have laid out lead me to believe that the current emphasis is largely wasteful of resources (again see Lawson, 1997; 2003). My point rather is that the reliance on mathematical modelling and on criteria like predictive accuracy, goes almost unquestioned throughout much of the economics academy, certainly within the mainstream and sometimes even beyond. And this is so despite the unrealistic concoctions that so far have almost always resulted from this endeavour along with the severe limitation of explanatory insight generated by (as opposed to being tagged on to) such activities. And it is so despite the ongoing crises leading economists of all persuasions to critically reflect upon the now-all-too-apparent failings of the academic discipline. All such features I suggest are strongly supportive of the contention that the belief/conviction that 'the only proper economics is a mathematical economics' is a prevailing form of ideology.

Explaining the ideology of mathematical technique in modern economics

If I am right about all this then the ideology I am identifying itself requires an explanation. This is easy enough to provide. But notice first that a feature (I believe it to be a strength) of the explanation of the state of modern economics that I am advancing is that I do not need to invoke a conspiratorial view of ideology (ideology$_2$); and specifically I do not at all view the mainstream as a body of dishonest individuals setting out to pull the wool over the eyes of anyone.

Nor of course do Guerrien and others who also emphasise the first interpretation of ideology (ideology$_1$), but who suppose that mainstream economist are 'blind' to the unrealisticness of their presumption that the political economic system is an efficiently functioning one. But unlike these contributors I also do not need to suppose that mainstream economists or anyone else continue to be blind to the increasingly all-too-apparent crisis-ridden state of capitalist economies.

Still I need to give some reason why mainstream economists may indeed be blind to the possibility that their methods of mathematical modelling are inappropriate to social analysis.

A large part of the explanation, I suggest, is simply that mathematics has been so successful in the history of human endeavour, and especially within (non-social) natural science, that its centrality to all science and serious and systematic investigation is, throughout wide sections of society, taken as an article of faith. Certainly a perception that, especially where measurable quantities are involved, all serious research requires a mathematical form has been widely in evidence since the Enlightenment. And economics is, more than any other social discipline, commonly interpreted as being concerned with measurable quantities (quantity of money, prices, output[13]). As such it is not surprising to find many economists both supposing that forms of mathematics are essential to economic science, and optimistic that economics can equally achieve significant mathematical successes eventually.

Thus, whilst Guerrien posits a blindness of mainstream 'intelligent' contributors even when the content of their models is regarded by him as so obviously 'stupid', I only posit a blindness in a situation where it may be understandably difficult for many to see clearly. With the neglect of ontological reasoning, recognition that the current emphasis on formal mathematical modelling in economics is misguided is not so obvious. This is especially the case in the light of the just noted and often emphasised post Enlightenment historical record of mathematical success throughout the various disciplines.

In fact, an acceptance of the idea that mathematics is essential to grounded knowledge has been a factor in sections of popular culture for rather longer even than the post-Enlightenment period. In the interests of brevity let me recall how Morris Kline sums up the introduction to his majestic *History of Mathematics in Western Culture:*

> In this book we shall survey mathematics primarily to show how its ideas have helped to mould twentieth-century life and thought. The ideas will be in historical order so that our material will range from the beginnings in Babylonia and Egypt to the modern theory of relativity. Some people may question the pertinence of material belonging to earlier historical periods. Modern culture, however, is the accumulation and synthesis of contributions made by many preceding civilisations. The Greeks, who first appreciated the power of mathematical reasoning, graciously allowing the gods to use it in designing the universe, and then urging man to uncover the pattern of this design, not only gave mathematics a major place in their civilisation but initiated patterns of thought that are basic in our own. As succeeding civilisations passed on their gifts to modern times, they handed on new and increasingly more significant roles for mathematics. Many of these functions and influences of mathematics are now deeply imbedded in our culture.
>
> (Kline, 1964)

The influence of mathematics is now so deeply ingrained within our culture, indeed, that many people (especially non-professional scientists) appear to suppose that anything stated in mathematics must be correct, whilst for things to be correct, reliable, insightful or scientific (or at least conferring of scientific status), they must be stated in mathematics[14]. For so many people it appears to be simply an unquestioned and seemingly unquestionable matter of faith that if a field of study is to be scientific or accorded status as a knowledge-producing activity, or otherwise regarded as serious, it must take a mathematical form.

Of course, the Enlightenment did give an important boost to this long-in-evidence perception. And in fact ever since Newton succeeded in uniting heaven and earth in equations, and Kant announced that the study of social phenomena requires its own Newton, the programme of mathematising economics has been underway (see Lawson, 2003, chapter 10).

Interestingly, John Henry (1997) recently observes that following the publication of Newton's *Principia,* readers "took for granted the validity of mathematics for understanding the working of the world". And he stresses that "although his book met with some fierce criticism, not a murmur was raised against it in [. . .] regard [to its emphasis on mathematical reasoning]" (p. 21).

Actually, from the point of view of understanding the acceptance of the emphasis on mathematisation as ideology, even more interesting is a critical response to Henry provided by Yves Gingras (2001) in his wide-ranging commentary on the history of mathematics. Addressing Henry's assessment that 'murmurs' of dissent against the mathematical formalism were absent from *Principia*, Gringras writes:

> As we will see, this was far from being the case but to recover these murmurs, one must look at actors who are now unknown precisely because they rejected the mathematization of physics and were thus excluded from the field (and its history) as it evolved in the eighteenth and nineteenth centuries.
>
> (Gingras, p. 385)

The point, then, is that a belief that mathematics is central to all science and serious study is a widespread cultural norm of long standing, one that emerged in the face of, and has been continually reinforced through, successes with mathematics throughout the disciplines. If the successes of mathematics has grounded a society-wide cultural belief in the general relevance of, and indeed need for, mathematics for scientific and all serious study, it is not surprising that economists enamoured of the idea of pursuing a serious and scientific economics have too fallen under its sway.

So my contention, in sum, is that the modelling emphasis of modern mainstream economics is explained by a largely unquestioning society-wide conviction (a form of ideology$_1$) that mathematics is fundamental to all science, a conviction or ideology that itself is in large part explained by the successes of mathematics in so many other domains.

The modern mainstream and the economic system

I have argued that the malaise of modern economics is not primarily due to ideology at the level of substantive political economy. I have also argued that ideology is present in the economics academy nonetheless, albeit at the level of methodology. Finally, I want to stress that in maintaining these views I do not at all suppose there is no relation between the mainstream stance (that is the insistence that mathematical techniques be everywhere employed) and the underlying economic system. Specifically, and despite the foregoing discussion, I do not at all deny that the mainstream practices can serve the purposes of sustaining the workings of the economic system. But let me be clear on how I think the two do relate.

First, I do not doubt that political-economic and cultural ideological factors in the sense of prevailing background beliefs (ideology$_1$) are in play in all societies or communities, and are manifest in the contributions and practices of us all. We are all situated and products of our time, place and culture etc. I do not doubt that such background ideology of this sort bears on the sorts of questions we ask, the orientations we adopt, the assumptions, including absences, we take for granted, the states of affairs we regard as 'normal', and so on. However, I do not think the very real ideological beliefs that prevail regarding the benefits or 'normality' of the existing political-economy system are primarily or even significantly responsible for the perpetual failings and acknowledged fictions of contemporary academic economics. This is just to repeat the foregoing. Most economists as academic researchers do not even seem interested in the economy as such anyway. Far more important is their prowess in manipulating mathematical models and such like. The dominant ideology in the economics academy, I am maintaining, is precisely the extra-ordinarily widespread and long-lasting belief that mathematical modelling is somehow neutral at the level of content or form, but an essential method for science, underpinning any proper or serious economics.

Second, and following on from the above, the scandal, of modern economics is *not* that it gets so many things *wrong*, but that it is so largely *irrelevant*. However in being irrelevant, and yet using significant resources that could have been used for research into the way the economy really works, then, at a time that the economy is in crisis and proving largely dysfunctional, the mainstream modelling orientation cannot but serve to deflect criticism from the nature of the *status quo* at the level of the economy and thereby work to sustain it (and would do so whatever that status quo happened to be). As Leamer, (already noted above) observes, no one takes anyone else's data analysis seriously. In truth, few people take any mainstream analyses seriously, except in economics faculties' promotion exercises.

Third, if however anyone *were* to pay much attention to mainstream analysis, it would serve to sustain, if not reinforce, the *status quo* in an additional way. The point here is that the emphasis on event regularities (necessitated by a reliance on forms of mathematical modelling), and so attachment to an implicit ontology of closure and atomism, entails that any references to social relationality, and so to (relational) issues of power, discrimination, domination, oppression, and conflict generally, are effectively masked over or hidden, or at best trivialised. For the framework is ill-equipped even to allow such categories to be seriously considered. Thus the very emphasis on mathematical modelling renders analyses of real conflict, power relations and social transformation effectively if inadvertently precluded.

The persistence of mathematical reasoning

I am accepting, then, that although the generalised malaise of modern economics does not reflect any ideological attachment to specific economic theories, the persistent irrelevance of academic mainstream economics, resulting from the emphasis on formal modelling, is nonetheless inhibiting of analysis capable of constituting meaningful constructive criticism of existing political-economic states of affairs. Moreover this consequence, which, I stress, I take to be largely unintended, does, I believe, contribute to explaining how the mathematical project persists in maintaining institutional power in the face of, and despite, its repeated failures and fictitious constructions. For government sponsored funding bodies and the like are actually less likely to withdraw funds from a project that provides no serious criticism of the government's actions.

Parenthetically, I believe this inability of the mathematical modelling project to challenge anything seriously or convincingly is a major factor in understanding how the project has survived as long as it has in the economics academy, and even how it originally came to dominate. Elsewhere, I address at length the reasons for the rise and persistence of a mainstream tradition that so clearly lacks a history of explanatory successes[15] (see especially chapter 10 of Lawson, 2003).

I stress once more, however, that in all this I am not suggesting that those who contribute to the mathematising project in economics do so, in the main, opportunistically. Rather I merely point out that whatever its advocates' intentions, the mainstream project (with its emphasis on mathematical deductivist modelling, and lack of criticality) may appear, and at times has indeed proven to be (see Lawson, 2003, chapter 10), conducive to those, especially outside the academy, seeking, for whatever reason, to deflect or minimise intellectual challenges to the underlying economic system. As such, this mathematical project, itself underpinned by methodological ideology, and not formulated by those pushing, or duped by, a political-economy ideology, might nevertheless be said to contribute ultimately to sustaining the *status quo*.

Conclusion

My contention, in short, is that contemporary *academic* mainstream economics is indeed often underpinned by ideology. But this ideology is first of all methodological in nature, being in effect the widespread cultural view that mathematics is essential to science. Incidentally I argue elsewhere not only that this ideology covers a false view in that successful natural science does *not* actually rest on the application of mathematics, but also that a nonmathematical economics can actually yet be a science in the sense of the successful natural sciences (see Lawson, 1997; 2003 and especially 2012).

I have suggested too that a possible, and indeed likely, reason the mathematical emphasis of the mainstream project does not come under more critical scrutiny from outside the academy is that the project's continuing irrelevance actually renders it harmless to political defenders of any prevailing *status quo* who might otherwise be drawn to more critical considerations in connection with funding and the like.

Although I have attempted here to explain the continuing misplaced emphasis on techniques of mathematical modelling in the economics academy I might add that I do not suggest that there are not yet factors at play additional to those I have identified. Amongst other things, the longish recent history of mainstream perseverance with the deductivist modelling techniques in the face of repeated failure has suggested to some that there may also be something pathological to what is going on, and that a psychological explanation is likely also of some relevance. Also, the pattern of behaviour in question seems to be gendered, with the mathematical modelling and prediction activities being relentlessly pursued largely by gendered males. This too seems to warrant explanation (again see Lawson, 2003, chapter 10). These are issues that are currently receiving attention elsewhere and in illuminating ways[16]. But that, as they say, is another story.

For now it does seem safe to conclude that the primary explanation of the numerous, long lived and continuing failings of modern academic economics is the (misplaced) emphasis on mathematical modelling. It is an emphasis underpinned by the cultural belief that a reliance on mathematical technique in science is somehow so normal or neutral or natural that any questioning of this emphasis can be ignored or swiftly dismissed as obviously far too radical if not nonsensical.

Acknowledgements

The writing of this paper benefitted from the financial support of the *Independent Social Research Foundation*. For helpful comments on an initial draft posted on the *Economic Thought* website I am grateful to Jānis Bērziņš, Frederico Botafogo, Thomas Bowen, Dick Burkhart, Lynne Chester,

Donald Gillies, Egmont Kakarot-Handtke, Roy Langston, Bruce Littleboy, Jamie Morgan and Patrick Spread.

Notes

1 This critique of detuctivism of course is not a denial that deductive reasoning can be appropriately employed alongside numerous other forms of logic, reasoning and analysis. In what follows I may occasionally refer not to deductivism but just to mathematical modelling or some such. For a discussion of deductivism as a form of scientific explanation see especially Lawson, 1997, chapter 2; 2003, chapter 1.
2 Brian O'Boyle and Terrence McDonough (2011) for example suggest that a "lack of an ideological-critique is perhaps the most glaring lacunae for the Lawsonian project, in light of its own philosophical project of critiquing mainstream economics". They add that "the Lawsonian project is unable (or unwilling) to entertain the possibility of an ideological function for mainstream economics" and, worse, that "to follow Lawson in his particular critique of the mainstream is to relinquish the very tools that are needed to uncover 'the anatomy and ideological function of orthodoxy' or indeed its contribution to neoliberal ideology". Other such critics include for example Kanth, 1999, and Guerrien, 2004 (see below).
3 Terry Eagleton (1991, p.2), for example, lists the following interpretations found in the recent literature: a process of production of meanings, signs and value in social life; a body of ideas characteristic of a particular social group or class; ideas which help to legitimate a dominant political power; false ideas which help to legitimate a dominant political power; systematically distorted communication; that which offers a position for a subject; forms of thought motivated by social interests; identity thinking; socially necessary illusion; the conjuncture of discourse and power; the medium in which conscious social actors make sense of their world; action-oriented sets of beliefs; the confusion of linguistic and phenomenal reality; semiotic closure; the indispensable medium in which individuals live out their relation to a social structure; the process whereby said life is converted to a natural reality.
4 Of course, when or where most people in a community think alike about certain matters, and even 'forget' that there are alternatives to the current state of affairs, we also arrive at Antonio Gramsci's concept of *Hegemony*.
5 As Muth himself puts it: "expectations, since they are informed predictions of future economic events, are essentially the same as the predictions of the relevant economic theory [. . . .] The hypothesis can be rephrased a little more precisely as follows: that expectations of firms (or, more generally, the subjective probability distribution of outcomes) tend to be distributed, for the same information set, about the prediction of the theory (or the "objective" probability distributions of outcomes)" (Muth, 1961, p. 316)
6 Thus, in contradistinction to Guerrien and others, Colander *et al.* (2004) call attention to what they see as the "changing face of mainstream economics" and criticise heterodox economists for failing to notice such ongoing developments. Specifically, these authors criticise heterodox contributors for adopting an overly "static view of the profession" (p. 486); for referring to the current mainstream as neoclassical; and for missing the "diversity that exists within the profession, and the many new ideas that are being tried out" (p. 487). In fact, Colander et al. insist that "Mainstream economics is a complex system of evolving ideas" (p. 489), and refer to the "multiple dimensionalities that we see in the mainstream profession" (p. 489).

7 See for example http://ineteconomics.org/initiatives/conferences/kings-college or http://www.youtube.com /watch?v=SdZgD1 DCNq4
8 See http://ineteconomics.org/video/conference-kings/agenda-reforming-economic-theory-joseph-stiglitz
9 Of course, the willingness to entertain unrealistic assumptions makes the whole project rather pointless (see Lawson, 2009a). If I am allowed to make unrealistic assumptions then after the event I can predict anything you want [if the outcome to be so 'forecasted' is X, then I can simply (or complexly) assume 1) Y implies X, and 2) Y]. Before the event then, in an open world, successful prediction, if it occurs (involving timing, – like earthquakes we all know crises can and will occur, and usually why) is mostly a matter of luck.
10 Coincidentally, as I was writing these lines I received via email a paper from INET written by Harald Uhlig (2011), based on his 2010 INET presentation, and entitled 'Economics and Reality' (the same title as my 1997 book). It is a philosophical paper so I thought this might be an exception in at least exploring the relevance and grounding of mainstream mathematical modelling. The author does, in a footnote on page 1, reference my book, and suggest that his piece may, in its philosophical orientation, be "more reminiscent of Lawson (1997)". But the author quickly adds, notably without any argument or explanation, "though I sharply disagree with his [Lawson's] rejection of formal, mathematical models to address the social reality of economics [. . .]"
11 Of course, I accept (indeed I continually argue) that (using the criteria of *explanatory* power) we can come to understand the workings of causal processes and mechanisms (see Lawson, 2009a; or 2003, chapter 4). And where we understand such mechanisms we can conditionally predict (contingent) *tendencies,* meaning the impacts of causal forces acting in certain ways or directions *whatever the actual outcomes.* Thus I predict that should planet earth survive without catastrophe into tomorrow then over large parts of the planet there will be gravitational tendencies in play working to 'pull' leaves to the ground, *tendencies that will be operative even as leaves fly over roof tops and chimneys.* But, excepting a lucky accident, only in a closure can we predict any actual outcome (in the case of the path of a specific leaf we must absent aerodynamic and thermodynamic tendencies, the wind, and so forth).

  I acknowledge, too, that because some tendencies are so powerful (relative to countervailing forces) we can even predict certain sorts of outcomes that will eventually occur. Thus given our understanding of the mechanisms behind earthquakes we can reasonably expect that the latter will continue to occur now and again on planet earth. And it is not difficult to understand that capitalism, being an inherently contradictory system, will repeatedly manifest crises. The specific forms and timing though are something else (in such cases the inability to predict outcomes matters little anyway, unless our one goal is to get rich through forms of gambling. Rather what we *need* to know is how best to locate and construct buildings that can withstand earthquakes; and how to best support social systems that are free of the sorts of contradictions that generate instabilities and crises; and so on. But these matters are not my focus here).

  Of course, as with all forms of gambling there is often some forecaster that picks a winner. As I write these lines (end of 2011) there are groups of economists predicting that the euro will collapse, though there is a range of predicted timings of this event; and there are others who expect the euro to survive. There are also anticipations of intermediate paths and outcomes. Each group or commentator is knowledgably analysing the nature of operative causal mechanisms. But the actual outcomes depend on so many contingent developments including factors yet to be determined. Of course, whatever happens, someone forecasting today will be found after the event to have been closest in their forecasting. But unless they possess the power to effect the result, such 'success' will inevitably be far more luck than judgement.

12 Though it seems to be something of an easy retort it is surely not wholly without significance, or totally unfair of me, to note that whilst the current paper was posted on the *Economic Thought* website the majority of comments it received advance the idea that the solutions to the problems I raise lie in continuing the search for more appropriate techniques of mathematical modelling.

13 As early as 1871 we find Jevons writing "My theory of Economics, however, is purely mathematical in character [. . .] To me it seems that our science must be mathematical simply because it deals with quantities" (p. 3).

14 Of course this view means turning a blind eye to (or forgetting) the clear scientific successes of the largely non-mathematical disciplines of chemistry and biology in the nineteenth century and indeed much of modern chemistry and bio-medical research (on all this and much that relates to the current paper see Donald Gillies, 2004).

15 In the context of the last 200 years of economic thinking, the fortunes of the project of seeking to mathematise economics have notably waxed and waned in line with changes in the relevant background academic environment, not least in responses to developments in forms of mathematics itself (again see Lawson, 2003, chapter 10).

But certainly no less important were changes in the political environment both inside and outside the academy. One significant feature of the latter was the influence of the political environment in the US following the Second World War. The situation in the US in this period is especially important to understanding the subsequent path of modern economics, just because the resources of the US in the early post-war period allowed it to dominate much of the post world war II international academic scene (in economics as in many other disciplines).

A very significant feature of the early Post World War II political environment was the emergence in the US of McCarthyite witch-hunts in the face of the Cold War. In this climate, the nature of the output of economics faculties became a particularly sensitive matter. And in such a context, the project of seeking to mathematise economics proved to be especially appealing. For although it carried scientific pretensions it was significantly devoid of any necessary empirical content (especially when carried out in the spirit of the Bourbaki approach – see Lawson, 2003).

The group most feared or resented by the McCarthyites were the intellectuals (see e.g., Erik Reinert, 2000). The formalising project with an emphasis on mathematical structure to the exclusion of almost any critical or reflexive content was clearly extremely attractive to those caught up in the situation. This was especially the case not just for insecure or fearful university administrators but also for the funding agencies of US social scientific research (who were especially important in this period – see for example, Bob Coats, 1992; Crawford Goodwin, 1998; Yuval Yonay, 1998).

In fact, historians of the US have long argued that McCarthyism and the Cold War were decisive in the growth of anti-intellectualism in the US in the twentieth century (see e.g. Richard Hofstadter's [1963] *Anti-Intellectualism in American Life;* or Alan Bloom's [1987] *The Closing of the American Mind*). My point here is simply that this environment impacted on the economics faculties as elsewhere, and was doubtless conducive to the spread of economics as merely a form of technicist manipulation, with little attachment paid to, or with little consistency in, economic content (see Reinert, 2000 for a similar conclusion). On all this see Lawson, 2003, chapter 10.

16 See for example Vinca Bigo, 2008.

References

Bigo, Vinca (2008) 'Explaining Modern Economics (as a microcosm of society)', *Cambridge Journal of Economics*, 32(4): 527–554.

Bloom, Allan (1987) *The Closing of the American Mind*, New York: Simon And Schuster.

Coats, A.W. Bob (1992) *On the History of Economic thought: British and American Economic Essays, Volume I*, London and New York: Routledge.

Colander, David, R. P. Holt and J. B. Rosser Jr. (2004) 'The changing face of mainstream economics', *Review of Political Economy*, vol. 16, no. 4, 485–500.

Colander, David, Hans Föllmer, Armin Hass, Michael Goldberg, Katerina Juselius, Alan Kirman, Thomus Lux, and Brigitte Sloth (2008), "The Financial Crisis and the Systemic Failure of Academic Economics", unpublished mimeo, available at: http://www.debtdeflation.com/blogs/wp-content/uploads/papers/Dahlem_Report_EconCrisis021809.pdf

Davis, John B. (2005) 'Heterodox economics, the fragmentation of the mainstream and embedded individual analysis', in Garnett, R. and Harvey, J. (eds.), *The Future of Heterodox Economics*, Ann Arbor, MI, University of Michigan Press.

Dixon, Huw (1990) 'Equilibrium and Explanation', in John Creedy (ed.) *Foundations of Economic Thought*, Oxford: Basil Blackwell.

Eagleton, Terry (1991), *Ideology: An Introduction*, London: Verso.

Fullbrook, Edward (2009) *Ontology and Economics: Tony Lawson and His Critics*, London and New York: Routledge.

Gillies, Donald (2004) 'Can Mathematics be used Successfully in Economics?' in Edward Fullbrook (ed.), *A Guide to What's Wrong With Economics*, London: Anthem Press, pp. 187–97.

Gingras, Yves (2001) 'What did Mathematics do to Physics?' *History of Science*, xxxix, pp 383–416.

Goodwin, Crawford. D. (1998) 'The Patrons of Economics in a Time of Transformation', in Morgan, Mary S. and Rutherford, Malcolm (eds.) *From Interwar Pluralism to Postwar Neoclassicism*, Annual Supplement to Volume 30, History of Political Economy, Duke and London: Duke University Press.

Guerrien, Bernard (2004) "Irrelevance and Ideology", *Post-autistic Economics Review*, issue no. 29, 6 December 2004, article 3.

Hahn, Frank H. (1994) 'An Intellectual Retrospect', *Banca Nazionale del Lavoro Quarterly Review*: 245–258.

Hahn, Frank H. (1970) 'Some adjustment problems', *Econometrica*, vol. 38, January; reprinted as pp. 1–17 in *Equilibrium and Macroeconomics*, Oxford, Basil Blackwell.

Hahn, Frank H. (1982) *Money and Inflation*, Oxford: Basil Blackwell.

Hahn, Frank H. (1992a) 'Reflections', *Royal Economics Society Newsletter* 77.

Hahn, Frank H. (1992b) 'Answer to Backhouse: Yes', *Royal Economic Society Newsletter* 78: 5.

Henry, John (1997) *The Scientific Revolution and the Origins of Modern Science*, New York.

Hofstadter, Richard (1963) *Anti-Intellectualism in American Life*, New York: A.A. Knopf.
Jevons, W. Stanley (1965 [1871]) *The Theory of Political Economy*, New York: Reprints of Economic Classics, Augustus M. Kelley.
Kanth, Rajani (1999) 'Against Eurocentred Epistemologies: a critique of science, realism and economics', in Steven Fleetwood (ed.), *Critical Realism in Economics: Development and Debate*, London and New York: Routledge.
Kirman, Alan (1989) 'The Intrinsic Limits of Modern Economic Theory: The Emperor has no clothes', *Economic Journal* 99(395), pp. 126–139.
Kline, Morris (1964) *Mathematics in Western Culture*, Oxford: Oxford University Press.
Lawson, Tony (1997) *Economics and Reality*, London and New York: Routledge.
Lawson, Tony (2003) *Reorienting Economics*, London and New York: Routledge.
Lawson, Tony (2005) 'The (Confused) State of Equilibrium Analysis in Modern Economics: an (Ontological) Explanation', *Journal for Post Keynesian Economics*, 27: 3 (Spring) pp. 423–44.
Lawson, Tony (2006) 'Tensions in Modern Economics. The case of Equilibrium Analysis', in Valeria Mosini (ed.), *Equilibrium in Economics: Scope and Limits*, London and New York: Routledge.
Lawson Tony (2009a) 'Applied Economics, Contrast Explanation and Asymmetric Information', *Cambridge Journal of Economics*, 33: 3, May, pp. 405–20.
Lawson, Tony (2009b) 'The Current Economic Crisis: its Nature and the Course of Academic economics', *Cambridge Journal of Economics*, 33: 4, July, pp. 759–788.
Lawson, Tony (2009c) 'Contemporary Economics and the Crisis', *Real-World Economics Review*, 50, pp 122–31.
Lawson, Tony (2010) 'Soros's Theory of Reflexivity: a critical comment', mimeo: Cambridge.
Lawson, Tony (2012) 'Ontology and the Study of Social Reality: Emergence, Organisation, Community, Power, Social Relations, Corporations, Artefacts and Money, *Cambridge Journal of Economics*, 36: 2, March, pp 345–386.
Leamer, Edward E. (1978) 'Specification Searches: Ad hoc inferences with non-experimental data', New York: John Wiley and Sons.
Leamer, Edward E. (1983) 'Lets take the Con out of Econometrics', *American Economic Review:* 34–43.
Muth, John F. (1961) 'Rational Expectations and the Theory of Price movements', Econometrica, Vol. 29, No. 3 (July, 1961), pp. 315–335.
O'Boyle, Brian and Terrence McDonough (2011) "Critical realism, Marxism and the Critique of Neoclassical Economics", Capital and Class, February, 35: 3–22: also found at http://goliath.ecnext.com/coms2/gi 0199–14565044/Critical-realism-Marxism-and-the.html
Reinert, Erik. S. (2000) 'The Austrians and 'The Other Canon'', in Backhaus, J (ed.) *The History of Evolutionary Economics*, Aldershot: Edward Elgar.
Rubinstein, Ariel (1995) 'John Nash: the master of economic modelling', *Scandinavian Journal of Economics* 97(1): 9–13.
Söderbaum, Peter (2009) 'A financial crisis on top of the ecological crisis: Ending the monopoly of neoclassical economics', *Real-World Economics Review*, issue no. 49, 12 March, pp. 8–19, http://www.paecon.net/PAEReview/issue49/Soderbaum49.pdf

Soros, George (2009) *The Crash of 2009 and What it Means: The New Paradigm for Financial Markets*, New York: Public Affairs.
Stiglitz, Joseph (2010) *An Agenda for Reforming Economic Theory*, presentation at 2010 INET Conference at Kings College Cambridge. See http://ineteconomics.org/video/conference-kings/agenda-reforming-economic-theory-joseph-stiglitz
Uhlig, Harald (2011) 'Economics and Reality', mimeo: University of Chicago, forthcoming: *Journal of Macro Economics*.
Yonay, Yuval P. (1998) *The Struggle Over the Soul of Economics: Institutionalist and Neoclassical Economists in America Between the Wars*, Princeton: Princeton University Press.

8 Tensions in modern economics: the case of equilibrium analysis

Modern mainstream economists distinguish themselves from both their predecessors and also the current heterodox traditions by their insistence on everywhere employing methods of mathematical deductivist modelling. So immersed in these modelling activities are mainstream economists that they regularly, or so I will argue, elide the distinction between properties of their models and properties of the domain of reality that economists are professing to study. Perhaps this might seem defensible if there were no means of accessing social reality other than via such models. However this is not the case; there are indeed numerous ways of getting to know social reality as testified by our numerous everyday knowledgeable and skilful activities. Acknowledging this we might still want to reason that the elision in question need not matter if we have reason to suppose that the methods in question were well tailored to conditions typical of social reality. Once more, though, we know this not to be so. Rather whilst we shall see that the methods in question are appropriate to a closed world of isolated atoms (terms I will elaborate upon below) social reality is found to be rather different in nature.

One result of this regular mismatch of method and subject matter is that the mainstream project of modern economics is characterised by repeated explanatory failure. This is an issue I have explored at length elsewhere (see Lawson: 2003). Here I focus instead on an alternative manifestation of the ill health of the discipline, the tensions or confusions that arise just because real world properties and those of models often become conflated. Such tensions furthermore even frequently carry over to the contributions of heterodox opponents, who often accept mainstream claims at face value and thereby engage in debates that miss the point.

My aim here is elaborate upon these contentions by way of considering how economists have employed one particular, albeit often central, category, that of (economic) equilibrium.

My argumentative strategy is to first identify tensions in the theorising of equilibrium. I then demonstrate that the factors already discussed serve, when further elaborated, to explain the identified tensions.

Equilibrium theorising in modern Economics

A review of the contributions to equilibrium theorising in modern economics in fact immediately reveals various *prima facie* problematic features, confusions or at least curiosities, some of the most significant of which I wish to focus upon here. These are all features that in due course I shall seek to explain.

A first notable feature of the modern discipline is that at any point in time many authors seem incapable of avoiding inconsistent accounts of the nature of their project. In particular many oscillate between i) supposing that an equilibrium exists and is something to be explained and ii) asserting that its existence is something to be established.

Thus, for example, Arrow and Hahn, in their *General Competitive Analysis,* (Arrow and Hahn: 1971 – one of the seminal contributions to general equilibrium theory) early on claim the heritage of Adam Smith (asserting that "Smith was a creator of general equilibrium theory", p. 2), and note that Smith's project was to explain an *a posteriori* state of affairs that was no part of anyone's design. Indeed they hold the view that Smith's

> notion that a social system moved by independent actions in pursuit of different values is consistent with a final coherent state of balance, and one in which the outcomes may be quite different from those intended by the agents, is surely the most important intellectual contribution that economic thought has made to the general understanding of social processes.
>
> (Arrow and Hahn, 1971: p. 1)

Yet no sooner do they assign to economics the task of explaining this state of affairs, one they interpret as an equilibrium, than Hahn, writing at the time Arrow and Hahn (1971) would have been in press, warns us to caution against supposing an equilibrium exists:

> it cannot be denied that there is something scandalous in the spectacle of so many people refining the analyses of economic [equilibrium] states which they give no reason to suppose will ever, or have ever, come about. It probably is also dangerous. Equilibrium economics... is easily convertible into an apologia for existing economic arrangements and it is frequently so converted.
>
> (Hahn: 1970, pp. 88–9)

A second feature of equilibrium theorising in economics is that there are various competing conceptions of equilibrium, with the range of notions apparently resistant to successful systematisation, despite the best efforts of some. The result inevitably is a lack of clarity over what is being discussed. Machlup (1991) sums this situation up with the assessment that equilibrium is "A term which has so many meanings that we never know what its users are talking about" (p. 43).

A third remarkable phenomenon is that, amongst economists who bother to concern themselves with notions of equilibrium, there is a polarisation of responses. Most contributors are either i) strongly in favour of retaining some equilibrium notion in economics or ii) strongly against doing so. This polarisation is *prima facie* somewhat surprising in a situation that both lacks a consensus about what the concept means and even supports a widespread awareness that interpretations are indeed multiple.

Yet examples abound. Thus Matchlup (1991) maintains that "it is impossible to exclude the terms 'equilibrium' and 'disequilibrium' from the economist's discourse" (p. 43); Hahn (1984) insists that "Wherever economics is used or thought about, equilibrium is a central organising idea" (p. 43); and Backhouse (2003) recently concludes that "The strongest defence of equilibrium analysis ... is that it is indispensable" (p. 8). In the opposite camp Kaldor writes of the irrelevance of equilibrium economics (Kaldor: 1972), Robinson states that the "metaphor of equilibrium is treacherous" (1956, p. 59) whilst Hayek eventually chooses to avoid it as "A somewhat unfortunate term" (Hayek: 1968, p. 184).

An interesting aspect of this situation also warranting explanatory comment is that those most insistent on maintaining the notion are contributors to the mainstream project of modern economics, whilst those rejecting the equilibrium notion are mostly associated with modern heterodox traditions.

That said, however, I should note that the figures with whom the modern heterodox traditions are most associated were often accommodating of the equilibrium idea initially, before becoming less enchanted over time. This I think is true of the likes of Joan Robinson, Keynes and Hayek, now ineradicably associated with modern heterodox reasoning. Thus, for example, Robinson came to contrast equilibrium theorising negatively to a preferred historical approach, while Hayek, for reasons I will discuss in due course, came to prefer the "concept of order ... to that of equilibrium" (1968, p. 15). This latter set of developments too calls for some kind of explanation or further insight.

My aim with this chapter is precisely to outline one way of rendering the phenomena expressed in these observations intelligible. That is, I want to advance and defend an interpretation of what is going on that can account for the:

1   recurrent incoherencies that arise in equilibrium theorising
2   various competing conceptions of equilibrium
3   polarisation of attitudes towards equilibrium theorising, including a tendency for heterodox figures to become increasingly sceptical over time

The elaboration of an account that can explain these observed features constitutes the objective of the main body of this chapter. In a final section I draw out implications of the analysis sustained.

Explaining the phenomena noted

My explanation of the phenomena under examination, briefly sketched above, follows from a broad thesis about the nature of modern economics that I defend elsewhere. Here I mostly outline relevant components of it. I shall not rehearse previous extended defences of the overall thesis (for this see Lawson: 2003, especially chapter 1) although I shall provide some motivation for it. However, I do interpret its ability (demonstrated below) to render intelligible the phenomena before us as further evidence of its explanatory power and so adequacy. The relevant components of this broader thesis are as follow:

1. The modern economics academy is dominated by a mainstream tradition the essence of which is an insistence on mathematical-deductive modelling.
2. As an intellectual project modern mainstream economics is not in a healthy state (it achieves few explanatory or predictive successes, is plagued by theory/practice inconsistencies, relies on constructs recognised as quite fictitious, and generally lacks direction).
3. The explanation of the situation noted under 2) is that mathematical-deductive methods are regularly applied in conditions for which they are not appropriate.
4. If the heterodox alternatives are defined by a reaction to the mainstream insistence on the ubiquitous employment of methods of mathematical modelling, the explanation of this opposition is a shared vision largely at odds with the (atomistic and closed-system) ontological presuppositions of methods of formalistic modelling.
5. The ontological nature of the heterodox opposition to the mainstream is undertheorised and very often unrecognised within the heterodox traditions themselves being manifest mostly in the defence of alternative economic categories.

Let me briefly give some feeling for why I accept these particular assessments.

The first claim – that the modern economics academy is dominated by a mainstream tradition that insists that mathematical-deductive modelling be everywhere utilised – surely no longer needs justification. Consider just the observations of Richard Lipsey, an author of a best selling mainstream economic textbook:

to get an article published in most of today's top rank economic journals, you must provide a mathematical model, even if it adds nothing to your verbal analysis. I have been at seminars where the presenter was asked after a few minutes, 'Where is your model?'. When he answered 'I have not got one as I do not need one, or cannot yet develop one, to consider my problem' the response was to turn off and figuratively, if not literally, to walk out.

(Lipsey: 2001, p. 184)

Simply put an insistence on formalistic modelling methods whatever the problem is an edict accepted by, but only by, the mainstream, and is the only recurring feature of the mainstream (see Lawson: 2003, chapter 1).

My second claim – that as an intellectual project modern mainstream economics is not in a healthy state – is again one that needs little substantiation, being a matter that the more reflective of mainstream economists seem increasingly prepared to acknowledge themselves.

Thus we find Nobel Memorial Prize winners noting that that "Page after page of professional economic journals are filled with mathematical formulas leading the reader from sets of more or less plausible but entirely arbitrary assumptions to precisely stated but irrelevant theoretical conclusions" (Leontief: 1982, p. 104); that "economics has become increasingly an arcane branch of mathematics rather than dealing with real economic problems" (Friedman: 1999, p. 137); that "Existing economics is a theoretical system which floats in the air and which bears little relation to what happens in the real world" (Coase: 1999, p. 2).

Further, the mainstream 'theorist' Ariel Rubinstein admits that "economic theory has not delivered the goods" adding that "the link between economic theory and practical problems ... is tenuous at best. (Rubinstein: 1995, p. 12) Indeed he concludes, "Economic theory lacks a consensus as to its purpose and interpretation. Again and again, we find ourselves asking the question 'where does it lead?'" (Rubinstein: 1995, p. 12).

Nor is the problem just the project's lack of direction and limited explanatory and predictive power. In addition the project's theory and practice are highly inconsistent. For example econometricians put huge resources into elaborating the methods they take to be appropriate and justified, yet their practices diverge wildly from their own methodological strictures (see e.g. Leamer: 1978, p. vi; Hendry et al: 1990, p. 179)

All in all the discipline is replete with theory/practice inconsistencies, fares poorly by its own criteria, and lacks any clear idea as to where it is going. It is also full of anomalies that range over its various sub-programmes. Consider the observations of Richard Lipsey once more:

> anomalies, particularly those that cut across the sub-disciplines and that can be studied with various technical levels of sophistication, are

tolerated on a scale that would be impossible in most natural sciences—and would be regarded as a scandal if they were.

(Lipsey: 2001, p. 173)

If a summary statement is required it is perhaps provided by Mark Blaug, a methodologically oriented economist, who has spent considerable resources throughout his career attempting to shore up the mainstream tradition. His current assessment runs as follows:

> Modern economics is sick. Economics has increasingly become an intellectual game played for its own sake and not for its practical consequences for understanding the economic world. Economists have converted the subject into a sort of social mathematics in which analytical rigour is everything and practical relevance is nothing.
>
> (Blaug: 1997, p. 3)

My third claim – that the disarray of modern economics follows because methods of mathematical-deductive modelling are regularly applied in conditions for which they are not appropriate – is something I shall elaborate rather than defend (for a defence also see Lawson: 2003, chapter 1).

All methods are appropriate in some conditions and not others. As Keynes long ago in effect recognised the sorts of mathematical methods economists use presuppose a closed world of isolated atoms (Keynes focused on the econometrics of Tinbergen of course). To describe a causal factor as atomistic in this fashion is not to make a claim about size, of course, but to indicate a presupposition that it exercises its own separate independent and invariable effect, whatever the context, thus guaranteeing that under some repeated conditions x the same predictable outcome y will always follow.

The point, of course, is that social reality does not comprise merely closed atomistic systems. Indeed it is easy enough to show that social reality is not only open (it consists in more than systems supporting event regularities) but also structured (irreducible to the course of events), intrinsically dynamic (its mode of being is as a process) and highly internally related (consisting of parts and wholes each constituted though [ever-changing] relations to other parts and wholes – think of positions of teachers and students, or employers and employees), amongst much else. From this perspective it is not at all surprising that attempts to analyse social life using only methods that presuppose a world that is closed and atomistic fare so badly.

The fourth and fifth claims can be run together. Here I am suggesting that heterodox contributions tend to presuppose a shared vision largely at odds with the (atomistic and closed-system) ontological presuppositions of methods of formalistic modelling. Rather the heterodox contributions tend to advance substantive, methodological and/or policy claims whose ontological presuppositions are essentially those of openness, structure, process, internal-relationality, and so on. However, (with a few important exceptions, most notably Paul Davidson's emphasis on non-ergodic systems[1]) the ontological nature of the heterodox opposition to the mainstream is under-theorised and very often unrecognised within the heterodox traditions themselves.

Thus, in post Keynesianism we find an emphasis on uncertainty (presupposing openness) in place of risk, in feminism the emphasis is on caring and identity relations (presupposing internal-relationality) instead of selfish individuals; and in old institutionalism the emphasis is on the evolutionary method (process) rather than theorising an equilibrating or teleological system. However, as I say the ontological presuppositions *per se* are rarely emphasised. I believe it is just because the ontological basis of heterodoxy goes unrecognised that its criticisms of the mainstream have usually been less effectual than they deserve.

A brief sketch of my explanation of the state of equilibrium theorising

Here I want to use this five-part thesis (which as I say is defended at length elsewhere – see e.g. Lawson: 1997, 2003) to explain the phenomena noted earlier. The nature of my argument is perhaps unfamiliar. So it may be useful at this point if I provide a schematic overview of its basic thrust and direction. It runs as follows.

The limited power of mathematical methods to illuminate social reality, the lack of fit of the former to the latter, necessarily results in mainstream economists inventing "a reality" of a form that their modelling methods can address (i.e., a world of isolated atomistic individuals possessed, for example, of perfect foresight, or rational expectations, omniscience, pure greed, and so forth). But this is not all. It also imparts meaning to macro or system-categories of a sort that is driven by the needs or constraints of mathematical modelling (rather than meeting with the more usual, historical or intuitive understandings of such categories). And this happens in ways that are often unappreciated (if ultimately explicable). We shall see that *equilibrium* is one such system-category that suffers such a fate (a further one of interest but not considered here is the econometric idea of a data generation process or DGP, see Stephen Pratten (2005); another is that of complexity, see Eugenia Perona (2004).

If I can use the term *theoretic* to denote the quality of being a feature of a model and the term *ontic* to denote the quality of being a feature of the world the economist presumes to illuminate, a more succinct way of describing the problem that arises through the prioritisation of the modelling orientation is a conflation of the theoretic and ontic, with the latter reduced to the former[2].

Now in mostly neglecting to engage in systematic ontological elaboration the heterodox opposition has tended to take the mainstream constructs at face value, and thereby to counterpoise alternative conceptions at the same (substantive or system) level, mostly failing to appreciate that the two sides to the discussion are talking about entirely different worlds.

Only with a turn to systematic ontology, however, can we make sense of the total situation. For only then are we in a position both i) to clearly distinguish the ontological presuppositions of the mainstream methods and those guiding heterodox traditions, and ii) to see that not only are they differently derived but also (given the lack of fit of social reality and the formalistic methods used) necessarily very different in character. And we shall see that it is only through sustaining the theoretic/ontic distinction that we can ultimately comprehensively explain 1) the confusions and inconsistencies that arise, 2) the variety of equilibrium notions on offer, and 3) the debates and polarisations (including trends to increased scepticism in the contributions of some) such as are observed. Let me now defend this claim in detail.

The explanation in detail

In the context of equilibrium analysis my central claim translates into the idea that some conceptions of equilibrium found in the literature are theoretic and others are ontic, but that this difference in the nature of the competing conceptions goes largely unnoticed.

To illustrate we can consider the most frequently occurring examples of contrasted notions of equilibrium in the economics literature, those of *system determinateness* on the one hand and *balance or order* on the other. For an examination of actual texts quickly reveals that those who have emphasised determinateness have mostly meant by this the *determinateness of particular representations or formalisations* of the economy, whilst those who have emphasised balance or order have interpreted this as *an aspect of the economy they are attempting to represent*. While the former is theoretic, a sought-after property of theories or more typically models, the latter is ontic, a property of society that the investigator is seeking to understand and explain.

However, it is a generalised failure to recognise that this is the nature of the distinction being drawn that has led to such confusion as abounds. Typically, the rhetoric of equilibrium analysis supports images of order or balance whilst its real content has concerned the properties of formalistic models. The failure to distinguish the two in a systematic way has resulted in a literature that is often incoherent, with contributors tending to talk past each other. Ultimately, we shall see, this state of affairs also throws insight on the plethora of equilibrium concepts in contention as well as the polarisations in attitudes to equilibrium theorising.

The equilibrium dichotomy

It is useful at this point to consider the classic statement of equilibrium theory in the modern period provided by Arrow and Hahn (1971). This is useful just because these authors start their book with a "historical introduction" which emphasises precisely the distinction just noted. Indeed their opening sentence runs as follows:

> There are two basic, incompletely separable, aspects of the notion of general equilibrium as it has been used in economics: the simple notion of determinateness, that the relations describing the economic system must be sufficiently complete to determine the values of its variables, and the more specific notion that each relation represents a balance of forces.
>
> (Arrow and Hahn: 1971, p. 1)

If we examine this passage closely we can indeed see the different nature of the two conceptions. The first criterion, *determinateness*, is precisely a property of a system of (mathematical) relations used to 'describe' the economic system, whilst a *balance of forces* is an aspect of the economy, one that each equation is said to represent. The former is a property of the theoretical conception; the latter thought to be a property of what the theoretical conception is about. The former is theoretic, the latter ontic.

Arrow and Hahn, though, like most modern economists, are so much oriented to the theorising aspect that they misunderstand the nature of the difference in the two conceptions they describe. As the noted passage also indicates, they suppose that the difference to which they are drawing attention is one of levels generality. Specifically, they emphasise that the idea of representing a *balance of forces* is a "more specific notion" than that of "determinateness".

Let me be clear on this. Contra the sort of interpretation advanced by Weintraub (2005) these authors do not claim that the historically prior notion (or aspects of a notion) concerning a "balance of forces" has now been replaced by the (more) modern notion (or aspect) of determinateness. Rather, as I say, they merely see the former as being the more specific concept; indeed they view the two conceptions as incompletely separable aspects of one notion.

Now, contra Arrow and Hahn I suggest that the categories in question are after all completely separable notions of equilibrium, that (what I am calling) the ontic notion is not simply (or at all) a more specific notion, but something quite different to the theoretic one. It is clear, though, that Arrow and Hahn do often run the two concepts together (as two inseparable aspects of one notion) just because the theoretic/ontic distinction is untheorised. Their primary concern is with model properties, with the determinateness of systems of equations. They think that any

178　*Tensions in modern economics*

attempt to theorise the whole of an economic system implies the acceptance of this conception of equilibrium. However, in illustrating the supposedly more specific notion of a balance, they unwittingly provide an ontic formulation. Consider more of Arrow and Hahn (1971):

> In a sense, almost any attempt to give a theory of the whole economic system implies the acceptance of the first part of the equilibrium notion; and Adam Smith's 'invisible hand' is a poetic expression of the most fundamental of economic relations, the equalization of rates of return, as enforced by the tendency of factors to move from low to high returns.
>
> The notion of equilibrium ('equal weight,' referring to the condition for balancing a lever pivoted at its centre) was familiar to mechanics long before the publication of *The Wealth of Nations* in 1776, and with it the notion that the effects of a force may annihilate it (e.g., water finding its own level), but there is no obvious evidence that Smith drew his ideas from any analogy with mechanics. Whatever the source of the concept, the notion that a social system moved by independent actions in pursuit of different values is consistent with a final coherent balance, and one in which the outcomes may be different from those intended by the agents, is surely the most important intellectual contribution that economic thought has made to the general understanding of social processes.
>
> (Arrow and Hahn: 1971, p. 1)

This passage (apart from the first clause referring to equilibrium as determinateness) deals solely with the way the economy works. The concern is with the balance of a social system. The focus has nothing to do with properties of models, and everything to do with the forces of society. Yet Arrow and Hahn move from this discussion to immediately suggest that "Smith was a creator of general equilibrium theory", a purely theoretic notion, thus indeed confusing the discussion of equilibrium theorising.

Thus we can see the source of the confusion noted at the outset. Smith and those adopting an ontic orientation are indeed concerned to explain an existing situation. Smith's objective is to explain such economic order as occurs in the social world. By referring to such a state of affairs as an equilibrium Arrow and Hahn and others are thereby suggesting at this point that an equilibrium always occurs and is something to explain. However, when they conceive of an equilibrium in terms of a consistency property of their models, as determiniteness, their concern is to show that such a property – an equilibrium – exists[3]. Thus the failure explicitly to distinguish the theoretic and the ontic produces conflicting statements about what is going on.

Consider again the passage from Hahn noted at the outset "... it cannot be denied that there is something scandalous in the spectacle of so many people refining the analyses of economic [equilibrium] states which they give no reason to suppose will ever, or have ever, come about" (Hahn: 1970, pp. 88–9).

Let us once more be clear. When Hahn here refers to an equilibrium that may never come about it perhaps appears at first sight that he is using an ontic notion. However, this is not so. He is really saying that in an imagined world consistent with his model there is nothing to ensure that an equilibrium position would result. Or more accurately, he is saying that if, for a set of equations used to construct a description of the economy, there is a manner – a specification – whereby the various equations are found to be mutually consistent, then the solution to the consistency question, stylised an equilibrium, is not a part of the model description, and so not a necessary outcome even in such a counterfactual (closed and atomistic) world as described by the model specification.

In short, the equilibrium is merely a solution to a system of equations. It is a vector that renders the equations consistent. Hahn's point is that there is nothing in the apparatus of the model to ensure that even if, *per impossible,* the model accurately represented the world, the equilibrium situation, expressed by the model's consistency condition, would emerge.

I do not want to suggest that Hahn intentionally misleads, or always fails to acknowledge the limits of his endeavour. Certainly, Hahn seems to have become increasingly clear with the passage of time on what his constructions entitle him to conclude. Indeed in a recent "Intellectual Retrospect" he is very clear about what is taking place in his theory contributions:

> The great virtue of mathematical reasoning in economics is that by its precise account of assumptions it becomes crystal clear that applications to the "real" world could at best be provisional. When a mathematical economist assumes that there is a three good economy lasting two periods, or that agents are infinitely lived (perhaps because they value the utility of their descendants which they know!), everyone can see that we are not dealing with any actual economy. The assumptions are there to enable certain results to emerge and not because they are to be taken descriptively.
>
> (Hahn: 1994, p. 246)

It seems reasonable to suppose that if Hahn had been clearer on this score from the outset, however, some of the earlier (non-connecting) discussion might have been avoided. Joan Robinson (for example 1978, p. 127) in particular might have been spared the effort of responding to Hahn in terms of outlining, and defending as more realistic, a particular (ontic) conception of an equilibrium.

180 *Tensions in modern economics*

To repeat, then, my explanatory thesis (conditioned on the description of modern economics described above) is that in modern economics there is an erroneous (if explicable) tendency to conflate theoretic and ontic features of an analysis. And this thesis can be seen to account for much of the incoherency of equilibrium analysis as abounds.

The remaining problematic features

How does this thesis account for the two remaining sets of observations noted above, namely of:

i) a plethora of competing equilibrium conceptions, especially of those conceptions that can be viewed as versions of system determinateness, and
ii) a polarisation of orientations, divided amongst mainstream/heterodox lines?

The plethora of conceptions is easily explained. For where equilibrium is merely a solution concept for a model, a property of a system of equations, there can clearly be as many definitions of equilibrium as there are possibilities for system-model construction. And scope for the latter seems limitless.

This situation is grasped by some but seemingly not by most. Thus a heroic attempt to bring clarity by Machlup ends up doing no more than rendering both the equilibrium as *balance* and equilibrium as *determinateness* notions as theoretic:

> Equilibrium, in economic analysis [is] a constellation of selected interrelated variables so adjusted to one another that no inherent tendency to change prevails in the model which they constitute.... As an alternative definition of equilibrium we may propose mutual compatibility of a selected set of interrelated variables of particular magnitudes.
>
> (Machlup: 1991, pp. 54–5)

But Dixon amongst others hits the nail on the head precisely: "At its most general, we can say that 'equilibrium' is a method of solving economic models. At a superficial level, an equilibrium is simply a solution to a set of equations" (Dixon: 1990, p. 356).

It is equally possible to explain our remaining puzzle, the polarisation of attitudes over the relevance of an equilibrium notion. I have already noted that attitudes have tended to divide along mainstream/heterodox lines, with the mainstream, unlike heterodoxy, insisting the equilibrium notion is essential, and with the heterodox opposition becoming increasingly marked over time. We now have before us the resources to understand why.

Consider first the mainstream insistence that the equilibrium notion be retained. The reason for this must now be clear. For this mainstream project is defined by its insistence that mathematical methods be everywhere and always employed, despite the dearth of explanatory successes to date. But in a situation where model equations are found almost always to be inappropriate to the analysis of the economic system what other goal can be accepted for modellers than the questioning of their equations' mutual consistency? Where the emphasis is on a formalistic system, attention is always going to turn to the question of whether the system has some sort of mathematical solution. And the natural, or anyway traditional, way to try and present this as an economic activity is to present the mathematical exercise as the search for an economic equilibrium. Associating the process with Smith is merely an attempt to grant the exercise a historical legitimacy, an endeavour that significantly misleads.

How about the heterodox rejection of the use of the term? If the mainstream was always going to require a notion to express the model-property of consistency or determinateness, was it equally predictable that heterodoxy was always going to abandon the term?

The answer I think is yes if not necessarily immediately. I earlier suggested that a feature of the heterodox traditions is that although they emphasise categories with ontological presuppositions different to those of the mainstream mathematical methods, they rarely acknowledge that this is so. Specifically, the mainstream methods presuppose a closed atomistic reality, whereas heterodox conceptions can be shown to be based on a vision of social reality as open, structured, processual, highly internally related, amongst much else (see Lawson: 2003). As I say, though, the ontological basis of the opposition has rarely been explicitly identified.

Even so heterodox economists have been oriented to ontic elaboration, focusing mostly on equilibrium as a balance or form of order. In consequence the tension between the conceptions of social order they have been seeking to explain and the more dominant definitions of equilibrium have usually been apparent, even if the ontological basis of the distinction remained un-theorised. This has resulted in equilibrium notions being employed, if at all, often in a hesitant and cautious manner. Joan Robinson provides an obvious example:

> The word equilibrium, in ordinary speech, describes a relation between bodies in space. The scales of a balance are in equilibrium when the balance is at rest. If we are continually throwing coppers at random into either scale, the balance is continually wobbling and

> never reaches equilibrium; but, at any moment, there is a definite equilibrium position which it would quickly reach if, from that moment, we left it alone.
>
> (1956, p. 57)

She concludes:

> Nor can we apply the metaphor of a balance which is seeking or tending towards a position of equilibrium though prevented from actually reaching it through constant disturbances. In economic affairs the fact that disturbances are known to be liable to occur makes expectations about the future uncertain and has an important effect on any conduct (which, in fact, is all economic conduct) directed towards future results. . . . A belief that a particular share is going to rise in price causes people to offer to buy it and so raises its price. . . . This element of 'thinking makes it so' creates a situation where a cunning guesser who can guess what the other guessers are going to guess is able to make a fortune. There are then no solid weights to give us analogy with a pair of scales in balance. The metaphor of equilibrium is treacherous.
>
> (1956, p. 59)

The more that the ontic orientation has been manifest in a sustained concern with the nature of the actually existing social order, the more heterodox economists have grasped the irrelevancy of the equilibrium framework. Thus, with time, of course, Joan Robinson turned from equilibrium thinking to history.

A second illustration is provided by the contributions of Hayek. Hayek is especially interesting here in that all along he recognises the theoretic or *a priori* nature of the dominant framework, interpreting it as a logic of choice, whilst being driven himself always to provide an ontic account. This is especially true of his work of the late 1930s. Specifically his 1937 "Economics and Knowledge" paper is a particularly ingenious attempt to reconcile two ultimately incompatible endeavours: an *a priori* logical framework (presupposing a closed system) and a desire for a realistic (open-system) vision of the actual social world.

Early on in this 1937 paper Hayek writes:

> I am certain that there are many who regard with impatience and distrust the whole tendency, which is inherent in all modern equilibrium analysis, to turn economics into a branch of pure logic, a set of self-evident propositions which, like mathematics or geometry, are subject to no other test but internal consistency.
>
> (Hayek: 1937, p. 35)

How is the noted tendency to turn economics into a branch of logic to be avoided? How is equilibrium analysis to be rescued as an ontic endeavour, as a project concerned with understanding social reality? Hayek hopes this can be achieved by way of economists seeking out a real world tendency to equilibrium:

> We shall not get much further here unless we ask for the reasons for our concern with the admittedly fictitious state of equilibrium. Whatever may occasionally have been said by over-pure economists, there seems to be no possible doubt that the only justification for this is the supposed existence of a tendency toward equilibrium. It is only by this assertion that economics ceases to be an exercise in pure logic and becomes an empirical science; and it is to economics as an empirical science that we must now turn.
> (Hayek: 1937, pp. 43–4)

The story is a long one. But it is sufficient to note here that eventually Hayek accepts that a tendency to equilibrium requires that individuals' expectations of each other become more and more accurate; whilst he admits that he does not know why or how such an eventuality should come about. As a result he comes close to abandoning the equilibrium project even in this early essay:

> But I am afraid that I am now getting to a stage where it becomes exceedingly difficult to say what exactly are the assumptions on the basis of which we assert that there will be a tendency toward equilibrium, and to claim that our analysis has an application to the real world. I cannot pretend that I have as yet got much further on this point.
> (Hayek: 1937, p. 47)

Not surprisingly perhaps, this failure spurred Hayek into a form of ontological reasoning. After initially trying to maintain an equilibrium idea Hayek's ontic orientation led him increasingly to appreciate its limitations. Some time after the "Economics and Knowledge" paper, in fact, Hayek was emphasising the idea of social order rather than equilibrium:

> The concept of 'order', which ... I prefer to that of equilibrium, has the advantage that we can speak about order being approached to varying degrees, and that order can be preserved throughout the process of change.
> (Hayek: 1968, p. 184)

Eventually, of course, Hayek elaborates a social ontology of rules and other aspects of social structure, and develops his conception of spontaneous order:

> What reconciles the individuals and knits them into a common and enduring pattern of society is that they respond in accordance with the same abstract rules ... What ... enables ... men to live and work together in peace is that the pursuit of their individual ends and the particular monetary impulses which impel their efforts ... are guided and restrained by the same abstract rules. If emotion or impulse tells them what they want, the conventional rules tell them how they will be able and allowed to achieve it.
>
> (1976, p. 12)

> A catallaxy is thus a special kind of spontaneous order produced by the market through people acting within the rules of the law of property, tort and contract.
>
> (1982, p.109)

This is no longer a conception of a state of order in which expectations are always met; rather it is one in which disappointments are unavoidable.

> In a spontaneous order, undeserved disappointments cannot be avoided.... It is only because countless others constantly submit to disappointments of their reasonable expectations that everyone has as high an income as he has.
>
> ibid, p. 128

With this being so, Hayek's conception is far more in line with the world we daily experience. It is quite different from Hayek's original notion, but reveals the sort of direction that is ultimately to be expected where there is a consistent emphasis on the ontic.

Implications and conclusion

Modern economics is not in a healthy state. And the reason for it is that it, or rather the dominant mainstream tradition, defines itself in terms of its method, that of formalistic-deductive modelling, and does so in a context where that method has little application. I have indicated before how this emphasis has resulted in limited explanatory successes, theory/practice inconsistencies and other pathologies. Here I have focussed on a further problematic feature created by the mainstream prioritising of modelling over illumination: the confusing of claims about models and their properties with properties of the reality that the models putatively aim to represent.

In truth, modern economics supports two broad sets of traditions, the mainstream project and the heterodox alternatives. The mainstream prioritises modelling whilst the heterodoxy prioritises social illumination. And because the implicit (though rarely examined) ontological commitments of the heterodoxy (of openness, structure, internal-relationality and process) are quite different to those (of atomism and closure) presupposed by the mainstream modelling emphasis, the two projects rarely find common ground.

However the true ontological nature of the differences is rarely explored. One of the many debilitating results of this is that when common categories are employed, the real nature of the differences in arguments mostly goes unrecognised resulting in participants in debates talking past each other. I have illustrated this theme in the context of equilibrium analysis.

If all parties agree that Adam Smith set (and contributed to answering) one of the fundamental questions of economics, namely how the fact of social order emerges in the absence of central or any intentional design, and indeed with individuals pursuing largely independent goals, it is clear that the inheritors of Smith's project are not economic equilibrium theorists concerned with formalistic modelling. Rather it is those working in the traditions of Marx, Keynes, Hayek and others who make the explaining of the actually existing social order the priority.

The project of formalistic modelling can be misinterpreted as one concerned with explaining the actual social order only if the atomistic presuppositions of the former go unrecognised, or their irrelevance remains unappreciated. Once we turn to social ontology, to theorising the nature of social reality, the impotence of the equilibrium notion becomes apparent. The real question, Smith's question in modern terms, is how social reproduction of complex, internally related, dynamic, social structures occurs in an open world of a multitude of unique if related individuals each seeking to realise her or his own objectives. As I say, this eventually was the concern of Hayek and Keynes as well as Marx. How successful they were in the details of their analyses, of course, is a different question.

Notes

1 See e.g., Davidson: 1989, 1996.
2 Elsewhere I have described this error as based on the *epistemic fallacy*. The fallacy in question is the supposition that questions about being can be always be rephrased as questions about knowledge (of being).
3 For example, they turn next to Walras to whom, they suggest, the "full recognition of the general equilibrium concept can be attributed unmistakably" (Arrow and Hahn: 1971, p. 3). Here we are in the realm of models. Things are confused because variables in models are referred to as prices, demand and supply, and so forth. However it is clear from the discussion that when equilibrium is now conceived as a set of prices, being those that equate supply and demand on each market under a given set of conditions, the category is a property of models not to states of affairs they are purported to represent:

"That there was an equilibrium set of prices was argued from the equality of the number of prices to be determined with the number of equations expressing the equality of supply and demand on all markets. Both are." (Arrow and Hahn: p. 5)

Bibliography

Arrow, Kenneth. J. and Frank H. Hahn, (1971), *General Competitive Analysis*, Holden-Day, San Francisco.

Backhouse, Roger, (2003), 'History and Equilibrium: a partial defence of equilibrium economics', unpublished mimeo.

Blaug, Marc, (1997), 'Ugly Currents in Modern Economics', *Options Politique*, September, pp 3–4.

Coase, Ronald, (1999), Interview with Ronald Coase, in: *Newsletter of the International Society for New Institutional Economics*, 2 (1), Spring issue.

Davidson, Paul, (1989), 'The Economics of Ignorance or the Ignorance of Economics?', *Critical Review*, 3, 467–487.

Davidson, Paul, (1996), 'Reality and Economic Theory', in: *Journal of Post Keynesian Economics*, Summer, 18(4), 479–508.

Dixon, Huw, (1990), 'Equilibrium and Explanation', in: John Creedy (ed.) *Foundations Of Economic Thought*, Basil Blackwell, Oxford.

Friedman, Milton, (1999), 'Conversation with Milton Friedman', in: Snowdon B. and Vane H. (ed.), *Conversations with Leading Economists: interpreting modern macroeconomics*, 124–44, Edward Elgar, Cheltenham.

Hahn, Frank H., (1970), 'Some adjustment problems', in: *Econometrica*, 38, 1–17, January, reprinted in Hahn (1984), (page references to the latter).

Hahn, Frank H., (1984), *Equilibrium and Macroeconomics*, Basil Blackwell, Oxford.

Hayek, F.A., (1937), 'Economics and Knowledge', *Economica*, IV: 33–54.

Hayek, Friedrich A., (1968), 'Competition as a Discovery Process', in: *Hayek*, 1978.

Hayek, Friedrich A., (1976), 'The Mirage of Social Justice', in: *Hayek* (1982).

Hayek, Friedrich A., (1978), *New Studies in Philosophy, Politics and Economics*, Routledge and Kegan Paul, London.

Hayek, Friedrich A., (1982), *Law, Legislation and Liberty*, Routledge and Kegan Paul, London.

Hendry, David F., Edward E. Leamer and Dale J. Poirier, (1990), 'The ET Dialogue: A Conversation on Econometric Methodology', in: *Econometric Theory*, 6, 171–261.

Kaldor, Nicholas, (1972), 'The Irrelevance of Equilibrium Economics', in: *Economic Journal*, 82, December. Reprinted in Nicholas Kaldor, (1978), *Further Essays on Economic Theory*, Duckworth, London.

Lawson, Tony, (2003), *Reorienting Economics*, Routledge, London and New York.

Leamer, Edward E., (1978), *Specification Searches: Ad hoc Inferences With Non-experimental Data*, John Wiley and Sons, New York.

Leontief, Wassily, (1982), 'Letter', in *Science*, 217: 104–7.

Lipsey, Richard G., (2001), 'Successes and failures in the transformation of economics', in: *Journal Of Economic Methodology*, 8 (2), June, 169–202.

Matchlup, Fritz, (1991), 'Equilibrium and Disequilibrium: misplaced concreteness and disguised politics', in: *Economic Semantics*, Transaction Press, New Brunswick, N.J., Reprinted in Donald Walker (ed.), (2000), *Equilibrium 3 Volumes*, Edward Elgar, Cheltenham.

Perona, E., (2004), 'The confused state of complexity in economics: an ontological explanation', Faculdad de Ciencas Economicas, Universidad Nacional de Cordoba.

Pratten, Stephen, (2005), 'Economics as Progress: the LSE approach to economic modelling and critical realism as programmes for research', in: *Cambridge Journal of Economics* vol. 29, issue 2, 179–205.

Robinson, Joan (1956) *The Accumulation of Capital,* London: Macmillan.

Robinson, Joan, (1978), 'History versus equilibrium', in *Contributions to Modern Economics,* Oxford: Basil Blackwell.

Rubinstein, Ariel, (1995), 'John Nash: the master of economic modelling', in: *Scandinavian Journal of Economics,* 97(1), 9–13.

Smith, Adam, (1975), *The Wealth of Nations,* Dent, London and Toronto.

Weintraub, Roy, (2005), 'On Lawson on Equilibrium', in: *Journal of Post Keynesian Economics,* 27 (3), 445–454.

9 Soros' theory of reflexivity: a critical comment*[1]

Introduction[2]

In a recent book George Soros (2009) proposes a new paradigm for economic thinking. In doing so he reveals himself to be somewhat wary of the emphasis of contemporary mainstream economists on methods of mathematical modelling, and stridently critical of certain prominent substantive economic theories, most especially those developed under the heads of rational expectations, the efficient markets hypothesis, and equilibrium theory.

Soros' contribution, I believe, contains insight. However in arguing his case Soros draws several questionable contrasts and these likely detract from the force of his insights. In this short note I briefly question some of Soros' background claims and assessments, and examine the contribution that remains once, or if, various unsustainable, and in fact unnecessary, claims are jettisoned. A critical commentary on the sustainable part of Soros' contribution then follows.

A central argument here is that Soros' criticisms do not quite go far enough. Though the shortcomings may seem minor, they bear implications regarding the sorts of contribution likely to be encouraged within Soros' recent venture, systematised as the *International Network for Economic Thinking* (INET). Despite Soros' intentions in sponsoring INET to improve the state of modern academic economics, I fear that unless the nature and implications of Soros' insights are better recognised, the net result, at the level at which it matters, i.e., that at which the discipline goes awry, will just be more of the same, a perpetuating of the most fundamental errors.

Reflexivity

George Soros' central contention, the core of his proposed 'new paradigm', is advanced under the head of *reflexivity*. Human beings, Soros observes, seek *both* 1) to understand reality and 2) to influence reality. He refers to the former as *the cognitive function* and to the latter initially as *the participating function* and, more recently, as *the manipulative function*. The essential point for Soros is that there is a two way exchange: 1) from reality (including humans and their interactions) to our understanding of it, and 2) from each human being armed with an understanding, back to (the rest of) reality. For Soros the term reflexivity is basically used to express or capture this two way relationship.

Soros' concern is that both functions of this two way relationship can be in operation at the same time, leading them to interfere with each other:

> When both functions operate at the same time they may interfere with each other. For the cognitive function to produce knowledge it must take social phenomena as independently given; only then will the phenomena qualify as facts to which the observer's statement may correspond. Similarly, decisions need to be based on knowledge to produce the desired results. But when both functions operate simultaneously, the phenomena do not consist only of facts but also of intentions and expectations about the future.
>
> (Soros, 2009, p. 4)

Soros' central contention does indeed contain insight, and it takes us beyond the standpoint of much modern economics. But there is a need for some clarification.

The nature of the problem

It is important to appreciate the real nature of the problem to which Soros is pointing. In effect Soros is identifying factors that contribute to rendering social reality inescapably open; he is indicating that the future, because dependent on what we are all doing, not least in anticipating and reacting to each other, is yet to be determined and inherently unpredictable.

I shall use the term closure or closed system to express a situation in which an event regularity, or correlation occurs; it is a condition for successful prediction. In the absence of conditions supporting event regularities the system can be said to be open.

The future, and indeed the present, of social reality are indeed open and unpredictable, and Soros emphasises reflexivity as one of the reasons why. However, in correctly identifying the feature of reflexivity Soros wrongly supposes thereby both that assessments about social phenomena are necessarily more fallible or imperfect than claims about natural phenomena, and also that a science of social phenomena and/or capable everyday human activity, are impossible.

Very briefly, all knowledge is fallible and imperfect whatever it is about. Even the seemingly most explanatorily powerful of natural scientific claims have usually been found to be inadequate in some ways in due course. Soros is surely right to emphasise that "our understanding of the world in which we live is inherently imperfect". But it confuses matters to suggest that such imperfection arises "because we are part of the world we seek to understand" (p. 3). Not only is all knowledge fallible, and our understanding of other worlds, say outer space, or that of the dinosaurs, imperfect, but it is not clear that our having been part of anything *necessarily* complicates our understanding of it relative to our understanding of anything else. Thus medical research into the human body is often seemingly comparably successful to some of the non-human or non-social sciences. Moreover it can reasonably be argued that we often have a greater insight into the social realm, i.e., that realm of phenomena whose existence necessarily depends at least in part on us, *just because it depends on us, and is intrinsic to our activities*.

We in fact find ourselves to be extraordinarily capable beings *qua* social beings, very adept at understanding and coping with the everyday complexities of social life. We are very skilful at acquiring language, negotiating the market place, motorways, forms of international travel, and communications, new technologies, the host of human institutions, and so forth. In fact, on examination, our ability to navigate a rather complex social reality is revealed to be really quite extraordinary (requiring many years of training).

How come we are so skilful at negotiating the world around us given that the latter is essentially open? We are so just because reality, both (the non-social) natural and social, is also structured. Although both realms are open in the sense that, away from experimental laboratories, event regularities (regularities of the form whenever event x then event y) rarely occur, behind surface phenomena in each domain lie deeper causal forces. Indeed it is often just because a multiplicity of causal forces governs any outcome that regularities at the level of outcomes or events rarely occur. Now the underlying causes in (the non-social) natural and social realms alike will often be relatively enduring, and frequently identifiable. For example, underlying and governing the paths of autumn leaves are causal factors such as gravity and aerodynamic forces; underpinning the symptoms of mad cow disease is the prion; and underpinning social practices are social structures such as collective practices, rule systems, social relations, and the like. And it is through seeking knowledge of these underlying structures that science and capable human practice alike are feasible.

Science, I have elsewhere argued (1997, 2003, 2010) is characterised precisely by the move from surface phenomenon of interest to identifying the underlying cause(s). In other words, its central goal is causal explanation. It is because the social realm, like the (non-social) natural realm, is structured that this move is as possible in the former realm, rendering a social science entirely feasible.

It is also precisely because reality, both (non-social) natural and social, is so structured, that capable everyday behaviour is feasible, despite outcomes or events being unpredictable in advance. For underlying and grounding social practices are causal structures such as social rules, and relations. And capable human agency is possible through people drawing on their knowledge of underlying social (and natural) structures, and adapting as they go along.

Thus when, for example, an individual embarks on a motoring journey, it is usually enough to know the rules of the Highway Code, how to drive, the causal forces represented by other vehicles, the way gravity operates, and so forth. Specifically, it is not necessary to predict in advance each configuration of vehicles etc., to be encountered throughout the journey. The latter feat would usually, of course, be impossible, because, despite its highly structured nature, even the motorway is ultimately an open system.

So what is the problem?

If openness of social (and non-social natural) systems proves not to be undermining either of the possibility of social science or of capable day-to-day human agency, what is the problem to which Soros is pointing with his notion of reflexivity?

I have indicated that social science and daily activities are viable because they are concerned with, and draw upon, understandings of the deeper structures. In particular human daily activities are conditioned upon these, and result from our abilities to adapt to immediate circumstances.

The sorts of problems that most interest Soros, however, arise because of a concern not (or not just or primarily) with (identifying and understanding) underlying causal structures, but rather and centrally with *predictions of specific concrete outcomes*. These *outcomes* are exactly the sort of phenomena to which financial speculation and investment are oriented; the focus is typically on future relative prices or relative price movements. However, because the financial system is open—and as we have seen Soros' insights systemised under the heading of reflexivity give reason to suppose that the financial system is in fact as open as any—such concrete outcomes are just the sort of thing that *cannot typically be known or successfully predicted in advance*, even if or when a knowledge of some significant underlying structures has been achieved.

Soros' criticisms

We are now in a position to more clearly understand the real nature Soros' concerns relating to modern economics. Despite Soros' various suggestions to the contrary, the fundamental problem to which he draws attention does not depend on any natural/social distinction or on a science/non-science opposition. If there is a contrast of relevance to be drawn it is between open and closed systems. Soros' concern boils down to the impossibility of successfully anticipating concrete outcomes in an open system, except maybe by chance, coupled with an apparent failure of many academic economists to recognise this.

In open social systems, such as the financial world, uncertainty is always rife; and specific outcomes such as relative prices cannot possibly be known in advance. Yet, as Soros notes, modern mainstream economics is awash with assumptions of perfect foresight or rational expectations, of efficient markets, and of market equilibrium, all, at least in the manner they are typically employed, essentially premised on the successful predictability of future outcomes; all supposing that in an open system actual outcomes can be effectively anticipated. Indeed all such endeavour in effect treats open systems as if they are actually closed.

This latter situation is the central focus of Soros' consternation. And his criticisms remain legitimate, despite the questionable nature of some of the contrasts he makes in motivating them. Thus Soros is correct when he writes:

> I contend that rational expectations theory totally misinterprets how financial markets operate. Although rational expectations theory is no longer taken seriously outside academic circles, the idea that markets are self correcting and tend towards equilibrium remains the prevailing paradigm on which the various synthetic instruments and valuation models which have come to play such a dominant role in financial markets are based. I contend that the prevailing paradigm is false and urgently needs to be replaced.
>
> The fact is that participants cannot base their decisions on knowledge. The two-way, reflexive connection between the cognitive and manipulative functions introduces an element of uncertainty or indeterminacy into both functions. That applies both to market participants and to the financial authorities who are in charge of macroeconomic policy and are supposed to supervise and regulate markets. The members of both groups act on the basis of an imperfect understanding of the situation in which they participate. The element of uncertainty inherent in the two-way reflexive connection [...] cannot be eliminated, but our understanding, and our ability to cope with the situation, would be greatly improved if we recognized this fact.
>
> (Soros, 2009, pp. 6–7)

Elsewhere Soros in similar vein, and with good reason, takes issue with the 'efficient market hypothesis':

> The prevailing interpretation of financial markets – the Efficient Market Hypothesis (EMH) – has been well and truly discredited by

the Crash of 2008. The current financial crisis was not caused by some exogenous factor – like the formation or dissolution of an oil cartel – but by the financial system itself. This puts the lie to the assertion that financial markets tend towards equilibrium and deviations are caused by external shocks. But the alternative theory of how markets work that I am proposing – the theory of reflexivity – has not taken its place. It has not even received serious consideration by the economics profession.

(Soros, 2009, p. 216)

Critical commentary

It could reasonably be asked why I have bothered to run through all this if Soros' main claims are found to stand up, despite some questionable background assessments offered in their support.

A first answer is precisely to pre-empt any rejection of Soros' insights on the grounds that the arguments made in their support are suspect.

But actually I want to go further. By clarifying the grounds of Soros' conclusions I think it is possible to show that Soros mostly does not go far enough in his criticisms; or that when he does so, there are grounds for his doing so in a rather bolder fashion than he appears hitherto to have felt is justified. Amongst other things, the comments which follow are significant for questioning whether Soros' proposed new *International Network for Economic Thinking* is, in seeking to improve the state of modern economics, truly getting at the crux of the problem.

It seems evident from the passages just reproduced, that Soros takes theories and/or assumptions like "rational expectations" and the "efficient markets hypothesis" to be serious claims about the economy, albeit false ones. This is understandable given that he is a practitioner in financial markets, and is on the receiving end, as it were, of the activities of those who follow economic theorising.

However, it should by now be clear that these sorts of theories are not so much causes of the sorts of failings of modern economics with which Soros is concerned, as manifestations. Because social reality is, for the sorts of reasons given by Soros in his theory of reflexivity, everywhere open, and because the emphasis on modelling and event prediction presupposes that social reality is everywhere closed, the sorts of theories that can be entertained by mathematical modellers are to a significant degree *necessarily* unrealistic. Whatever conceptions that modellers come up with, core features will inevitably be fundamentally implausible.

To formulate matters somewhat more generally, the emphasis on mathematical modelling and event prediction in modern economics, presupposes that closed systems of event regularities or correlations everywhere occur (notice, incidentally, that these closures are as much presupposed or required by the 'newer' approaches to mathematical economics, those often referred to as non-linear modelling, complexity modelling, agent-based modelling, model simulations, [most of] behavioural or neuro-economics, and so on, as they are by the more traditional forms of micro, macro and econometric modelling). Such event regularities would be guaranteed if social reality consisted of systems of isolated atoms. By *atom* here I mean an entity that exercises its own separate, independent, and invariable effect, whatever the context. By positing such atoms it follows that each time some triggering event or condition X occurs the same induced response, Y say, follows, and this response is the actual outcome *unless some other countervailing force interferes*. To theoretically discount the possibility of such an interference is the role of the assumption that the atoms act in *isolation*. Although, the twin assumptions of atomism and isolationism are not strictly necessary, they do provide the guarantee that most modellers seek, and it is difficult to think of any other assumptions that can do the trick. In any case it is easy enough to see that it is theories implicitly couched in terms of worlds of isolated atoms, that dominate the actual economics literature (see, for example, Lawson, 2003 for an extensive analysis of all this.)

There are many reasons for supposing that the presumptions of atomism and closure are invalid as characterisations of the basic nature of social reality. Soros' account of reflexivity, as noted, is a specific, if important, example. It is because all economic theories attached to formalistic modelling endeavours must be consistent with worlds of isolated atoms that all are necessarily unrealistic. The problem is not intellectual failing or ideology at the level of economic theory, but philosophical failing or ideology at the level of scientific method and (implicitly at least) social ontology.

In fact, it is important to appreciate that the theories of which Soros is so critical were originally produced not because their formulators sought to capture something about the economic world but merely because they capture a form of internal consistency at the level of modelling practice.

For example, John Muth's (1961) intention in forming the rational expectations hypothesis, was merely to constrain the predictions attributed to human individuals or firms that are modelled to be *consistent* with the predictions generated by the economic model within which the same agents are theorised. As such the proposal is more a technique for consistency in modelling than anything else. As Muth himself formulated the 'hypothesis':

> expectations, since they are informed predictions of future events, are essentially the same as the predictions of the relevant economic theory [. . . .] The hypothesis can be rephrased a little more precisely as follows: that expectations of firms (or, more generally, the subjective probability distribution of outcomes) tend to be distributed,

for the same information set, about the prediction of the theory (or the "objective" probability distributions of outcomes).

(Muth, 1961, p. 316)

Any assertion that these expectations (and model on which they are imposed) are essentially correct, is a step that is *additional* to assuming rational expectations. Actually, just because social reality is open and economic models are constructed on the presumption that it is closed, it is no surprise that typically the projections of formalistic models are found everywhere to be wide of the mark. It follows that the processes of rendering the expectations of agents modelled consistent (in the noted sense) with these model projections ensure that these agents' expectations too are typically wide of the mark. Thus the presumption by so many commentators that the hypothesis of rational expectations is effectively equivalent to assuming that expectations are accurate is ironic in the extreme.

The hypothesis, I repeat, is not about realisticness but consistency. If the modeller changes the model specifications, then necessarily (with rational expectations assumed) the modelled expectation generating mechanism changes too, to retain consistency. That is about all that can be said of the hypothesis.

Of course, certain ideologically inclined economists have sought to exploit this property. Specifically models have been formulated in terms of variables with certain values termed 'natural rates', and where, by assumption/design, the variables in question are allowed to depart from the natural rates only where or if the modelled agents form expectations of the values of these variables that 'mistakenly' depart from these natural rates. Thus, as part of the model's design specifications governments are able to influence the variables in question, to get them to depart from natural rates, only through fooling people into making systematic 'mistakes' of the noted sort. Into this highly contrived framework rational expectations are introduced thereby seemingly rendering ineffective even this limited role granted to government. Though such manipulations are clearly designed to exploit properties of the rational expectations hypothesis, they rest fundamentally on ideologically contrived specifications that are additional to the hypothesis itself. The latter I repeat is merely a device for achieving model consistency.

In similar fashion any interest in equilibrium theorising in modern economics is motivated by concerns that have little to do with substantive concerns, relevance or realisticness and everything to do with modelling consistency (see e.g., Lawson, 2005, 2006). Economic models often comprise sets of equations, each of which is notoriously found to have little relation to what happens in the real world. Despite their lack of realisticness, however, one question that keeps economists occupied with such models, is whether the different equations of a system of such formulations are mutually consistent – in the sense that there 'exists' a vector of values of some variable, say prices, that is consistent with *each and all* the equations. Such a model 'solution' has tended to be called an *equilibrium*. This, though, if to repeat, is not a hypothesis about the world but merely a (possible) property that a set of equations may or may not be found to possess.

Of course, if not all economists always recognise this, those who have contributed to the formulation of equilibrium economics are often clear enough. Consider, for example, Frank Hahn on the matter:

> it cannot be denied that there is something scandalous in the spectacle of so many people refining the analyses of economic [equilibrium] states which they give no reason to suppose will ever, or have ever, come about. It probably is also dangerous. Equilibrium economics [...] is easily convertible into an apologia for existing economic arrangements and it is frequently so converted.
>
> (Hahn, 1970, pp. 88–9)

Or consider Huw Dixon who summarises matters as follows:

> At its most general, we can say that 'equilibrium' is a method of solving economic models. At a superficial level, an equilibrium is simply a solution to a set of equations.
>
> (Dixon, 1990, p. 356)

Nor can much more be claimed for, or of, the efficient markets hypothesis. Consider for example the manner of its defence by William Sharpe, a Nobel Memorial Prize Winner in economics, writing in his famous article on capital asset pricing. Here he acknowledges that the claims required to generate the conclusion that capital markets are 'efficient' are:

> highly restrictive and undoubtedly unrealistic assumptions. However, since the proper test of a theory is not the realism of its assumptions, but the acceptability of its implications, and since these assumptions imply equilibrium conditions which form a major part of classical financial doctrine, it is far from clear that the formulation should be rejected[...].
>
> (Sharpe, 1964, p. 434)

If mathematical economic modelling retains any interest it has nothing to do with providing insight into the real world. Basically, formulations are constructed to enable certain sorts of results considered desirable to emerge. Consider Hahn again in his "Intellectual Retrospect":

The great virtue of mathematical reasoning in economics is that by its precise account of assumptions it becomes crystal clear that applications to the "real" world could at best be provisional. When a mathematical economist assumes that there is a three good economy lasting two periods, or that agents are infinitely lived (perhaps because they value the utility of their descendants which they know!), everyone can see that we are not dealing with any actual economy. The assumptions are there to enable certain results to emerge and not because they are to be taken descriptively.

(Hahn, 1994, p. 246)

The problem is that practical modellers just seem unable, in the main, to grasp or accept this, or they somehow think that it does not matter. Soros clearly does recognise that the lack of realisticness and relevance of modern economics matters. The reason I run through all this is simply to bring home the fact that the theories or assumptions that so concern Soros are effectively of secondary importance compared to, and indeed constructed just to be supportive of, the practice of mathematical modelling *per se*. It is the overwhelming emphasis on mathematical modelling in modern economics that is the real cause of the problems that concern him.

Implications for Soros

So the fundamental point I am wanting to draw out here is that because the modern insistence on methods of mathematical deductive modelling presuppose, for their usefulness, a ubiquity of closed systems, whereas the social world in which we live is quintessentially open, the emphasis on mathematical modelling itself is subject to the sorts of criticisms that Soros makes of its recently most prominent theories.

Moreover, not only are the substantive theories and questions derivative of the formalist emphasis, but, like all fashions, they come and go with some rapidity. However, the mathematical deductive modelling emphasis itself, the ultimate source of all the problems, remains largely unchallenged (see Lawson, 2009b).

Indeed Soros notes in a passage reproduced above that the rational expectations hypothesis is 'no longer taken seriously'. So too equilibrium theorising is out of vogue. But, as I say, the mathematical emphasis of the discipline remains. My concern, however, is that Soros does not fully, or consistently, appreciate that it is the insistence on formalistic modelling *per se* that is the source of all the problems, and that the endeavour to produce new forms of mathematical modelling, incorporating revised economic theories, will necessarily mean merely more of the same.

In this light I cannot help but note that most of the members of the advisory board of Soros' new *Institute for New Economic Thinking* have been, and continue to be, mathematical modellers. There is a real danger,

198 Soros' theory of reflexivity

I fear, that many and perhaps even most of the recipients of the funds of the *Institute* will seek to produce more of the same: more mathematical models and techniques of economic modelling, if no doubt justified as being different sorts of mathematical models and different types of modelling methods to those currently on the scene. If this is indeed the outcome then the enterprise will very likely be found to be as irrelevant as projects that have prevailed all along.

At times Soros (2009) does seem critical of the emphasis on mathematical modelling *per se* in economics. But relevant criticism appears to be advanced only with notable hesitancy and often a degree of ambiguity. For example following passages reproduced above, Soros questions why his theory of reflexivity "has not even received serious consideration by the economics profession" (p. 216). Soros rightly recognises that this is because his theory is seemingly inconsistent with the project of mathematical modelling, but he seems to want to combine his theory with a formalistic modelling approach nonetheless. Specifically Soros writes:

> Those who are most sympathetic to my views explain to me that my theory is not getting more attention because it cannot be formalized and modelled. But that is exactly the point I am trying to make: Reflexivity gives rise to uncertainties that cannot be quantified and probabilities that cannot be calculated. Frank Knight made that point a century ago in *Risk, Uncertainty and Profit*, and John Maynard Keynes recognized it, too. Yet market participants, rating agencies, and regulators alike came to depend on quantitative models in calculating risks.
> (Soros, 2009, p. 217)

So far so good. But then Soros adds:

> One question I am seeking an answer to is whether it is possible to model reflexivity, or whether one should continue using quantitative models but take reflexivity into account by adding a margin for error due to incalculable uncertainties. My hunch is that we need to do both. Reflexivity cannot be modelled in the abstract, but it should be possible to model specific instances of it, such as the effect of the willingness to lend on real estate prices. At the same time, quantitative models may be useful for calculating the risks that prevail in near-equilibrium conditions, while remembering, particularly for regulatory purposes, that conditions may occasionally veer quite far away from equilibrium. These are questions that need to be explored.
> (ibid, p. 217)

Here I think Soros reveals himself to be ultimately insufficiently critical of the emphasis of the formalistic modelling endeavour. What does it even mean to be in "near-equilibrium conditions"? As Soros points out himself over and again, social reality is what we make it; it is path dependent. There is no set of outcomes that would somehow simply prevail if we were not involved.

Nor does it make sense to make reference to counterfactual states of affairs that could not come about (for example those in which we all have perfect foresight or rational expectations) and which have no bearing on anything that happens. Soros is rightly critical of those who respond to his contribution by merely suggesting that his "theory of reflexivity merely states the obvious, namely that market prices reflect the participants' biases", adding:

> That is an obvious misunderstanding of my theory, which holds that mispricing in financial markets can, in specific circumstances and ways, affect the fundamentals that market prices are supposed to reflect.
>
> (p. 216)

But a matter about which the qualifier "supposed" seems to reveal recognition is that there is no obvious meaning to the notion of fundamentals here, not if fallible and mistaken ideas and practices *constitutively* influence whatever happens. There is just a social system moving (or being moved) along, with all of us collectively drawing upon, and inadvertently or otherwise, reproducing, as well as transforming aspects of, that which has gone before in a non-predetermined way, in a manner in part captured by Soros' theory of reflexivity[3].

Soros continues by anticipating that behavioural economics and evolutionary systems theory constitute new ways of economic thinking, but is rightly cautious about their formalistic orientation. However, he finishes up a discussion of these projects writing:

> I am eager to understand better the connection between evolutionary systems theory and reflexivity. I posed the question at the Santa Fe Institute, which is devoted to the study of complexity, but I have not yet found the answer. That is another question I wish other people would think about.
>
> (Soros, 2009, p. 222)

Complexity theory as studied at the Santa Fe Institute is of course but another form of mathematical deductive modelling (if of a largely non-linear variety). It will thus be unable to meet Soros' concerns. Yet Soros seems not to appreciate this. Evolutionary theory *per se*, in contrast, seems entirely an appropriate framework for Soros' notion of reflexivity, albeit the evolutionary theory of Darwin rather than the very distant cousin found in modern economics. This, though, is too long a story to enter into here (though see Lawson, 2003, especially chapters 5 and 10[4]).

Final comments

In advancing his theory of reflexivity George Soros often appears to rest his case on various contrasts which, I have suggested, are not only overstated or incorrect but also inessential to his argument. Because of the importance of his central claims, and because his book seems to be widely influential, I have taken the time to indicate that Soros' main contentions stand up anyway. Hopefully, this will prevent these insights being rejected either by those sympathetic to Soros' position but unconvinced by the surrounding arguments, or by those opposed to Soros' central contentions and who might seek to use questionable (supplementary) arguments to detract from them.

In particular, I have suggested that Soros' contrast between the nature of (non-social) natural and social phenomena as formulated is too sharp and not especially relevant to the analysis, and nor is his science/non-science differentiation.

To be fair to Soros, there are times when I believe he appreciates all this himself. Thus towards the end of his 2009 book he comments:

> Here, I must introduce a cautionary note about my own argument. I am troubled by the sharp distinction that I have drawn between human affairs and natural phenomena. Such sharp dividing lines are not characteristic of nature, but of human efforts to make sense of an infinitely complicated reality. This is also in accordance with my postulate of radical fallibility.
>
> (Soros, 2009, p. 222)

And a few lines later he adds:

> I am willing to admit that reflexivity does not meet the currently accepted standards of scientific theory [. . .]. I contend, however, that we must either modify the standards or study financial markets in a non-scientific way. The former may be difficult, because it would involve a loss of status for economists.

Here Soros is right to suggest that we must modify the accepted standards, but wrong about his concept of reflexivity not meeting the important ones. Soros' conception expresses an efficacious causal process that Soros himself demonstrates, throughout his writings, to be empirically grounded. As I have argued over again elsewhere the only standards that require modifying are those of mainstream economists and other commentators who misconstrue the nature of science (see e.g., Lawson, 1997, 2003, 2010).

Outside the discipline of economics many mock the pretentiousness and irrelevance of the emphasis of modern economists on formalistic practices⁵. Mathematical methods are not essential to science even if they are sometimes found to be useful (Lawson, 2010). In modern economics, however, mathematical modelling methods are usually accepted uncritically and mostly serve to get in the way of insight and understanding.

If there is a central moment to the practices of the successful sciences it involves first identifying 'interesting' and typically puzzling phenomena, and then unearthing their causes. Just because such causal explanation involves moving from one type of phenomenon (the one to be explained) to a typically very *different type* of phenomenon (the causal factor[s] responsible), mathematical reasoning cannot do the job. Rather at such a point in the explanatory process more creative forms of human endeavour, like reasoning by analogy and metaphor and guess work, come to the fore.

These ways of proceeding may conform little to the typical economist's (misplaced) ideas of fundamental scientific practice, but if, in response to Soros' initiatives, a (greater) take up of such causal explanatory research were the case, the result would likely nonetheless actually represent something of a return of economics to scientific ways.

Notes

* This chapter previously published as Tony Lawson, "Soros's Theory of Reflexivity: A Critical Comment", *Revue de philosophie économique* (2013) 14(1). © Revue de Philosophie économique/Review of economic philosophy, 2013 © Librairie Philosophique J. Vrin, Paris. http://www.vrin.fr
1 Published *Revue de Philosophie Economique*. 2013. For generous funding support for preparing a revised draft of this paper I am grateful to the *Independent Social Research Foundation*.
2 On March 20th 2010, three weeks or so before attending a conference hosted by George Soros' *Institute for New Economic Thinking* (in Kings College Cambridge—starting April 8th), I set off for a lecture tour of Japan. Having inadvertently left my intended travel reading behind, and finding George Soros' (2009) book at Heathrow airport, I purchased it. In so doing, I was mindful both of the forthcoming conference, and that a close friend had repeatedly recommended Soros' book over the previous year as an important read. Indeed the latter is the case. This paper is basically an engagement with Soros produced in the confines of various forms of transit as I travelled to and from, and around various parts of, Japan. No doubt the style of the paper, and the fact that there are few references other than to Soros (2009) and to my own writing, reflects that confinement/context.
3 For a systematic elaboration of this process of transformation see Lawson, 1997, 2003.
4 Let me, however, make a very brief comment. It is worth recalling the central and great Darwinian insight is that a subset of members of a population may come to flourish relative to other members simply because they possess a feature, which others do not, that renders them relatively suited to some local environment. Fundamentally, the question of the intrinsic worth of those who flourish most is not relevant to the story.

We can briefly recall an example from biology. Consider the case of the varying fortunes of spotted grey and dark moths against an environment of UK industrialisation. Prior to the nineteenth century the spotted grey was more common than the dark moth. When resting on the lichen covered trees in their habitat the spotted grey moth was effectively invisible to birds, unlike the dark moth which was easily spotted against the light coloured trees and eaten. With nineteenth century industrialisation, however, pollutants killed the lichen on the trees in certain areas and rendered the bark of trees in the relevant vicinities a dark colour. Both types of moth continued to rest on trees. But with the spotted grey now more easily recognisable to birds, there was a shift in the relative proportions of the two populations from the spotted grey towards the darker variety. In a sense the pollution-darkened barks protected the darker moths from the danger of the moth-seeking birds.

A significant feature of this process is that certain individuals are found to fare better than others just because they are of a type, or possess a trait, relatively suited to their local environment, not because they are successful in any wider or absolute or more laudatory sense.

In the social realm, as I have elsewhere argued (Lawson, 2003) the variety to be selected amongst typically exists amongst certain human practices of interest, and the selecting environment is the sum total of all the practices. The latter determine which of the variety are selected as successful. Which are selected can usually only be discovered *a posteriori*. This applies to new processes of production, etc., but also to speculations where the 'winning bets' in financial systems depends precisely on the sum total of what everyone chooses to do. It also applies to the longevity of mainstream mathematical modelling project, which has clearly been unsuccessful in terms of results, but has been selected on grounds more to do with the acceptability of formalism *per se* in a given institutional context. It also applies to the *specific* (formalistic) theories within this explanatorily unsuccessful project, which get selected according to some needs of the academic environment that are found to be determining *a posteriori* (all this, of course, is a very long story, one elaborated in detail in Lawson, 2003, chapter 10). Hopefully these few comments are enough to indicate that an evolutionary framework is indeed a likely relevant one for Soros' concept of reflexivity that is so tuned, as it is, to processes of human interaction in an inescapably open social system.

5 Nor is this a recent phenomenon, see for example Richard Parker (1993) or David Howell (2000). We might recall, too, commentaries in the March 1994 edition of *The Times Higher Education Supplement* which carried the heading "No reality please. We're economists". The (U.K.) *Observer Magazine* (20th September 1992, p. 7) concluded that "there's no such thing as economics. It's all voodoo, bluff and pseudo-science". *New Scientist* (October 31 1992, pp. 26–31) even carried sketches of economists forecasting economic variables by reading lines on the palms of their hands and of econometricians pushing numbers around while blindfolded.

References

Dixon, Huw. 1990. "Equilibrium and Explanation", in John Creedy ed., *Foundations of Economic Thought*, Oxford: Basil Blackwell.

Hahn, Frank H. 1970. "Some adjustment problems", *Econometrica*, 38: 1–17, January, reprinted in Hahn, 1984. (page references to the latter).

Hahn, Franl H. 1984. *Equilibrium and Macroeconomics*, Oxford: Basil Blackwell.

Hahn, Frank H. 1994. "An Intellectual Retrospect", *Banca Nazionale del Lavoro Quarterly Review*, vol. XLVIII. no. 190: pp. 245–58.

Howell, David. 2000. *The Edge of Now: New questions for democracy and the network age,* London: Macmillan.

Lawson, Tony. 1997. *Economics and Reality,* London and New York: Routledge.

Lawson, Tony. 2003. *Reorienting Economics,* London and New York: Routledge.

Lawson, Tony. 2005. "The Confused State of Equilibrium Analysis in Modern Economics: an Ontological Explanation", *Journal for Post Keynesian Economics,* vol 27, no. 3, pp. 423–44 .Spring.

Lawson, Tony. 2006. "Tensions in Modern Economics. The Case of Equilibrium Analysis", in Valeria Mosini ed., *Equilibrium in Economics: Scope and Limits,* London and New York: Routledge.

Lawson, Tony. 2008. "Social Explanation and Popper", in Tom Boylan and Paschal O'Gorman, eds, *Popper and Economic Methodology: Contemporary Challenges,* London and New York: Routledge.

Lawson, Tony. 2009a. "Applied Economics, Contrast Explanation and Asymmetric Information", *Cambridge Journal of Economics,* 33: 3, May, pp. 405–20.

Lawson, Tony. 2009b. "The Current Economic Crisis: its Nature and the Course of Academic economics", *Cambridge Journal of Economics,* 33: 4, July, pp. 759–88.

Lawson, Tony. 2010. "Economics and Science", *The Transatlantic: Journal of Economics and Philosophy,* 1, pp. 8–13. Online version at: http://thetransatlantic.org/

Muth, John F. 1961. "Rational Expectations and the Theory of Price movements", Econometrica, Vol. 29, No. 3 July, 1961, pp. 315–35.

Parker, Richard. 1993. "Can Economists Save Economics?", *The American Prospect,* Vol. 4, Issue, 13, March 21.

Sharpe, William. 1964. "Capital Asset Prices: A Theory of Market Equilibrium Under Conditions of Risk", *The Journal of Finance,* XIX: (3) September, pp. 425–42.

Soros, George. 2009. *The Crash of 2009 and What it Means: The New Paradigm for Financial Markets,* New York: Public Affairs.

10 Ontology, modern economics, and pluralism

In *Reorienting Economics* (Lawson 2003a) and elsewhere (e.g. Lawson 2006a), I defend a specific ontological conception and use it to interpret the nature of both the mainstream and heterodox traditions in economics. Various commentators suggest that my position in all this is insufficiently pluralist. In this short chapter, I hope to convince otherwise. Specifically, I will seek to allay any concern that I defend a conception in which heterodoxy is somehow discouraged from engaging others, is necessarily oriented to replacing the mainstream with an undesirably monolithic paradigm, and/or is encouraging of isolationism.

A conception of heterodoxy in contemporary economics

Let me start by briefly summarizing the position defended in *Reorienting Economics*. I take it to be analytic to the notion of heterodoxy that it involves the rejection of some doctrine held to be true by a prevailing orthodoxy. That is simply what it means to be heterodox. And it is clear that the self-identifying heterodox traditions in modern economics not only all ardently oppose the mainstream output currently but also have done so persistently over a lengthy period of time, even through changes in the mainstream forms. Thus, it seems reasonable to conclude that the heterodox opposition stands against some feature that is enduring and central to the modern mainstream; certainly it is opposed to something common to, or presupposed by, all its contributions.

In order to distinguish the modern economic heterodoxy qua heterodoxy I thus start by identifying the (set of) feature(s) of the modern orthodoxy or mainstream that is common to all its contributions. The assessment I defend in *Reorienting Economics* and elsewhere is the following. The project that has dominated the discipline of economics for the last forty years or so is one that, although highly heterogeneous in detail, and fluid in revising its manifest form, is united and stable in, *but only in,* adhering to the following single doctrine or edict. This is an insistence that mathematical methods be more or less always employed in the study of economic phenomena. This insistence often runs over to claiming that any contribution that does not take the form of a mathematical model is not proper economics (see Lawson 2003a, chapter 1).

This is not to say that there is not an elite within the mainstream who feel their privileged positions allow them sometimes to set out some less-than-overly formalistic pieces, especially in presidential addresses and such like. But it is only in virtue of their previous, and other, formalistic contributions that such deviations are rendered legitimate. Such individuals may even introduce their favorite non-mathematical associates into the mainstream scene. But whilst the latter chosen few are few indeed, they are not really part of the mainstream as such and are seemingly mostly included/tolerated only because of their associations with powerful others who are. Even here, though, the mathematical contributions of their patrons (or matrons) constitute the essential condition.

If an oppositional stance to the noted orthodox doctrine (that formalism is normally compulsory) is the nominal essence of the current heterodoxy, what is its real essence, the explanation of this opposition? It is the recognition (albeit one that is often no more than implicit) that the universal application of the sorts of mathematical methods that mainstream economists formulate presupposes an untenable account of social reality as everywhere composed of systems of isolated atoms.

In *Reorienting Economics*, I argue that underpinning this heterodox oppositional stance is an implicit (and sometimes reasonably explicit) commitment to the alternative sort of social ontology I defend in that book. According to the latter, social reality is appropriately viewed as *structured*, in that it does not reduce to atomistic human practices but is constituted in large part by *emergent* social properties including social rules, relations, institutions, and so forth; as intrinsically *dynamic* or *processual*, in that its mode of being is a continual process of becoming; and as ubiquitous in *internal relationality* in that economic agents are what they are and/or can do what they do, by virtue of the constitutive relations in which they stand to each other (e.g. as in relations between employer and employee, parent and child, landlord or -lady and tenant, buyer and seller, etc.) (see Lawson 2006a).

So in short, if the only common and so distinguishing feature of the current mainstream is its continuing insistence upon forms of mathematical deductivist reasoning, the real essence of the heterodox opposition (qua heterodox opposition) is an accepted (but rarely explicitly acknowledged) ontological conception. It is a conception that is at odds with the implicit (closed-system and atomistic) ontology of mainstream deductivist reasoning, and so ultimately accounting for the heterodox oppositional stance.

Notice, though, that I do *not* distinguish the individual heterodox traditions from each other according to ontological commitments; indeed I suggest that ontological presuppositions are something they broadly hold in common. Nor, incidentally, do I believe that the features that serve to identify the heterodox groups as separate and distinct traditions lie at the level of substantive theories, results, methodologies, principles, policy stances, and such like. Rather my assessment is that old institutionalism, post Keynesianism, feminist economics, Austrianism, Marxian economics, etc., are each best distinguished/identified in terms of *questions and issues traditionally addressed* within their own program.

Thus old institutionalism, I argue, is an economics project concerned first and foremost with questions of stability and change. Hence its traditional and ongoing concerns are especially with technology (perceived as an important source of change), habits and institutions (seen as important sources of stability), evolutionary science, and so forth (see *Reorienting Economics*, chapter 8, and also Lawson 2002, 2003a). I return to this issue of characterizing the different heterodox traditions below.

With this heterodox emphasis on questions and interests (rather than principles, methods, or answers and so forth), there is scope both for different members of any given heterodox tradition to produce competing accounts of some phenomenon, as well as for the best-substantiated contributions to be continually improved upon. So the conception I defend is quite consistent with the sort of (shifting) variety of contributions we find within any heterodox tradition.

Notice, too, that I do not suggest that heterodox contributors do not, or should not, experiment with mathematical deductive techniques and the like. Social conditions may occasionally arise that are locally of a sort presupposed by methods of formalistic modeling. If I characterize the mainstream in terms of its usual *insistence* that (for a contribution to count as economics) various sorts of mathematical deductivist methods be everywhere and always employed, I conceive heterodoxy as an (implicitly) ontologically motivated rejection of *the universalizing and dogmatic aspects of this stance,* not as a refusal ever to experiment with formalistic methods or to employ them where conditions indicate their relevance.

The mainstream itself is pluralistic within its constituting constraint, of course. Despite the best advice of those economists associated with the Bourbaki school, it is impossible to pursue a mathematical economics purely in the abstract. There has to be content, and this is found to be highly variable. Indeed, both the substantive programs pursued by the mainstream and the sorts of mathematical deductivist methods employed (along with their interpretation) are highly variable (Lawson 2005). There are those who argue that *within* orthodoxy there exists a dominant and relatively enduring (though by no means fixed) "neoclassical core" or some such. But assessments of what this entails vary quite significantly (see, for example, Fine 2006, Hodgson 2006, Arnsperger and Varoufakis 2006, or Fullbrook 2005). For the purposes at hand, I do not need to consider these matters further here.

Pluralism

Before turning to prominent criticisms of my position that contend that I am not sufficiently pluralistic, let me indicate the type of pluralism that I believe to be of concern here. I take it that, generally speaking, by pluralism is meant something like the affirmation, acceptance, and encouragement of diversity. Clearly, such a notion itself has a plurality of meanings or inflections, of which two in particular are worth distinguishing.

One such is the notion of pluralism as description, as a claim about the way (some domain of) reality is. It is important to realize that any claim to be a pluralist in this sense needs a fair bit of elaboration. Consider for example the notion of *ontological pluralism,* which is sometimes mentioned by those who question my own orientation. This can have various meanings. One such conception designates the claim that multiple non-overlapping worlds exist (see Erlich 1986: 527). A second notion of *ontological pluralism* has it that our *one* reality contains an (at least synchronically) irreducible multiplicity of constituents.[1]

Now a *prima facie* oppositional position to an ontological pluralism is the idea that at the base of everything is one substance, say energy, or vibrations. To hold to this is to be a monist rather than pluralist in some metaphysical sense. Many Eastern religions support a monistic rather than a pluralistic philosophy. But it seems to me that, allowing for the phenomenon of emergence, either of the two conceptions of ontological pluralism just described may (or may not) be consistent with such a monistic metaphysics.

Clearly, this is not the place to attempt to elaborate an account of all the various kinds of descriptive pluralisms imaginable, and to indicate where I might stand with respect to them. I mention the foregoing merely to indicate the complexities of the topic, and ambiguities of any personal declaration to be a pluralist.

A second inflection on the term pluralism interprets it as a (normative) orientation, one of inclusiveness, of supporting and encouraging the participation of all interested parties, whatever their differences, within some process. The latter could be a society, or an academic conversation, a sports club, or whatever.

It is possible that because this second notion expresses an orientation rather than a state of affairs it is best captured by the adjective pluralistic. In any case, the two conceptions appear distinct. For it seems to me that no matter how pluralistic an individual might be in the second sense, they could still be led to the view that some domain of reality is, as a matter of fact, monistic in nature.

In any case, it is this second inflection of pluralism, or "being pluralistic," that seems most relevant here. For we shall see that each of the commentaries to be discussed is motivated by the worry that, by virtue of my conceiving heterodoxy in oppositional terms, my position is necessarily insufficiently pluralistic in the sense of somehow excluding, or showing insufficient respect or tolerance for or engagement with (the views of) certain others in the academic conversation. Let me then address the relevant critics. Below I examine in turn the concerns of John Davis, Robert Garnett, and Jeroen Van Bouwel.

Replies to critics

John Davis

In his recent *Post-Autistics Review* critique of my *Reorienting Economics*, Davis (2006) suggests that traditional heterodox economists have two options: to "look inwards" within the discipline and engage the mainstream (his preferred strategy) or to look outwards and develop alternatives of a different sort. Davis presents this as a choice between "chipping away at the core on a gradualist schedule" or "betting on a big scientific revolution." Davis prefers the former fearing that if the traditional heterodox programs do not take this route, any future change in the mainstream will be on terms determined by those pushing the "new approaches" to economics (behavioral economists, experimentalists, neuroeconomists, etc.), an outcome that is likely to be undesirably more conservative:

> traditional heterodox economists have two choices. They can maintain their outward-orientation, so that if change occurs in economics it will likely be on the terms determined by behavioral economists, experimentalists, and others in the new approaches. The risk here is that these movements may become more conservative as their success at influencing the core improves. Alternatively they can reverse their orientation, and turn to trying to shift what exists in the core, looking for allies in the "new heterodoxy" along the way, so as to improve the chances of successful change for both.
>
> (Davis 2006: 28)

From this perspective, I am criticized both as preventing the emphasized choice from emerging and for unhelpfully counseling an outward orientation:

> Lawson's view of heterodoxy, in my view, does not allow this choice to emerge. As a point-in-time, shared characteristics conception, it misses the heterogeneity and dynamics of heterodoxy, both traditional and new. Moreover, by asserting, "there is a set of characteristics by virtue of which any tradition qualifies as heterodox" (Lawson 2006a: 484), and by associating these shared characteristics with the rejection of the core of economics, he counsels an outward orientation. And with the recommendation of an outward orientation, he bets on the

unlikely big scientific revolution, so that, should traditional heterodox economists in any great number accept his advice, the chances of gradual change in economics being more conservative are increased."
(Davis 2006: 28–9)

The problem, as Davis perceives things here, is that I adopt the wrong strategy. Indeed, he finds the approach I adopt to be insufficiently pluralistic. Instead of looking for unity within the differences found amongst the heterodox (and other) projects, a position Davis attributes to me, we should accept a pluralism of strategies for changing economics. Thus in his final paragraph, Davis (2006: 29) asserts:

> For many [an expression of pluralism] seems to mean an open stance toward the different heterodox research programs associated with ICAPE [the International Confederation for Pluralism in Economics] that seeks to promote a unity within difference. This stance seems to me to be shortsighted and anti-pluralist in important respects.

And Davis ends by hoping that "ICAPE will become an increasingly pluralist organization in strategy as well as membership."

Engaging the mainstream: a reply to Davis

Davis essentially focuses upon strategies adopted in the effort to transform modern economics. As noted, he himself counsels an inward orientation of engaging with the mainstream. He criticizes me for supporting the traditional heterodox stance of advancing an alternative approach to the mainstream, rather than trying to gradually amend the latter from within. Davis advances his position in the name of both pluralism and efficacy in bringing about a more successful economics. Let me consider these two aspects (pluralism and efficacy) of his critique in turn.

First, just because heterodox traditions are constituted as heterodox traditions through their rejection of some orthodox doctrine, it does not follow that engagement with orthodox practitioners is thereby rendered necessarily infeasible or undesirable. Nor need communication be other than open and respectful. The possibilities for exchange will depend on context and on the nature of the differences. But this will be so however heterodoxy is constituted. I myself have never wished to discourage respectful engagement with others. The stance is not inherently anti-pluralist.

To be more concrete, it is clear that a rejection of the defining doctrine of contemporary orthodoxy does not involve a rejection of all endeavors to explore the usefulness of formalistic methods. Heterodoxy qua heterodoxy, as I conceive it, involves a necessary opposition *not* to the use of formalism, but only to *the dogmatic insistence that only these sorts of methods be used, irrespective of their ability to illuminate*. I do not see how a pluralist can accept this insistence, this orthodox doctrine, in the circumstances. Indeed, in rejecting this one enduring orthodox doctrine, heterodoxy, qua heterodoxy, is inherently pluralistic in its very constitutive orientation (whether or not specific heterodox contributions remain pluralistic in all other respects). If, however, individuals within or outside the traditional heterodox groups wish to explore new formalisms, or methods of any kind, who is going to object?

To date, formalistic methods that presuppose an atomistic ontology have met with very little success, and from the perspective of the ontological framework I defend, this is none too surprising. But even if the ontology I defend is roughly right, there may yet be pockets of social reality that provide the appropriate conditions for successes when utilizing methods of formalistic modeling, as I regularly acknowledge. In addition, of course, I recognize that the ontological conception I defend may yet turn out to be significantly mistaken in various ways; all knowledge claims are fallible. So no one wants to inhibit any serious methodological experimentation, whether involving formal techniques or otherwise. All that is being rejected by heterodoxy, on my conception, is the orthodox constraint on a pluralistic approach to economic analysis. This takes on a special significance just because the mainstream is constituted through this constraint. But if that is the nature of the beast, we just have to accept that opposing the mainstream (rejecting its constitutive doctrine) is a pro-, not an anti-, pluralistic stance.

I turn to the question of the efficaciousness of different strategies. Let me first emphasize that any desire to engage does not mean heterodox economists must resort to constructing formalistic models (although of course there is no reason not to try that route if there is thought to be some promise of success). In particular, meta-theoretical discussion is at least as valid, where feasible. This can take the form of engagement via publications. Other forms depend on context.

I well understand the problems. As Richard Lipsey reminds us, if anyone presents an economics seminar without formulating a mathematical model it is not unknown for the mainstream economists "to turn off and figuratively, if not literally, to walk out" (Lipsey 2001: 184). But not all mainstream contributors are like this, especially the more thoughtful ones, despite appearances. While I was originally formulating my critique of the mainstream, Frank Hahn was head of the Cambridge (UK) economics faculty in which I am located. Hahn's commitment to the mainstream is clear enough from his retirement speech to the *Royal Economic Society*, where he famously gave advice to students to "avoid discussions of 'mathematics in economics' like the plague" (Hahn 1992a, see also Hahn 1992b), adding that we should "give no thought to methodology." Elsewhere, as I have often observed, Hahn writes of any suggestion that the emphasis on mathematics may be a problem that it is "a view surely not worth discussing" (Hahn 1985: 18). But appearances or rhetoric can mislead. This set of beliefs did not prevent Hahn himself, on various occasions, accepting invitations to talk at the *Cambridge Realist Workshop*[2] that I co-ordinate. In that forum, a genuine exchange of ideas took place on the sorts of issues here in contention, with large audiences of mostly Ph.D. students listening (and indeed joining) in. I mention this just to reinforce the idea that possibilities for engagement depend very much on people and context. In particular, there should be no presumption that we always hide our real critique, or perpetuate approaches we actually think are very unlikely to reveal insight, to be able to engage.

Davis, though, believes it strategically more efficacious to engage the orthodoxy on its own terms. He seems to contend that a failure to do so, and specifically if the traditional heterodox traditions maintain their outward-orientation, then any change achieved will be on the terms determined by the "new programs," namely: behavioral economists, experimentalists, and others in the new approaches. He worries that the "risk here is that these movements may become more conservative as their success at influencing the core improves." He believes that if the traditional heterodoxy changes its orientation and challenges the core, meaning the sort of formalism practiced, this would "improve the chances of successful change."

This statement begs various questions. What does it mean to say the new programs are likely to become more "conservative" as they influence the core? Why are the new programs likely to become more "conservative" as/if they influence the core? Is there any reason to suppose that if the traditional heterodoxy oriented itself more towards the core it could thereby achieve changes worth having?

I presume that by "more conservative," Davis means something like becoming more sympathetic to, and having minimal or reduced impact on, the current mainstream insistence that formalism be everywhere used.[3] If so, Davis is surely correct that it is only through adopting such an inward orientation that proponents of the new programs will be accepted by the mainstream. But this is the case whatever orientation is adopted by the traditional heterodoxy. Putting forward a formalistic program is the only basis on which the current mainstream has been found to accept change. Furthermore, the traditional heterodoxy is, by its nature, opposed to the insistence that formalism be everywhere involved. The only way it could thus orientate itself to the mainstream in the manner Davis suggests is to drop this opposition and relinquish its generalist heterodox status. But then it is unclear why any changes subsequently wrought by such a transformed project, should any occur, would be any less "conservative" than any brought about by the new approaches acting alone.

Fundamental to all this is the question of the sort of plurality we seek. If it is a plurality of mainstream approaches, if the goal is a variety of modeling endeavors pursued by those who insist that formalistic methods only be followed, then Davis's approach seems appropriate. Having said that we should acknowledge that at this level the mainstream is already pluralistic; the sorts of mathematical-deductivist endeavors being followed within the mainstream are regularly shifting. Our real difference here seems to be that I am more concerned that we create space for that which is largely absent: nonformalistic approaches to economics. These are lacking because of the anti-pluralistic maneuvers of the dominant mainstream. It is not yet clear that engaging the mainstream on the question of which form of mathematical modelling to use in conditions where none of the available options seem especially appropriate will bring about much of an improvement.

In any case, I hope it is clear that there is nothing in my approach that discourages active engagement with the mainstream. I do not think that formulating mathematical programs is the only way of doing this. Nor do I think such engagement is likely to be extremely fruitful. But there is nothing in my position that argues against it happening. On grounds of efficacy, as well as in the interests of pluralism, let a multitude of strategies be followed.

Rob Garnett

In addition to some of the sorts of views aired by Davis, Rob Garnett (2006), the ICAPE Secretary and Conference Organizer from 1999 through 2007, provides a further line of criticism. In an important and wide-ranging (and I believe overall a very fair) contribution, Garnett criticizes those heterodox "paradigmist economists" who seek to replace a mainstream paradigm with their own hopefully superior one. Garnett worries that my own approach carries residual traces of such a vision:

> Even the open system pluralisms of [...] Lawson carry residual traces of this paradigmist vision, insisting that heterodox economics define itself as the Other of orthodox economics. This is Cold War paradigmism in a different guise but still the same oppositional project, with the same truncated pluralism: offering intellectual openness and respect to persons and arguments within our own paradigm communities but not to outsiders. To define heterodox economics in this way is to warrant the charge that heterodox economics has no positive identity, that it defines itself only in terms of what it is not, rather than in terms of what it is (Colander et al. 2004: 491). This keeps us in the reactive position of "permitting the mainstream to set the heterodox agenda for heterodox economics... to define its structure and content" (King 2004). It also demonstrates that our professed commitments to pluralism are fundamentally ill-conceived, insincere, or both.
> (Garnett 2006: 531–2)

Paradigms and the like: a reply to Garnett

In response to Garnett, I must emphasize that it does not follow that, just because heterodoxy is characterized by its rejection of some orthodox doctrine, heterodox conceptions need be monolithic, monist, paradigmist, or whatever. In principle, such heterodox projects can be as small, partial, open, multifaceted, fragmented, transitory, and inclusive as you like. Having said that, I see nothing inherently anti-pluralistic about specific individuals exploring the possibility of creating a successful substantive paradigm of any sort.

Perhaps, though, it will be said that I am being less than pluralistic in supporting one specific social ontological conception above others. I hope it is clear that the conception I defend is consistent with many modes of explanation and forms of substantive theorizing. Indeed, I would describe my position as one that is, if ontologically bold, then epistemologically and substantively very cautious. But still some might worry that my defense of a specific ontology, and my resting my arguments for inter-, or across-, group collaboration upon it, constitutes an undesirably anti-pluralistic stance in itself.

I do not think it does though. I am of course not suggesting that alternative ontological conceptions are not possible. Clearly they are. And to the extent that competing conceptions are produced, the point, once more, is to do whatever it takes to encourage all parties to constructively engage. But if one ontological conception can be shown to be better grounded than available alternatives, is that not a reason for drawing on it? Would anyone counsel a different approach in any other walk of life? Yes, let us leave options open. Let us also (repeatedly) try out alternatives, where appropriate. Certainly, let us include everyone in the conversation, whether it is oriented to the nature of ontology, substantive work, the nature of pluralism or being pluralistic, or whatever, and seek to do so with respect for, and encouragement of, each other. But *if*, when the time comes to make use of an ontological conception, one such conception (whatever the focus) seems to be significantly more appropriate than others, not least because it is found to be far more explanatorily grounded, then it seems reasonable (for at least those that believe in it) to make use of the latter. This applies to our theories of the natures(s) of pluralism(s), of how we ought to be pluralistic, as well as to everything else.

Concerning Garnett's further point that to "define heterodox economics" in opposition to orthodoxy is to warrant the charge that heterodox economics has no positive identity, it does not follow for any heterodoxy characterized by its rejection of specific orthodox doctrine(s) that it must thereby be a purely reactive program, lacking identity and defining itself purely in terms of the orthodoxy. It does mean that heterodoxy can be *identified as heterodox* in virtue of the opposition (its nominal essence). But if the opposition is to a specific set of doctrines, rather than opposition for opposition's sake, there will typically be a determinate cause, or set of causes, of this opposition rooted in the nature of the opposed doctrine(s), revealing something more fundamental about the heterodoxy qua heterodoxy (its real essence).

And over and above any rejection of specific orthodox doctrine, including the reasons for this rejection, any heterodoxy or heterodoxies can be as complex and heterogeneous as you like. As a project in its own right, each separate heterodox grouping can have its own identity, set its own agenda, and be continually evolving. Moreover, this can be so even if, throughout this variety and evolution, a rejection of fundamental orthodox doctrine is sustained.

Now this, indeed, *is precisely my conception of the situation of modern heterodox economics.* As I understand it, heterodoxy is a (group of) project(s), each primarily motivated by its own agenda (not by any desire to oppose the mainstream per se), and each concerned with questioning social reality without supposing the latter's nature everywhere conforms to the closed worlds of isolated atoms that the mainstream insistence on formal modeling presupposes. More positively, my assessment is that contemporary heterodoxy is a set of projects concerned to develop substantive theories consistent with the sort of social ontology that I believe receives the most philosophical grounding.

As I say, only if it were the case that any opposition to orthodox doctrine was caused solely by a desire to be oppositional for opposition's sake irrespective of doctrine would it follow that heterodoxy is purely reactive. If some commentators do hold to such a conception of the heterodoxy of modern economics, I am not amongst them.

Rather, on my understanding contemporary economic heterodoxy possesses deep-seated and valid reasons for its enduring and widespread opposition to specific orthodox doctrine. But this is an *a posteriori* response to a mainstream insistence that methods other than mathematical deductivist modeling are inappropriate. If the relevant orthodox doctrine were to be abandoned, this would be reason for the traditional heterodoxy to abandon the heterodox ascription, not for its seeking some other doctrine to oppose, nor for its abandoning the constructive endeavor by virtue of which each division of this heterodoxy constitutes one particular heterodox group rather than another.

Jeroen Van Bouwel

Somewhat more trenchant in his criticism is Jeroen Van Bouwel (2005). After distinguishing five different motivations for declaring oneself a pluralist (the ontological, the cognitive limitations, the historical and geographical, the pragmatic, and the strategic motivations), Van Bouwel worries about the motivation for my support for pluralism:

Lawson's quest for heterodox economics is not so much focusing on elaborating compatibility and complementarity with *mainstream* (or neo-classical) economics, but rather creating his own alternative, that would be the new (monist) standard.

If we call Lawson's contribution pluralist, as he does, we can distinguish two different forms or conceptions of pluralism. Firstly, Lawson's work is pluralist in the sense that it provides us with an alternative to the mainstream, and as such we have more than one alternative (hence we have plurality). Secondly, we can understand pluralism as engaging in a conversation, as exchanging ideas, and not merely developing different isolated (and essentially monist) alternatives.

Lawson's account does not defend this second kind of pluralism. He does not develop a form of pluralism that shows how the different schools or alternatives can be used for different occasions. He rejects the *mainstream* completely, without considering possible positive contributions. He does not elaborate a form of pluralism that might show the complementarity of the schools or make us understand the origin of the differences between [them].

(Van Bouwel 2005)

In his conclusion, Van Bouwel adds:

I claim that a *really* pluralistic approach should engage in a conversation, in spelling out compatibilities and complementarities between the mainstream and the heterodox approaches (both sides should be engaged). The pluralism of Lawson risks leading us to an isolated diversity, to a lack of exchange of ideas.

(Van Bouwel 2005)

Isolationism: a reply to Van Bouwel

As well as airing the concern (addressed in my responses to Davis and Garnett) that I discourage engagement with the mainstream, Jeroen van Bouwel further complains that my approach encourages an isolationist stance within the heterodoxy. According to Van Bouwel, specifically, I do not "develop a form of pluralism that shows how the different schools or alternatives can be used for different occasions," that I do "not elaborate a form of pluralism that might show the complementarity of the schools or make us understand the origin of the differences between [them]." I have actually had much to say on this not only in *Reorienting Economics* (Lawson 2003a), but also in Lawson (2004, 2006a). Let me briefly outline my position.

The basic thesis I advance concerning the (traditional) heterodox projects is that they are actually best conceived as divisions of labor in one overall project. Remember I do not think the heterodox projects can be distinguished by the answers given (within any given tradition these are far too variable, both at any point in time and over time). Rather I argue that the individual heterodox traditions, like, I think, research endeavor in almost all other disciplines, are identifiable more by the sorts of questions asked (see Lawson 2003a, 2006a). It is with this understanding of heterodoxy in mind that we can view the separate traditions as divisions of labor.

Central to this interpretation is the ontological conception that I defend, one that I also believe these heterodox traditions mostly implicitly presuppose. This conception has many facets. Social phenomena are, for example, viewed as bearing emergent powers, being structured, open, processual, highly internally related, comprising value, carrying meaning, and so forth. The various heterodox traditions I believe are best viewed as exploring, if implicitly, specific aspects of this ontology (whilst maintaining a commitment to the whole).

Post Keynesians, for example, make fundamental uncertainty a central category. This clearly presupposes an ontology of openness as many post Keynesians have in recent years come increasingly to acknowledge. Such a focus has involved examining the implications of uncertainty or openness for the development of certain sorts of institutions, including money, for processes of decision-making, and so forth. At the level of policy, the concern may well include the analysis of contingencies that recognize the fact of pervasive uncertainty, given the openness of social reality in the present and to the future, etc. For those influenced by Keynes, especially, a likely focus is how these matters give rise to collective or macro outcomes, and how they in turn impact back on individual acts and pressures for structural transformation, etc. (see Lawson 1994, 2003a, chapter 7).

By similar reasoning, and as already noted earlier in this chapter, I believe that it is best to distinguish (old) Institutionalism, following Veblen especially, as concerned with the processual nature of social reality, and so as focusing especially on those forces working for stability and on others working for change. This orientation has taken the manifest form of a traditional concern with evolutionary issues, and with studying those aspects of social life that are most enduring, such as institutions and habits, along with those that are most inducing of continuous change, such as technology (see Lawson 2002, 2003a, chapter 8; 2003b, 2006b).

Feminist economics, I believe, is best distinguished in terms of a focus on social relationality. Relations of care are of course a central issue. But relationality in itself seems central to most feminist concerns. Very often feminist economists have identified their own project as one that first of all concerns itself with women as subjects (which may include, for example, giving attention to differences among women, as well as between genders) and takes a particular orientation or focus, namely on the position of women (and other marginalized groups) within society and the economy. In practice this project includes an attention to the social causes at work in the oppression of, or in discrimination against, women (and others), the opportunities for progressive transformation or emancipation, questions of (relations of) power and strategy, and so forth.[4]

Austrians may perhaps be best identified in some part according to their emphasis on the role of inter-subjective meaning in social life (see Lawson 1997, chapter 10), and so on.

I suggest, then, that at least some heterodox traditions are most easily viewed as primarily (though not exclusively) concerned with different aspects of the properties of social phenomena (openness, processuality, internal relationality) uncovered and explicitly systematized through philosophical ontology.

Others traditions, though, seem to be more interested in elaborating the nature of specific social categories, and in particular how the features uncovered through philosophical ontology (openness, relationality, process, etc.) coalesce in certain social items of interest within that particular tradition. An obvious example is Marxian economics, a project primarily concerned to understand the nature of the relational totality in motion that is capitalism. But we also find a significant Austrian interest in the nature of "the market process" and entrepreneurship in particular. And as already noted there is significant post Keynesian interest in the nature of money, institutionalist interest in institutions and technology, feminist interest in care, and so forth.

How does the current mainstream join the party? Clearly its *insistence* that mathematical deductivist methods be more or less always and everywhere used and by all of us, is ill fitted to this pluralistic picture. Of course, the argument that only formalistic methods be used can be heard, but there can be no compulsion for anyone to follow. But those who experiment with formalistic methods, without insisting that others always and everywhere do so, certainly have a place. It is my assessment that formalistic endeavor will likely be most fruitful where social conditions most approximate the atomistic ontology that such endeavor presupposes. In *Reorienting Economics* (chapter 1), I sketch the sorts of scenarios under which the emergence of such conditions appears most feasible and wherein, indeed, some successes seem occasionally to have been achieved.

I hope it is clear, then, that there is a place for more or less all types of existing research practice on the conception I defend; I am not at all advancing a vision of (or seeking to encourage) isolated practices.[5] To the contrary, according to the conception I am advancing it is actually vital that the various divisions perpetually keep in touch with each other's contributions and developments. For all are working on aspects of the same whole, and each tradition requires some understanding of the whole (and so of each other's contributions) in order to carry out its own division of labor competently.

Conclusion

My view that heterodoxy is most appropriately identified through its opposition to a specific orthodox doctrine does not, I believe, preclude or undermine the possibility of maintaining pluralistic orientations of the sort that most seem to concern Davis, Garnett, Van Bouwel, and others.[6] In fact, the realizing of a more pluralistic discipline, I hope it is clear, is something towards which, in advancing the position defended, I too aspire.

Acknowledgments

I am grateful to Vinca Bigo and an anonymous referee for helpful comments on an earlier draft.

Notes

1 Typically, it is also held that each constituent or entity can be known only fallibly and partially, in various ways, under various competing descriptions, with all ways of knowing reflecting the situatedness and specific capacities of the "knower," etc.
2 For a listing of the program for the last ten years or so, including several presentations by Hahn, see www.econ.cam.ac.uk/seminars/realist/previous_workshops.htm.
3 Thus, I assume Davis does not mean politically conservative. Davis explicitly rejects the idea that we should relate distinctions in the sorts of economic programs pursued (and in particular any differentiations as to whether they are orthodox or heterodox) to political differentiations/allegiances.
4 In turn, of course, this focus, reflexively adopted, has come to affect the ways some feminists at least are committed to developing pedagogical approaches that acknowledge and explore (typically hierarchical) relations not just in society at large but also within the academy.
5 This indeed is something I have endeavored to emphasize over and again (see, for example, Lawson 2006a).
6 This is not, of course, to imply that things couldn't be improved (for an argument that heterodoxy could be more pluralistic, see Holcombe 2008).

References

Arnsperger, C. and Varoufakis, Y. (2006) "What is Neoclassical Economics?" *Post-Autistic Economics Review*, issue 38, July: 2–13.
Colander, D., Holt, R., and Rosser, J. (2004) "The Changing Face of Mainstream Economics," *Review of Political Economy*, 16: 485–99.
Davis, J. (2006) "The Nature of Heterodox Economics," *Post-Autistic Economics Review* issue 40, December 1, 23–30.
Erlich, B. (1986) "Amphibolies: On the Critical Self-Contradictions of 'Pluralism,' " *Critical Inquiry*, 12(3), spring: 521–49.
Fine, B. (2006) "Critical Realism and Heterodoxy," unpublished paper, University of London, School of Oriental and African Studies.

Fullbrook, E. (2005) "The RAND Portcullis and PAE," *Post-Autistic Economics Review*, issue 32, July 5, Article 5.
—— (2006) "Paradigms and Pluralism in Heterodox Economics," *Review of Political Economy*, 18(4): 521–46.
Hahn, F. (1985) "In Praise of Economic Theory," the *1984 Jevons Memorial Fund Lecture*, London: University College.
—— (1992a) "Reflections," *Royal Economics Society Newsletter*, 77.
—— (1992b) "Answer to Backhouse: Yes," *Royal Economic Society Newsletter*, 78: 5.
Hodgson, G. (2006) "An Institutional and Evolutionary Perspective on Health Economics," unpublished paper, presented at the *Cambridge Realist Workshop*, November.
Holcombe, R.G. (2008) "Pluralism versus Heterodoxy in Economics and the Social Sciences," *Journal of Philosophical Economics*, 1(2): 51–72.
King, J.E. (2004) "A Defense of King's Argument(s) for Pluralism," *Post-Autistic Economics Review*, issue 25, March 18: 16–20.
Lawson, T. (1994) "The Nature of Post Keynesianism and its Links to other Traditions," *Journal of Post Keynesian Economics*, 16: 503–38. Reprinted in Prychitko, D.L. (ed.) (1996) *Why Economists Disagree: An Introduction to the Contemporary Schools of Thought*, New York: State University of New York Press.
—— (1997) *Economics and Reality*, London: Routledge.
—— (2002) "Should Economics Be an Evolutionary Science? Veblen's Concern and Philosophical Legacy," The 2002 Clarence Ayres Memorial Lecture, *Journal of Economic Issues*, 36(2): 279–91.
—— (2003a) *Reorienting Economics*, London: Routledge.
—— (2003b) "Institutionalism: On the Need to Firm up Notions of Social Structure and the Human Subject," *Journal of Economic Issues*, 37(1): 175–201.
—— (2004) "On Heterodox Economics, Themata and the Use of Mathematics in Economics," *Journal of Economic Methodology*, 11(3): 329–40.
—— (2005) "Reorienting History (of Economics)," *Journal of Post Keynesian Economics*, 27(3): 455–71.
—— (2006a) "The Nature of Heterodox Economics," *Cambridge Journal of Economics*, 30(2): 483–507.
—— (2006b) "The Nature of Institutionalist Economics," *Evolutionary and Institutional Economics Review*, 2(1): 7–20.
Lipsey, R. (2001) "Successes and Failures in the Transformation of Economics," *Journal of Economic Methodology*, 8(2): 169–202.
Van Bouwel, J. (2005) "Towards a Framework for Pluralism in Economics," *Post-Autistic Economics Review*, issue 30, March 21, article 3.

11 The varying fortunes of the project of mathematising economics: an evolutionary explanation[1]

How are we to account for the rise to, and continuing, dominance of the mathematising project in modern economics? Not, I think, in terms of this project's successes at illuminating the world in which we live. For the evidence is that these are rather few. Indeed, as even (the more reflective) spokespeople of this modern 'mainstream' project acknowledge, as a scientific endeavour it is in a state of some disarray and unclear even as to its own rationale (see e.g. Bell and Kristol, 1981; Kirman, 1989; Leamer, 1978, 1983; Leontief, 1982; Rubinstein, 1991, 1995; Wiles and Routh [eds.] 1984). Thus Rubinstein observes that:

> The issue of interpreting economic theory is ... the most serious problem now facing economic theorists. The feeling among many of us can be summarized as follows. Economic theory should deal with the real world. It is not a branch of abstract mathematics even though it utilises mathematical tools. Since it is about the real world, people expect the theory to prove useful in achieving practical goals. But economic theory has not delivered the goods. Predictions from economic theory are not nearly as accurate as those by the natural sciences, and the link between economic theory and practical problems ... is tenuous at best.
>
> (Rubinstein, 1995, p. 12)

He concludes:

> Economic theory lacks a consensus as to its purpose and interpretation. Again and again, we find ourselves asking the question 'where does it lead?'
>
> (Rubinstein, 1995, p. 12)

And more than ten years earlier, Leontief, a Nobel Memorial Prize winner in economic science, was already bemoaning the project's continuing failure to advance understanding:

Page after page of professional economic journals are filled with mathematical formulas leading the reader from sets of more or less plausible but entirely arbitrary assumptions to precisely stated but irrelevant theoretical conclusions.... Year after year economic theorists continue to produce scores of mathematical models and to explore in great detail their formal properties; and the econometricians fit algebraic functions of all possible shapes to essentially the same sets of data without being able to advance, in any perceptible way, a systematic understanding of the structure and the operations of a real economic system.

(Leontief, 1982, p. 104)

Blaug formulates matters at least as starkly:

Modern economics is sick. Economics has increasingly become an intellectual game played for its own sake and not for its practical consequences for understanding the economic world. Economists have converted the subject into a sort of social mathematics in which analytical rigour is everything and practical relevance is nothing.

(Blaug, 1997, p. 3)

And Friedman, also a Nobel Memorial Prize winner, admits:

economics has become increasingly an arcane branch of mathematics rather than dealing with real economic problems.

(Friedman, 1999, p. 137)

How, then, has the project managed to survive in such a dominant fashion over a longish period of time, in the face of its numerous failures? This is my question here and I want to give at least a sketch of an answer, to identify (what I suspect is) an essential part of the total cause.

Background

I have advanced a partial explanation before (which I further ground below). Specifically, I have previously identified an impetus to the noted situation, the one I believe to be the most significant. This is the enormous, almost uncritical, awe of mathematics in modern Western culture (Lawson, 1997a, 1998). This impetus is a cultural phenomenon pervasive in society at large. Indeed, for so many people it seems to be simply an unquestioned and seemingly unquestionable matter of faith that if a field of study is to be scientific or accorded status as a knowledge-producing activity, or otherwise regarded as serious, it must take a mathematical form. There is little reason to doubt, I think, that the staying power of the mathematising project in economics owes something to this acceptance of the drive to mathematise which is so prominent in Western culture.

222 The varying fortunes of the project

Interestingly enough since I produced a first draft of this paper the teaching and content of economics has become a topic of a lively public debate; at least this is so in France, and especially in the pages of *Le Monde*. The debate was sparked by economics students based in the Grandes Ecoles in Paris protesting at the lack of pluralism in their courses, and noting the almost exclusive concentration on methods of mathematics, in particular. Many university lecturers, including some Nobel Memorial Prize winners in economics, have responded to the students' criticisms, and a good proportion have done so expressing some sympathy with the students' concerns. However, there has been a notable reluctance to question the role of mathematics. Most respondents to the students' concerns not only insist that economics must be scientific but appear to believe unquestioningly that mathematics is essential to science. A few of them do allow, along with Sen (*Le Monde*, 31/10/2000), that mathematics may not be a unique foundation of science. But most believe it is essential[2].

I have demonstrated often enough that mathematics is not after all an essential component of science. However, I do not intend to go over this ground here (although see Lawson, 1997b). My point at this stage is just that a major explanation of the phenomenon of the mathematising project continuing to gain converts despite its poor record at illuminating the social world, is an awe of mathematics in society at large, coupled with a belief that mathematics is a necessary component of all science.

I should probably emphasise at this point that I have no wish to belittle mathematics here. To the contrary I am enthraled by its elegance and power. But it is possible to recognise the latter without thereby concluding that mathematics be promulgated uncritically and without limit. As I say, I am here drawing attention to what I see as the current uncritical reception (or granting of scientific authority to the perpetrators) of anything mathematical. This is an orientation that is embedded in Western culture at large, and in the habits, norms and power structures of the modern economics academy in particular.

A further puzzle

My thesis to date, then, has been that it is this culturally-based idea of science as mathematics that drives the mathematising project on in economics. Now although the fact of this widespread perception of a link between mathematics and science (and indeed all serious thought) does throw light on how the mathematising project persists despite its dearth of successes, it is clear that some problems remain for the thesis advanced; the account so far given is, at best, highly incomplete. For the rise to prominence of practices concerned with mathematising the study of social phenomena occurred only in the twentieth century. Yet the cultural embracing of mathematics to which I refer was evident long before this time. And this latter observation holds true in parts of the world with amongst the longest and strongest traditions in economics. In France, in particular, the cultural impact of mathematics has, since the Enlightenment at least, been very powerful. Yet even in France it is only since the early twentieth century that the attempts to mathematise economics have risen to dominance.

From the viewpoint of the thesis I have been putting forward, then, an important puzzle which remains to be resolved is why, if the cultural forces I identify are really so significant, the mathematical project in economics did not rise to prominence at an earlier stage. Why furthermore did it eventually rise to dominance when it did, given there were no notable breakthroughs in its ability to illuminate at that time (or since)? Or, to look at the puzzle from a different angle, how can my thesis account for the fact that the project of mathematising the subject does now survive as the dominant approach, given that the place of mathematics in Western culture has not always brought this result? In short, what explains the relative fortunes overtime of the mathematising project in economics? If the effect of culture has long been in play and is as important as I suggest, why have the fortunes of the project not been the same throughout? Why in particular has the mathematising project in economics fared significantly better after the start of the twentieth century?

The nature of the expanded explanatory thesis

Here I want to suggest an explanation of the relevant course of events, focusing in particular on developments in France. It is an explanation that, in part at least, can reasonably be construed an evolutionary one, incorporating elements analogous to a Darwinian mechanism of natural selection. Indeed, the fact that the project of mathematising economics rose to prominence and survives *with few if any notable explanatory successes being achieved along the way,* immediately suggests that elements of a natural-selection evolutionary process may be in play. For the central and great Darwinian insight is that members of a population can, by way of a natural selection mechanism, come to survive and flourish merely because they are relatively suited to some local environment; the question of the intrinsic worth of survivors need not be (and typically is not) relevant to the story. I shall argue that a natural-selection mechanism of this sort is indeed a part of the explanation of the varying fortunes of the mathematising project in economics. But at the same time I shall indicate that such an evolutionary mechanism is *no more than a part of the story;* the episode also helps indicate that borrowing from biology, where relevant, is likely to contribute only partial insights at best.

Evolutionary explanation

In order to illustrate what I understand by 'natural selection', and to indicate why survivors of a natural selection process (typically) do not warrant

224 The varying fortunes of the project

being regarded as successful in any sense other than their surviving, it may be useful, briefly, to recall an example from biology. Consider, the widely observed case of the varying fortunes of spotted grey and dark moths against an environment of UK industrialisation. Prior to the nineteenth century the spotted grey was more common than the dark moth. When resting on the lichen covered trees in their habitat the spotted grey moth was effectively invisible to birds, unlike the dark moth which was easily spotted against the light coloured trees and eaten. With nineteenth century industrialisation, however, pollutants killed the lichen on the trees in certain areas and rendered the bark of trees in the relevant vicinities a dark colour. Both types of moth continued to rest on trees. But with the spotted grey now more easily recognisable to birds, there was a shift in the relative proportions of the two populations from the spotted grey towards the darker variety. In a sense the pollution-darkened barks protected the darker moths from the danger of the moth-seeking birds. Darwin provides similar examples:

> When we see leaf-eating insects green, and bark-feeders mottled-grey; the alpine ptarmigan white in winter, the red-grouse the colour of heather, and the black-grouse that of peaty earth, we must believe these tints are of service to the birds and insects in preserving them from danger.
>
> (Darwin, 1964 [1859], p. 84)

Notice, however, that although the tints or colours in question may indeed be of service to their possessors, the main natural selection mechanism works neither by way of the variety generation (here genetic mutation) conditions affecting the environment, nor by way of the environment conditions affecting those of variety generation (mutation). Rather, the central causal mechanism in question involves certain environmental factors bearing differentially on (i.e. 'selecting' amongst) the independently produced variety at the level of the individual. In our example the noted environmental factor selects not at that level at which mutations in types of moth are possible but rather at the level of individual moths. And through such a natural selection mechanism a matching of (surviving) individuals and environment emerges. This is a matching which is no part of anyone's design; nature has the appearance of design so long as it makes an appearance at all.

Now a significant feature of this process, to return us to the point of the discussion, is that certain individuals 'survive' better than others just because they are of a type, or possess a trait, relatively suited to their local environment, not, or not necessarily, because they are successful in any wider or absolute or more laudatory sense.

As I say, the explanation I want to advance of the rise to, and continuing, dominance of the modern mainstream or mathematical project in economics (in the face of continued failure to add much in terms of social understanding) takes much the same form. The way in which the project has been received over the last two hundred years or so, has been related to shifts in the relevant local environment in some way; changes in the nature of its reception have had little to do with changes in the project's explanatory merit or performance.

The natural selection model

Put differently, the possibility I want to examine here is that there is a general process or model of change, one which is well illustrated by biological examples or tokens, but which has social manifestations as well. Specifically, I want to suggest that such a general model can indeed be identified and that one social manifestation of it is the history of modern economics, or at least of (significant aspects of) its (currently mainstream) mathematical component. Let me then proceed at this point by very briefly abstracting out essential components of the more generalised natural-selection evolutionary story. For the remainder of this section and all of the one that follows I develop a fairly abstract model of a natural selection mechanism. Only once this is accomplished do I turn to the task of examining the adequacy of a natural selection story for accounting for concrete details of the varying fortunes of the project of mathematising economics.

First of all, of course, in any model capable of incorporating a natural-selection mechanism there has to be *variety* in a relevant *population*. The natural-selection evolutionary account is one in which, within a population, individuals with a particular trait come to dominate or flourish largely because either i) the particular trait is a newly emergent one and found to fit relatively well to the environment into which it is born', or ii) the particular trait was always present but environmental conditions shift (independently) towards those which in some relevant sense favour the trait in question. If there is only one type of individual or trait in contention there is no basis for change as evolution via natural selection. If evolution is to be continuous, there must be a continuous source of variation within a population.

Second, if individuals with an environmentally (relatively) apt trait or characteristic are to come to dominate in a population over a period of time, there must be a mechanism whereby the characteristic in question (colour or whatever) is *reproduced* from one generation to another. Following Dawkins (1976, 1978) I shall call an item whose structure is replicated a *replicator*.

Third, there must be a way in which individuals with different aspects interact with their environments. Without such interaction there could be no process whereby a particular subset of individuals is *selected* in the sense of being found to fit or survive better than others within this environment. Notice I am referring here not (or not just—if we are to capture a natural selection story) to interaction between variety generation (mutation) conditions and the environment, but to interactions between the environment and all the developed individuals within it. Following Hull (1981) I shall call the mechanism for this the *interactor*. All aspects are essential for an explanation along evolutionary lines.

The PVRS model

Let me label an abstract model which supports these features a population-variety-reproduction-selection or PVRS model. Clearly for the model to capture a natural selection story where *a posteriori* fit is not (wholly) a product of design, it must be the case that the V (variety generation) and S (environmental selection) conditions are largely independent.

Now to suggest that such a PVRS model can have relevance not only in the biological realm but also in the social, is not to suppose all aspects of the manner in which such a model may be concretised in the biological realm carry over to the social domain. Indeed, if the model has relevance at all to the social realm, it will be concretised quite differently in the latter than in the biological realm. Most clearly any processes of innovation, reproduction, interaction and selection as occur in the social realm can be achieved only though the mediation of human agency. Social systems are nether self-reproducing nor naturally produced. Rather reproduction of the social system results from capable and purposeful human beings going about their daily business, interpreting their everyday tasks and the pertaining social order in very definite ways.

A second major difference between the two realms (that will be reflected in the form of any PVRS model developed) is that any variety generation and selection conditions will be more, or more often, interconnected in the social domain than in the biological. Although much of what occurs in the social realm is unintended and perhaps misunderstood, intentionality is far more significant in the social than natural domains.

Let me refer to a PVRS model which constrains variety generation (or mutation) and selection conditions to be strictly independent of each other as a strict, or polar (or neo-) Darwinian version of the model; alternatively put it is the PVRS model with purely Darwinian features. It is this particular polar model, or close approximations to it, which are usually thought to have most relevance in modern evolutionary biology. Certainly it is the version of the PVRS model which best illuminates the natural selection mechanism in which I am here interested. For this version of the model makes it clear that order, a fitting of individual and environment, or part and whole, can emerge even where variety generation and environmental conditions are totally unrelated.

Of course, it is possible to specify versions of the PVRS model that do not conform to the polar Darwinian conception. Let me call a PVRS model which allows environmental selection conditions (S) to feed back into the process of variety generation (V) a feed-backward or S-to-V model[3]. An example conforming to such a model for the social domain is any situation in which market research and its results, or other anticipations of environmental conditions, are fed back into the variety generation process.

Further we can refer to a PVRS model where (conditions or mechanisms affecting) the variety of traits (V) causally influence the selection conditions (S), the feed-forward or V-to-S model. An example here is a situation in which advertising, or indeed any form of persuasion, including use of power structures, are used to 'manipulate' the environment of selection.

I repeat, the version of the PVRS model that I refer to as the Darwinian natural-selection conception is one in which V (variety generation) and S (environmental selection) conditions are independent at least to significant degree. Thus I do not restrict it to the polar-Darwinian version, but to any in which the environment, and the factors or traits on which latter comes pivotally to bear, are to a significant extent independently determined.

In the social realm, of course, it is to be expected that, to the extent that the evolutionary or PVRS model has relevance at all, it will never be purely or polar-Darwinian (which would entail that human practices and differentiated survival rates are autonomous of human intentionality); nor purely feed-backward, i.e. backward *determining* (the functionalist mistake of the modern mainstream); nor purely feed-forward, i.e., forward *determining* (voluntarism or putty-clay environment). But if it is to be expected that feed-forward and feed-backward mechanisms will each have some role, in a world that is complex, holistic and incompletely understood, such as ours, we should not be surprised if, in any PVRS situation, a Darwinian natural-selection element emerges as significant on occasion.

So, to sum up this brief discussion, the Darwinian natural selection model—by which, to repeat, I mean a PVRS model in which V (variety generation) and S (environmental selection) conditions are to a significant degree independent—promises to be a useful source of redress against those who would see everything that happens in terms of intentionality. It is a counter model to any which presumes that all outcomes are optimal in some way, and that this presumed optimality (in a world of rationally calculating individuals) is effectively its own explanation. However, in any social explanatory context where the PVRS model does prove appropriate, it seems extremely unlikely that a natural (or environmental) selection mechanism acting on the individuals of the analysis will ever constitute the whole of any socio-explanatory story, even if sometimes it is highly explanatorily significant.

Such considerations, then, suggest that if a successful social-evolutionary explanation is possible, it will likely identify modes of interaction between

228 *The varying fortunes of the project*

only relatively independent variety generation and selection conditions. Strict Darwinian separation of modes of mutation and selection will give way to processes of causal interdependency and interpenetration to some degree. Any such explanation, in other words, can be expected to involve shifting patterns of both harmony and tension, of accommodation and rejection, as individuals and ultimately environment interact in a process of continuous reproduction and transformation.

But to recognise this is not to preclude the possibility that of mechanism analogous to that of Darwinian natural selection having a role in the social realm, and perhaps even a quite significant one. Whether such a possibility is ever actualised is something that can be determined only empirically. As it happens, I believe that the process I have in mind concerning the eventual rise to dominance and ensuing survival of the mathematising project in economics is just such a case of this kind. Let me now turn directly to the task of explaining this particular phenomenon.

Modern mainstream economics

To recap, given that this formalistic modelling approach has tended to produce little by way of explanatory successes, its emergence and continuing survival provide a particularly interesting set of phenomena to explain.

Indeed, I believe the history of the modern mainstream, the rise to dominance of formalistic modelling practices and an account of the 'survival' of this project, constitutes a central chapter in the history of academic economics that remains largely unwritten. The one significant exception to this of which I am aware is the excellent study of the history of general equilibrium economics by Ingrao and Israel (1990), an account that ties in very much with my own reading of the relevant episode in the history of economics. Here I can only give the briefest sketch of certain relevant developments.

Basic components of the social evolutionary story

What first of all might be the relevant population of the account I am proposing? What is the population of individuals with a variety of characteristics, only some of which will be favoured by specific environmental shifts? The population I have in mind is that of research practices undertaken by those who study social (including economic) phenomena. And the sub-group of population members whose (varying) fortunes I am particularly interested in here, is that set of practices concerned with mathematising the study of social phenomena.

Now a fundamental component of my account is a recognition that it was not the case that one fine morning in recent times a great economist awoke with the idea of mathematising the discipline. Rather attempts to so formalise the study of society and economy have been under way for a rather long time. Thus such attempts should be recognised as but one set of long existing research practices amongst the *variety* of practices continually in competition within the *population* of all academic or serious research practices.

However, it is only relatively recently that practices oriented to mathematising social phenomena have caught on in a significant way, as we shall see. Clearly, then, if an evolutionary explanation is appropriate here it will be the version which involves a (relatively autonomous) environmental shift (favouring the mathematising practices already in place); it will not involve the introduction of a new sort of practice found to be especially suited to the environmental conditions. And indeed, I shall argue precisely that the varying fortunes of the mathematising project over time reflect in some significant part (autonomous) changes that occurred in the relevant environment; that we do have something of an evolutionary story of the natural-selection sort. As an essential first step in developing and substantiating such a thesis, I need to ground the specific claim that practices concerned with mathematising the study of society and economy, practices which form part of the lineage of modern mainstream economics, have indeed been long under way.

The drive to mathematise

I do not claim to know where, in the history of those research practices that ultimately gave rise to modern mainstream economics, the formalising tendency first took root. However, it is clear that an important impetus to the process was Newton's success in uniting the heavens and the earth in mathematics. Even Kant came to argue thereafter that a science of society was required and this necessitated a social-scientific Newton or a Kepler to identify the laws of society. And in the euphoria of the achievements of the Enlightenment, indeed, the 'mathematisation' of the social sciences became a major theme of contemporary Western culture.

I must emphasise, though, that the influential role of mathematics in (especially) Western culture predates the Enlightenment by a long way. As Morris Kline summed up his findings in the preface to his *Mathematics in Western Culture* written almost half a century ago:

> In this book we shall survey mathematics primarily to show how its ideas have helped to mould twentieth-century life and thought. The ideas will be in historical order so that our material will range from the beginnings in Babylonia and Egypt to the modern theory of relativity. Some people may question the pertinence of material belonging to earlier historical periods. Modern culture, however, is the accumulation and synthesis of contributions made by many preceding civilisations. The Greeks, who first appreciated the power of mathematical

reasoning, graciously allowing the gods to use it in designing the universe, and then urging man to uncover the pattern of this design, not only gave mathematics a major place in their civilisation but initiated patterns of thought that are basic in our own. As succeeding civilisations passed on their gifts to modern times, they handed on new and increasingly more significant roles for mathematics. Many of these functions and influences of mathematics are now deeply imbedded in our culture.

(Kline, 1964)

Indeed the influence of mathematics is now so deeply ingrained within our culture that many people, as I earlier noted, appear to suppose that anything stated in mathematics must be correct, whilst for things to be correct, reliable, insightful or scientific (or at least conferring of scientific status), they must be stated in mathematics. This certainly is the view that pervades modern academies of economics, as I have already stressed. In fact, in the writings of modern mainstream economists, mathematical modelling is even synonymous with the idea (it is considered to comprise the totality) of 'theory'. Thus a recent article in the *Journal of Economic Literature*, entitled "The Young Person's Guide to Writing Economic Theory", concentrates only on the elaborating of formal models (Thomson, 1999).

Strassmann in a critical commentary on this situation conveys the essentials of it well:

> To a mainstream economist, theory means model, and model means ideas expressed in mathematical form. In learning how to "think like an economist," students learn certain critical concepts and models, ideas which typically are taught initially through simple mathematical analyses. These models, students learn, are theory. In more advanced courses, economic theories are presented in more mathematically elaborate models. Mainstream economists believe proper models – good models – take a recognizable form: presentation in equations, with mathematically expressed definitions, assumptions, and theoretical developments clearly laid out. Students also learn how economists argue. They learn that the legitimate way to argue is with models and econometrically constructed forms of evidence. While students are also presented with verbal and geometric masterpieces produced in bygone eras, they quickly learn that novices who want jobs should emulate their current teachers rather than deceased luminaries.
>
> Because all models are incomplete, students also learn that no model is perfect. Indeed, students learn that it is bad manners to engage in excessive questioning of simplifying assumptions. Claiming that a model is deficient is a minor feat – presumably anyone can do that. What is really valued is coming up with a better model, a better

theory. And so, goes the accumulated wisdom of properly taught economists, those who criticize without coming up with better models are only pedestrian snipers. Major scientific triumphs call for a better theory with a better model in recognizable form. In this way economists learn their trade; it is how I learned mine.

Therefore, imagine my reaction when I heard feminists from other disciplines apply the term *theory* to ideas presented in verbal form, ideas not containing even the remotest potential for mathematical expression. "This is theory?" I asked. "Where's the math?".

(Strassmann, 1994, p. 154)

Of course, mathematics *has* been extraordinarily successful in helping us understand and transform the world. However, the perception thereby gained that mathematics is the only way forward does not follow in logic, at least not without some additional argument turning, amongst other things, on ontology. But, as I say, this is not how most people seem to see it. That mathematics is central to all scientific progress is an accepted element of modern Western culture.

Now different types of culture (whether artistic, macho, twentieth-century-UK-working class, racist, capitalist-competitive, family-cooperative, etc.) give rise to, are embedded within, and/or are reinforced or transformed through, certain types of practice. And this is no less true of the culture of mathematics, including the societal respect for it, and indeed, belief in its ubiquitous relevance. This culture both underpins the practices of those who would apply mathematics to almost anything, and it is reinforced every time a further success is achieved or at least proclaimed. (No doubt too the difficulty that many profess to experience in the doing of mathematics reinforces the latter's aura and authoritative appeal.)

The generative role of this culture of mathematics is certainly widely in evidence today. It is the idea or notion or edict that any serious economics must be formulated mathematically that I take to be in effect the *replicator* of the evolutionary account I intend to defend. And the pervasive practices thereby sustained, the attempts to mathematise ever wider spheres, are the *interactors* of my evolutionary account. The relevant environment of interaction, of course, includes the shifting mix of competing research practices in play at any time. Whether or not, or the extent to which, a drive to mathematise held sway throughout the last 2000 years or more of Western history, there is little doubt that the successes of the Enlightenment did give a significant boost to this mathematising orientation, encouraging, thereafter at least, the widespread idea that further possibilities for the role of mathematics lay beyond even the uniting of heaven and earth.

Certainly during the period of the Enlightenment the endeavour of mathematising the study of social life was taken up by some in a relatively big way. According to Ingrao and Israel (1990), in fact, the:

historiography of philosophical thought has long identified the "mathematisation" of the social sciences as one of the major themes of contemporary culture generated and moulded in the rich melting pot of the Enlightenment.

(p. 34)

France was pivotal in this development as I have already briefly noted, especially with regards to those aspects of this history that can now be recognised as lying in the direct lineage of modern economics. Let me indicate something of this history, if only to indicate that the drive to mathematise the discipline is really something that long preceded the widespread acceptance of that project in the twentieth century.

The drive to mathematise economics in France

Most are aware of Walras's eventual contribution to the mathematisation of the discipline through his formulating the theory of general equilibrium. But he was neither the first nor the last significant contributor to the mathematisation of the subject, even in France. Any list of French contributors prior to Walras, and influenced by Enlightenment achievements, would include the Physiocrats or Physiocratic 'sect', especially Quesnay (1694–1774). Quesnay supposed that the political and moral basis of society is regulated by an inescapable force established by the creator, or at least taking the form of natural law, a view which underpinned his *Tableau économique* or "arithmetical formula" of the annual reproduction of the nation's wealth. But such a list ought also to include numerous others.

For example, Turgot (1727–1781), a contributor close to the Physiocrats but not a member of the sect, developed the Physiocratic metaphor of blood circulation in suggesting a connection between the operation of markets and the dynamics of fluids. Dupont de Nemours (1739–1817) who argued that because everything happens in the order established by the creator of nature, it is possible to apply physico-mathematical methods to the moral sciences. Condorcet (1743–1794) attempted to found a *mathématique sociale*, aiming to achieve an objective science of subjective phenomena formulated in terms of the probability calculus. Achylle-Nicolas Isnard (1749–1803) produced his own table of arithmetic to demonstrate, as a departure from Physiocratic thought, that manufacturing industry, like agriculture, may also generate a surplus, one that accrues to not only landowners but also owners of scarce productive resources. Canard (1750–1833), in works on social mathematics and on political economy, provided (or anyway attempted to provide—some dispute his achievements) the first explicit formulation, and dynamic treatment, of the notion of economic equilibrium, the first application of marginal analysis, and a conception of the connection between the ideas of mechanical and economic equilibrium. Dupuit (1804–1866), contributed to the development of general equilibrium theory by providing a mathematical foundation for the idea of the measurability of utility (a quality of the good depending upon the attitude of the economic individual). And Cournot (1801–1877) demonstrated how to apply functional analysis to economic phenomena in a manner that required specifying only the most generalised features of the functional forms utilized. He also provided a statement of a supposed law relating the quantity of a good demanded and the latter's monetary price in a single market. And it was Cournot who introduced concepts eventually known as the elasticity of demand and marginal cost, and ideal types of market forms (perfect or unlimited competition, etc.), amongst much else.

Walras (1834–1910) remains the central figure in this early French history, of course, at least in terms of modern day renown. But we can already see that in formulating a mathematical theory of general equilibrium, Walras was developing the work of others, most especially the contributions of Canard, Isnard and Cournot (although only the latter is explicitly acknowledged by Walras)[4].

I have no need to go into the details of Walras's contribution here, which are in any case well known. At this point I am merely concerned with identifying relevant threads in the early history of the current mainstream; I am wanting to draw attention to the fact that practices concerned with mathematising the discipline of economics have long been under way. And the driving force, the generative motor, was societal culture. This bore as heavily on Walras, as on his predecessors more than hundred years earlier. The historical analysis of Ingrao and Israel indicates well:

> how deeply attached Walras was to the main trends in French culture that had inspired the application of mathematics to economics and, in particular, the early development of economic equilibrium theory. Despite his reluctance to acknowledge his precursors ... there are numerous passages clearly showing his awareness of belonging to a French cultural tradition inspired by a project of applying a Newtonian model of physical and mathematical science to the social sciences.
> (Ingrao and Israel, 1990, p. 142)

We might note, too, that when Walras resigned from his teaching obligations in Lausanne in 1893, he was succeeded by Pareto (1848–1923), born in Paris but eventually raised in Italy, who was also concerned with the mathematisation of the social world. For Pareto, at least as much as for Walras, an understanding of mechanical equilibrium served as a model for theorising general economic equilibrium. In attempting to construct a rational mechanics of economic behaviour using methods of physics and mathematics, Pareto aimed to give the former the same analytical foundation and empirical grounding as rational mechanics.

In France's intellectual history especially, then, a part of the lineage of modern economics is to be found. However, although important contributions to the modern situation emerged during this early French episode, none were especially well accepted in their own time (even if Walras was occasionally prone to making extravagant claims to the contrary). Of course, as we now know, the goal of mathematising the discipline, including that of developing a formalistic equilibrium theory, did eventually become widely accepted, even if mathematical modelling methods have never proven to be particularly successful or fruitful as ways of investigating and understanding social reality. Walras in particular, albeit long after his death, was eventually to achieve the recognition he had, for much of his life-time, felt he deserved. Samuelson, for example, was to interpret him as the only economist on the level of Newton. And Schumpeter declared him "the greatest of all economists". However, before there was to be a widespread acceptance of mathematical economics in general, and of the importance of Walras's contribution in particular, a new methodological framework was to be adopted, and the focus of attention switched away from France to interwar Vienna, Britain, Sweden and ultimately the USA.

Before examining various relevant aspects of these developments, I might reemphasise my objective here. I am proposing a socio-evolutionary explanation of the development and persistence of modern mainstream economics interpreted as the project concerned to formalise social/economic phenomena. To this point I have merely indicated that amongst the *variety* of practices within the *population* of methodological practices of economists, endeavours to mathematise the study of social phenomena have long been in evidence. If this, at least in part, is an evolutionary story I need to demonstrate how the environment has played a role in selecting out the *a posteriori* successful practices (or equivalently, in filtering out those which, at any point of time, were unsuccessful). I emphasise that I do not take a deterministic stance here. Changes in the environment do not have to play such an influential role. My argument is just that, in the case of the rise of modern mainstream economics, it turned out *a posteriori* that they did.

The culture of mathematics in France

In fact a question I must first address is why the euphoria of the achievements of the Enlightenment gave rise to such an impulse to mathematise the social sciences *in France* in particular. Of central relevance here, I believe, is the Cartesian heritage of that country. Newtonianism was initially wielded as a weapon in the intellectual struggle against Cartesianism (Voltaire, 1738). But, as is so often the case in a debate where each side contains insight, the outcome was a project modified very much in the light of criticisms of, and so conforming to, the other. Thus it was, that on emerging from its encounter with Cartesianism, Newtonianism (in its particular guise of a concern with elaborating laws[5]) assumed quite unique features in France, being substantially transformed in line with the opposition. In particular, whereas the empiricist orientation of England gave rise to small-scale empirical research, the French physico-mathematical approach adopted the goal of furthering the mathematical analysis of Newton's laws of Physics. Moreover those who accepted this goal were quite successful in their pursuit of it. So much were they so, in fact, that (at a time when the English *Royal Society* was in decline) the French *Académie des Sciences,* very much bound up with the development of (this form of) Newtonianism, became established as the leading scientific institution in Europe.

As might be expected, this achievement of French science had knock-on effects in society at large. Science came to be seen as the most prestigious sphere of French life and thereby proved to be widely influential. In its mathematical-Newtonian guise science came to be seen as an ideal for all branches of study and for culture more widely, giving an impulse not least to the idea of the possibility of a mathematical-scientific approach to the governance of society, and, as a condition for this, to understanding its conditions. In their historical overview Ingrao and Israel summarise the ensuing situation in France as follows:

> [With the successes of the 'French physico-mathematical school'] the scientific intellectual became the model intellectual and the scientific community the model community for scholarly communities. In the reformist view of the values and decrepit institutions of absolutism, Newton's scientific philosophy and the model of the scientific intellectual established in France became points of reference for an ideal renewal of the whole of society. In its Newtonian garb, science put itself forward as the *centre* of society and the *driving force* of reform, promising new horizons in all fields of knowledge to which the new methods of scientific thought could be applied. This scientistic (in the full and broad sense) vision was thus projected beyond the confines of traditional science, and under the urgent prompting of institutional, economic and social problems—first under the *Ancien Régime* and then during the Revolution—the question of the *scientific* government of society and economy achieved full status also in theoretical terms.
> (Ingrao and Israel, 1990, p. 36)

The environment

If Western culture in general, and French post Enlightenment culture in particular, held mathematical practice in such high esteem, it is not surprising that attempts to formalise economics took place in such conditions.

It may be thought a puzzle, then, that such practices failed to win widespread approval within the academy at an earlier time, especially in France. If the culture placed a premium on the reproduction and proliferation of mathematical practices, including in economics, why did they not flourish more in that field in the immediate Enlightenment period, and on the scale they do today?

The answer, I now want to argue, has something to do with the *specific local academic environment* in which the mathematising economists existed. Let me indicate something of the context in which the early post-Enlightenment attempts to formalise the study of social phenomena occurred in France.

In fact, in the period immediately following the Revolution the academic climate in France was particularly open to ambitious projects of political and educational reform. At this point, the application of mathematics, as opposed to many literary activities, was interpreted as accessible to people from all backgrounds or classes, and so desirable, and social mathematics found some space in the educational system. In particular, the Academy of Moral and Political Sciences of the Institut de France concerned itself in a very significant way with the application of mathematics to the study of society.

But Enlightenment culture not only prompted attempts to mathematise all areas, it also required criteria of verification in all fields; there was a demand that descriptive or explanatory accuracy be demonstrated. From early on, even in France, there was significant opposition from the sciences at large, and from within mathematics especially, to the use of mathematics in areas considered unsuited to it. As the early optimism of the Revolution turned to the harsher realism, even academic intolerance, of the Napoleonic order, there was less emphasis on encouraging certain academic practices for their own sake, or for the sake of those who prosecuted them. Greater emphasis, instead, was put on accepting academic practices for their perceived relevance.

The demand for descriptive or explanatory relevance was to prove, then as now, beyond the means of those striving to mathematise the social realm. And this was widely recognised. Laplace, in particular, came to view the attempt to mathematise the social realm as an intellectual mistake. He had suggested some support for the idea at the time of the Revolution. But with further study and reflection his attitude turned to one of outright hostility. So hostile was he, in fact, that when, with the death of Lagrange, he achieved near supremacy in scientific matters in France, especially at the Institut de France's Class of Geometry, Laplace set about actively purging what remained of the programme of mathematising society.

In this period, with Laplace's influence large, the scientific world largely lost interest in applying mathematical methods outside of physics; only the physico-mathematical sciences were accorded any serious status. The project of mathematising the social world continued, of course. But the result of developments in the physico-mathematical sciences was that all attempts at constructing an autonomous discipline were abandoned. Instead such attempts as persisted followed the official model as laid down by the physico-mathematical sciences; all became oriented to traditional mathematical tools and concepts and deterministic methods of mechanics. All traces of Condorcet's probabilistic approach, for example, had for the time being disappeared.

However, it was not just in mathematics and the physical sciences that the idea of mathematising social phenomena was to become rejected as misguided. The conclusion that mathematical methods provided a barrier to understanding social reality, came to be accepted closer to home.

Say (1767–1832) and the French Liberal school he in effect founded, a school that was to dominate the field of social study for most of the nineteenth century, took much the same position as well. They even made an opposition to the mathematisation of social phenomena a central plank of their broader philosophy. For members of this school, reality is captured by the data of experience, so that methods, including modes of reasoning, must be in tune with the latter. It was observed, however, that when mathematical methods were applied to social categories, the results were such that facts of experience were always ignored. Say argued for example:

> Without referring to algebraic formulas that would obviously not apply to the political world, a couple of writers from the eighteenth century and from Quesnay's dogmatic school on the one hand, and some English economists from David Ricardo's school on the other hand, wanted to introduce a kind of argumentation which I believe, as a general argument, to be inapplicable to political economy as to all sciences that acknowledge only experience as a foundation. By that I mean the argumentation that lies on abstract ideas. Condillac has rightly noticed that abstract reasoning is nothing but a calculation with different signs. But an argument does not provide, nor does an equation, the data that is essential, as far as experimental sciences are concerned, to get to the discovery of truth. Ricardo set it in a hypothesis that cannot be attacked because, based on observations that cannot be questioned, he imposes his reasoning until he draws the last consequences from it, but he does not compare its results with experience. Reasoning never wavers, but an often unnoticed and always unpredictable vital force diverts the facts from our calculation. Ricardo's followers. . . . considered real cases as exceptions and did not take them into account. Freed from the control of experience, they rushed into metaphysics deprived of applications; they have transformed political economy into a verbal and argumentative science. Trying to broaden it they have led only to its downfall.
>
> (Say, 1971, p. 15)

As Ingrao and Israel have also observed, this "rejection of the mathematization of social science was pushed by Say almost to the point of the idiosyncratic rejection of mathematics *tout court*" (Ingrao and Israel, 1990, p. 60). It is relevant to inquire why. After all, the French Liberal School which Say founded was primarily concerned with particular substantive theories and policies. And the obvious, and sufficient, orientation for a realist to adopt, is opposition to any dogmatism on the part of others who neglect the real world; there is no obvious reason to prevent (as opposed merely to critically engaging with) all mathematising tendencies.

In truth, explaining the nature of Say's opposition to social mathematics is a somewhat complicated story (as Arena, 2000a makes clear). Although, the period 1790 to 1870 saw the rise to prominence of the French Classical or Liberal School, with Say as the founder and figurehead, Say's initial project was not to establish a new school at all but something rather different. His purpose was merely to disseminate the insights of Smith's *Wealth of Nations* in Continental Europe, albeit with some extensions introduced for purposes of clarity (Say, 1803).

But Ricardo and Malthus adopted similar projects, albeit providing different interpretations of Smith. This introduced a kind of rivalry, especially between Say and Ricardo. Over time this led Say to re-evaluate his own contribution. First he revised upwards the degree of originality of his contribution; he reinterpreted his project not merely as disseminating Smith's writings but also as advancing Say's own scientific discoveries. And eventually he came to argue explicitly for a different approach to that of Ricardo and other heirs of Smith. Although Ricardo did not use mathematics in his contributions, he did adopt a deductivist style of argument. It is a mode of argumentation that would lend itself to easy mathematisation by later mathematical economists, and suffers from the same problems of connecting with social reality as experienced with mathematical methods in economics. It was an opposition to this deductivist method, in particular, that Say emphasised, and which emerged thereby as a central plank of French classical thought. As Arena summarises matters:

> This dissent from Ricardo's method was considered by Say as a fundamental issue and this view was then adopted by most of Say's French Liberal followers, forming therefore one of the crucial components of the liberal theoretical framework in France.
> (Arena, 2000a, p. 207)

Certainly most of Say's followers took his lead in opposing the Ricardian deductive approach, with some of them, especially Wolowski (1848), Reybaud (1862) and Baudrillart (1872) being opposed to the use of mathematics in particular[6]. According to Reybaud, for example, the Ricardians were only out "to feed principles with equations and give political economy a false air of algebra in order to impress minds who look for deep thinking" (Reybaud, 1862, p. 301)

The reasons for the rise to dominance of the French liberal school, with its fundamental opposition to mathematical methods, need not concern us here (and are well documented in Arena, 2000a, especially pp. 215–218). The point to emphasise, rather, is that once it achieved dominance this school developed strategies to maintain its position. For example, liberals attempted to control educational institutions that played any role in the teaching of political economy. At some point or other, they carried significant and often total influence in the Athénée, l'Ecole Spéciale de Commerce, l'Ecole Commerciale, the Conservatoire des Arts et Métiers, and the French Grandes Ecoles, with the peak of their sway culminating, in 1871, in the creation of the Ecole Libre des Sciences Politiques. The liberals also significantly influenced the constitution of scientific societies. They created the Société d'Economie Politique in 1842, and became prominent amongst the members of Académie des Sciences Morales et Politiques after its reestablishment in 1832. And liberals also either dominated, or very significantly influenced, the major journals read by economists. These included *Le Censeur, Le Libre-Echange, L'Economiste Français, Le Globe, Le Journal des Débats, Le Siècle* and most significantly *Le Journal des Economistes*. The latter, which was created by the liberals in 1841, defended the liberal viewpoint until its demise during the second world war. The effect of all this on the contemporary practices of economics in France is once more well summarised by Arena:

> French liberal economists, however, were jealous of the influence of their approach. Therefore, they built and implemented a strategy for the diffusion of this message. The liberal school thus formed a homogeneous group unified by familial links, friendship and participation in common Societies and Journals. This participation strongly contributed to the diffusion of the liberal central message. It was however decisively reinforced by the strategy of control of educational institutions. This control helped French liberal economists to diffuse their views and act as if they were the only ones who could be considered "economists," as such. Their cultural, political and social predominance was no longer questionable. Economists who did not accept the liberal views were proclaimed to be "heretics": they became "socialists" or "prohibitionists"; they actually lost their right of belonging to the realm of political economy.
> (Arena, 2000a, 219)

So important was the liberal school's influence, including its amplification of Say's rejection of attempts to mathematise the social sciences, according to Ingrao and Israel (1990), that "Say's methodological views were long to weigh upon French culture as an impediment to any further attempt to use mathematical models in economics" (p. 60).

Thus from the beginning of the French classical period to the time of Walras, the relevant academic environment presented difficulties for would-be mathematisers of the study of social phenomena. In French society at large the idea of mathematics as an essential feature of any respectful discipline prevailed. Yet within relevant branches of the academy the reception afforded the would-be mathematisers of social phenomena was continually hostile. For the natural sciences and their mathematicians this did not require a demotion in the importance of mathematics, merely a recognition that economics required something different. For Say and his followers, in contrast, there likely was a rejection of the view that mathematics is an essential component of all serious process of knowledge production. But in either case, attempts to mathematise the study of social phenomena were viewed as misguided and, more significantly, actively resisted.

Still, attempts to mathematise the social sciences did nevertheless continue throughout, as we have seen. Variety in social research practices was always present, and the wider cultural forces ensured that the range of practices followed included at least some of this mathematising sort. But it was always difficult for the would-be social mathematicians. The influence of Laplace, as I say, resulted mainly in a forced concentration on the strictly deterministic approach of mechanics based on methods of infinitesimal calculus. And the fact of the near total dominance of Say's school within economics, along indeed with, in the late nineteenth century, the growing influence of historicism and institutional analysis, in addition to the scientific community's eventual near total dissociation from the mathematisation of the social sciences project, rendered any contribution to the latter a somewhat isolating and wearisome endeavour. It was precisely these conditions which Walras himself was to encounter.

The reception of Walras

It is against a backdrop of such forces and developments, then, that we must interpret the reception of Walras's efforts. Not surprisingly, when in 1873 Walras presented his first attempts at formulating a mathematical economics at the Insitut de France's Académie des Sciences Morales et Politiques, it was largely met with either disinterest or outright hostility. The economic historian Levasseur was especially critical. In particular, he ridiculed Walras's application of mathematics to phenomena which, as he saw it, do not lend themselves to such a treatment, concluding that "one gets a far better idea from thinking than from the author's mathematical formulae" (Levasseur in Walras, 1874, p. 117). Levasseur also warns of the:

danger that lies in the desire to bring together, as a unit, at any cost, things that are complex by their nature, as in wishing to apply to political economy a method that is excellent for the physical sciences but could not be applied indiscriminately to an order of phenomena whose causes are so variable and complex and that above all involve one eminently variable cause that can absolutely not be reduced to algebraic formulae: human freedom.

(Levasseur in Walras, 1874, p. 119)

Other economists proved hardly more charitable in their reception of Walras's formulations.

Thus ignored or dismissed by economists Walras turned his attention to seeking the approval of physicists and mathematicians. This is not to say that Walras no longer sought the approval of economists as well. But perceiving that mathematics was the dominant and most influential discipline, Walras reasoned that if the mathematician's could be brought on side, the economists would sooner or later follow. But persuading mathematicians that his approach had relevance was no easier than persuading economists. Although some were interested, most were not. Walras, ever the optimist, eventually claimed Poincaré as amongst the more positively inclined. But this was really an exaggeration. In a short letter he sent to Walras in 1901, commenting on the copy of *Eléments d'economie politique pure* that he had recently received from Walras, Poincaré observed:

at the beginning of every mathematical speculation there are hypotheses and that, for this speculation to be fruitful, it is necessary (as in applications to physics for that matter) to account for these hypotheses. If one forgets this condition, then one goes beyond the correct limits.

(Poincaré, 1901)

It is this realist condition, of course, that mathematical economists have been unable fully to satisfy either prior to, or since, this time. Against Walras's *Eléments*, specifically, Poincaré, picking up on features that are still prominent in much modern economic theorising, observed:

You regard men as infinitely selfish and infinitely farsighted. The first hypothesis may perhaps be admitted in a first approximation, the second may call for some reservations.

(Poincaré, 1901)

In truth, after several years of self propaganda by Walras and often fierce rejections of the idea of mathematical economics by mathematicians, the dialogue between the two groups, mathematicians and those economists keen to formalise the study of social phenomena, became severely curtailed. Ten years into the twentieth century, indeed, it seemed that the goal of extending support for the application of mathematical methods beyond the borders of physics, certainly to the social sciences, was widely (though never universally[7]) regarded as impossible.

Yet, despite these setbacks, the story was, at this point, far from over; as we know the mathematisation project in general, and general equilibrium analysis specifically, were yet to rise phoenix-like from the ashes. How could this be? In particular how could this be if, amongst other things, and as I have noted all along, the project was never to achieve much success in terms of illuminating the social world?

A shifting environment: reinterpreting mathematics

A significant part of the answer lies in a shift that occurred in the relevant environment, i.e., in the environment of academic practices within which attempts to mathematise the discipline competed with others. I have already noted how the criticisms of Laplace and others led those economists who continued with the mathematisation project to adopt the model of the contemporary paradigm of physics, basically mechanics. However, at this time, this classical reductionist programme (the programme of reducing everything to the model of physics, in particular mechanics) was itself coming into disarray. With the development of relativity theory and especially quantum theory, the image of nature as continuous came to be reexamined in particular, and the role of infinitesimal calculus previously regarded as near ubiquitous within physics, came to be reexamined even within that domain.

The outcome, in effect, was a switch from an emphasis on mathematics *as an attempt to apply the physics model,* and specifically the mechanics metaphor, to an emphasis on *mathematics for its own sake.* As classical physics itself went into crisis, developments in mathematics were to reduce the dependency of mathematisation projects on physics altogether. Mathematics, especially through the work of Hilbert, became increasingly viewed as a discipline properly concerned with providing a pool of frameworks for *possible realities.* No longer was mathematics seen as the language of nature, abstracted from the study of nature. Rather it was conceived as a practice concerned with formulating systems comprising sets of axioms and their deductive consequences, with these systems in effect taking on a life of their own. The task of finding applications was henceforth regarded as being of secondary importance at best, and not of immediate concern.

This method, the axiomatic method, removed at a stroke various hitherto insurmountable constraints facing those who would mathematise the discipline of economics. Researchers involved with mathematical projects could, for the time being at least, postpone the day of interpreting their preferred axioms and assumptions. There was no longer any need to seek the blessing of other economists or of mathematicians and physicists who might insist that the relevance of metaphors and analogies be established at the outset. A need to match method to the nature of social reality was no longer regarded as a binding constraint, or even a matter of any relevance, at least for the time being. Nor, it seemed, was it possible for anyone to insist (with any legitimacy) that the formulations of economists conform to any specific model already found to be successful elsewhere (such as the mechanics model in physics). Indeed, the whole idea of prior models, metaphors, even interpretations, came to be rejected by some economic 'modellers' (albeit never in any really plausible manner).

Probably the most famous (though certainly not the only[8]) influential contribution to the formalisation of economics since Walras remains Debreu's (1959) axiomatic treatment of (the existence and uniqueness) of general equilibrium, a contribution that gained its author the Nobel Memorial Prize in economic science. Even today the language and symbolism of Debreu's *Theory Of Value* is found in many axiomatic papers. And Debreu's contribution rests for its legitimacy precisely on the claim that axioms are not in need of any interpretation. As Debreu expresses these matters himself:

> *Allegiance to rigor dictates the axiomatic form of analysis where the theory, in the strict sense, is logically entirely disconnected from its interpretations.* In order to bring out fully this disconnectedness, all definitions, all hypotheses, and the main results of the theory, in the strict sense, are distinguished by italics; moreover, the transition from the informal discussion of interpretations to the formal construction of theory is often marked by one of the expressions: "in the language of the theory," "for the sake of the theory," "formally." Such a dichotomy reveals all the assumptions and the logical structure of the analysis. It also makes possible immediate extensions of that analysis without modification of the theory by simple reinterpretation of the concepts; ...
>
> (Debreu, 1959, p. x, emphasis added)

If the decline in the classical reductionist program and the rise of axiomatic mathematics laid the conditions for the eventual proliferation of mathematical economics, advances along these lines came only gradually. And it is perhaps significant that the project of mathematising economics received the greater stimulus at this juncture not in France, with its close links with the classical reductionist programme, but in Austria and Germany, where the new physics, revised conception of role of mathematics, and a specific emphasis upon axiomatic mathematics, had originated and now flourished. In particular, it was here that von Neuman, Wald, Morgenstern and other mathematicians made their initial contributions.

And although approaches such as those of Wald and von Neumann were different in kind, they were later reconciled in the US where many of the early contributors had emigrated under the Nazi threat.

Of course, France itself eventually witnessed significant related developments as well. I have already mentioned the contribution of Debreu. Although Debreu's *Theory of Value* was produced after his move to the US Cowles Commission in the 1950s, Debreu was very much a product of the French Bourbaki 'school' (a group of French mathematicians[9] who argued that mathematical systems should be studied as pure structures devoid of any possible interpretations). It was at the Ecole Normale Superieure in the 1940s that Debreu came into contact with the Bourbaki teaching. And once trained in this maths, but with his interests aroused by economics, Debreu sought a suitable location to pursue an interest in reformulating economics in terms of this mathematics. It is perhaps not insignificant that his move to the Cowles Commission coincided with the latter's effective acceptance of Bourbakism.

The fine details of the latter and all other developments cannot be elaborated here[10]. My general point, though, is common to most if not all such individual pathways, and can be stated without filling in all the specific links. It is that in the Western academies at least, the constraint of social reality on mathematical modelling was at this point postponed until some 'tomorrow'. And with this being the case, the possibilities for mathematical modelling were, for the time being anyway, restrained almost solely by the ingenuity of the protagonists.

Let me briefly take stock. I have argued that the formalising tendency has been in play long before the twentieth century, albeit meeting with little success in the area of formalising the study of society. In the earlier to middle twentieth century, however, its fortune, in terms of approval rating, started to improve remarkably. This however occurred not as a result of any improved explanatory performance. Rather it was the climate of its reception that shifted. Fundamental here were changes in the way mathematics was interpreted, or the criteria according to which mathematical reasoning in any sphere were considered justified.

Of course, a multitude of factors not considered here will also have played a role in shaping eventual outcomes, or at least in shaping the manner in which things happened. No doubt, as I have already acknowledged, the life paths of specific individuals will have made differences, often fortuitously. And one especially significant development in the midst of all this was the emergence of cheap computing facilities allowing the speedy development, initially of econometrics, and later of computer simulation models and the like.

However, I do not need to recount the precise steps whereby, in the changed and changing, more conducive environment, mathematical economics came to be accepted and indeed grew to become dominant. Nor do I really want to. For I am not suggesting a deterministic account, that what happened had to be. My aim is merely to indicate that, as it turned out, the environment of other relevant practices often had a very significant bearing in the determination of which practices in economics were, or were not, able to survive comfortably enough to flourish. Although there was no inevitability about anything that happened, it is clear, I think, that the changes in the environment made a significant difference, that the account of them sketched above has significant evolutionary-explanatory power; if the environmental shifts which occurred did not determine the outcome they did serve to make what in the end happened more likely. The drive to mathematise the study of social phenomena has for a long time been a dominant force in Western culture, a force that has been manifest in the academy. However, prior to the twentieth century, this drive was essentially constrained by the dominant view that research practices ought to be relevant to the object of study, that reality ought to constrain the analyses prosecuted. With the reconceptualisation of mathematics in the earlier twentieth century, this constraint of reality on the mathematising project in the social sciences was lifted. Thus unconstrained, the project achieved a spell of dominance, a spell that still continues.

Of course, the important point, here, from the perspective of establishing an evolutionary story, is that the conditions responsible for the noted shifts in the environment had little to do with the conditions generating the variety of research practices which economists followed; the conditions of variety generation and environmental selection are largely independent.

Feed-forward and feed-backward mechanisms

The topic of this illustration does warrant further comment at this point, however. For although the axiomatic approach allowed a postponing of the day when the axioms and assumptions were to be given a realistic interpretation, it was always expected that the day of reckoning would eventually come. Yet we are still waiting; illuminatory successes, as noted throughout, are hard to find. How, then, after more than half a century of the 'new' approach to mathematics, is modern mainstream economics managing to survive, despite its unhappy record in providing social illumination?

To this point I have focused very much on the role of the environment of all practices serving to select or reject those of mathematical economics. Of course, once any project has achieved a certain level of dominance the opportunity may well exist for its agents to affect variety and selection conditions in its favour. And if and where this occurs we must recognise that the natural selection model is limited in its explanatory contribution, or at least that the degree of dependence between conditions of variety production and environmental selection is relatively high.

246 *The varying fortunes of the project*

We have already seen, for example, how the dominance of Say's school made it very difficult for the early mathematising project to gain proper consideration, or even to get started, and how the influence of Laplace made it difficult for any endeavour that did not conform to the standard model(s) of physics. These are cases of the feed-backward version of the PVRS model having significant relevance, of selection conditions significantly affecting the variety in play.

There are also numerous historical examples whereby the feed-forward version of the PVRS model is appropriate, of variety-generating factors influencing, or at least being brought to bear in an attempt to influence, the selecting environment as well. One such is Walras's well known attempts to publicise his own approach. He appealed not just to Poincaré, but to almost any economist or (more often) physical scientist or mathematician of influence, who might find an interest in it. As Ingrao and Israel note:

> An examination of Walras's published correspondence provides confirmation of the turning point reached in 1874. It was precisely in that period that he began an intense promotional campaign largely through his letters in an attempt to open channels of scientific exchange and possibly to win pupils and create a number of 'Walrasian schools'. His method was to establish networks of correspondents in various countries (Britain, the United States, Germany, Austria, Italy, and France). His greatest efforts were, as usual, directed to his home country and now in particular to the scientists, while not neglecting his traditional relations with economists. A brief glance immediately reveals where he found listeners and where not, where interest was sometimes followed by disappointment. While the German-speaking world proved fairly indifferent to mathematical economics, greater interest was displayed in Anglo-Saxon circles, albeit only amongst economists. In this sphere, his most important exchanges were with Jevons and Edgeworth, and both brought disappointment and difficulty....
>
> (p. 148)

And if a century ago, possibilities for new approaches to mathematising the study of social phenomena, or for influencing the environment of selection, were rendered difficult, today the boot is on the other foot. In modern times it is the traditions that maintain realisticness or social illumination as the primary goal which fail to receive a sympathetic hearing; indeed they rarely get a hearing at all.

In other words, I think it is fair to say that, within the economics academy, there are instances where this mathematising project maintains itself by closing off lines of intellectual competition, where it manipulates conditions both of variety generation and environmental selection. During the period of the dominance of mathematical economics, for example, we have tended towards a position where university courses in faculties of economics (in the UK at least) cover little more than methods of mathematical modelling (especially at the post graduate level); most journals regarded as prestigious have acquired gate-keepers who effectively bar non-mathematical expositions; appointments in academic economic departments and the like usually advertise specifically for (econometric, micro- or macro-) modellers; and for committees charged with allocating resources or effecting promotions, etc., non-mathematical contributions are rarely treated seriously at all.

In my experience mathematicians, philosophers and other social scientists who are aware of the situation of modern economics side heavily with heterodox criticisms of the (concentrated emphasis on the) mathematising tendency within economics. However, the mainstream of modern economics preserves itself in a situation of significant isolation from other disciplines. And until recent times, at least, such a situation has appeared sustainable. To the uniformed the mathematical emphasis gives an aura of technical sophistication that is perhaps intimidating, whilst the degree to which the project dominates the modern discipline encourages the response that surely so many people (most of mainstream economists) cannot be wrong. Also economists' representatives on the relevant research assessment committees and funding bodies are themselves chosen from within the mainstream.

However nothing stands still, especially in the social realm. Whilst contributions from heterodox groups persist (and in truth it is usually all too easy to win any intellectual debate as occurs with the mainstream), other tendencies are in train. Student enrolments in economics faculties are currently in decline in many parts of the world. This has certainly coincided with the growth of business schools, and a reorienting of departments of human geography, sociology and the like, which now provide opportunities for people to teach and study aspects of life considered to be economic, but to do so without insisting that it all be carried out in a formalistic fashion. Also there are commentators in the media and elsewhere increasingly aware of the plight of the discipline. It seems likely, certainly possible, that such pressures will lead to a pro-intellectual reorientation sooner or later (especially as the main mainstream response, as far as I can see, is currently no better than to suggest a 'need' to pay their professors higher wages. This presumably is intended to make the goal of becoming an economic professor more attractive financially, even if holders of such posts are largely constrained from illuminating social and economic life).

Overview and concluding remarks

I hope that I have by now covered enough ground to indicate that the rise to prominence of the mathematising project in economics conforms (or has aspects which conform) to a significant degree to the (Darwinian) evolutionary model, to the natural-selection metaphor. It is indeed a success story for the practices concerned in terms of their eventual rise to dominance. But it does not appear to be a success story by any wider or more laudatory criterion. In fact if measured against the criterion of progress in knowledge and understanding of the social realm, modern economics is something of an unfortunate episode.

The evolutionary example discussed here illustrates not only that social evolution is (of course) continually mediated by human agency. It indicates as well that any social process that does manifest evolutionary, or natural selection, tendencies will almost inevitably be one of continual accommodation and resistance, attraction and rejection, fit and mismatch, harmony and disharmony of subject and object or of 'individual' and environment, as changes in each interact with the other, as new practices emerge, and selections and selecting environments adjust. The social evolutionary process, then, will inevitably be one of sifting, slipping and sliding.

There can be no presumption that any *a posteriori* underlying direction of longer term change is necessarily irreversible of course. We are sometimes encouraged to think of the development of life on earth, including the emergence of humans, or of developments in some branches of knowledge as, by and large, stories of irreversible progress. But there is no reason to suppose that all evolutionary episodes conform to such examples if so interpreted; reversals of fortunes are always possible. Such a reversal, of course, is precisely the outcome many heterodox economists are attempting to facilitate in the context of modern economics. The aim is so to reorient the discipline, to reinstall the goal of explanatory adequacy, even of truth, as primary once more, as well as to achieve a more pluralistic, intellectually open and tolerant, forum.

Of course, reversals in fortune are not unheard of even in the biological realm; indeed they are rather common. I referred earlier to the varying fortunes of spotted grey and dark moths in the UK in the nineteenth century. In particular, I noted how, with nineteenth century industrialisation, pollutants killed the lichen on the trees in question and rendered the bark a dark colour, leaving the spotted grey at a relative disadvantage compared to dark moths because more easily recognisable to moth-eating birds. With the increase in pollution control in the twentieth century, however, lichen is again growing on trees in relevant areas, and I understand that once more the dark moth is on the decline relative to the spotted grey.

The noted increase in opportunities for students to study economics, without the constraint of reducing all to formalistic modelling, in business or management schools, departments of human geography, sociology and the like, and the openings equally provided for researchers more interested in social illumination, may mark an analogous case of re-switching in the environment of academic economic practices. And as I noted earlier, students at some of the elite schools in France have started a protest against the excessive mathematisation of the modern economics discipline[11]. Perhaps it will all make a difference.

However that may be, the evolutionary model does seem capable of providing a framework for understanding certain significant aspects of developments in the modern economics academy. Of course, the explanatory sketch provided here, though an extension of an argument found in previous contributions, remains (like any explanatory account) somewhat partial. Indeed (and again as with any explanation) new questions are thrown up by the answer(s) suggested. For example, why did the mathematising tendency not take off in a bigger way in the other branches of social science? Is the fact that most social phenomena which are measurable tend to be regarded as 'economic' sufficient to explain this? And why in the last fifty years especially, have *specific* forms of mathematical economics (and not others) taken off, and why have they taken off when they have? For example, why has game theory risen to prominence only relatively recently given that the basic principles were developed rather a long time ago? I have my own particular views on these and related issues. But, whilst all answers generate yet more questions, the truth is the historical documentation and explanation of the mathematising tendency in economics is a task that largely still lies in the waiting.

Here I have merely provided a sketch of what I believe is one set of explanatory ingredients in the historical episode. But it is an important set in that the features noted seem, in some significant part, to account in a coherent way for the relatively recent rise to prominence, and indeed continuing dominance, of the formalising project in the absence of any obvious measure of success other than its current widespread acceptance. Moreover, this explanatory coherence is achieved in a context where it is difficult to find, or easily imagine, any convincing alternative explanatory story.

Notes

1 For helpful comments on an earlier draft I am grateful to Richard Arena and Leonard Bauer.
2 Thereby encouraging the headline in Le Monde of 31/10/2000: "Les mathématiques, condition nécessaire mais suffisante aux sciences économique".
3 A biological token being the Lamarckian model.
4 In an autobiographical note Walras records how the wishes of his father convinced him to devote his career to continuing his father's work and produce a pure political economy "in mathematical form" (Walras, 1893). Though his idea for a science of mathematical economics had been clear about 15 years earlier it was in his Eléments d'economie politique pure, published between 1874 and 1879, that Walras's major contribution to the mathematisating project appeared.
5 Of course even at the level of methodology there is more to Newton's contribution than this form of 'Newtonianism'. Indeed, Newton's method

of analysis and synthesis was very much oriented to identifying the underlying causes of phenomena. It just so happens that some of his most spectacular findings lend themselves to mathematical representation. An unfortunate result of this has been a widespread tendency to conflate Newton's method with a way of presenting some of his results (on all this see Montes, 2001).
6 There were though exceptions. Dupuit pursued the mathematisation project but supported the remainder of the liberal programme, and seems to have received some accommodation.
7 Gide for example established with Walras the Revue d'Economie Politique. And Colson attempted to save the mathematising project by providing a synthesis of liberalism and mathematics.
8 Contributions of the likes of Samuelson and Hicks cannot be overlooked for example. To some extent these contributors can be viewed as attempting to provide a general framework in which the various competing positions could be embedded and contrasted.
9 The group met in secret and took the name of a nineteenth century French General whose name was already given to the street in which they met.
10 But for an account of post war French developments centring on the 1950s see Arena (2000b).
11 And as I proof read these lines I note that Ph.D. students in Cambridge UK have circulated a petition decrying the lack of discussion concerning the mathematisation of modern economics.

References

Arena, R. (2000a) "J-B. Say and the French liberal school of the nineteenth century: outside the canon?" in S. Peart (ed.) *Refections on the Classical Canon: Essays in Honour of Samuel Hollander,* London: Routledge (forthcoming).
Arena, R. (2000b) "Les économistes français en 1950" *Revue économique,* vol. 51, no. 5, septembre, pp. 969–1007
Baudrillart, H. (1872) *Manuel d'Economie Politique,* Paris: Guillaumin.
Bell, D. and Kristol, I. (1981) *The Crisis in Economic Theory,* New York: Basic Books.
Blaug, M. (1997) *Ugly Currents in Modern Economics,* Options Politiques, Septembre, pp. 3–8.
Darwin, C. (1964 [1859]) *On the Origin of Species,* Harvard University Press: Cambridge Massachusetts, USA.
Dawkins, R. (1976) *The Selfish Gene,* New York and Oxford: Oxford University Press.
Dawkins, R. (1978) 'Replicator, Selection and the Extended Phenotype', *Zeitschrift für Tierpsychologie,* 47, pp. 61–76.
Debreu, G. (1959) *The Theory of Value,* New York: Wiley.
Friedman, M. (1999) in Snowdon, B., and Vane, H., (eds) *Conversations with Leading Economists: Interpreting Modern Macroeconomics,* Cheltenham: Edward Elgar.
Gee, J.M.A. (1991) "The Neoclassical School", in Mair, D. and Miller, A.G., *A Modern Guide to Economic Thought: An Introduction to Comparative Schools of Thought in Economics,* Aldershot: Edward Elgar.
Hull, D. (1981) 'Units of Evolution:' A metaphysical essay' in Jensen, U.J. and Harré, R (eds.) *The Philosophy of Evolution,* pp. 23–44, Harvestor Press

Ingrao, B. and Israel, G. (1990), *The Invisible Hand,* Cambridge MA: MIT Press.
Kanth, R. (1999) "Against Eurocentred Epistemologies: a critique of science, realism and economics", in Fleetwood, S. (ed.) *Critical Realism in Economics: Development and Debate,* London: Routledge.
Kirman, A. (1989) "The Intrinsic Limits of Modern Economic Theory: The Emperor has no clothes", *Economic Journal* 99(395).
Kline, M. (1964) *Mathematics in Western Culture,* Oxford: Oxford University Press.
Lawson, T. (1997a) *Economics and Reality,* London: Routledge.
Lawson, T. (1997b) "Horses for Courses", in Arestis, P., Palma, G., and Sawyer, M., (eds.) *Markets, Unemployment and Economic Policy: Essays in honour of Geoff Harcourt, volume two,* pp. 1–15, London and New York: Routledge.
Lawson, T. (1998) "Critical Issues in *Economics as Realist Social Theory*", *Ekonomia;* reprinted in Fleetwood, S. (ed.), 1999, *Critical Realism in Economics: Development and Debate,* London: Routledge.
Leamer, E.E. (1978) "Specification Searches: Ad hoc inferences with non-experimental data", New York: John Wiley and Sons.
Leamer, E.E. (1983) "Let's take the Con out of Econometrics", *American Economic Review:* 34–43.
Leontief, W. (1982) Letter in *Science* 217: 104–7.
Poincaré, H. (1901) Letter to Walras, in W. Jaffé (ed.) (1965) *Correspondence of Léon Walras and Related Papers,* vol. 3, letter 1496a, Amsterdam: North Holland, pp. 162–5.
Reybaud, L. (1862) *Les économistes modernes,* Paris: Guillaumin.
Rubinstein, A. (1991) Comments on the Interpretation of Game Theory, *Econometrica,* Vol. 59, No.4, pp. 909–924.
Rubinstein, A. (1995) "John Nash: the master of economic modelling", *Scandinavian Journal of Economics* 97(1): 9–13.
Say, J-B (1803) *Traité d'Economie Politique,* First edition, Paris: Crapelet.
Say, J-B (1971 [1826]) 'Discours Préliminaire', in *Traité d'économie politique,* 5th edn, with a preface by G. Tapinos, Paris: Calmann-Levy.
Strassmann, D.L. (1994) "Feminist Thought and Economics; Or, What do the Visigoths know?", *American Economic Review, Papers and Proceedings:* 153–158.
Thomson, W. (1999) "The Young Person's Guide to Writing Economic Theory", *Journal of Economic Literature,* Vol. XXXVII, pp. 157–183
Walras, L. (1874) "Principe d'une théorie mathématique de l'échange" in *Compte-rendu des Séances et Travaux de l'Académie des Sciences Morales et Politique,* séances du 16 et 24 Août 1873, January 1874, pp. 97–120.
Wiles, P. and Routh, E. (1984) *Economics in Disarray,* Oxford: Basil Blackwell.
Wolowski, L. (1848) *Etudes d'économie politique et de statistique,* Paris: Guillaumin.

Index of names

Académie des Sciences (France) 235
Académie des Sciences Morales et Politiques 236, 239–40
AHE (Association for Heterodox Economics) 25
Allais, M. 38
Arena, Richard 238–9, 250n10
Arestis, P. 27
Arnsperger, Christian 95n4
Arrow, Kenneth 170, 177–8, 185n3
Aspromourgos, Tony 87, 94n3, 96n8, 97n17

Backhouse, Roger 171
Basel Accord 119, 126–7n10
Baudrillart, H. 238
Baumol, William 49n6
Beasley, C. 51n16
Becker, Gary 9n45
Bentham, Jeremy 69
Bigo, Vinca 125n3, 166n16
Blaug, Mark 13, 49n4, 174, 221
BNP Paribas 120, 127n12
Boisguilbert, Pierre le Pesant, sieur de 70
Bourbaki school 165, 206, 244

Cairnes, John Elliott 69–70, 72, 74, 78, 98n23
Cambridge Realist Workshop 211
Canard, Nicholas-François 232–3
Cartesianism 234
Chick, Victoria 126n4
Clark, John Bates 82
Coase, Ronald 3, 34, 36, 173
Colander, David, on neoclassical economics 101n32

Colander, David *et al.*: debate with Lawson 131–4; on heterodox economics 28, 95–6n5, 212; on mainstream economics 32, 34–5, 57, 163n6; on mathematical modelling 106–9, 112, 130, 140, 156
Colson, Clément 250n7
Condillac, Étienne Bonnot de 237
Condorcet, Nicolas de 232, 237
Courbet, Gustave 7
Cournot, Antoine Augustin 232–3

Darwin, Charles 199, 224
Das, Satyajit 127n11
Davidson, Paul 50n10, 175
Davis, John 32, 57, 208–9, 211–12, 218n3
Dawkins, Richard 225
Debreu, Gérard 243–4
Dixon, Huw 150, 180, 196
Dobb, Maurice 94n3
Dow, Sheila 27, 126n4
Dupuit, Jules 232, 249n6

Eagleton, Terry 163n3
Eichner, A. S. 27

Fayazmanesh, Sasan 87, 94n3, 96n8, 97n17
Fine, Ben 89, 95n4
Fitch Ratings 117–18
Föllmer, Hans 106, 130, 156
Friedman, Milton 3, 34, 173, 221
Fullbrook, Edward 101n31, 131–2, 137

Garnett, Robert 208, 212–14
Gide, Charles 250n7
Gingras, Yves 159
Goldberg, Michael 106, 130, 156

Index of names 253

Gowan, Peter 119, 126n7
Gramsci, Antonio 163n4
Guerrien, Bernard 29, 59, 145–7, 151, 157–8, 163n2
Guesnerie, Roger 49n6

Hahn, Frank: on equilibrium theory 149, 170–1, 177–9, 185n3, 196; *General Competitive Analysis* (with Arrow) 170; on mathematical modelling 33, 154, 196–7, 210–11; on neoclassical theory 30, 88–9, 94n4
Hass, Armin 106, 130, 156
Hayek, Friedrich 171, 182–5
Henry, John 159
Hicks, John 93n2, 96, 250n8
Hilbert, David 84, 242
Hodgson, Geoffrey 27, 95n4
Holt, Richard 28
Howell, David 202n5
Hull, D. 225

ICAPE (International Confederation of Associations for Pluralism in Economics) 25, 209, 212
INET (Institute for New Economic Thinking): alternative projects of 9; and Soros' reflexivity paradigm 188, 193; use of mathematical modelling 96–7n16, 155–6, 197
Ingrao, B. and Israel, G. 228; on mathematisation 231–3; on prestige of science 235; on Say's resistance to mathematisation 237, 239; on Walrasian networks 246
Institut de France 236
Isnard, Achylle-Nicolas 232–3

Jevons, William Stanley 93n2, 94n3, 165n13, 246
Juselius, Katerina 96n11, 106, 130, 156

Kaldor, Nicholas 171
Kant, Immanuel 159, 229
Kanth, Rajani 29, 49n5, 147–8, 151, 163n2
Keen, Steve 93n1
Keynes, John Maynard: and actually existing reality 185; on atomisation 39; on classical economics 70; and equilibrium theory 171; and levels of abstraction 22–3; and mathematical modelling 123–5, 174; and post-Keynesianism 27, 216; and reflexivity 198; and uncertainty 46
Keynes, John Neville 77–9, 81
King, J. E. 212
Kirman, Alan 31–3, 106, 130, 154, 156
Kline, Morris 158, 229–30
Krugman, Paul 93n1

Laplace, Pierre-Simon 236, 240, 242, 245
Lavoie, M. 27–8
Leamer, Edward 31, 33, 36, 151, 160
Leontief, Wassily 3, 34, 36–7, 173, 220–1
Levasseur, Pierre Émile 240–1
Lipsey, Richard 33, 172–4, 210
loans, moving off balance sheet 118–20
Lux, Thomus 106, 130, 156

Malthus, Thomas 238
Marshall, Alfred: and equilibrium theorising 88; and marginalism 93n2; on mathematical methods 18; and neoclassical economics 67, 76–8, 97; taxonomic approach of 78–81, 87, 99n26
Marx, Karl: and actually existing reality 185; against naturalisation of capitalism 100n29; on appropriate tools for economics 37, 109; on classical economics 70, 82–3, 98n22, 100–101n29; and commodity exchange 20; and tendency of rate of profit to fall 23
Matchlup, Fritz 171, 180
McDonough, Terrence 163n2
Menger, Carl 93n2, 94n3
Mill, John Stuart 45, 69–70, 72, 98n23
Moore, G. E. 124
Morgan, Jamie 126n7
Morgenstern, Oskar 243
Muth, John 149, 163n5, 194–5

Nemours, Dupont de 232
Newton, Isaac 159, 229, 234–5, 249n4

O'Boyle, Brian 163n2

Pareto, Vilfredo 233
Parker, Richard 202n5
Partnoy, Frank 127n11
Paulson, Hank 119
Perona, Eugenia 175
Petty, William 70

Poincaré, Henri 241, 246
Pratten, Stephen 10n19, 99, 175

Quesnay, François 232, 237

Reybaud, Marie 238
Ricardo, David 70, 237–8
Robinson, Joan 94n3, 171, 179, 181–2
Rosser, J. Barkley Jr 28
Rubinstein, Ariel 31–2, 36, 151, 173, 220
Rutherford, Malcolm 48–9n4

Saber, Nasser 126n8
Samuelson, Paul 94, 234, 250n8
Santa Fe Institute 199
Sawyer, M. 27
Say, Jean-Baptiste 237–9, 245
Schumpeter, Joseph 94, 234
Sen, Amartya 222
Sharpe, William 113–14, 196
Sloth, Brigitte 106, 130, 156
Smith, Adam: disseminators of ideas of 238; and equilibrium theory 170, 178, 181, 185; and ontology 100–1n29
Söderbaum, Peter 147
Solow, Robert 49n6
Soros, George: author's engagement with 201n2; and INET 9, 96n16; on mathematical modelling 155, 197–8; on natural and social phenomena 189–91, 199–200; new paradigm of 188–9
Stigler, George 49n4, 94n3
Stiglitz, Joseph 155–6

Strassmann, Diana 49–50n6, 230–1

Thomson, William 33
Tracy, Count Destutt de 144
Turgot, Anne-Robert-Jacques 232

Uhlig, Harald 164n10

Van Bouwel, Jeroen 208, 214–15, 218
Varoufakis, Yanis 95n4
Veblen, Thorstein: on classical economics 70–4; conception of social reality 85; concept of neoclassical economics 56, 59–61, 66–7, 75–7, 81–3; and evolutionary economics 22; and institutionalism 216; on marginalism 99–100n27; specific neoclassical thinking discussed by 77–9, 91–2
von Neuman, John 243

Wald, Abraham 243
Walras, Léon: and general equilibrium theory 185n3; and marginalism 93n2, 94n3; and mathematisation of economics 232–4, 240–1, 246, 249n4
Weintraub, Roy 89, 94–5n4, 177
Williamson, Oliver 49n4
Wolowski, L. 238

Zafirovski, Milan 94n3

Index of subjects

abstraction, levels of 21–3
academic economics: changing trends in 248; and Cold War 165–6n15; and global crisis 105, 131, 142; and ideology 152; and mathematical modelling 10, 106, 123, 125n1, 133; and neoclassicism 56, 94; and neo-liberalism 4; power structure of 139, 141, 161, 246–7; return to Keynes 125
agent-based modelling 62, 143, 194
animism 69–71
anti-intellectualism 165n15
asset-price bubbles 116, 119
assumptions: justifying by conclusions 8–9, 113–14, 196–7; taboo on questioning 2, 50n6, 230; *see also* unrealistic assumptions
atomisation: and optimisation 62; presupposition of 175, 185, 194; and rationality 5, 29, 87–8, 147–8; use of term 39; *see also* isolated atomic worldview
Austrian economics: distinguishing features of 46, 217; as heterodox 26; and neoclassical economics 67, 76, 97n19
axioms: formulating sets of 84; in neoclassicism 57

balance, and equilibrium 176, 178, 180, 182
banking: remuneration in 126n9; shadow system of 121
Basel Accord 119, 126–7n10
behavioural economics 126, 199, 208, 211
biology, as non-mathematical 165n14

capital asset pricing 113, 196
capitalism: depiction as optimal 147–8; economic science of 29, 148; mainstream economics' defence of 149; Marx's understanding of 100n29
capital markets, efficiency of 113
caring: in feminist economics 42, 46; in mainstream economics 43
Cartesianism 234
causal mechanisms: as goal of science 17; isolating effects of 18, 20; multiple 15
causal-processual ontology: and evolutionary science 83; and heterodox economics 64–5; in modern economics 90; in neoclassical economics 79, 82–3, 86, 89–90; use of term 62–3
causal sequence: closures of 38, 41; cumulative 68, 80; and empiricism 72; in evolutionary thinking 92; in mathematical deductivism 109
ceremonial adequacy 72–3
chemistry, as non-mathematical 165n14
classical economics: modernised 76–7; and neoclassicism 56, 60, 67; and normality 72–4; ontology of 71–2; Veblen's use of term 70–1
closures and closed systems: and atomism 39–40; of causal sequence 38, 41; conditions for 136–8; and deductivism 38, 136, 143; and isolationism 63, 66, 87, 112, 143; local 65; and mathematical modelling 182, 192–3, 197; as substitutes for heterodox claims 43
Cold War 165n15
collateralised debt obligations 116–18, 120–1

Index of subjects

common sense: as basis of interpreting regularities 72–3; Colander et al.'s use of 107, 133; economics as 10; mathematical modelling as 4
complexity modelling 143, 194
complexity theory 34, 199
computer simulations 34, 244
contrast explanation 18–19
correlations: in classical economics 73; fixation on seeking 93; in neoclassical economics 81; *see also* event regularities
credit and debt, role of social positions in 115–16
credit rating advisory services; 117; *see also* rating agencies

Darwinianism: and Marx 100; and natural selection 201–2n4, 223, 226–8; and neoclassicism 79–80
data generation process 175
deductivism: appropriate use of 163n1; in classical economics 73–4; and correlations 86–7; and mathematics 83; in modern economics 91; in neoclassical economics 82, 86, 88–90; pathological attachment to 162; Say's use of 238; use of term 58, 61; *see also* mathematical deductivism
deductivists, non-dogmatic 91
dependent variables 22, 38
derivatives, over-the-counter 116–17, 127n11
determinateness 176–8, 180–1

ecological economics 34
econometrics: actual practices of 173; and atomisation 39; and classical statistics 34; and computing technology 244; Keynes on 124; limitations of 14, 31, 37; varying conclusions in 151
economic crisis *see* global economic and financial crisis
economic journals: as gate-keepers 246; mathematical modelling in 33, 36, 106
economic modelling: functional relations in 14, 17; presupposing preferred conclusions in 64, 113, 135; *see also* mathematical modelling
economic narratives 143
economic policy analysis 105, 154

economics: alternative projects in 8–9; author's definition of 51n14; deeper structures in 20–1; as logic 182–3; methodological problems of 2–4; object of 87; ontological presuppositions in 67–70; quantitative study in 158; as science 16–18, 45; teaching of 10–11, 49–50n6, 94–5n4 (*see also* academic economics); *see also* heterodox economics; mainstream economics; modern economics
economic theory: direction of mainstream 31–2; and ideology 145; substantive 3, 22
economic variables, correlations between 14
Efficient Market Hypothesis (EMH) 188, 192–3, 196
emergence: in social ontology 41, 62–3, 216; use of term 96n12
empiricism, and classical economics 72
enlightened self-interest 32, 57
the Enlightenment, and mathematics 83, 158–9, 223, 231, 236
entrepreneurship 46, 217
environmental selection 226–7, 245–6
epistemic fallacy 185n2
equilibrium: in classical economics 74; in financial markets 192–3; Hayek on 182–4; and isolated atomic worldview 126n6; mainstream/heterodox polarisation over 180–1, 185; and mathematical modelling 88–9, 195–6; in neoclassical economics 57, 88–9; theoretic and ontic conceptions of 176–80; as unrealistic 150, 154
equilibrium theory: and formalistic modelling 175; in modern economics 169–71, 177; problems with 171–2; Soros' critique of 188; *see also* general equilibrium theory
ethics and morality, in economics 9–10
event prediction *see* forecasting
event regularities: accidental 138; in classical economics 72–3; functions expressing 89; presupposition of 38, 41, 61, 68–9, 109–10, 193–4; rarity in social realm 14–16, 110–11, 136, 190; and social relationality 161
evolution: and causal sequence 92; Darwinian *see* Darwinianism; and interactors 231; and Marshall 77–9;

and natural selection 223–6; and neoclassical economics 79–83; and PVRS model 227–8; and replicators 225, 231, 233; social 226, 228, 234, 245–9; and teleology 71–2, 74, 81, 100–1n27, 175; Veblen on 67–9, 73–5, 83
evolutionary concepts: in institutionalism 46; in mainstream economics 43
evolutionary economics 22, 100n29
evolutionary method 42, 75–80, 98n21, 98–9n24, 101n30, 175
evolutionary science: preconceptions of 75, 80; Veblen on 68, 83
evolutionary systems theory 199
experimental control 9, 14, 17–20, 111
experimental economics 34
explanations: causal 20, 190, 201; contrast 18–19; evolutionary 223–5, 229; political-economic ideology 148–52; psychological 162; socio-evolutionary 227, 234; in terms of individuals 30

feed-backward 226–7, 245
feed-forward 227, 245–6
feminist economics: caring and relationality in 42, 64–5, 175, 216; distinguishing features of 46–7; as heterodox 26
feminists: and non-mathematical models 231; pedagogy of 218n4
finality, grounds of 68, 76, 92
financial assets, ratings of 120
financial crises, inherent causes of 107; see also global economic and financial crisis
'The Financial Crisis and the Systemic Failure of Academic Economics' 106–8, 130, 156
financial globalisation 121
financial markets: deregulation of 113, 122; Soros' critique of 192–3, 199–200
financial speculation 191
financial system: behavioural patterns in 122; dominant institutions of 120–1; possible reforms to 123; in social totality 112, 115
forecasting 4, 165n11, 192
formalistic-deductive framework 32
formalistic methods: and closed systems 38, 194; in heterodox economics 36, 209–10; ontological preconditions of 42–3; and social reality 175
formalistic modelling: in economics teaching 246; failures of 109, 131, 141; in finance industry 125n3; mainstream insistence on 130, 156, 173, 211, 217; new forms of 105–8, 132–3, 139; theoretic and ontic in 175; as unrealistic 114, 123, 185
France: academic institutions of 239; Cartesianism and Newtonianism in 234–5; and classical economics 70; early social sciences in 236–8; mathematisation of economics in 223, 232–3, 239–40, 243–4; protest against mathematisation in 222, 248
French Liberal School 237–9
functional relations: attempts to formulate 23; and mathematics 17; posited by deductivism 38; and social phenomena 14–15
functions, mathematical 14, 101n30

game theory 34, 243, 249
gender, and attachment to deductivism 162
general equilibrium, two notions of 177
general equilibrium theory: Adam Smith and 170, 178; and atomised worldview 126; history of 228; and mathematisation of economics 232–3
generalisations: in classical economics 72; in taxonomic science 69
Germany, and mathematisation of economics 243
global economic and financial crisis: economists blamed for 105; and mainstream self-criticism 154–5; mechanisms contributing to 116–18; responses to 122–3; reward for predicting 156; and social ontology 114–15; Soros on 192–3
global economic system, and mainstream economics 29–31, 148, 160–1
God, in classical economics 71

hedonism 71, 81
heterodox, use of term 28
heterodox economics: acceptance of mathematical modelling 66, 112–13, 125–6n4, 134–5, 155–6; attitude to mainstream 34–6, 63–4, 95–6n5, 112,

134–5, 204–5, 212–14; connections between traditions 51n13; differing traditions of 25–8, 44–8, 58, 205–6, 214–17; and equilibrium theory 171, 181–2; methodological pluralism of 6; ontology of 37, 42–4, 48, 64–5, 172, 174–6; pluralism in 207–9, 218; recent developments in 25
historical school 76
historicism 240
history, causal 18, 38
human agency: and social evolution 226, 248; transformative 40
human nature 6, 10, 71
hypothetical science 74

identity relations 175
ideology: and failure of economics 144; in mainstream economics 29, 145–7, 162; mathematical modelling as 4, 152–4, 157, 160; use of term 29, 144–5, 163n3
independent variables 38
individual behaviour: axioms of 88; optimisation of 31
individualism: mainstream commitment to 31–2; methodological 50n9
inference, theories of 33
infinitesimal calculus 83, 240, 242
innovation: conditions of survival 80–1; and natural selection 226
institutional analysis 240
institutionalism: distinguishing features of 46, 65; old 26, 48–9n4, 206, 216; and processuality 42
institutions: development of 46; and game theory 34
interactor 225–6, 231
internal relationality: in causal-processual ontology 63; in modern capitalism 136; ontology of 42–3; of social reality 143; use of term 40
investment banks 116, 118–21, 127n13
invisible hand 178
isolated atomic worldview: adjustments to 122; and event regularities 61–2, 86–7, 110, 194; heterodox rejection of 205; and mathematical modelling 3, 40, 87, 124–5; as preconception 41–2, 66; as unrealistic 62–4, 143, 175
isolation: condition of 15, 126n6

isolationism, in heterodox economics 204, 215

knowledge: grounded 158; individuals with perfect 57; and reflexivity 189–90, 192

laissez-faire ideology 29, 89, 147
language, as processual system 16, 40, 111–12, 137
Le Monde 222
leverage, expansion of 118–19, 125n3
Levy processes 133
loans, moving off balance sheet 118–20

mainstream economics: attachment to mathematical modelling 3, 61–3, 108–9, 153–4, 157–9, 230–1; developments in 34–5, 163n6; disciplinary definition of 17, 45; distinction from heterodox 6, 27, 63–6; as dogmatic deductivism 38–9, 91; and equilibrium theory 5, 30, 32, 94n4, 171, 181; explanatory failure of 36–7, 59, 169, 192, 220; general theories in 46; heterodox engagement with 209–12, 217; invented reality of 175; as irrelevant 160–2, 173–4, 197; as neoclassical 145; ontological assumptions of 37–8; purpose and direction of 29–32, 149–52; self-criticism of 155; social evolution of 228, 234, 245–9; use of term 28–9, 58
mainstream economists, 'elite' among 35, 205
marginalism, and neoclassicism 67, 82, 93–4n2, 97n17
markets, Austrian interest in 46, 217
Marxian economics: as heterodox 26; and nature of capitalism 65, 217; use of mathematical methods in 49n5; Veblen on 76
mathematical deductivism: alternatives to 18, 137–8; and failure of economics 143–4, 152; heterodox use of 206; inappropriate use of 48, 109, 114, 132, 135–6, 172; mainstream economics as 23, 35, 48, 63; and modelling 131; and neoclassicism 58–9, 85–6; and policy analysis 105–6; power's insistence on 139, 141; rise to pre-eminence 84, 90; as taxonomic science 92

mathematical economics: autonomous tradition of 83; and closed systems 143, 193–4; evolutionary success of 243–6, 249; Walras' promotion of 240–1

mathematical modelling: alternative forms of 9, 108, 138–40, 143, 155–7; Colander et al.'s support for 132–4; as common thread of mainstream economics 47–8, 58, 152, 169, 172–3, 184; complexity theory as 199; and deductivism 85; in economics education 49–50n6; empirical failure of 109–10, 137, 140, 161–2; and finance industry 107, 123; inappropriate use of 18, 48, 174; internal consistency of 182, 194; misallocation of resources to 130–1, 135; myths and fallacies of 5–9; ontological presuppositions of 37–43, 61–2; seen as indispensable 11, 23, 33, 154, 160, 204–5; social reality as constraint on 244; Soros' critique of 188; survival of 202n4

mathematicians, Walras' appeal to 241

mathematics: axiomatic method in 83–4, 242–5; culture of 231; deductive 17; as essential to science 49–50n6, 153, 157–9, 162, 221–2, 229–31; rejection of 237–8; as useful tool 142–3

mathematisation of economics: closing off competing trends 246–7; and Cold War 165n15; desirability of 32; early failures of 235–6; harmful consequences of 8; history of project 6, 83–4, 159, 232–3; reception of 224–5, 228–9; rise to dominance 220, 222–3, 228, 241–5; student protests against 222, 250n11

McCarthyism 165n15
meta-axioms 57, 95n4
metaphysics, Veblen's use of term 67
meta-theory 57, 94–5n4
methodological experimentation 210
methodological principles 26, 44–8
modelling consistency 150, 195
model simulations 143, 194
modern economics: basic divisions in 90, 184–5 (*see also* heterodox economics; mainstream economics); crisis of 142, 148–9, 220–1, 247; explanatory failure of 3–4, 64; fundamental problem of 13, 108, 130–1, 142; future of 248; inappropriate methodology of 13–14, 105; institutional problems in 140; myths and fallacies of 1–3, 15; natural selection process in 225; other sciences' critiques of 247; over-generalisation in 23; strategies for changing 209; unrealistic assumptions of 112

monism 207, 213, 215
moths, natural selection of 201, 224, 248

natural law 69–70, 78, 98n23, 232
natural rates 195
natural sciences: event regularities in 14–16; experimental practices in 110–11, 136; mathematics in 83, 157, 162; non-mathematical 165n14
natural selection 75–6, 223–9, 245, 247–8
natural theology 71
near-equilibrium conditions 198
neoclassical economics 27; alternative categorisations of 86–9; continuity with classical economics 75–7, 87, 94n3; heterodox opposition to 66; as ideology 147; as inconsistency of ontology and method 79–82, 84–6, 92–3; mutual accusations of 93n1; as unneeded category 58–61, 90–1, 93; use of term 4, 27, 34, 56–7, 64; *see also* mainstream economics
neo-liberalism 4
neo-Ricardianism 27–8
neuro-economics 5, 143, 194, 208
Newtonianism 233–5, 249n5
Nobel Memorial Prize winners: on efficient markets 196; on explanatory failure 3, 220–1; on mathematical modelling 34, 173; on pluralism 222
non-ergodic systems 175
nonlinear modelling 143, 194
normality: in classical economics 73–5; of global economic system 160; in neoclassical economics 78; presupposition of 68–9; in social reality 85
normative pluralism 207–8

ontological pluralism 207, 213
ontological presuppositions: heterodox 43, 175, 181, 205–6; mainstream 7, 176; of mathematical modelling 40,

48, 61, 65–6, 84; of taxonomic method 79; Veblen on 67
ontology: of Adam Smith 69–71; atomistic 210, 217; causal-processual *see* causal-processual ontology; of classical economics 71–2; economics' neglect of 6, 64, 66, 158, 176; of heterodox economics 37, 42–4, 48, 64–5, 172, 174–6; of internal relationality 42–3; philosophical 50n12, 217; social *see* social ontology; and social sciences 6; use of term 37; Veblen on 67–70, 86
openness, of social reality 16, 46–7, 143, 174, 189, 216
optimality, presumed 227
optimising individuals 29, 35, 148
order, and equilibrium 171, 176, 178, 181–5
outcomes, optimal 29–30, 147–8

paradigmist economists 212
physics: mathematics in 36; as model for science 83–4; as paradigm of mathematical economics 235, 242
Physiocrats 69–70, 232
pluralism: in academic economics 10, 222; in mainstream economics 151–2, 211–12; and mathematical modelling 7–8, 155; methodological 36; use of term 207, 215
polyvalence 41
post-Keynesianism: assumption of openness in 42–3, 64, 175; differences within 27–8; distinct features of 46, 216–17; as heterodox 26, 134
power relations: obscured by mathematical modelling 161; preventing intellectual advance 139; and social position 96n13
price mechanism 21
prices: 'fundamentals' of 199; movement of relative 191–2
processuality: as generalisation 22; and heterodox categories 43; in language system 16, 40; of social reality 47, 143, 181, 205, 216
proprietary trading 121, 127n13
purposeful behaviour 32, 57
PVRS model 226–7, 245–6

quantum theory 83, 242

rates of return, equalization of 178
rating agencies 117–18, 120–1, 123, 198
rational behaviour, in neoclassicism 57
rational-choice Marxists 30
rational expectations: and consistency in modelling 149–50, 194–5; and financial crises 107; Soros' critique of 188, 192–3, 197; as unrealistic assumption 5, 137
rationality: as axiom 5, 30, 88, 94; in ecological economics 34; mainstream economics commitment to 4–5, 29, 31–2
realisticness: lack of 146, 148, 195, 197; of mainstream economic assumptions 5, 135; traditions maintaining 246
Real World Economics Review 147, 156
reductionism 242–3
reflexivity, in Soros' new paradigm 188–9, 191, 194, 198–9
relativity theory 83, 242
Reorienting Economics 45, 204–5, 208, 217
replicator 225, 231, 233
representative agents 107, 133, 137–8, 146
Revere Award for Economics 156
rigour, multiple forms of 140
risk, and uncertainty 43
risk assessment 118

science: and causal explanation 190; disciplinary definitions in 45; and event regularities 38; evolutionary and taxonomic conceptions of 68–9; and mathematical modelling 8, 17–18; non-mathematical methods in 200–1; ontological preconceptions of 68, 75–6, 87; prestige of in France 235; primary objects of 16–17; *see also* social sciences
securities, structuring of 117–18
securitisation 119–20
selfishness 32, 57
simulation analysis 9
social analysis, and mathematical methods 37
social atomism 50n9; *see also* atomisation
social economics 26, 58
social life: ability to cope with 190–1; as networked 111
social mathematics 174, 221, 232, 236, 238

social ontology: and crisis of economics 61–2, 194; and equilibrium 183, 185; and heterodox economics 10, 43, 205; overview of theory 40–2; processual *see* causal-processual ontology
social phenomena: assessments of 189; intrinsic stability of 15–16
social positions: as concern of economics 6; network of 111, 115; relationality of 40–1, 136–7
social reality: appropriate tools for analysis 7, 13; causal-processual model of 62–3, 85; and closure conditions 135–7; and economic models 84, 109–12, 242–4; forecasting 3–4, 19; in heterodox economics 40–2, 46, 181, 214; mathematics as obscuring 5, 161, 169, 193–5, 237; natural selection in 225–7; path-dependence of 198; and risk assessment 118; and social sciences 45; as totality 115
social relations: constituent 62; internal 40
social sciences: division of labour within 45; mathematisation of 231, 234, 236–7, 239–41, 245, 249; object of 47; and ontology 6; possibility of 9, 190–1
social systems, reproduction of 226
special purpose vehicles 119
speculative arbitrage 116
spontaneous order 183–4
standard models 107, 131–3, 155, 245
statistics, limitations of classical 34
structural transformation 46, 115, 122, 216
structuredness, of social reality 41, 174, 190–1, 205
sufficiency conditions 136
sustainability 32, 57
system determinateness 176–7, 180

Tableau économique (Quesnay) 232
taxonomic approach: in modern economics 90; Veblen on 75, 78, 92, 97–8n20
taxonomic science: classical economics as 69, 73–5; neoclassical economics as 77–80, 86, 92; preconceptions of 75; Veblen's conception of 68
taxonomists, non-dogmatic 91
technology: institutionalist view of 42, 46, 206; use of term 40
teleology 69, 71–2, 100n27, 101n29
tendencies: identifying 21; use of term 17
theoretic/ontic distinction 175–8, 180, 182–3

uncertainty: fundamental 27, 42, 46, 216; Keynes on 22; mainstream economics dealing with 43; in post-Keynesianism 175
uniformity: and deductivism 58; in neoclassical economics 78; statements of 80–1
United States, post-war environment of 165n15
unrealistic assumptions: deliberate insertion of 113–14; of economic system efficiency 157; in mainstream economics 3, 5, 134–5, 137–8, 164n9, 192–3; specific cases of 5, 109; Stiglitz's use of 156
utilitarianism 71

VAR (vector autoregression) 122, 133
variety generation 224–7, 245–6
verification, criteria of 236
vulgar economy 70, 98n22, 100–1n29

Wall Street, and asset-price bubbles 116, 120–1
women, and feminist economics 47, 216–17

eBooks
from Taylor & Francis

Helping you to choose the right eBooks for your Library

Add to your library's digital collection today with Taylor & Francis eBooks. We have over 50,000 eBooks in the Humanities, Social Sciences, Behavioural Sciences, Built Environment and Law, from leading imprints, including Routledge, Focal Press and Psychology Press.

Choose from a range of subject packages or create your own!

Benefits for you
- Free MARC records
- COUNTER-compliant usage statistics
- Flexible purchase and pricing options
- 70% approx of our eBooks are now DRM-free.

Benefits for your user
- Off-site, anytime access via Athens or referring URL
- Print or copy pages or chapters
- Full content search
- Bookmark, highlight and annotate text
- Access to thousands of pages of quality research at the click of a button.

ORDER YOUR FREE INSTITUTIONAL TRIAL TODAY

Free Trials Available

We offer free trials to qualifying academic, corporate and government customers.

eCollections

Choose from 20 different subject eCollections, including:

- Asian Studies
- Economics
- Health Studies
- Law
- Middle East Studies

eFocus

We have 16 cutting-edge interdisciplinary collections, including:

- Development Studies
- The Environment
- Islam
- Korea
- Urban Studies

For more information, pricing enquiries or to order a free trial, please contact your local sales team:

UK/Rest of World: **online.sales@tandf.co.uk**
USA/Canada/Latin America: **e-reference@taylorandfrancis.com**
East/Southeast Asia: **martin.jack@tandf.com.sg**
India: **journalsales@tandfindia.com**

www.tandfebooks.com